"*Born From War* is the story of a father and son at war. The story of Vietnam is told through the eyes of one soldier by his son who relates his father's conflict through the prism of his own wartime experience in Iraq. It is the personal and moving story of the timelessness of war for fathers and sons despite the differences in their respective conflicts. It is an engaging human story highly recommended for anyone seeking to understand the real-life impact of America's wars from those who fought them and their families back home."

—James H. Willbanks, PhD, Vietnam Combat Veteran and author of *Abandoning Vietnam* and *A Raid Too Far*

"*Born From War* is a compelling, first-hand account of how the experience of conflict has an enduring impact on the families of those who serve. Patrick Naughton offers an understanding of the Vietnam War for a new generation who themselves have just lived through decades of conflict. He candidly rips open, and lays bare the experiences of a father and son during America's fight against communism and terrorism. Naughton's narrative jolted me back once again to the reality of a sometimes calm, frequently confusing, occasionally frightening, never-forgettable tour as an ARVN infantry battalion advisor with his father in Vietnam. The creeping redefinition of objectives in Vietnam over time by political and military leadership was a tragedy and cost many lives. The same mistakes were then made later in Iraq and Afghanistan. Naughton astutely recognizes the foreseeable and missed similarities between Vietnam and then America's global war on terror. This is a must-read book for anyone looking to understand how Vietnam, and now Iraq and Afghanistan, will continue to influence the families of those who served and foreign policy decisions for decades to come."

— Richard Keller, Lieutenant General, US Army (Ret.), Chief of Staff of US European Command, and a veteran of the Vietnam War

"*Born From War* deftly weaves parallel American wartime experiences between a father (Vietnam) and a son (Iraq). The book is a deep, unflinching examination of what made these two combat veterans and, in the larger sense, two wars tick. It's an intriguing read that I highly recommend."

—Chris McKinney, author of the Water City Trilogy and *The Tattoo*

"Told through one Hawai'i family's experience in Vietnam and America's global war on terror, Patrick Naughton provides an interesting and thoughtful analysis about the generational influence of service. The author's father and I voluntarily went through Reserve Officer Training Corps together and then served in Vietnam at the same time, thereby proudly joining the ranks of thousands of others from our island home who fought for our country. From the draft to the all-volunteer force, this story will resonate with the countless Hawai'i families whose sons and daughters answered the call to serve in both conflicts."

—Clarence M. Agena, Brigadier General, US Army (Ret.) and a veteran of the Vietnam War

"Naughton traces the legacies and lessons of two wars—his and his father's—in this thoughtful, insightful, and important book. *Born From War* is a must read for anyone interested in America's modern wars."

—Dr. Robert K. Brigham, Shirley Ecker Boskey Professor of History and International Relations Vassar College and author of *ARVN: Life and Death in the South Vietnamese Army*

"Fathers and sons have gone to war for America for generations, yet none has shared their journey like Patrick Naughton's *Born From War*. From the jungles of Vietnam to the streets of Baghdad, Naughton takes us through America's longest and most controversial wars, detailing the pain and sacrifice of families in the name of freedom. This is a must read especially for those who never got affected by these modern overseas conflicts."

—Quang X. Pham, author of *Underdog Nation: Zero in on Effort and Results for Success* and *A Sense of Duty: Our Journey from Vietnam*

"This book should be required reading for any policymaker faced with the prospect of sending Americans to war with a cause that is worthy of their sacrifice. There is no better source for understanding war than an army officer who has been on the ground in a combat zone trying to relate his father's experience as an officer with the 82nd Airborne in Vietnam. Teachable points abound in these well-researched pages, which are laden with uncanny parallels of wars fought three decades apart. Nothing is learned by forgetting."

—Robert J. Dvorchak, journalist, army veteran, and author of *The Golden Brigade: The Untold Story of the 82nd Airborne in Vietnam and Beyond*

"*Born From War* is a powerful, thought-provoking book. Naughton declares that this is not an anti-war book, but rather it is an attempt at reconciliation. In this he is successful in reconciling his own war experience with that of his father's; writing that 'the relationship between a father and son can be tricky. Emotions and words are often left unspoken, but the bond is ubiquitous and unbreakable.' Naughton weaves his own Iraq experiences with his father's in Vietnam, expertly highlighting the similarities and differences. Additionally, in his concluding chapter, Naughton coins what he calls the Brown Principle, named after a soldier with whom his father served and died in Vietnam. Naughton states the principle is as follows: 'if you cannot with a straight face explain to hometown ma and pa that a conflict is worth their child's life, then it is not.' A simple yet powerful guide to policy makers about maintaining the support of the people when the decision for war is taken. Naughton's book made me think. It is a worthy contribution to not only American military history, but also a thoughtful work on how going to war changes people and their families."

—Kevin Benson, Colonel, US Army (Ret.), author of *Expectation of Valor: Planning for the Iraq War*

BORN FROM WAR

A Soldier's Quest to Understand Vietnam, Iraq, and the Generational Impact of Conflict

PATRICK W. NAUGHTON JR.

CASEMATE
Pennsylvania & Yorkshire

Published in the United States of America and Great Britain in 2025 by
CASEMATE PUBLISHERS
1950 Lawrence Road, Havertown, PA 19083
and
47 Church Street, Barnsley, S70 2AS, UK

Hardback Edition: ISBN 978-1-63624-514-0
Digital Edition: ISBN 978-1-63624-515-7

A CIP record for this book is available from the British Library

Printed and bound in the United Kingdom by CPI Group (UK) Ltd, Croydon, CR0 4YY

Typeset in India by Lapiz Digital Services, Chennai.

For a complete list of Casemate titles, please contact:

CASEMATE PUBLISHERS (US)
Telephone (610) 853-9131
Fax (610) 853-9146
Email: casemate@casematepublishers.com
www.casematepublishers.com

CASEMATE PUBLISHERS (UK)
Telephone (0)1226 734350
Email: casemate@casemateuk.com
www.casemateuk.com

For our son, Tommy, you need not follow in our footsteps … unless you want to.

Contents

Acknowledgements

It would take a full chapter to name all the soldiers, non-commissioned officers, and officers who have had a positive influence on my life. If we served together and you are reading this, know that I immensely value and treasure you as a brother or sister. We all voluntarily answered the call of our nation. For that we should hold nothing but pride in our hearts.

Thank you to my family for their patience in answering my numerous questions about growing up under the shadow of Vietnam. I am sorry for the scabs that may have been ripped off because of it. A heartful thank you to those who answered my cold calls and emails about long lost loved ones: Bob Boyce, James Brewer, David Compton, Bruce Dyer, Everett Emery, Charlie Gadd, Patrick Hiu, Joseph Lampara, Karen Wager, and Nguyễn Ngọc Sơn. Those who you knew killed in that conflict are now immortalized in these pages forever.

The skills developed to write this book are due solely to the patient mentorship via my various writing endeavors over the years by the Art of War faculty at the Army's Command and General Staff College and the guidance from various Army Center for Military History historians. Additionally, thank you to the ultimate polisher my proofreader Ed Crocker, and Vietnamese translator Nhan Phan. To the Casemate team, Ruth Sheppard, Elke Morice-Atkinson, and Daniel Yesilonis, thanks for taking a chance on this unorthodox book. To my wife's sister Katie Lipscomb, you are a marketing genius.

To the combat veterans of Vietnam who let me into my father's war, please know that the nation now appreciates and values your service: Joe Hindle, Richard Keller, Larry Lockeby, Alic Tahir, and Doyle Wilkins. Thank you for your unfiltered tactical, operational, and strategic perspectives on the conflict.

Of course, thank you to my father for sharing his painful memories about Vietnam. You have been a constant reminder of what it truly means to be a good man. Thank you to my mother Jeanie and my best friend, my sister Leanne, for their unwavering support throughout my life as well.

Thank you to my amazing wife Sheila for giving me time. The countless late-night hours and weekends spent writing this book as she cared for our infant son with zero complaints are beyond appreciated. Additionally, her constant encouragement through various episodes of writer's block and moments of self-doubt made this book possible. It is through her support that this work came to fruition.

Lastly, as my brother in arms David Briseno once said shortly before his death, "Be like a tank in life," forever a tanker he was, "it may not be the fastest or sexiest thing on the field of battle, but it always advances no matter what is thrown at it." To all who have served in any of our nation's conflicts, just keep going with your rucksack on, shoulders hunched, and your head held high. We will all push forward together against anything that may come against us.

Prologue

> "By God, we've kicked the Vietnam syndrome ..."
>
> PRESIDENT GEORGE H. W. BUSH

In the three-foot gap between a bookshelf and a worn-out living room couch lay a place of wonder for a young boy. The slope of the couch, combined with the dark carpet and placement of the living room lamp, created a murky cave where I would spend hours deciphering my discoveries. There, tucked away on a bottom shelf, treasure abounded. Interspersed between old books on geography, cooking, and exercising—untouched for years—were secreted small, green binders with United States (US) Army emblems in gold. In these folders, browned with cracked edges, were slips of musty-smelling paper embossed with symbols I did not understand about a place called Vietnam.

As I sounded out words such as Combat Infantryman's Badge, Heroism in Ground Combat, and All the Way, they soaked into my psyche. As I grew older, I began to understand these were military medals—earned by my father Patrick W. Naughton on faraway battlefields discussed only in hushed tones. I attempted to recreate my own combat scenarios in the lush hills surrounding the town of Hilo, Hawai'i. Dressed in camouflage and carrying plastic guns, my friends and I chased an imaginary enemy and carried out our own heroic deeds.

One time, when my mother was once again complaining about my grandmother's husband's lack of amicability, my father finally spoke up. "I get along with him just fine," he quietly said. My mom sucked her teeth followed by a loud "cha"; the inimitable sound of a Jamaican native after they have heard something ridiculous. "And why does he only get along with you?" she demanded. "Because we are both combat veterans," he calmly replied—my grandmother's husband was an Iwo Jima survivor with a wicked scar from shrapnel up his left arm. "We have a connection." My child-mind was not sure what he meant but I curiously replayed it in my head. Lying behind the couch on my belly with my feet in the air and medals spread out in front of me, that conversation reverberating in my subconscious, I thought that, surely, the Army is how one becomes a man.

As I matured and served in my own war, I began to wonder about Vietnam—along with my entire generation, who have only known conflict for the past 20 years in various corners of the world. Like most my age, everything I knew about the conflict was learned from movies. Films such as *Platoon*, *Full Metal Jacket*, *Hamburger Hill*, *The Deer Hunter*, and *Casualties of War*, and television shows such as *Tour of Duty* informed all I knew about the war. Movies such as *Rambo* and *Missing in Action* filled out my knowledge.

These and a slew of other 1980s war flicks completed my opinion of Vietnam—it was ugly, wrong, and everyone who served in it suffered from some type of post-traumatic stress disorder (PTSD). As I progressed through the ranks, my professional military education in the Army taught me there was nothing to be learned from the conflict, which was just an ugly speed bump between the Korean War and First Gulf War. Nothing to see here; best to move on.

Years on from the cave behind my parents' couch, with my own medals tucked away in a dusty corner and my own war tucked under my belt, I sat in my living room with tears flowing down my face—my wife shocked at the spectacle of both her husband and the news as we watched our allies being abandoned in Afghanistan. As the media screamed, "Saigon, 1975, all over again!" my curiosity about my father's war grew. This is not an anti-war book. Rather, it is an attempt at reconciliation. A quest to understand war and its enduring generational impact, ugliness, and all.

Vietnam: an event that has haunted America and its military for decades. Even as a young infantry soldier with the 101st Airborne (Air Assault) pre-September 11th, I understood that it cast an omnipresent shadow over everything we did. As we patrolled the training areas of what was then called Fort Benning, Georgia and Fort Campbell, Kentucky—as well as the big game prior to the wars on terrorism, the proving grounds of the Joint Readiness Training Center at Fort Polk in Louisiana—it was obvious the hold the war still had on us. It was clear, even to an 18-year-old private, that we were still in many ways fighting our old foe the North Vietnamese Army (NVA) and its elusive guerrilla wing and ultimate insurgent force the Viet Cong (VC). Even with the war long over, somehow these menaces now stalked the woods and swamps of the southern US. Their influence was hard to shake even as we readied ourselves to face more conventional threats after the end of the Cold War.

As my military career progressed I, like my father before me, became an officer, eventually even being assigned to Congress. It was here I noticed the specter of what some dubbed the Vietnam Syndrome, which I found to be present at all levels of national security. People's memory of Vietnam was of a war fought without the full weight of the military behind it, clearly defined political objectives, or the backing of the American people. I observed in Congress how simply throwing the word into any foreign policy discussion shut down discourse, frightened participants, and doomed many a proposed strategy—especially in regard to Iraq and Afghanistan.

Despite this, most senior military leaders of the late 20th century were Vietnam veterans who attempted to use their experience to positively shape military policies. This was demonstrated by one Vietnam warrior during America's next large-scale conflict in the deserts surrounding Iraq. "We're not going into this with one arm tied behind our backs," General Norman Schwarzkopf fumed to his commanders in 1991 before assuring them that, unlike Vietnam, they were there to destroy the enemy with everything at their disposal.[1] The great soldier and statesman Colin Powell concurred and took this notion one step further. He credited the war with shaping his doctrine and vowed that, when his generation's turn came to lead at the senior level, "we would not quietly acquiesce in halfhearted warfare for half-baked reasons that the American people could not understand or support."[2] History will judge if he successfully lived up to his mantra in the global war on terrorism.

The ghost of Vietnam also extended into the political arena. Ronald Reagan noted it as an omnipresent barrier to any type of discussions involving possible foreign military intervention.[3] Future politicians recognized its influence as well. "It's a proud day for America," declared President George H. W. Bush at the conclusion of the First Gulf War. Having promised all along that this conflict would not descend into another prolonged debacle that would divide the country, he declared the struggle won. "By God," a jubilant Bush continued to standing ovations, "we've kicked the Vietnam syndrome once and for all."[4] Years later, at the height of my own war, his son would evoke the memory of leaving Vietnam to a room full of veterans to justify the US staying in Iraq, calling it crucial to "American credibility."[5] George W. Bush would be chastised for his analogies between the two wars by many people, including a future president, who stated that Bush's policies were "pushing us toward another Saigon moment." Little did then-Senator Joe Biden know that he himself would later face the ghoul of Vietnam head on.[6]

As the nation's commitments in Iraq waned and involvement in Afghanistan increased, future presidents found themselves fighting off the phantom. Laying out his strategy for Afghanistan in 2009, President Barack Obama hit back against critics who called the war "another Vietnam."[7] In July 2021, when asked by reporters about the similarities between the two wars regarding the imminent withdrawal, now-President Biden defensively declared there were: "None whatsoever. Zero … there's going to be no circumstance where you see people being lifted off the roof of an embassy." He continued, "It is not at all comparable."[8]

As the departure from Afghanistan descended into chaos, Biden evoked Vietnam to defend the similarities being broadcast live into American homes, claiming that unlike leaders during the Vietnam era, he would not have asked Americans to serve in the first place in a "military action that should've ended long ago."[9] His political foe and predecessor, Donald Trump, seized on Biden's attempt to deflect the parallels. On his favorite media channel, Fox News, Trump described the scene at the Hamid Karzai International Airport in Kabul as one "that blows the helicopters in Vietnam away," further calling it one of the nation's most "humiliating" moments.[10]

Unfortunately, it appears that recently, America's experience in Vietnam has digressed from one that offers very real warnings and lessons for the future use of military force to misused historical analogies and political fodder. "Those of us facing the assignment to write the official history of the war in Vietnam," began an epigraph from Charles MacDonald, the Deputy Chief Historian of the US Army Center of Military History at the start of an official synopsis of the war from 1969. Curiously, this was the first document I accessed when I set out to learn about my father's year in Vietnam. What did MacDonald see dominating the narrative for all historians undertaking this task? "Jungle, inundated rice paddies, and punji stakes." Even then he anticipated the future negativity that would accompany this war, "but with a liberal portion of chastened optimism," he concluded, "we will find a path."[11]

Thanks to the grandiose strategizing and negative connotations it encouraged in barrel-chested generals, political opportunists, and pop culture pundits, it is easy to forget that the Vietnam War was fought by real people who left behind families and loved ones, sometimes never to return. People like my father, whose service was the sole reason I joined. A trove of letters and a detailed diary document his year at war. As I read through them and connected with those mentioned, I was shocked at how timeless and familiar his military service was compared to mine.

As a teenager, I remember him sitting at the dinner table, suddenly staring off into space. "I once saw someone step on a mine and pieces of him flew in the air," he blurted out of nowhere. My sister and I froze mid-bite and grew quiet, unsure what had prompted this revelation, but my father carried on eating as though nothing had happened. Armed with some of MacDonald's suggested optimism about the possibility of understanding Vietnam and now my own generation's wars, I needed to know more.

Chapter 1

"What are you going to do with your life ...?"

MILILANI HIGH SCHOOL TEACHER

Communism. To my generation, it is mainly a trigger word thrown around in the social media sphere to insult the left—if you want to paint a liberal into a corner, call them a commie and watch them try to squirm their way out. However, during my father's time it was deemed a very real threat to the capitalist way of life. Political pundits and strategic theorists of the era shrieked about the danger this philosophy posed to the free world. Soon, the supposedly Cold War that ensued from this ideological dichotomy started heating up in several places, including a little-known flashpoint on the periphery of Asia where Frenchmen were dying: Vietnam.

"You have a row of dominoes set up, you knock over the first one, and what will happen to the last one is the certainty that it will go over very quickly," noted President Dwight Eisenhower in 1954 when asked about the importance of Vietnam not falling under the sway of communism. With the Korean War just ending and the communist expansion in Asia halted there, "you could have a beginning of a disintegration that would have the most profound influences," he confidently declared, thereby laying the foundation for all subsequent treatments of the region.[1]

This was the notorious Domino Theory, born from the containment policy of the Truman Doctrine and nurtured by a slew of strategic whizzes over the years. If all of Korea had fallen, and now the tottering Vietnam, surely Southeast Asia would be next. Then the Philippines, Japan, Australia, New Zealand; heck, what's the next black and white game piece ready to topple after that? Hawai'i. This could not be allowed to happen; communism must be stopped in its tracks.

But what was the genesis of the Vietnam War? There was no *Lusitania*, Zimmermann telegram, Pearl Harbor or 9/11—no seminal event that shook the nation to its core and propelled it to war. Rather, Vietnam slowly burned in the background, growing in the periphery until suddenly it was an inescapable part of everyday American life. "My generation of students was led down the chute-to-chute in the catastrophe of a WWII [World War II] which could have been prevented," later noted the secretary of state for much of the Vietnam conflict, Dean Rusk. Communist hot spots continued to flare up all over the globe after this worldwide struggle. Events in Azerbaijan, Turkey, Greece, Czechoslovakia, Berlin, Cuba, and Korea preceded Vietnam and painted a dire picture of communist expansion indeed. US participation in and support to these clashes "was the key to prevention of World War Three," or so Rusk and others liked him believed.[2]

As this ideological struggle possessed the great national security minds of the time, my family grew up in paradise, oblivious to the simmering conflict on their doorstep.

Mililani High School, Mililani, Hawai'i; May 1996: In the nineties, joining the military was not in vogue. The economy was booming, and cell phones were on the rise. Home video games and the internet were taking off, Oprah Winfrey began to tell the nation what books to read, and everyone wanted to be a hip-hop gangster or alternative rocker. Lost in this noise was a 17-year-old kid trying to find his way. The product of a broken home and some tough neighborhoods that few *haole* (Hawaiian slang for white) boys would have survived, I found myself enrolled in special programs for disciplinary problems with the other troublemakers in high school.

"What are you going to do with your life?" yelled a frustrated teacher at the end of an especially vexing conversation about not doing my schoolwork. I thought back to my father and my youth spent playing Vietnam-driven soldier scenarios in the jungled forests on the slopes of Mauna Kea. Then, trying to look and sound tough to the other kids so I didn't become a victim (a well-honed survival tactic) I blurted out my just-formed life plan: "Fuck you! I'm going to join the Army!"

Red-faced and fuming, the teacher marched to her desk at the back of the room. Two minutes later, she interrupted my slouched-in-my-chair-quiet-tough-guy act: "Patrick, you have a phone call." Surprised, I walked to her desk and took the receiver. "Hello, this is Staff Sergeant Kamakahi, I will meet you at the flagpole after school," said a confident voice on the other line that was not going to take no for an answer. This simple phone call set me on my path to follow in my father's footsteps. Once all the papers were signed, the green Army folder adorned with pictures of smiling troops sitting on tanks sat on our coffee table. The date "July 23, 1996" was handwritten in permanent marker on a white sticky label affixed to the top right-hand corner—my ship date, a constant reminder for months of a looming unknown.

The Center for a New American Security's 2017 report, titled *Generations of War: The Rise of the Warrior Caste and the All Volunteer Force,* argues that today's military recruits primarily come from families with a history of service.[3] This certainly rang true for me. Service ran strong in my family. On my father's side, my grandfather was an Irish immigrant, but his sister served on Eisenhower's staff during World War II with the Women's Army Corps. My grandmother's family can trace their military roots back to a signer of the Declaration of Independence, Richard Stockton, and then forward to soldiers in almost every conflict including the American Revolution, Civil War, both World Wars, and Korea. Even my mother's side of the family served. Born and raised in Jamaica as part of the British Empire, her brother dedicated his life to Her Majesty's Army.

"I thought it was a good move," my mother told me years later about my decision to follow those before me in our family and join the Army. "It would keep you out of trouble. It would give you discipline because you were on the wrong track, drinking alcohol in rooms in Waikiki and getting drunk," she irritatingly told me. "You were out of control," she accurately concluded when assessing my then 17-year-old self.[4]

Regardless of my wayward past, if my family had no history and my father had not been a soldier, the thought of joining would never have crossed my mind, and I probably would have ended up in jail or worse. I have a recurring nightmare where I wake up in a prison cell and realize that all the positive things I have done in my life were actually just a dream. If I had not enlisted, I would have never seen the sands of the Middle East and the mega city of Baghdad; I would never have moved my family across the country multiple times on short notice to places we would never have chosen on our own. None of it would have happened. Unknowingly, Vietnam set the course of my life, and, in turn, it may set that of my son's—when he matures and is met by a recruiter near a flagpole of his own.

Mānoa Valley; Oahu, Hawai'i; 1960–1961: The Hawai'i of my father's youth was nothing like today. In place of the surf slippers, shorts, and t-shirts, accompanied by the musical cadence of Hawaiian pidgin on the playground of my childhood, was a strict dress and language code for both boys and girls. Despite the tropical climate, long pants, shoes, collared shirts, and below-the-knee dresses comprised the daily attire. Colorful madras fabric clothing, purchased at India Imports from the Ala Moana Center, was all the rage and allowed for some limited expression to break this monotony. Due to mandatory Reserve Officer Training Corps (ROTC) classes at Mānoa Valley's Roosevelt High School, even this small rebellion was stifled as the boys all had to have short hair and wear full dress uniforms every Tuesday—whether they wanted to or not.

My Uncle John and my father spent their youth in the Cub and Boy Scouts. My aunts Noreen and Eileen (the latter known affectionately by her Hawaiian middle name Momilani, or Momi) were Brownies and Girl Scouts. My grandmother, later known by all as Tutu (Hawaiian for Grandma) was always the Scout leader. All grew up in the faculty housing of the University of Hawai'i (UH), where my grandfather taught in the chemistry department and was a renowned scientist. This was a thrown-together neighborhood composed of repurposed World War II Army buildings and old prefabricated cottages transplanted from sugar cane plantations, known as "Haole Camp" by the locals. It was nestled next to what would become the Punchbowl Cemetery and the university's teaching farm, so fresh produce and boundless adventures were just a short walk away.[5]

As they grew older, the siblings morphed into their own personalities and joined the timeless Hawai'i High School cults. The daily ecosystem included tanned surfers, preppies in Madras, band nerds, and *mokes* and *titas*, which were tough guys and girls with attitude (hippies never quite took hold).[6] John was the cool-guy champion swimmer and borderline *moke* who all the girls lusted after. Noreen pursued her orchestral and art dreams—in between surfing Waikiki and, to the displeasure of the hotel staff, sprinting through their lobbies to get to the beach, dodging the likes of Tony Curtis and David Niven in the process.[7] Momi, the baby prep, was a soloist at church, high school, and with the Honolulu Opera Chorus, slowly learning and echoing Joan Baez protest songs as the '60s progressed.[8]

Meanwhile my father—the self-described ugly duckling—entered the high-stakes world of band and served as drum major. One day he would name me after him, at which point he became Patrick Senior. By the mid-1960s, the family were all deeply involved in romances and life, all the while experiencing an idyllic youth in paradise.[9]

Mānoa Valley, Oahu, Hawai'i; 1962–1965: Just like high school, up until the late 1950s most major universities required all male students to attend ROTC classes as part of their mandatory curriculum for their freshman and sophomore years. This waned a little due to various societal pressures, but with the passing of the ROTC Vitalization Act of 1964—which aimed to make it an enticing part of academia—the program was accelerated to meet the demands of the growing involvement in Vietnam.[10] UH was one of the few institutions across the nation in the early 1960s that never removed the ROTC mandatory requirement for all males throughout their first two years of college. Prior to their junior year, men would make the choice of whether to stay with the program to earn a commission or else end their military experience there. Graduating high school in 1962, after a brief stint contemplating becoming a drama major when he starred in a play with the then unknown Bette Midler, my father soon found himself two years into a degree in Geography in UH and at this very ROTC crossroads.[11]

"The draft was beginning to breathe down all single guys' necks," he recalled when asked why he stuck with it after he contracted for the final two years of ROTC at UH in 1964.[12] Family history also played a part in his decision, as it did mine, to put on a uniform. As he put it, military blood—going back to the American Revolution—ran thick in the family. "Military service was expected," he shrugged, "and if you have to go, better to be as an officer."[13]

As with many across the country, Momi wrestled with the draft and what she saw happening to her brothers. "Above all else," she wrote in a senior year high school homework assignment, "I am grateful I was born a girl." She witnessed young men scrambling to either go to college (with no degree in mind) or else find some other avenue to escape the draft. At 17, with President John F. Kennedy's words "ask not what your country can do for you, but rather what you can do for your country" still ringing in her ears, Momi continued to question the government and the support expected of Americans towards the growing war. "The boys of America will not have the complete democracy that the girls have," she despairingly wrote about their upcoming graduation, "and so they will be drafted."[14]

On July 28, 1965, the president reinforced my father's choice to control his own military destiny and not have it defined for him. To a crowded press room, wearing a dark blue suit and tie, Lyndon Johnson answered that infamous letter from a "woman in the Midwest" on "why Vietnam." He somberly announced to a nation, many of whom could not even find the country on a map, that he was raising the draft call from 17,000 a month to 35,000.[15] My Uncle John, as noted by his sister, took a risk and tried a different tack to avoid the draft. He successfully managed to join the Coast Guard a week before he received his notice in the mail.[16] By 1965, he was well entrenched in the maritime service and safe from the call up.[17] With one son in ROTC and the other tucked securely in the bosom of a Coast Guard cutter as a rescue swimmer, the family seemed safe from the ever-expanding Vietnam War.

My life growing up in paradise was similar, although my military journey was different. Joining the Army was an unusual move for most in my social group. No one was going to fight in a war—the world had moved on from that. Looking back now on the rise of radical Islam, it is almost shocking how we missed all the signs. As I matured, the rise of violent extremist groups was omnipresent while simultaneously invisible, just as communism was during my father's day. As his generation tried to contain communism, mine would do the same with terror. Who knew that we would end up fighting a conflict against it for over 20 years and counting.

Chapter 2

"Get out of this house ..."

JOOP DENEEVE

Emily Perez was the first person I knew who was killed in the global war on terror. I was not close to Perez, who died from a roadside bomb while leading a convoy in Al Kifl in September 2006, but she was in my platoon in officer basic at Fort Sam Houston, Texas. She was in first squad while I was in second; I spent the last four months of 2005 standing just behind her at our daily formations. I remember her telling me about the Army's plan to rush her to the 4th Infantry Division immediately following graduation so she could make their deployment to Iraq. A West Point graduate, she had plans to go all the way in the Army—and now she was dead.

Numerous other friends had been wounded, most from roadside bombs known as Improvised Explosive Devices (IEDs). This was a new term from my generation's war that is now part of the daily American lexicon—Vietnam had booby traps and punji stakes; Iraq and Afghanistan, IEDs. I remember a high school buddy telling me that years later, his body was still pushing small pieces of shrapnel in his legs to the surface. Another relayed how an explosion flipped the 5-ton armored vehicle he was in three times in the air like a toy. Finally, one of the toughest infantrymen I knew told me of how he still wakes up screaming each night, reliving a close-quarter Taliban ambush where he was wounded by AK-47 fire.

I watched month after month as the war churned and grew around me and more friends I knew were killed or wounded, several from suicides. I later learned that my family had already gone through the exact same thing, only on a much larger scale. The growing war in Vietnam became harder to ignore as casualties started to increase in homes across the nation. It turns out that a war fought with minimal troop commitment fed by volunteers—my war—churns out casualties at a much slower rate than a bloated one filled with draftees—my father's war.

Mānoa Valley, Oahu, Hawai'i; early 1966: "Why must our men die and kill in Vietnam?" asked a pamphlet in the *Honolulu Star Bulletin* delivered to the family's new home in Parker Place in Mānoa Valley. The full-page broadside, full of bold letters and emotional taglines, decried the still little-known war to the family as "cruel and senseless."[1] This was a rare anti-war event for a state that was staunchly military friendly due to its memory of Pearl Harbor in World War II and the storied 442nd Regimental Combat team: Hawai'i held service in high esteem.[2] However, it was not the leaflet that caught the family by surprise; rather, it was who signed it. Names they knew well were signatories—influential people such as the family's close friends the Banners, neighbor and music professor Raymond Vaught, and even Noreen's cello teacher Allen Trubitt. It was an initial sign that something was happening outside the confines of their beautiful tropical valley.

My family, like many around the nation, found itself split in support of a war that eventually grew to dominate the national conversation. My grandfather John (who all called Jack) and Momi were against Vietnam, whereas Tutu and my Uncle John Jr. were supportive, which "made for some lively dinner conversations," groaned Momi years later.[3] Noreen mainly focused on her music and art, which shielded her from the war. One night, family friends were in attendance, sharing drinks and playing cards with my grandparents, when the conflict came up. Joop DeNeeve (a World War II Dutch veteran whose son Pete was in Vietnam), and my grandfather had one too many and began arguing. Joop jumped to his feet and screamed at Jack to "get out of this house!" Tempers cooled and drunken chuckles erupted once he realized that he was not at his house but theirs. Ironically, once Pete returned from Vietnam, he became one of the biggest anti-war demonstrators in the islands.[4] This was a sign of a rift slowly growing in many homes around the US.

Near Trung Lập, Vietnam; April 1966: Besides some antiwar newspaper pamphlets, boozy outbursts, and lively dinner conversations, the war remained an abstract idea miles away from Hawai'i which had not impacted my family directly.

On April 4, Second Lieutenant (2LT) Thomas Blevins, known as Hawaiian Eye by his friends and labeled as the "Man with a Future" in his high school yearbook, placed his platoon into a defensive position about 2,000 meters northwest of the settlement known as Trung Lập. Blevins graduated with honors from UH with an economics degree, where he completed ROTC. Despite being only one year ahead of my father, he was already a seasoned platoon leader. Occupying abandoned enemy trench works arranged in a rectangle around a small farm, 3rd Platoon, A Company, 2nd Battalion, 27th Infantry (Wolfhounds) of the 25th Infantry Division settled in for the night.[5]

As part of Operation *Circle Pines*, the Wolfhounds were ordered to provide a linear blocking force across the axis of advance of the 1st Battalion, 69th Armor, who were tasked with sweeping the routes toward Trung Lập.[6] Unfortunately, two armored personnel carriers were disabled by mines, robbing the initiative from the advance and halting forces for the night until the vehicles could be recovered and the route cleared of mines.[7]

A tense and sleepless night ensued for the Wolfhounds, whose small patrols made contact throughout the evening with several enemy elements, proving the bad guys were there. At about 4:00am on April 5, a combined force of NVA soldiers from the 1st Battalion, 165 A (Main Force) Regiment, and VC fighters with a hodgepodge of uniforms and weapons snuck up on the unsuspecting company. At 4:20am they unleashed a barrage of small-arms fire, hand and rifle grenades, recoilless rifles, mortars, and rockets on the surprised Americans.[8]

As the enemy blasted away, VC soldiers—unarmed and unencumbered with gear and dedicated solely to hurling grenades and dragging away captured US weaponry—bombarded 3rd Platoon's position. Despite the deafening noise and debris being kicked up by exploding munitions, Blevins slowly stuck his head above the trench parapet to check on his men and was immediately struck by a piece of shrapnel. As their lieutenant lay unconscious on the trench floor, covered in dirt and spent shells, 3rd Platoon engaged in hand-to-hand fighting for the next 30 minutes as they tried to beat back the enemy horde.[9] Artillery was called in to their position to try to thwart the attack. A heavy barrage of almost 500 rounds, some landing as near as 50 yards from their positions and known as a danger close fire mission, finally gave the beleaguered men a brief reprieve.[10]

As an uneasy calm descended over the battlefield, the Wolfhounds could hear the enemy shouting orders, arguing, weeping, and moaning as they licked their wounds after the deadly volley. Expecting a final human wave at any moment, the men of A Company redistributed the ammunition taken off their dead and wounded. With stern handshakes and quietly mumbled prayers, they said their goodbyes to their comrades and made peace with their maker. At 5:25am, the silence was broken by a shrill whistle, followed by a single bugle call. Expecting the worst with this obvious signal, the besieged Americans were shocked when the enemy broke contact and retreated—thus ending what later became known as the first battle of Trung Lập.[11]

Recorded in the unit's summary as a "battle far more important than the mere size of the elements involved," it was the first time the enemy had massed its forces and risked a battalion-sized offensive against the 25th.[12] It was recorded as a "deliberate, well planned, and coordinated" attack aimed at annihilating the unit, which was thwarted only by the "fighting qualities of the officers and men of Company A."[13] A feather in the cap of the Wolfhounds for sure, but little solace to a family from Hawai'i.

Days before over a dinner of *poi* and *laulau*, Hawaiian staples sent to Blevins by his family back home, his father and uncle gave the young officer some advice.[14] "Don't be a hero," instructed his father, a World War II and Korean War veteran, "just do your job the best you can."[15] Chief Warrant Officer Four James Blevins and his uncle Sergeant John Ka'aihue, both also in Vietnam with the 25th, tried their best to connect with the young Blevins as often as they could. "My son never complained about the war," the elder Blevins later explained, "he knew he had a job to do in Vietnam."[16] His mother concurred, recollecting how their son wanted the Army to be his life and felt that he, like his father before him, was doing his duty.[17]

The younger Blevins received a minor bullet wound in the buttocks on February 4 but only spent two weeks in the hospital, yearning to get back to his unit the entire time.[18] Many wondered why he wanted to get back, but as his father, a personnel warrant officer, explained, "All the wounded men want to get back to their outfits as soon as possible. Thomas was always concerned about the welfare of his men." This was demonstrated by his actions during the onslaught of fire the platoon endured, peeking over the parapet to check on them. The older Blevins spent 10 hours holding the hand of his unconscious son in the field hospital before he passed. "I have seen many men die," he recalled, "but seeing my own son dying was the hardest thing I had to face up to."[19] Having turned 23 only weeks before, on April 6, Thomas succumbed to his wound.

When asked about the war, cracks had started to show in even the opinions of career soldiers. "Horrible," the older Blevins called the conditions in Vietnam when asked. A veteran of two wars, he labeled it a different kind of conflict, one with no clearly defined frontlines. Despite this and his son's death, he was disgusted with the growing anti-war protests at home and believed in the war, claiming that the men in Vietnam "resent such demonstrations."[20]

Blevins was buried in the National Memorial Cemetery of the Pacific, known as Punchbowl to the locals. In attendance was the entire UH ROTC class who knew him. "Losing him so early after his commissioning," remembered one cadet, "served as a personal motivator to all of his ROTC classmates."[21] Many of these classmates, like my father, were on the path to eventually join the war themselves. Blevins was also the first person the family knew who died in Vietnam.

My father did not know it then, but this would also be his initial introduction to a place he would grow to know well, Trung Lập. Like the Wolfhounds, he also took note of one telling lesson on the ferocity of Vietnam from the battle, "the bayonet for the M-16 rifle should be issued as soon as possible."[22]

Not long after Blevins's death, a new anti-war pamphlet appeared, this time in the Roosevelt High School newspaper. A now yellowed old broadside, flattened and folded in four from many years spent tucked away in family papers, depicts a scared young Vietnamese girl holding a baby boy. "We are tired of acting like members of a Greek chorus," stated the leaflet, "standing at the side watching a tragedy take place and merely offering occasional comments." The work, titled "America Second—Humanity First," decried the war as unjust and declared that the US was better than this. Unexpectedly, a new signer familiar to the family appeared on this declaration: Momilani Naughton.[23]

Vĩnh Thạnh Valley, Vietnam; August 1966: Life went on; the siblings had all completed high school and were working their way through various advanced degrees. John had moved on from college and landed a dream job working in the marine biology field, in which he would spend the rest of his life. No one imagined that Vietnam would force its way violently into their tiny world again so soon.

Delphine Funn and Momi grew up together through elementary and high school within the confines of the lush and safe Mānoa valley.[24] Delphine's older brother by one year, Gary Funn, shipped off to Vietnam in the fall of 1965.[25] A large, tough local boy, he was assigned to carry the M-60 machine gun. Lugging this 23-pound behemoth through the tough terrain and wicked heat of Vietnam could easily break a lesser soldier, but Gary carried it with pride. He knew that in a firefight the gun—or the pig, as it was affectionately called—would spit a massive amount of lead toward the enemy and protect his fellow soldiers.

While with A Company, 2nd Squadron, 12th Cavalry, 1st Cavalry Division, Gary fell victim to the scourge of the Vietnam combat soldier—malaria. After being hospitalized for two months in Hong Kong, Gary found himself back with the 1st Cav on search-and-destroy missions between Suối Cả and the Vĩnh Thạnh valleys.[26] With the pig cradled in his arms like a guardian sentinel, he watched over his unit with keen eyes as they searched for the enemy in the heavily jungle-covered hills and low-lying areas infested with 10-foot-tall elephant grass. It was there on August 10, 1966, that Gary would be killed by enemy small arms while providing suppressive fire with his M-60. "He died protecting his machine gun," remembered his comrades later in life. "What else could a good soldier do?"[27]

News of Gary's death in a war that many still knew little about again shocked the tight-knit Hawai'i community. Relatives and friends, many of whom worked with the local telephone company and Sears warehouse, honored Gary and his family with support and flowers; all shaken by this unexpected event.[28] For the Naughton family, Gary's death was appalling, but it soon faded with the hectic schedule of college social life and schoolwork.

"The 1966 twentieth-century man, too, is on a great adventure," began the final message around the same time of Gary's death to the UH graduating class from my father's year. Amid the great space race with the Soviet Union, many in the nation began to look to the heavens for inspiration and to explain their lives. "The search for a unified, complete picture of the universe is accomplished by an equally significant search," continued the sage advice to his class, "for a better understanding of another realm—human nature—and also for a more meaningful and satisfying existence."[29]

However, something kept distracting this skygazing generation away from the heavens; a nagging feeling that something wasn't quite right. Inklings of this tiny tear in US society are evident even in my father's yearbook in 1966. As the family garnered him with flower leis at his graduation and Tutu pinned 2LT bars on my newly commissioned father, some of his classmates protested the war. Tucked away in the back of the book are examples of this growing rift: on one spread, pictures of students peacefully holding signs declaring "Americans in Vietnam in the Defense of Freedom" and "We Must Support US Policy in Vietnam"; on the other, placards that shouted, "No More War" and "Stop the War in Vietnam."[30]

Camp Zama, Japan; May 1967: Blevins's father, a veteran of three wars, was correct about most things except one: not all wounded men wanted to get back to their units as soon as possible. As my family lived their lives, the war continued to grow. First Lieutenant (1LT) Everett Glick was well known by the Naughtons. His father was a sociology professor, and he grew up in faculty housing with the family. He too went to Vietnam and was wounded in action seriously enough to be evacuated to recover in Camp Zama, Japan.[31]

After several months on the mend, he got news he was to be returned to Vietnam and his unit, the 4th Infantry Division, the same one my friend Emily was killed in decades later. The thought of returning to the war was too much to bear. The division operated in horrendous terrain which included triple canopy jungle and excessive heat. It was tasked with protecting the border of South Vietnam; the first line of defense against any forces traveling down the infamous Hồ Chí Minh Trail. However, before he could be transferred, out of nowhere his family was notified he had died. "We really don't know," reported his mother frantically as his cause of death was withheld, "we are waiting for more details."[32] For a time, even Army officials in Hawai'i were uncertain whether he had succumbed to his earlier gunshot wounds or if he had died from something else.[33]

Eventually, word would filter out through all who knew him that, rather than return to Vietnam, Glick had committed suicide. Years later, my aunt still remembers the shock and sadness on learning of his fate.[34] He left behind a wife, a four-year-old daughter, and a three-year-old son. What would drive a man to leave two little babies behind? Something was definitely not quite right.

Chapter 3

"He never wanted to worry me ..."

MONIQUE EVARTS

His face had a permanent awkward look to it, as though he didn't know whether to smile or cry. He appeared to be going through the motions of walking, almost zombielike, shuffling through our headquarters in Baghdad when I recognized him. He was a man I knew well; I immediately rushed to him to try to offer some comfort. We hugged in an awkward way that only two guys with deep-rooted repressed emotions from birth can. After all, only days earlier his best friend had killed himself. When this happens overseas, the body is rushed home as soon as possible so the family can grieve. For the friends left behind—it is back to work, no breaks allowed.

I knew Major (MAJ) Michael Evarts well. A former football player and wrestler, his square-jawed barrel-chested freedom fighter facade hid a huge heart. "Man, that guy looks hardcore," remembered one new soldier assigned to the Combat Support Hospital we were in before getting to know the huge teddy bear everyone called MAJ Mike.[1] A family man with a wife and two young boys at home in Ohio, he loved them more than anything—which is why it was such a shock to everyone when he took his own life in Tikrit, Iraq on January 17, 2011. His young boys were outside playing in the snow when the official Army party arrived at the Evarts' household to inform them of their father's passing. "I saw a strange car in the driveway," his wife Monique remembered. "You saw the soldiers walking up and you knew. I don't even remember what they said, I was just in shock."[2]

"The circumstances surrounding his death are still being investigated," stated an official Army spokesperson to local inquiries from his hometown of Concord Township, Ohio.[3] Questions continued as his body was flown home five days later.[4] On a snowy and freezing cold January day, throngs of people bundled up against the frigid temperatures and lined the route that his body took to the funeral home. The procession watched with gratitude as well-wishers waved American flags and held salutes while some sang *God Bless America.* With silent "thank yous" mouthed to the strangers in the crowd by the Evarts family as they drove past, MAJ Mike received a hero's welcome. "We can stand out in the cold for someone who was willing to give their life [for our country]," stated one somber participant with her young children when asked why they had attended the impromptu vigil.[5]

With an Army honor guard in full dress uniform and black earmuffs to protect against the frigid temperature, Evarts was laid to rest in the Mentor Cemetery. A picture in the local newspaper depicts his two little boys wrapped up against the cold looking on, bewildered, as their mother receives a folded American flag from an Army Chaplain—not quite understanding what had just occurred. I still tear up when I view it.[6]

With 17 years in the Army Reserve, a growing family, and a promising civilian career, no one understood what had happened to Evarts. Although this was his second tour in Iraq and not as dangerous as his first, in many ways this one was harder, recalled his wife—"the first time, it happened real fast"—whereas for the second, he had more time to prepare and realized how much he was going to miss his family. "He was struggling to go, but he had to finish one more year before he could retire," his wife stated at his wake. "It was important to him to finish and to be able to get benefits … support his family." She had no idea that her husband was suffering in Iraq. He never mentioned anything to her. "He didn't tell me," Monique said through tears, "he never wanted to worry me."[7]

As late as April, three months later, the official line of the Army was that the investigation surrounding the death of Evarts would likely take a few more months to complete. After repeated requests by the local newspaper, the answer they finally got was that it would be up to the family, not the Army, if more information could be released. "And they have said they do not want to do so," stated the Army in an email, "the official military classification is that it was a noncombat-related death."[8] Just like Glick, the Evarts family had to wait a long time to get answers. I have seen these investigations play out time and time again and I have never understood why they take so long. As they progress, the Army sticks to the canned line that they cannot talk about an open investigation, so they just remain silent. While this may be true, it does not mean that a little empathy cannot be displayed throughout the process.

What happened in Iraq to MAJ Mike? I honestly have no idea. I heard many rumors, but I will not repeat them here. All I know is that he used his service-issued pistol to end his life. I reached out to his best friend to try to learn the truth, the man I encountered in our headquarters days after Evarts's death. Unfortunately, even years later it is too painful for him to talk about, which I respect completely. Buried in Evarts's online obituary is what I believe to be an anonymous message from his best friend's wife. "I'm writing this for my husband who served with you on your last tour," it begins. "He was and still is deeply affected by your death. He dreams about you and misses you dearly," the caring note continues; "he hopes to see you in Heaven someday and your endearing smile he talks about."[9]

I considered MAJ Mike a mentor and friend. He called me days before he died to ask me a question. I remember being extremely busy and not being able to help him in the same way I had done many times back in the US. He seemed disappointed, but I did not think anything about it. Days later he was dead. While part of me is sure our phone call had nothing to do with his death, I can't help but feel a sense of guilt; and I worry that it was just another thing in a litany of mounting disappointments which added to his depression. I also feel remorseful on a more personal level. He was a shared friend with my ex-girlfriend, who I had broken up with just before we deployed. I used his death as a pathetic excuse to try to reconnect with her. For that selfishness I am utterly ashamed.

There is probably not a soldier in the Army that does not have a similar story like this. A week after Evarts's death, Monique was contacted by another grieving widow. Five months earlier her husband Sergeant Thomas Penn had killed himself. Just before the unit deployed, it went to the rifle range to qualify. As the supply sergeant, Penn was responsible for securing the extra ammo in the arms room until it could be turned back into the ammunition supply point. But this never happened. Instead, Penn opened the arms room early the following morning and used one of the 5.56 bullets on himself. "I know how hard it is now, but I am telling you it gets a little easier day by day and sometimes minute by minute," was the supportive advice Penn's wife offered, "then it becomes hour by hour and so on."[10]

One can't discuss the global war on terror without also talking about suicide, the scourge that has seemed to attach itself to my generation's conflicts and has never let go. Glick's death made me realize that I know more people who died from suicide in the Army than from combat-related activities.

In the most recent Department of Defense (DoD) statistics tracked by the under secretary of defense for personnel and readiness through the Defense Suicide Prevention Office (DSPO), service member suicides have been on the rise. In 2021 alone, 519 service members and 202 family members died by suicide, as noted in its annual account on suicide in the military.[11]

The Veterans Affairs (VA) also tracks similar data but focuses on veterans in its annual numbers. In its most recent report from 2022, there were 6,146 veteran suicide deaths. This is 57.3 percent higher than the figure for non-veteran adults. Shockingly, suicide is the 13th leading cause of death among veterans overall and the second for veterans under the age of 45.[12]

A recent study in academia confirms the VA's findings, calling the trend of recent military suicides "deeply alarming." It notes that while suicide rates from among the public have steadily increased over the past 20 years, the numbers from among those who have served post-9/11 have easily outpaced the general population. "High suicide rates," the study scathingly concludes, "mark the failure of the U.S. government and U.S. society to manage the mental health costs of our current conflicts."[13]

To its credit, the DoD has attempted to lower suicide rates, establishing the DSPO in 2011, which is tasked with working with a myriad of government departments, non-governmental agencies, and non-profit organizations to try to reduce the risk of suicides in the military. Through an array of medical and non-medical resources, it seeks to prevent, intervene, and help those left behind heal from these deaths.[14] "Mental health is health," declared Secretary of Defense Lloyd Austin when outlining the DoD's three-pronged approach to countering the scourge: breaking down the barriers for those seeking help, addressing the stigma of doing so, and building healthy command climates where all can thrive.[15]

In addition to the DSPO, the US government also established a toll-free 24-hour crisis line for all service members, their family, and veterans. You only need dial 988 and then press 1 to reach a responder trained in crisis intervention and military culture.[16] In addition, the Army has its own initiative, called the Army Suicide Prevention Program. It includes a host of resources for prevention, intervention, and support for unit commanders, soldiers, and their families. The most famous is the ACE (Ask, Care, Escort) slogan. Branded on posters and wallet-sized cards for ease of carry, it instructs soldiers on how to ask someone if they are going to commit suicide, how to care for them if so, and then ways to escort them safely to get help.[17]

In contrast to the accusation leveled by the academic study at the government's and society's failure to manage the mental health costs of the past two decades of war, it appears the US government is taking the threat seriously and trying to address it. As is the civilian population. There are a host of non-governmental and non-profit organizations seeking to raise awareness about this issue and assist veterans and service members in obtaining help and support if needed. Who can forget the 22 Pushup Challenge that swept social media from 2014 to 2016?

All this begs the question—why has this tragedy impacted my generation so severely? Our conflicts were no easier or worse than previous ones. Is it a data collection anomaly or truly a generational issue? "No, I don't remember any suicides—in Nam or afterwards," replied my father when I asked if he personally knew anyone who had taken their own life due to Vietnam (even after I reminded him of Glick).[18] I took this to mean he was implying that this is a problem unique to my generation and not his.

"You are doing God's work killing these bastards," forcefully declared a soldier my dad served with when I asked him about the suicide discrepancy between the two wars, "you ought to be proud of yourself." He compared the Islamist extremists we faced to the "atheistic assholes" from his war and how they both raped, pillaged, and plundered the civilian populations at will. He credited popular culture in the US as being the reason why so many killed themselves from my generation's conflicts, shamed into believing that our actions overseas were fundamentally wrong no matter the reason. "To go home and commit suicide is pretty goddamn dumb," he declared about US efforts to stop the barbaric acts the enemy perpetrated during both conflicts. "You've done a wonderful thing ... you'll never lose a night's sleep if you understand that."[19]

Personal hard-assed opinions aside, I leave the answer to this question to academia and social scientists; however, no amount of statistics, suicide training, phone numbers, posters, or handouts can take the place of knowing your soldiers.

One of my most respected mentors once told me, "Under no circumstances, ever, do you befriend a subordinate on social media." He further emphasized, "You may one day have to order them to their deaths; you are their leader, not their friend." While I respect his advice tremendously, on this point I disagree. Today's generation of junior soldiers live out their entire lives online. If depression has set in or they are contemplating harming themselves or others, chances are they will drop hints or beg for help through their various platforms. While it should never replace personal and direct leadership, it is certainly a powerful tool that a leader can use to monitor their soldier's mental health. I have personally intervened three times and successfully prevented a possible suicide because of what I read in a post. Leaders must adapt to the times and go where their soldiers are—and sometimes that is the made-up world of social media.

But back to my family, their war, and the growing impact it was having on their lives. For Momi, one event soon ripped her eyes away for good from the dreamlike heavens mentioned in my father's yearbook message. By now married and settled into family life and completing school, she had kept in touch with an ex-boyfriend who was serving in the Army. It became harder to look to the stars, as the yearbook advised, with bullets zipping by friends on the ground in Vietnam, especially when more started dying.

Chapter 4

"Singing when the lights went out ..."

MOMILANI NAUGHTON

Thoughts of a perfect tropical beach filled his dreams each night as 22-year-old Lieutenant Jan Doxey lay sleeping in his bunk just west of today's Hồ Chí Minh City (formerly Saigon), before starting his day as a communications officer with the 25th Infantry Division.[1] An exceptionally talented singer who starred as the lead in numerous high school plays with Momi, Jan also felt the same societal pressure of service that my dad did. Unable to afford college, he was originally slated to sing for the United Service Organizations (USO), but with a career Marine Corps colonel as a father, there was a strong expectation that he serve in another capacity.[2] Instead of entertaining and raising troop spirit with his voice as part of USO acts, he found himself at basic training at Fort Ord, California and then Officer Candidate School (OCS) at the then-named Fort Gordon, Georgia.

"We spend every day marching and attending classes," Jan wrote to Momi about his lack of communication, "all the free time we have seems to be spent polishing brass and leather."[3] Upset about his lack of singing opportunities, he complained that he could only do that in one of two places: church and the shower. "And since I take a shower with at least 3 other guys and as many as 5 others, I don't sing long there," he joked.[4]

Despite not being with the USO, later in the tough crucible that is OCS Jan was offered a similar opportunity to boost morale. When the training, advising, and counseling (TAC) officers—the officer version of a drill sergeant—discovered that Jan loved singing and operettas, something alien and scary to the olive drab world of the army, they hatched a plan to embarrass him. Forcing him to the front of the class of a group of exhausted officer candidates, the TACs belittled him for his passion and ordered him to sing. Thinking this would be the ultimate form of humiliation and a great lark, they were quickly dumbstruck into silence as all stared on with open mouths. Without hesitation, Jan began to expertly belt out the exuberant "Drink, Drink, Drink" from *The Student Prince.*

"To this day in my mind I can still picture everything as it occurred," remembered his classmate at OCS. "There was total silence among the candidates and the TAC officers until Jan had finished." From that point on, no one made fun of him. In fact, quite the opposite: after the lights went out at the end of each grueling day, Jan would sing to ease the homesickness of his bunkmates until they fell asleep. "In the quiet and silence of the barracks his voice would penetrate and resonate throughout, bringing peace and a sense of calm," recalled a friend decades later. The lights out rule, normally a time of total quiet, was just this once allowed to be broken by the TACs.[5] "Please write if you can or whenever you can," pleaded Jan to Momi as he battled his own melancholy, "because it's pretty lonely here without people you know and love."[6]

"One day when we had a rare moment to relax," remembered Joseph Lampara, a friend from OCS, Jan showed him a photo of the young woman he had been writing to. He could not remember what the girl looked like, except to say that despite their breakup, Jan was still fond of her. A yellow manila envelope from my Aunt Momi arrived for me on a warm Texas January day. Among its contents from a long-ago war that my aunt had saved, it contained several old pictures of a young couple. In a beautiful pink gown, with a *pikake* lei made of tiny, small ball-like white flowers, stood my aunt. Next to her in black pants and a white tuxedo suit was a smiling Jan. "It is really good to see it," Joe replied after I emailed him a copy. "I remember Jan, but after so many years I had forgotten how young we all were … I will save this photo among my others from that long ago time."[7]

As Jan slept and rested his extraordinary voice on a February morning in 1968, perhaps dreaming of past days spent on the beautiful beaches in Kailua on Oahu, the Tet Offensive was 22 days old. The massive surprise attack, launched during the most important holiday in Vietnamese culture, caught US forces off-guard. "Over 5,000 Viet Cong and North Vietnamese troops started moving southward from Phuoc Long Province on 20 February," noted the Central Intelligence Agency's (CIA) situation report on the week's activities. The troops swarmed south to attempt another thrust to seize Saigon, set to begin on February 22, the same morning that Jan slept peacefully in his bunk.[8]

In the quiet early morning hours, as part of this offensive an NVA team maneuvered a new weapon onto the battlefield, the Chinese-manufactured-and-supplied Type 63 multiple rocket launcher. With its 12 tubes mounted in three rows of four on a towable chassis, it looked like a medieval contraption designed to shoot arrows. The arrows, however, were 107-millimeter rockets that could saturate an area the size of a football field with each salvo.[9] As each rocket burst from its tube with a loud swoosh, one of them slammed into the roof directly above Jan, wounding his bunkmate but killing Jan as he slept.[10]

In late February 1968, Momi was visiting Waikiki beach when she heard a familiar group called "Up with People" playing at the old Queen's Surf Restaurant and Nightclub. She decided to go listen and say hello to her performing friends. Before she could do so, she was stopped by the band director and Hawai'i music legend Shigeru Hotoke, a former teacher of Jan's. Emotionally distraught, with tears in his eyes, he delivered the news that Jan had just been killed in Vietnam.[11] Years later, she is still saddened by his death and the loss of a talent that might have been world-changing. "I just hope he was still singing when the lights went out," she reflected, "and perhaps did the night he died ... just a hope."[12]

Quảng Điền Province, Vietnam, March 1968: As the Tet Offensive continued to rage, another Hawai'i boy was caught up in its whirlwind. Twenty-two-year-old 1LT Frank Rodriguez graduated from UH a year after my father. He knew him well as they were both in ROTC and majored in geography together. There, Rodriguez was the drill team commander for their ROTC program. Awarded a broken rifle stock as a jest by his teammates at a graduation party just before he left to join his first unit, he was liked by all.[13]

In December 1967, as a sign of the growing war, the US tapped into its strategic reserves and summoned the final two brigades from the 101st Airborne Division to join the fighting in Vietnam. One brigade had already been present since 1965. Rodriguez, along with over 10,000 other Screaming Eagles, was a part of Operation *Eagle Thrust*, the largest airlift in the war. Two brigades of personnel and equipment were airlifted from Fort Campbell, Kentucky directly to the war zone. This brought the total troop count in Vietnam to about 475,000, larger than the peak of 472,800 soldiers during the height of the Korean conflict.[14]

Cutting a striking figure in combat fatigues and helmet, and with a .45 caliber revolver and dagger tucked into his belt, the division commander, Major General Olinto Barsanti reported to General William Westmoreland, commander of Military Assistance Command, Vietnam (MACV) from 1964 to 1968. With a confident salute and the declaration, "The 101st Airborne Division is present for combat in Vietnam," their war began.[15] Some officers love this theatrical stuff. They've seen too many war movies and think if they look like a character their soldiers will think they are tough and follow them. Sometimes it works, sometimes it doesn't; for Barsanti though, it worked like a charm. With a gleam in his eye at seeing the former division he commanded prior to the war, Westmoreland welcomed what he dubbed "a formidable fighting force" to support what he called a "right and just" cause for freedom.[16]

Three months later and miles away from the parade field, led by Rodriguez, 3rd Platoon, A Company, 1st Battalion, 501st Infantry from the 101st slugged it out with NVA and VC forces in what they called "Eight Klick Ville." It was so named for the 8-kilometer area peppered with small villages infested with enemy forces that they constantly air assaulted in and out of. As my father would learn all too well, whack-a-mole was the name of the game. Intelligence would find out about possible enemy locations in one of the villages and the 101st would cobble together a team and throw troopers at them.

On March 29, in one of these rural communities, 3rd Platoon found the enemy. As the gunfire rang out, word quickly spread through the ranks that their platoon leader had been hit. Telling his squad to stay put, Sergeant Charlie Gadd worked his way toward his last known location. As he crept forward, he noticed a wounded NVA soldier trying to crawl out of his spider hole. Not wanting to give away his position, Gadd quietly flung a grenade into the pit, blowing the enemy soldier out of it. He then advanced and came upon Rodriguez, who had died instantly from several rifle shots to his chest and face. His radioman was beside him, shaken but still alive.[17]

Despite 2nd Platoon trying to warn 3rd of the hidden fighting position, Rodriguez had walked right up on the spider hole only feet away from the rifle muzzle that killed him. As the rest of the platoon coalesced on the area and slugged it out with any remaining enemy in their hidden positions, Gadd tagged the Russian-designed SKS semi-automatic rifle that he took from the dead enemy he had killed with his grenade, suspecting that it was the weapon that had killed their leader. He sent it to battalion with the intent of taking it home as a war trophy, but some rear area puke got to it first and took it for themselves. Rodriguez was killed along with another officer and a private in an unremembered operation in an unnamed firefight.[18]

This was another funeral for current cadets and UH ROTC alumni to attend, including my father. One night while visiting his grandson he relayed to me his memory of Rodriguez being buried at Punchbowl and how they helped each other graduate with the same geography degree. Another cadet also credited Rodriguez's tutoring being responsible for him making it through school. He also recollected seeing him off before he left for Vietnam. "I am not coming home," Rodriguez remarked chillingly before entering Honolulu airport. Even then "he knew," remembered his friend.[19]

Years later, three of the men from his platoon recalled what a shocking loss his death was. Rodriguez was a highly respected officer who led from the front and set an example in all he did. "We were very fortunate to have such exceptional leaders," they thankfully told me.[20] One relayed how he still remembers kneeling besides his body to say goodbye before he was loaded on the evacuation helicopter.[21] Rodriguez was the 108th person to die in the war from the State of Hawai'i.[22] And the fifth loss for the family from a war that continued to sneak up on them.

University of Hawai'i; Oahu, Hawai'i; May 1968: Events like this were occurring all over the nation. Combat deaths, combined with the fact that Vietnam was the first conflict to be broadcast live into every home each night with the evening news, propelled antiwar protests beyond simple newspaper pamphlets and sign holding into outright physical demonstrations—even in normally quiet Hawai'i. From May 20–30, the UH campus erupted into its own anti-Vietnam sit-in that lasted for ten days. "That was probably the most difficult of stands to take in Hawai'i," later recalled student organizer Linda Delaney, "because the military presence was more overwhelming than it is now and World War II was still fresh in the community's mind."[23] Occupying Bachman Hall on the main UH campus, around 200 faculty and students expressed their views via a peaceful protest. Eventually, 160 of them were hauled out and arrested by police in a surprise raid that left them feeling betrayed by the administration and community.[24]

More sobered by the war now, Momi watched on with sad eyes, and even stoically listened to some of the impassioned speakers—but thanks to Jan, she just didn't have the heart to join in.[25] Noreen remained submerged in arts and music, with Vietnam remaining a background abstraction—so much so that her only memory was lugging her heavy cello case as she stepped over the sleeping students occupying Bachman Hall on her way to the music department.[26]

While all of this was happening in the US and Hawai'i, my father received a "delay to active duty" of two years from the Army and left to attend a master's program in Geography at the University of Alberta in Canada. He watched from his college in Canada and tried to focus on his studies, knowing he still owed the Army time. John and Momi were both married, and Noreen was in a serious relationship and working her way toward marriage herself. Sadly, all this would be once again shattered by a war that refused to go away.

Bình Định Province, Vietnam, June 1968: A huge smile beamed from the senior Roosevelt High School class photo of Algernon Ka'akimaka, known to his classmates and my family as Algie.[27] He was an aspiring artist and author who had several of his paintings exhibited at the Honolulu Academy of Arts and a poem about a trip he took to Lahaina published in the local *Beacon Magazine* before he left for Vietnam.[28] Algie also had a huge heart and loved everything about the ocean and his Polynesian heritage.[29] These were the details his friends remember most as he spent his last week before leaving for the military at various house parties and watching movies at the Varsity Theater in Mōʻiliʻili.[30]

Algie was one of those who Momi watched with concern as he was drafted into the Army. After a 10-day leave in 1967, enjoying the ocean he loved, Algie ended up in Vietnam as an infantry sergeant with the 173rd Airborne Brigade, opposing the NVA and VC every step of the way as they tried to advance during the Tet Offensive.[31] As part of the effort to halt communist forces, in March 1968 the 173rd initiated Operation *Cochise* in the Bình Định province. The operation had two objectives: to rid the heavily jungled mountain areas of the NVA and to destroy the VC in the bountiful, rice-producing lowlands.[32] After several months of hard fighting, the brigade eventually drove NVA conventional forces out of the area.[33]

By May 1968, Algie had also grown disillusioned by his experience in the Vietnam War. "I have so much to say that I'm delirious with anxiety," he wrote to journalist Jesse Sartain from overseas. Sartain was the editor of *Young Hawaii* magazine, a venue aimed at Hawai'i's booming youth culture. "I've witnessed some goings-on that would definitely call for a congressional investigation," continued Algie. "The black market, senseless killings, corruption among our leaders, info about pot … I want to expose everything, but would like your advice since I was planning to use your paper to do so."[34] Algie would never get the chance to expand on his charges as the operational environment in Bình Định shifted suddenly, with disastrous consequences for the aspiring author.

"It became obvious in June," noted 173rd intelligence reports, "that the 3d NVA Division had pulled out of the area to receive replacements, reequip, retrain and recover from the beating inflicted by the Brigade. It left behind small units to aid the local VC in sniping, bobby-trap and mining operations and terrorist attacks."[35] This was an unfortunate development that would impact Algie firsthand.

In a glossy book produced by the brigade, illustrations and descriptive prose recorded and memorialized the fourth year of war for the 173rd. It was something a civilian would hardly recognize and dub a yearbook, but operational maneuvering, body count statistics, and tales of valor replaced sports team victories and student club achievements in the military's clumsy attempt to normalize horrendous combat conditions into something familiar; almost comfortable. I have my own glossy yearbook from Iraq tucked away.

In its snazzy pages, accompanied by action shots, the yearbook explained, "The war in Vietnam has had its big battles, but most of the action comes in company-size or smaller contacts known as firefights … in almost every firefight, someone has to become a hero. Someone endangers himself to knock out a machine gun or silence a sniper, crawl under fire to bring needed supplies or rescue a wounded man. But as they say," it flippantly continued, "it's no big thing, it happens all the time."[36] Unfortunately, it was a big thing to the Ka'akimaka family. After surviving some of the roughest fighting in the war, on June 1, 1968, Algie was killed by one of the snipers left behind by the enemy to harass the Americans.[37]

This was another awful reminder to the Naughton family that the war was very real, growing, and getting very close. No matter what they did, the war kept yapping and snapping at their heels like a demented stray dog, howling, "Look at me, I have something to say."

Chapter 5

"A little pissant war ..."

PATRICK W. NAUGHTON SR.

The weather made it feel as though I was swimming through boiling water. Fort Benning, Georgia (as it was then called) was a long way from home. For a teenager used to drinking shoulder-tapped purchased beer with friends behind the local convenience store in Hawai'i, the hot oppressive humidity of a summer in the south was a different world.

As I conducted one of the countless foot marches during basic training in the middle of the day, my heavily recycled web gear—stained with the sweat of countless's privates before me—dug into my tender flesh. The punishing march is the main tool of an infantryman, like a scalpel to a surgeon or a laptop to a tech geek. An infantry soldier fights and survives on their feet with a rucksack strapped to their back. In certain spots my gear chafed the skin raw, where the salt from my perspiration and dust from the red Georgia clay rubbed into the wound, causing a new level of discomfort unknown in civilian life. The Army was like a sand blaster to the face, completely stripping me of my self-identity. No longer knowing who I even was anymore, I thought to myself, "What am I doing here?"

My Kevlar helmet seemed too heavy on my head, forcing my eyes to the ground. Prickly heat set in along the band. Not that it would have helped even if I could have looked ahead: a steady flow of sweat poured into my eyes, making the world one big shimmering blur. The M-16 A2 rifle thrust into my hands on day one caused my biceps to burn as I strained to keep it at the ready. A slight dip of the rifle's barrel resulted in a string of unpleasant expletives from the drill sergeant. One can only hear "Get that weapon at the ready, fuck-stick!" screamed in one's ear so many times a day. "How much further can I go?" I debated with myself. My one-size-too-small, issued combat boots—size eight was all they had left for a size nine 18-year-old boy—intensified the pain in my already infected blisters and aggravated the growing stress fracture in my right middle metatarsal.

This was an injury that could have got me sent home. An injury I told no one about except for a choice few in my platoon who I trusted. They snuck me 800 milligram ibuprofen or muscle relaxers issued to the other privates when they could.

"What the fuck are you doing?" exclaimed my bunk mate, a California beach bum in his previous life. "You're going to cause permanent damage to your foot, go to sick call," he pleaded.

"No," I calmly replied, "they will send me home." This was my worst fear, worse than death: being sent home a failure. I imagined the disappointment in my father's eyes as I walked through the working-class neighborhood of Kaimuki, just outside of Honolulu, that we moved to just before high school. I imagined seeing the confused looks of everyone I ran into. "Eh, brah, I thought you went Army?" they would ask in the sing-song cadence of Hawaiian pidgin that was my native tongue, learned on the hardscrabble streets of Hilo on the Big Island. "I did, but I nevah made it," I would have meekly replied as I hung my head in shame. The thought of all that was too much to bear. No. I decided I would I push on until either my foot fell off or I became a soldier.

Fort Benning, Georgia, home of the United States Army Infantry School, has been training soldiers since 1918.[1] Officers and enlisted men alike cut their teeth on this same terrain. There, the only objective is to take in a pile of civilian jelly and spit out a hardened soldier in mind and body who can march all day with any weight through any environment—and still fight when they get there. As I painfully plodded along, surviving my own personal crucible to reach this goal, my mind began to wander. My head hung low as I felt sorry for myself, and I soon noticed the 20-inch-deep ruts in the clay on the side of the road. Formed through the tread of countless soldiers before me, these paths accompany almost every road in Kelly and Sand Hill, the main areas where all infantry training was and still is housed.

It suddenly occurred to me: I was literally walking in the footsteps of my father as he trained for Vietnam. My web gear and weapon were nearly identical to what my father wore and carried during the conflict. I could do this: soon I would be a man; soon, like my father before me, I would be a grunt. An infantry soldier in the greatest army the world has ever known. My eyes rose as I cleared the sweat from my eyes with a filthy sleeve. My back straightened and my rifle steadied. I could take one more painful step after all. Now, I remembered, this was what I was doing here.

Eventually my skin toughened up and the soles of my feet became hard as rocks. After I had chewed some of the same dirt that my father had, I was assigned to my first unit. The 101st Airborne Division, the Screaming Eagles—underdogs who bore the brunt of the full fury of Hitler's counterattack and thumbed their noses at him with the simple phrase, "nuts." The unit came to fame in World War II as countless American families huddled around their living room radios, listening to stories of the division's scrappy Alamo-like stand during the Battle of the Bulge.

For a young man fresh out of basic training, nothing could beat wearing this black, white, red, and gold storied patch featuring a defiantly shrieking eagle's head. It was just a piece of cloth, but oh how it infused one with pride. I couldn't help but compare it to my own father's unit that he served with in Vietnam, the celebrated 82nd Airborne Division (nicknamed the All Americans). Surely, I thought, my own patch would make him proud.

The infantry of the late 1990s was a mere shell of its once great self. The mechanized hordes of the First Gulf War and the strategic airpower demonstrated there and during Yugoslavia's breakup lulled many military minds into thinking they had found the answer to putting grunts on the ground; found a way to eliminate the chance of a Vietnam ever happening again. "You will always need infantry to take and hold terrain," empathically declared my young and eager platoon leader as we stood around dejectedly dividing up 100 rounds of blank ammunition between each squad—11 rounds for each man—which was supposed to last us for two weeks of field training.

An air assault unit supposedly on the cutting edge of helicopter operations, we were told we had no money to fuel our helicopters (known as birds to a soldier) so we would simulate flying into battle on the back of trucks. The trucks would stop, and we would all pile out and imagine we had just left a bird as it drove off into the distance. Then we were told we had no money for fuel for the vehicles, so we would walk and simulate riding on trucks, which were still simulating the helicopters—my first intro to military logic was an interesting one. Woe be upon the private who asked why we didn't just skip simulating the truck and go back to mimicking the bird landing instead.

By this point in the Army, Vietnam combat veterans only existed at the very senior levels of Army leadership. The infantry had a slim slice left from the First Gulf War but very few had seen any actual combat there. What my unit, Charlie Company of the 2nd of the 502nd, did have was two of the best non-commissioned officers (NCOs) I have ever served with: Sergeant First Class (SFC) Kenneth P. Boorn, my platoon sergeant, and Company First Sergeant (1SG) Sean T. Watson. Both were veterans of the battle in Mogadishu made famous by the book and movie *Black Hawk Down*. These two men watched our diminishing combat prowess and plummeting morale with concern and decided to do something about it.

A game of good cop/bad cop ensued as these two NCOs sought to better the unit. I still look back and feel like I was in some type of sick, fucked-up war movie family triangle with these two as my surrogate fathers; my own personal battle for the possession of my soul as depicted in Oliver Stone's 1986 classic *Platoon*.[2] SFC Boorn we loved: he was like Gunnery Sergeant Highway in Clint Eastwood's *Heartbreak Ridge*—a crusty old nonpolitically correct combat veteran who would do anything for his men. Once, after the company commander lambasted us for 30 minutes on not firing from the prone enough during maneuvers, he pulled us aside. "Fuck that shit," he said. "I was kneeling when I was shot. Had I been lying down I would be dead. You do what the fuck you want, men."

We despised 1SQ Watson, a relentless taskmaster who commanded perfection in everything we did. There was no escaping his demanding eye. He drove us day and night to ensure we understood how to survive and thrive in combat conditions. "I know I rode you all hard," he humbly informed our group of tired infantrymen when he left the unit. Informally huddled on the side of the company area with no officers or senior NCOs present, he bared his soul. "Combat is horrendous, men. One day you will see what I was trying to do." Years later, I would run into a buddy from this time. "Bro, 1SG Watson and what he taught us saved my life," I said. A silence passed before my friend, who despised him the most out of all of us, quietly answered, "He saved mine, too."

Both only wanted to keep us alive by teaching us what they had learned on their own faraway battlefields.

Behind all of this, a quiet voice whispered—Vietnam. An experience buried behind my father's sad eyes as he watched me join the Army. The same green folder affixed with a ship date on our coffee table not only reminded me of my fate but must have also impacted my father. "Vietnam was just a little pissant war in 1964 when I signed up for advanced ROTC," he recalled, when I finally had the courage to start asking him about the war and why he voluntarily joined the army during a time of conflict.[3] In this, he was unknowingly echoing what President Lyndon Johnson raged to his generals in 1965 on hearing their lack of solutions "for this damn little pissant country."[4]

Fort Benning, Georgia; July 1968: As my father slugged through graduate school and watched what was happening at home from afar during his two-year delay, the Army finally came for its due. Fort Benning, home of the infantry, became his new home, just as it did for me. The family saw him off at the Honolulu airport. The event was captured in a photo that still exists—everyone dressed loosely in floral patterns for the tropical climate, my father in full uniform with the prerequisite flower leis stacked around his shoulders up to his ears. After Basic Infantry Officer School, he found himself teaching there as part of the Recoilless Rifle and Missile Subcommittee—running men through the same ruts I would later tread.

Bored out of his mind by office work and range safety duties, he called Infantry Branch and volunteered for Vietnam with the little old admin lady in tennis shoes who answered the phone. The fact that he volunteered to go to war when he did not have to was something he hid from the family for years. He was given the choice of going to Ranger School or the Jungle Operations Training Center (simply called Jungle School) before shipping out. As the latter was shorter, he prepared to depart for steamy Fort Sherman in Panama to begin his training.[5] He later snidely joked that he "should have gone to the rice paddy warfare school" as that was where he saw much of his combat.[6]

Vietnam knocked on my family's door one last time before my father stepped foot in country, by way of another one of his former classmates and junior ROTC friends, Herbert Cho. After high school he had moved to the mainland and joined the Los Angeles Police Department while taking classes at the University of California.[7] There he received his draft notice. It could have been deferred by his police service, but he decided to go anyway. Like my father, societal and family pressure had exerted itself on the once all-star guard and Roosevelt High School football team captain.[8]

Herbert became a sergeant and served with the 1/50th Infantry Battalion under the 9th Infantry Division. As part of an elite group called a Long Range Reconnaissance Patrol unit or LRRP (pronounced by rhyming it with burp), he searched for enemy forces by stealthily penetrating deep into their territory to bring the fight to them. A seasoned combat veteran by late 1968, Herbert and his LRRP unit found themselves patrolling the Mekong Delta region with one of South Vietnam's elite counterinsurgency Provincial Reconnaissance Unit (PRU) teams, who were supporting the CIA's controversial Phoenix Program. This was a long way from home for the island boy from Mānoa Valley.

Cho was expected home for leave in a couple of weeks. Tragically, the ingenuity of the VC struck once again before that could happen.[9] While on patrol with his LRRP unit and PRU team just outside their base camp at Đồng Tâm at 0815 September 25, 1968, they struck a booby trap, which riddled them all with shrapnel. Three Americans and one PRU member were wounded by a claymore mine.[10] This US-made weapon was probably stolen by the VC from the very perimeter of the American camp. Cho, peppered with steel ball bearing-sized projectiles in his neck and chest, quickly bled out and died on site.[11] This was a final reality gut punch for my father. "Hey," it said, "this shit is for real, ask Tom, Gary, Everett, Jan, Frank, Algie, and Herbert. No one cares about the pamphlets your family and friends signed, or who shut down UH for ten days, or who's whining about the war." With a combat boot to the ass, my father was on his way to Vietnam, Republic of.

There has been nothing sadder than researching the men who died during the war that impacted my family. Most of their stories can be found in the various online memorial pages created to remember those who were killed in Vietnam. There, family members, friends, and strangers can post pictures and leave messages for their loved ones. It was an emotional roller coaster to dig through the posts and find old photos of smiling young men cut down in their youth. Reading the short notes from old friends and sweethearts who posted every year on their birthday or death anniversary was truly heartbreaking, especially as you notice how the messages fade out over time as those who knew them pass themselves or reluctantly move on with their lives. I can't help but wonder if the same thing will happen to those I loved who gave their all in the wars against terrorism.

Chapter 6

"He cried on the way home …"

PATRICK W. NAUGHTON SR.

My generation's war started on a Tuesday. Early that day I had to drive to Tripler Army Hospital in Hawai'i for a medical appointment. No longer on active duty, I had hurt my wrist the weekend before with my Army National Guard Infantry Regiment where I was a sergeant. It was one of the most cohesive units I had ever served with, thoroughly united through its history and island pride. In the tiny apartment I shared with my sister, my father slept on a mattress wedged in the corner. He was visiting for the week so I couldn't turn on the lights or make any noise. As I quietly prepared a bowl of cereal and tried to navigate the 2-foot space between fridge and counter, bowl, milk, and Cheerios splashed across the kitchen floor. A strong believer in omens, I silently muttered to myself as I quietly cleaned it up: "Fuck. This is going to be a bad day."

As I drove my truck to Tripler, I hit dead-stop traffic on the H2, extremely unusual for that time of day. Early mornings in Hawai'i are the best; I usually kept the vehicle silent so I could drive with the windows open and soak in the cool tropical morning breeze as paradise came alive. With that ruined, I turned on the radio. By that time, the second tower had already fallen in New York, the Pentagon had been struck, a plane had crashed in Pennsylvania, and the US was in full crisis mode trying to determine what was happening. Quickly finding the next exit, I called the apartment four times before my father finally answered. "Dad, turn on the TV, we're under attack!" I yelled. By then I was bursting through the front door, waking him and my sister.

Without thinking, I started packing my military gear, believing the Russians, Chinese, or maybe aliens (I love that sci-fi stuff) were about to fall from the sky and shatter the perfect Hawai'i sunrise. Calling my Guard unit in pidgin, the unofficial language you had to speak to truly be accepted, I excitedly bellowed, "I ready brah, we going war or what?" Just pack your bags and be prepared, they replied, with no hesitation. I'm way ahead of you, I thought. I tossed my combat boots, still caked in muck from the weekend training, into the slop sink next to the washer and furiously scrubbed the mud off. Funny how ingrained discipline works. The world could be ending, but the perpetrators weren't going to catch me without spit-shined boots. The world changed and my life along with it; my generation's war had begun. Come to think of it, I never did get my wrist looked at.

Reading about my father's send-off to war caused me to reflect on my two most important military departures—for basic training and then Iraq. The first occurred at 3:00am when the recruiter picked me up from home to take me to the Military Entrance Processing Station (MEPS). My little sister, who I thought was still asleep, came flying downstairs and clutched me, crying, afraid she would never see me again. Reluctantly prying myself loose from her grasp, I shook my father's hand and went off to MEPS. At the airport he hugged me and whispered in my ear that he was proud of me. Unlike my father, no flower leis for my send-off.

Iraq was different. The family all met in San Diego, where emotions were even more constrained. All I remember about the goodbye is eating a nice dinner the night before I left. My mother took us all to a fancy joint, held my hand, and quietly said, "I just wanted to take you someplace nice before you go so that your last memory is a pleasant one that you can always think back on." And I did just that, Mom.

The past two decades have hosted more than their share of soldiers in airports going to war. It used to be a common sight to see them in droves in terminals across the nation. Some weren't flying overseas but wore their uniforms anyway: shameless junkies for the attention; free coffees and meals bought and "thank you for your services" thrown their way. A trained eye could tell the difference between soldiers travelling internally stateside and those going overseas—a subdued American flag on their right shoulder meant they were deployed, the colored one meant not. In addition, for Army personnel, no patch on the right sleeve meant they had never deployed. And finally, they were really clean.

Dallas and Atlanta airports were gateways where soldiers on leave from war or individual deployers traveled through as they came and went. They were a strange crossroads where those coming from overseas first re-entered the civilian world. They were also one of the few places where most of the US population ever ran into service members during the entire global war on terror. It was always jarring how little the world had changed each time you re-entered that airport gateway back into normal American life.

By the time you land you are usually exhausted from the travel and just want to sleep before catching your next flight. It was always amusing to watch soldiers slink off to their next gate, find a corner, curl up on the floor without a second thought to it, and fall fast asleep. It was also fascinating to see how rapidly society got used to this phenomenon. Businesspeople with their laptops propped open smashing out deals on their cell phones with several dirty service members crashed out in the fetal position a few feet away became a common sight. I did this several times myself; only to be woken up by civilians or airport employees checking on me to make sure I didn't miss my flight. Annoyed but appreciative, I would thank them for the well-meaning wake up. Time to shoulder my pack, get some real food, and ignore the cheesedicks with their non-combat patched sleeves and colored flags seeking out civilian paparazzi to feed their ego.

Panama Canal Zone, Panama; 2014: The familiar orderly layout of buildings, each marked by large numbers that you find on every US base that has ever existed, sped past as we headed into the jungle to visit the Emberá tribe. They were a native indigenous group that, due to urban encroachment and conflict, had settled in the Panama Canal Zone. "Are we on a military base?" I wondered aloud to my future wife on a tour in Panama in 2014. Our guide overheard me and confirmed that we were indeed on the old Fort Sherman, an American base that used to be the home of the US Army's Jungle School.

After a short boat ride, we entered a deep lush wilderness that blocked out the sun and wrapped you completely in its hot and humid arms. There we met some of the Emberá, who explained to our group, now dripping in sweat, how their people had survived this harsh terrain for generations. As a sign of how times have changed, the tribespeople, draped in brightly colored, mass-manufactured, store-bought clothing meant to mimic their traditional garb, proudly described how at one time, their forefathers had passed on this knowledge to American soldiers on their way to Vietnam.

Looking out over the jungle through the massive floor-to-ceiling windows in the lobby of a posh hotel we had lunch in on the way back, I couldn't help but wonder what my father experienced here before he left for Vietnam. After all, technically, this was where his war began. My thoughts were interrupted by our tour guide who asked me, "So, how hot was it in Iraq anyway?"

Panama Canal Zone, Panama; April 1969: Decades earlier, government buses—not unlike the Diablo Rojos death traps of today so famed in the region that we saw in 2014, just without the jarring paint motifs—rumbled unremarkably across the isthmus. This was a daily occurrence during America's time controlling the canal, when troops constantly crisscrossed the territory. It was also the primary transportation mode between Howard Air Force Base on the Pacific side (now the Panamá Pacífico International Airport) to Fort Sherman at Toro Point on the Caribbean end of the Panama Canal, directly opposite Colón. Their cargo? Eighty-seven Army lieutenants bound for Class 69-18A of Jungle School. For the next 13 days, they would learn how to survive and thrive in this unforgiving terrain, absorbing skills that would hopefully be useful to them in Vietnam. The newly minted officers, including my father, were shocked by the squalor they saw outside their windows. The stark difference between the rich living in the cool hills and everyone else living in rickety shacks was astounding: "There was no in between people, just very poor and very rich," my father remembered.[1]

As the noise of the engines and cultural shock drowned out the awkward attempts to start conversations, each man sat quietly reminiscing about the lives they had left behind. For my father, the crushing humidity in Panama and the warm, dirty-brown waters of the canal and jungle streams were in stark contrast to the beautiful and clear Queen Surf's Beach in Waikiki, where the family spent each Sunday afternoon. His thoughts drifted to the two-week vacation he had just enjoyed at home. His somber message for the family now: "Aloha from the deep deepest south y'all."[2]

"Talk about miserable," he decried in a letter home. Panama and his time in the jungle made Hawai'i "feel like the north pole."[3] Like all island boys when away from home, we sniff out others like us. We must have a unique swagger, or perhaps it's the mispronunciation of certain English words that are forever warped by the intonation of growing up speaking pidgin, instantly giving a local boy away. He found all the soldiers from the Hawai'i National Guard and his old ROTC classes and rapidly buddied up. He must have been a strange image to an outsider—a 6'1" giant white guy with a bunch of short, brown islanders. It was a sight which soon earned him the nickname "Big Pineapple."[4] This was no different than my own childhood experience, minus the height.

Over the next two weeks, everyone attempted to gain the 1,000 points required to be considered a Jungle Expert and be allowed to graduate from the course. The evaluated tasks consisted of events such as swimming in or dangling over alligator-infested rivers on ropes, rock cliff rappelling, boat crossings, and the general misery of living in the jungle. The culminating event was an escape and evasion course called Field Training Exercise Black Panther.[5] The Army to this day loves to devise tough-sounding and imaginative names for maneuvers and operations. As we saw with Frank Rodriguez and the 101st, the soldiers must have had a field day with the name Operation *Eagle Thrust.* Once, to poke an especially annoying senior leader in the eye, we named an exercise Operation *Wild Chicken.* Regardless of the cool name, my father breezed through the events with only one minor hiccup, a bee sting which paralyzed his arm but only kept him out of the field for a day.[6] The biggest lesson he learned? Underclothes, humidity, and the jungle don't mix. "Leave all underwear and stuff in Hawai'i," he informed his family when they wanted to send him replacements, "don't use that kind of stuff here."[7]

Jungle School complete—next stop, Vietnam. The Army gave my father several days to get to the embarkment station. Its location? Honolulu, Hawai'i. Rather than rely on the military's travel arrangements, he rushed to the airport and booked his own flights that would get him there the fastest. The only available tickets were first class from Charleston to Atlanta to Los Angeles and then home—well worth it to spend a couple more days with family.[8]

Hickam Air Force Base; Oahu, Hawai'i; May 1969: A brand new white 1969 American Motors Rambler 440 station wagon traveled down Route 92, known as the Nimitz Highway after famed World War II Admiral Chester Nimitz, on its way to Hickam Air Force Base (AFB) on Pearl Harbor. Before he entered the boxy machine, Momi suppressed the horrid thought that she would never see her brother again and sent him off with as much aloha as possible.[9]

In his common time-off attire of shorts, slippers, and a wild aloha shirt, my grandfather quietly drove his son to war. "Be safe and come home," he stoically told my father as he dropped him off at the military terminal. A light kiss on the cheek was the response received, which surprised the normally unemotional man; "We just weren't demonstrative in those days," my father recalled. With that brief goodbye, and wearing his short-sleeved khaki uniform, low quarter shoes, and garrison cap, he shouldered his one small bag full of shaving gear and walked into the terminal and off to Vietnam. Years later, from my Tutu, we learned that my grandfather deeply sobbed all the way home.[10]

Chapter 7

"I finally had my war ..."

PATRICK W. NAUGHTON JR.

After a steep stomach-churning descent to avoid small arms fire, the giant C-130 rumbled to a sudden halt at Baghdad International Airport (BIAP). As the back ramp dropped, the heat hit my face like an open oven. Fortunately, after spending nearly two weeks acclimatizing in the barren, almost white-hot flats of Camp Buehring, Kuwait, I was used to the weather. My time at the theater gateway to Iraq consisted of sleeping on green cots in giant white circus tents, walking around the camp in circles, and watching the entire first two seasons of the motorcycle outlaw drama *Sons of Anarchy* in the morale, welfare, and recreation (MWR) tent. Finally, word came that we were crossing the berm, entering the box, going downrange, headed north—these were some of the ridiculous Army euphemisms spewed out by the team rather than just say we were being flown into Iraq.

The hustle and bustle of the military side of BIAP was like any other tarmac, except instead of transporting goods, tourists, businesspersons, or families visiting loved ones, its trade was soldiers and the subsistence of war—of which Iraq was a ravenous and insatiable beast. Large upright concrete barriers buffered by sandbags topped with camouflage netting replaced the comfortable whitewashed walls drowning in elevator music of a normal airport terminal.

As we were the advance party of my unit, our team was small. We hitched a ride on the cargo plane with a host of other hodgepodge groups, who were clearly returning to a war they knew well. By the time the back ramp was settled securely on the tarmac, we were the only ones left standing at its base. The four of us stood huddled in our still crisp digital pattern Fire Resistant Army Combat Uniforms (the biggest joke of a uniform in the history of any army—basically pajamas with pocket-pasted Velcro tabs which stopped working after one wash) with a lost look on our comparatively untanned faces. We were clearly different to the sunbaked skin and almost-bleached-white-from-the-sun uniforms and body armor of our compatriots, who had scurried off the plane as soon as they could.

The war on terror was handled differently to my father's time in Vietnam. Then, soldiers were rotated in and out of country for a year as individuals, earning the criticism that the war was being fought in one-year increments seen through the lens of only one person. Compare this to my time, when entire units were rotated yearly as one complete entity, with a week overlap between each unit. Rather than a two-decade continuous conflict against terror, some argue we fought 20 separate wars over that time. No doubt historians and security strategists will spend decades comparing the successes and failures of both policies.

"Welcome to BIAP," said a short, African American, no-nonsense female staff sergeant with a clipboard in hand to our bewildered group, still loitering on the boiling hot tarmac. "Please follow me," she added. She led us to a small square space surrounded by T-shaped walls (6-meter-high concrete walls that looked like upside down Ts) topped with camouflage netting to provide some type of shade. Under this barely effective barrier from the sun were placed about 20 folding chairs with two tables full of random MWR items. This was a common sight in just about every building in Iraq occupied by Americans: kind donations of magazines, snacks, and just about anything the folks from home thought we would need.

We settled down for what we thought would be a lengthy wait in the dusty space (literally everything is covered in a fine layer of sand in Iraq) and hoped it wouldn't be long. Within two minutes, we were surprised by the huge smiling faces of several members from the unit we were replacing. Unlike the normal Army hurry-up-and-wait routine that had defined our movement to Iraq so far, these soldiers were going to ensure we were on time. The quicker we assumed control of the mission, the faster they could go home. After some vigorous hand shaking and back slapping, they took us to our new home for a year, the headquarters of Task Force Medical, under United States Forces-Iraq (USF-I). Once a dining facility for the Iraqi Army near Saddam Hussein's old Al Faw Palace on Victory Base Complex, it now housed our unit, which would provide command and control for most medical assets during the final months of the war.

As we drove to our headquarters, I couldn't help but notice the signs of past conflict everywhere. It's funny how fascinated you get with the remnants of war when you first see it—it has a pull which makes you want to stop and stare. It's even worse today because my generation has to post everything on social media. "You have to get the perfect war shot to prove to everyone you were in the shit," I thought as I looked back at a picture of me in Iraq posing before a bullet-riddled wall I had nothing to do with.

We were immediately linked up with the people we were replacing and began what the Army calls its week-long left seat/right seat activities, meaning the outgoing personnel (right seat) would theoretically act as a passenger as the inbound individual began to drive (left seat). Backseat driving at its extreme. After several days of this you become so annoyed you want to bark at the well-meaning person you're replacing, "Dude, I fucking got it already. Let me take over and go away!" As they attempted to rapidly mind dump a year's worth of knowledge into our brains, the air was pierced by a loudspeaker just above my new desk. "Incoming, incoming, incoming!" a mechanical voice shrieked. "What. The. Fuck. Does that mean?" I silently asked myself as everyone instantly hit the ground.

My training quickly kicked in as I flopped to the floor. As I lay there, mouth open, fingers covering my eyes the best they could to protect them from debris and palms clamped over my ears so that my brain wasn't compressed by a nearby strike, I intently gazed under my new desk at what must have been 2 inches of built-up sand and trash. "Doesn't anyone clean up around her?" I thought to myself. Funny the dumb stuff you notice when someone is trying to kill you. That fleeting thought was suddenly replaced by the fear of dying. Lying helplessly on a nasty floor while some assholes dropped a rocket on me was not how I wanted to go, and I just wanted out of there now. I quickly slammed that fear deep down into my gut; I was an officer and, like my father before me, I must be brave in front of everyone. Having remembered that, this brief moment of cowardice was my first and only in Iraq.

As the radar guided Counter Rocket, Artillery and Mortar System (C-RAM) sprang into action, it attempted to shoot down or destroy any incoming projectiles before they impacted the base. A weapon originally made for naval ships, it was quickly found to be effective as a land-based system to defend against what its initials stand for. Like something out of a Star Wars movie, the highly effective R2-D2 lookalike—if the Star Wars robot had a 20-millimeter Gatling gun for a penis capable of firing 4,500 rounds per minute—was something we grew to love as it protected us every day. As it fired it mimicked a loud and sustained belch which would make any frat boy jealous with envy. The sound of the C-RAM quickly faded as did the distant thud of rockets being blown out of the sky. The all-clear notice soon broadcasted over the intercom, and those we were replacing acted as though nothing had happened. "Wait, should we at least talk about that?" I wondered. "Huh, guess not, well back to work." Our first day in country—nice.

That night, in my Containerized Housing Unit (known as a CHU but pronounced Choo)—an aluminum box about the size of a 20-foot shipping container lined with untreated wood split in half which slept two people as roommates on each side—I contemplated what the next year might be like. Lying on my sagging single bed with my one wall locker, bare walls, and roaring air conditioner, I was soon serenaded to sleep. The unit was so loud that over the next year, my roommate and I would sleep through multiple mortar or rocket attacks and fail to check in with the unit as required. Many a night a pissed-off soldier muttering about those stupid lieutenants would have to hammer on our door to check we were still alive. I finally had my war.

Tân Sơn Nhứt, Vietnam; May 1969: Two postcards arrived at the Naughton family home in Mānoa which tracked my father's progress as he traveled from Hickam to

Vietnam, to a conflict that had slowly shifted from being called "Johnson's war" to now "Nixon's War" in a nod to the President who had just assumed office five months earlier.[1] The first card, hurriedly dropped in the mail during a brief stop at Anderson AFB in Guam, showed a scenic view of Orote Point, where the US naval base known as Big Navy is located. The second depicts a young Filipino boy riding a water buffalo and was sent from Clark AFB in the Philippines.[2] It was a feeble attempt to alleviate the family's fear through real-time updates as their son went to war. I had email and Skype. My father? Twenty-five-cent postcards.

At 10:15am on May 9, just like my own experience with a steep descent to avoid small arms fire, a chartered civilian airplane shuddered to a stop at Tân Sơn Nhứt AFB (Saigon International Airport) Vietnam. On its manifest was young 2LT Patrick W. Naughton.[3] At the door to the exit ramp, the young, attractive female stewardesses wished the men good luck as they disembarked. "I saw eyes full of fear, some with real terror," recalled one of these women years later, remembering how she attempted to put on her best smile for the departing soldiers. "And maybe this sounds crazy," she continued, "but I saw death in some of those eyes."[4]

Ten days earlier, the Vietnam War had reached its peak troop strength of 543,482.[5] My father was a part of this number. He also arrived in Vietnam just as the monsoon season was set to begin. The seasonal prevailing winds of Southeast Asia blew in from the southwest between May and October and drenched everything in continuous rain.

All were quickly herded off the plane and shuffled past torn-up concrete holes from recent enemy rocket and mortar attacks towards waiting buses. The cherries—brand new soldiers to a combat zone; the Army is not known for its political correctness (PC)—all stopped to gawk and take pictures. This was not allowed by the greeting party of veterans who, while shaking their heads at the stupid new guys, moved them along efficiently before shoving them into seats.[6]

As my father sat in another nondescript government bus, not unlike the ones in Panama or the countless others ridden throughout his years of officer training, he noticed one difference when looking out the window. To prevent explosive devices being shoved through the aperture, the normally unobstructed glass was replaced with wire mesh.[7] Thankfully the VC did not dabble heavily in IEDs. Interesting addition, my father thought as they left the air base.

The buses traveled along Route US 1 on their way to Long Binh Post and the 176th Replacement Depot (most called it Long Binh Junction due to its location between the two large air bases of Biên Hòa and Tân Sơn Nhứt). As the vehicle briefly passed through the outskirts of Saigon, my father peeked through the little squares of rusted wire and took in the sights. At each bridge he noticed reinforced bunkers manned jointly by US and Vietnamese guards.[8] In combination with the white-shirted Saigon National Police (Cảnh Sát or White Mice, as many called them for their clothing and supposed lack of bravery) they sought to thwart VC infiltration and saboteur activities and generally control the flow of the city.

He also noted the strategically placed flash towers soaring over his head. These converted water towers and rooftops, both lined with sandbags, were manned 24 hours by binocular spectacled soldiers from the Capital Target Acquisition Battery. Their only job was to spot flashes from launched enemy rockets and mortars with the naked eye. They would then call in counter battery fire to attempt to neutralize the shooter. It was a far cry from the radar guided R2-D2 penis C-RAM of my war.[9] However, most of all what my father remembers is the sheer humanity packed into the city and the utter poverty; the same thing I do from Baghdad.[10]

Back to Long Binh, the largest base in Vietnam. It was considered an oasis away from the war due to its restaurants, snack bars, photo labs, wood shop, post office, swimming pools, athletic courts, golf course, laundromats, banks, nightclubs, bars, and other adult-oriented establishments.[11] Compare this with my time—because the Iraqi government frowned on those sorts of comforts and the barely working personal internet service we paid for in our CHUs blocked anything enjoyable, my only adult entertainment consisted of a smuggled-in removable hard drive of porn. If you want to learn about your buddy, ask to borrow his fun drive. You'll most likely be shocked by what they are into and never shake their hand again. Despite the available entertainment, unfortunately my father would only have one night in this haven.

On his first night in Vietnam, he lay in a wooden barrack right next to Long Binh's main perimeter fence, packed behind 6 feet of sandbags stacked to the roof. The Army loves to layer everything in sandbags in a war zone; a truism even today as I was hard pressed to find an un-sandbagged building in the Middle East. Harassment and interdiction artillery rounds popped off all night as my father tossed and turned and tried to sleep. Set to hit key terrain or areas of interest, the rounds were randomly fired with the hope they would strike something of importance, or at the very least slightly annoy the enemy. A monstrosity of mines and tangled barbed wire 10 feet deep—with beer cans full of rocks as elementary early warning devices—lay between him and the outside world.

My father struggled to sleep as tomorrow he would find out where he was going in Vietnam. When I went to war, I knew exactly what unit I was with. I can't imagine lying there and not even knowing your future. If he was staying in the local area he would be told at 0730; if he was being sent up or down country he would know at 1900.[12] Nothing like efficiency in the Army.

Chapter 8

"A breaking point …"

HENRY KISSINGER

I still remember the glossy, 16-panel fold-up pocket GTA (graphic training aid) called the *Iraq Cultural Smart Card* being thrust into my hands just after I received a class on how a paperclip stashed on your body was the only tool you needed to escape if captured. Surely that card would give me everything I needed to function in a completely foreign environment and not make any mistakes that reverberated across social media or the 24-hour news cycle.[1] That, combined with my paperclip secreted within one of my many Velcro pockets, would be all I'd need to thrive and survive in ancient Mesopotamia. As I learned more about my father's war, it was comforting to learn that during Vietnam, the Army felt it was just that easy too.

In a modern war of grand stratagem stretched across multiple time zones, I quickly realized that with little to no training, junior leaders were expected to perform simultaneously as warriors, statesmen, economists, agriculturists, and anthropologists. The main difference with Vietnam, however, was our preparation. For the most part, the training and informational pamphlets of the 1960s that my father saved for decades were gone, replaced by omnipresent and dull PowerPoint slides and online classes to prepare us to function in faraway lands. With each "next slide" announced by the presenter to a half-asleep audience, or each online class we quickly clicked through as we watched unrelated videos on our phones, we were to be transformed into Patton-Albright performers.

Along with these clumsy training sessions, metrics have dominated my time in the Army. I was shocked to discover it was the same for Vietnam. "The more statistics you assemble the greater your appetite becomes for even more statistics," General Creighton Abrams once fumed to his staff during the war; "somehow you feel that, in the end, you can solve the whole goddamn problem if you just had enough statistics!"[2]

Red, amber, green stoplight PowerPoint slides and Excel sheets quantifying data dictated policies and strategies during my wars, as did the pressure exerted to achieve the ever-elusive green metric—the unicorn during the global war on terror. It seemed at times that extremism could only be wiped out by this hue. Its beautiful radiance on an overhead projector or printed report was so alluring that it forced many a senior leader to pressure their subordinates to fudge their numbers or just outright lie, thereby proving to their boss that their unit was the top dog or that they deserved praise and advancement.

Among the statistics from Vietnam, the most controversial was the number of enemies killed. This was colloquially known as the body count, a term General Westmoreland claimed he abhorred. Like most data desired from senior leaders, by the time it is translated to ground level it morphs into something else altogether. I can't tell you how many meetings I have sat in with senior military officials and politicians where something was said offhand, or a question left unanswered that takes on a life of its own. When I would return to the field, all would be chaos as a berserk colonel demanded the world be moved to obtain an answer for the general or senator. "Whoa, this was not the intent or result desired from that meeting at all," I would think to myself. I believe this is what occurred with the body count in Vietnam. A genuine desire to measure progress transformed into something ridiculous and irrational by the time it hit the front lines.

As I reviewed the strategies implemented for Vietnam, I found them just as overwhelming and confusing as those created for Iraq and Afghanistan. Massive mind-maps with intersecting cause-and-effect lines and fancy graphics aside, at the end of the day I believe that at its core, communities being destroyed by collateral damage and the loss of their loved ones to combat operations just desire security above all else. Whoever can provide this will win their support, despite the rhetoric of those providing the safety (communist, Islamic extremist, or those selling democracy).

Vietnam, much like Iraq and Afghanistan did for my generation, presented senior military leaders and civilian strategists with a puzzle they could never quite crack. One well-regarded theorist even suggested that a moat be built around Saigon to keep out the Viet Cong.[3] As frustrated National Security Advisor Henry Kissinger once declared to his staff, "I refuse to believe that a little fourth-rate power like North Vietnam does not have a breaking point."[4] Was the end goal to just secure the South from communism or to destroy the North? It was never quite clear.

The Domino Theory briefed well, but the reality in Vietnam was much more complicated. By the time my father was on his way to the war, Secretary of Defense (SECDEF) Clark Clifford had just completed a tour through Southeast Asia. To his utter amazement, he learned that none of the countries in the region agreed with the theory; that, in fact, "the dominos didn't believe in the domino effect."[5] Added to this, direct foreign intervention in Vietnam was getting old. The Chinese had tried for a thousand years, then the French, the Japanese, and the French again. Unlike Korea, where the communist horde was being kept at bay at the 38th parallel, the same was not happening at the 17th in Vietnam. Their efforts to infiltrate conventional forces and foster guerrilla activity well south of this boundary placed them on a collision course with the US.

In 1965, Clifford's predecessor and SECDEF for most of the war, Robert McNamara, directed an assessment on how, if committed, the US could win the war. Led by Army General Earle Wheeler, the chairman of the Joint Chiefs of Staff, and assisted by Assistant Defense Secretary John McNaughton, its conclusion set the course for much of the conflict. Westmoreland's report to the study group on the South Vietnamese military, especially the Army of the Republic of Vietnam (ARVN), was not flattering, and claimed they had been "chewed up" by the enemy so far and demonstrated a "reluctance to engage in offensive operations."[6] He warned that without direct US intervention on the ground "we are headed toward a VC takeover of the country."[7] With this assessment in hand, the group formulated a strategy based on the assumption that the ARVN could not and would not be able to be serve as the main effort in any operations against determined enemy forces until they were further built up.[8]

The results of the group's study presented to McNamara planted the seeds from which US troops were committed and a strategy to fight the Vietnam War was grown. "I saw no solution," Westmoreland later stated about stopping communist expansion in South Vietnam, "other than to put our own finger in the dike."[9] The strategy suggested by the group consisted of two concurrent lines of effort that outlined how forces would be arrayed. First, operating out of secure bases, US troops would undertake the bulk of the fighting and conduct deep land and air offensives to locate and destroy NVA/VC forces and other supporting organizations.[10]

Meanwhile, the ARVN (except for a few crack units) would squat and hold, along with the rest of South Vietnam's military forces. In the areas it already occupied, it would attempt to solidify its grip and conduct offensive action against local VC units if possible. It was thought that allowing ARVN forces to focus their efforts on maintaining and extending the areas currently under their control would allow for them to regroup, reconstitute, train, and "engender the buildup of an offensive spirit."[11] This would therefore regulate the ARVN to a supporting role for much of the war, which would have disastrous consequences later.

As the US continued to be drawn into the conflict, the NVA and the VC implemented the same basic strategy that Mao Zedong used in China: control the rural areas and their people and restrict the South Vietnamese government's sway to the urban centers. The US strategy played right into this. The ARVN would hold the populated areas while American forces were sucked deeper into the countryside, straining their lines of communication and requiring more and more troops to control terrain.

In contrast, the North Vietnamese had one simple objective: unite Vietnam under communist rule. Their strategy consisted of three lines of effort to support this. First, nurture and support an insurgency in the South. Second, garner support by any means possible for the revolution among those still uncommitted to either side. Lastly—and something the Americans never fully grasped or could counter—turn the tide of US public opinion against the conflict. As Mao noted in his writings, "We further our mission of destroying the enemy by propagandizing his troops."[12]

These three efforts would eventually wear down their opponents to the point that conditions were favorable for the North to pivot to (and back and forth between) conventional warfare when and where they saw fit to achieve their main objective: classic Mao and his People's War strategy. Or, as the North Vietnamese called it: *tiến công và nổi dậy, nơi đây và tấn công* (attack and uprise, uprise and attack through the use of VC or infiltrated main forces); *nơi đây đồng loạt* (simultaneous uprising between both the VC and NVA); and *dứt điểm* (to take over a target completely, the pivot to conventional warfare seen towards the end of the war and attempted with Tet 1968).[13]

Mao clarified his point about the relationship between the people and combatants in his writings, which also pertained to Vietnam. "The former may be likened to water," noted the experienced insurgent leader, "and the latter to the fish who inhabit it." In an insurgency, it is imperative that both willingly coexist, as "like the fish out of its native element," the insurgent cannot survive without the support of the populace.[14] To their credit, many US military and civilian strategists recognized this relationship. "People, more than terrain, are the objectives in this war," noted Westmoreland.[15] "The war in Viet Nam," also wrote Samuel P. Huntington, considered one of the greatest political scientists of the twentieth century, "is a war for the control of the population."[16]

Huntington, in his oft-cited 1968 article in *Foreign Affairs*, noted a curious fact about the steady increase of the population falling under the control of the government of South Vietnam. By the time my father arrived, this was the good-news statistic constantly touted by senior military leaders as being the direct result of US combat operations. "This change," however, noted Huntington, "has been largely, if not exclusively, the result of the movement of the population into the cities rather than the extension of the Government's control into the countryside."[17] For the first time in Vietnamese history, the population count of those living in metropolises outnumbered the rural areas. People were driven to the cities for economic reasons since much of the countryside and arable land had become free-fire zones, been deforested by tactical herbicides, or required local inhabitants to live under the constant fear of a random airstrike or a harassment and interdiction artillery round landing on their head.

Large population centers such as Saigon appeared to be under control. However, few understood that through the VC, North Vietnam fostered a parallel government known as the Viet Cong Infrastructure (VCI) that ruled over most rural areas outside the metropolitan areas. Communist dissenters and agents had infiltrated every town and hamlet in South Vietnam. The VCI collected taxes, controlled local insurgent units, and provided intelligence and logistical support to the NVA—another driver that compelled the population to move to the cites.

In his article, and to the horror of many a reader, Huntington noted that maybe the US had inadvertently stumbled on a solution to win the war. "The effective response lies neither in the quest for conventional military victory nor in the esoteric doctrines and gimmicks of counter-insurgency warfare," he wrote. "It is instead forced-draft urbanization; removing the water from the fish, instead of the other way around."[18] This urbanization, as it became known, could in theory remove the population from communist influence.

Little did the outraged public realize that Huntington was far from the first to suggest or implement a form of urbanization to win the war. From the late 1950s, the failed Agroville Program forcibly relocated peasants to areas where they could be guarded against communists for their own good. This soon morphed into another failed attempt in the early 1960s, the Strategic Hamlet Program. A different name with the same goal—protect the population by physically segregating them from the VC. Then came the Revolutionary Development Program of 1965–1966; instead of moving the communities the ARVN and US would send cadre to them to help stimulate their own self-defense and raise their standard of living. There was a common theme here—either fortify existing villages or consolidate the people into new ones where they can be controlled, and communist influences eliminated.

These and a host of other programs, strategies, and theories were supposed to win the war; obviously by 1969 they still had not.

Pacification was still the strategic buzzword by the time my father arrived in Vietnam. Borrowed from the French during their conflict in what they called French Indochina and the British in Malaysia, it was adopted, dusted off, and then rebranded as uniquely American. The II Corps commander, when presented with the 1969 version of pacification, called it "reinventing the wheel by another name," noting that it was essentially the oil spot theory from Malaysia (clear and hold one area and then move to another) rebranded. After criticizing it during a commanders' conference, he meekly conceded that he supposed it was "hard to dream up anything new."[19]

General Wheeler, when briefed on these same revisions, was not overly impressed. "We have tried innumerable programs, variations of programs, concepts, devices, stratagems, with differing success," he declared, speaking slowly and haltingly after the commander and staff at MACV presented their updates; "some of them flat failures, some have shown some success, some have shown a great deal," he continued, before concluding that he thought this latest round in a long list of ideas was "worth a try."[20] Historian and onetime Under Secretary of the Air Force Townsend Hoopes was a little less positive in his analysis, derisively calling pacification a "transparent monstrosity, an example of American optimism and messianic zeal gone off the deep end."[21]

As Wheeler noted, many a grand approach, operational plan, and policy was drafted in Washington and by senior military officials to enthusiastically achieve pacification. Actually implementing these efforts were the junior leaders, young lieutenants, and sergeants who were supposed to understand these plans and policies and execute them at the tactical level. The Army's answer at the time to translate these abstract ideas into tangible concepts? The tried-and-true Informational Pamphlet and Graphic Training Aid (GTA).

Upon arrival in Vietnam, my father was handed Command Information Pamphlet 12-69, titled *Pacification*. This zealotic newly dubbed state-of-the-art US strategy offered the "quickest ticket home," it claimed.[22] The official intent of the 17-page booklet, with a kaleidoscope collage on its covers of smiling Vietnamese of all ages and sexes, was to "fill a gap" to ensure all American personnel understood the self-acknowledged complicated and extensive objectives of the strategy. Even looking at it today, with its professionally organized pages and expertly presented argument, we might ask how in the world the war was not won.[23]

Winning the hearts and minds of the people, argued the *Pacification* pamphlet, was still the "best way to end the conflict satisfactorily."[24] This reinforced the cliché the Vietnam War is best remembered for; one I heard often unofficially whispered in Iraq. The emphasis was now on the people and not on material things, continued the treatise. It further stressed that every American in Vietnam had a part to play in the pacification process, supporting the idea that only the government of South Vietnam and not communism offered its citizens a path to a free and peaceful life.[25]

"Pacification is a military, political, economic and social process," the pamphlet declared—but what did that mean to the sweat-soaked grunt on the ground charged with its execution, some with no more than a high school education? To further define it, it was expounded on in detail: "Establishing or reestablishing local government responsive to and involving the participation of the citizens; Providing sustained credible security; Destroying the enemy's underground government; Asserting or reasserting GVN political control; Involvement of the people in the central government; Initiating economic and social activity capable of self-sustenance and expansion."[26] Some definite mouthfuls of bold goals; ones that would swell the heart of any post-Camelot and Kennedy-child true believer.

In 1969, the pacification campaign was adjusted from past efforts by the addition of a single guiding principle, which seemed to be pulled straight from the hippie counterculture of the time: community spirit. This spirit was based on cooperation between the people, government, and the various official agencies. It placed special emphasis on the role of the Vietnamese people as participants in all military, political, economic, social, and educational efforts.[27] Community spirit would be achieved through eight pacification objectives: "1) Provide Territorial Security. 2) Establish Local Government in Villages. 3) Organize People's Self Defense. 4) Increase the

Number of Hoi Chanh (Chiêu Hồi). 5) Reduce the Viet Cong Infrastructure. 6) Intensify Information and Propaganda Efforts. 7) Stimulate the Rural Economy. And lastly, 8) Reduce the Number of Refugees."[28] It was this guiding principle and its supporting objectives which were supposed to direct all my father's actions over the next year.

Finally, the pamphlet identified the 1968 Tet Offensive as a direct response from the enemy to the success of pacification so far.[29] As the snazzy booklet, which would make any advertising agency executive proud promised, all these efforts combined aimed "at shattering the VC organization, restoring public security, and ultimately, in establishing a stable and viable Republic of Vietnam."[30]

If the Tet Offensive was the direct result of pacification efforts, then the creation of the Capital Military Assistance Command (CMAC) to protect Saigon was as well.[31] Formed to prevent a recurrence of 1968, CMAC was established as a permanent tactical command solely focused on protecting Saigon.[32] Utilizing ambushes, rocket and mortar detection systems, water denial, and bridge security, its main mission was to prevent indirect fire attacks and saboteurs from infiltrating the capital to destroy infrastructure.[33] CMAC realized that any successful ground or rocket attack against Saigon would provide the enemy with a publicity and propaganda victory through the media.[34]

By the time my father arrived in Vietnam, the 3rd Brigade of the 82nd was the only US unit left under the operational control of CMAC and involved in the protection of the capital.[35] "When the people come to the cities, they remove themselves from enemy influence and control," stated one naïve US advisor about this phenomenon. "You might say we are winning the war through urbanization."[36] Never mind, as already discussed, that this mass exodus was actually due to insecurity in rural areas rather than the desire to support the South Vietnamese government.

Despite this migration, decades of colonial domination and mismanagement had left the government of South Vietnam with a weak economy rife with corruption, nepotism, and inefficiency, unable to support its new inhabitants. One journalist critical of Saigon called it "a seething cauldron in which hissed and bubbled a witches' brew of rival French and American imperialisms spiced with feudal warlordism and fascist despotism."[37] Guess the cities were not as desirable as they seemed.

CMAC saw its role in pacification, as advertised in its own glitzy informational pamphlet that far surpassed its guiding strategy document for creativity and colorfulness, as helping the people aid themselves. It seems the whole war could be immortalized by its plethora of pamphlets alone. Through the coordination of tactical maneuvers, civil affairs, psychological operations, and civic action, every CMAC effort was "directed toward helping the Vietnamese people build a democratic nation, rebuild their society and end the war."[38]

Lastly, their pop-artsy booklet, which would have made even Andy Warhol cringe, pointed out, "Vietnamese citizens, now nearing middle age, have never known the tranquility of their country at peace. CMAC realizes this, and perhaps its most complex mission is the restoring of confidence to these war-weary people."[39] A lesson that we as Americans in our comfortable and safe lives often forget.

Vietnam was a messy operational environment with an equally complicated strategy to match it that, like my generation's wars, was never fully appreciated. In a conflict without easily measurable objectives, a host of statistics were created to gauge its progress. Our western military minds, trained on pioneering Napoleonic military theorists Antoine-Henry Jomini and Prussian Carl von Clausewitz, demanded it as did McNamara, a self-described numbers guy.[40] Later, Westmoreland would lay this voracious desire for more numbers to gauge the war's progress at the feet of the SECDEF, claiming that he "constantly prodded for more and more statistics."[41]

Weapons captured, lines of communication opened, percentages of the population under government control, and the proficiency ratings of South Vietnamese military units were some of the data points measured. This data gathering to quantify the war effort was and still is highly criticized. "In a conflict with no conventional front lines," Westmoreland later wrote in his memoir defending these information-gathering efforts, "statistics, were, admittedly, an imperfect gauge of progress." However, "How else to measure it?" he asked.[42]

Data could be gathered but then it had to be analyzed. And therein lay an issue. One example of the dangers of this misanalysis concerned weapons captured on the field of battle. Many US analysts opined that abandoned weapons meant the enemy lacked the capability or manpower to haul them away after an engagement—an indicator of their low morale or diminished fighting prowess. "Every battlefield was considered as a 'hot market place'," subsequently reported Wilfred Burchett, a journalist and author who dedicated several books to reporting on the perspective of the North Vietnamese. Enemy commanders allegedly laughed at this statistic as the field was the best place to "exchange 'old for new', often discarding even usable weapons in favor of those needed to standardize a unit's equipment."[43]

The body count was another metric disaster. A desire to know death rates due to military operations is understandable; however, it implied that the US could kill its way out of the war: just keep knocking down bad guys until they run out of humans to arm. The press soon got hold of this statistic and twisted it into something macabre that now defines the conflict.[44] By the time my father arrived in 1969, cracks in statistics gathering had begun to show in even the most hardline of Army institutions. "One thing should be made absolutely clear: attrition is not a strategy," cynically wrote one instructor in a new textbook introduced in 1969 at Westmoreland's alma mater West Point. "It is irrefutable proof of the absence of any strategy," continued the teacher to the new cadets. Pulling no punches, it "uses blood in lieu of brains" it concluded.[45]

Abrams himself commented to his staff about the obsession with metrics at this point in the war. "It finally gets to the point where that's really the whole war," he raged during a meeting about the worshipping of data in Vietnam, "fucking charts ... somehow the chart itself becomes the whole damn war, instead of the people and the real things." Instead of looking past the numbers, he realized his subordinate commanders were solely trying to push them in the right direction instead of actually addressing what they were measuring.[46]

Number counting or not, Brigadier General George Dickerson, commander of the 3rd Brigade 82nd Airborne, acknowledged the assigned mission for his brigade and their part in the pacification and overall war effort: secure the western approaches to the capital and prevent ground and rocket attacks against Saigon and the Tân Sơn Nhứt complex.[47] Preventing attacks on Saigon, he noted, strengthened the "legitimate government's image in the villages and hamlets."[48] He also understood that the rockets themselves did little damage to the city; however, "a rocket slamming into the Capital City of Saigon is certain to merit attention in the world press and gives the nonmilitary audience an exaggerated picture of Viet Cong capabilities."[49]

It was in the rural areas surrounding Saigon that each of the brigade's battalions (known as regiments in the 82nd) were strategically placed on firebases to best conduct ambushes and searches, aimed at preventing the enemy from pre-positioning materials needed to launch rocket or mortar attacks. Or, as the commanding general better described his tactical efforts, rooting the enemy from his hiding places by day and preventing him from moving during the night.[50]

The 1/505th Infantry Regiment, where my father would soon be assigned, did their part from Firebase All American I, which they constructed just northwest of Saigon.[51] Their mission in support of the brigade and pacification: prevent infiltration; interdict enemy movements; identify and eliminate any VC infrastructure; and, most importantly, focus on any personnel or equipment that could be used in indirect fire attacks.[52]

Taking Dickerson's guidance to heart, the regiment saturated their area of operation with night ambushes and day patrolling or, in their own words which echoed the boss's guidance, they "prevented the enemy from having access to its area of responsibility by night and hunted him and his caches during the day." The regiment created and adopted a new mantra for Vietnam with pride, "Travel Light—Fight by Night."[53]

In addition to kinetic action, Dickerson claimed they further embraced pacification guidance and executed numerous civic action programs and self-help projects as well as Medical Civic Action Programs (MEDCAPS) and Dental Civic Action Programs (DENTCAPS).[54] All were aimed at trying to address social rifts and loosen the grip of the VCI over the peasants—trying to win those hearts and minds through shots, checkups, and root canals.

While the 82nd fought, the new SECDEF appointed by President Nixon to replace Clifford, Melvin Laird, completed his own tour of the conflict just before my father arrived. "Mr. Laird may have gone out looking for a miracle. They all do," anonymously noted one seasoned White House official of several administrations, "but he came back perplexed, like all the others."[55] Another official called his return "purposely gloomy," adding that he told the hawks in DC to "stop dreaming about victory."[56] The MACV commander had a different assessment: "I'm not trying to be a Pollyanna about this," excitedly declared General Abrams to his staff about pacification efforts in 1969; "but the truth of the matter is that since 1964 it has never looked so good."[57] My father was about to see for himself firsthand the conditions in Vietnam.

Chapter 9

"Huh, looks like Vietnam ..."

PATRICK W. NAUGHTON SR.

A massive sprawling complex consisting of a cluster of bases surrounded BIAP. It had everything a soldier away from home could need—bazaars, restaurants, masseuses, gyms, barbers, and even a racetrack for remote-controlled cars. Victory Base Complex (VBC): much like what Long Binh had been to Vietnam, VBC was to Iraq.

My first month in Iraq I met a girl—a fellow soldier who worked on the other side of the sprawling VBC. Every chance I got I would sneak out to pick her up in one of our civilian sport utility vehicles (which technically I guess I stole for short periods of time). Not that we really had anywhere to go, but it was still nice to drive in circles around the base when we could. It was so massive that when traveling in our borrowed vehicle, we couldn't always tell where the perimeter was or when one base started and the other ended. Parked in our hidden spots like teenagers in heat, we would often be interrupted by a strange vehicle slowly passing by that probably should not have been on VBC. We shrugged it off with an "Oh well, they did not try to kill us"; back to making out.

As we drove endlessly in circles, I formed my first impression of my home for the next year. The signs of war were everywhere. Half buried and destroyed T-72 tanks and armored vehicles littered the perimeter. Being a former Iraqi government complex, every building of note had a collapsed roof and bomb damage due to precision strikes early in the war. Those buildings not beyond repair were repurposed for American use, to include the grand Al-Faw Palace. Built to commemorate the victory over the Iranians in 1988, this soon-Americanized building came to symbolize the war for many who served there. I too took the mandatory picture of myself sitting in the huge wooden throne-like chair that Saddam had received from Palestinian leader Yasser Arafat.

All structures were surrounded in a maze of upside-down T-walls buttressed by green or tan sandbags. White 20- or 40-foot trailers were everywhere and served every function you could think of. About every 150 meters, in between the trailered Subways, Pizza Huts, CHUs, laundries, and working areas, bunkers were built, the insides of which I grew to know well. The heat was miserable, rain was rare, and dust storms were common. Despite the $5 footlongs and a variety of available junk food (the best pizza I ever had came from a small Pizza Hut trailer on VBC), it was drab, dreary, and sandy. Even the fish originally stocked by Saddam in the many manmade lakes on VBC were pissed to be there. Meanwhile, over the tall wall in between rolls of razor wire trees, the bustle of everyday life could be seen. Another tenet of the American way of war: we bring a little bit of home with us everywhere we go.

Long Binh, Vietnam; May 1969: With the start of the monsoon season still days away, May 10 dawned hot and dry with a vengeance, setting the conditions for the foreseeable future: "sweat, sweat, and sweat."[1] The 0730 call came and went; "To add insult to injury the bums assigned me to the 3rd Brigade, 82nd Airborne Division," my father reported to the family after the assignments occurred at 1900.[2] He was unhappy because he thought it meant that he would need to go to airborne school and yet more training, when he would rather get his war on. Luckily, the brigade was not on airborne status, and most were straight legs (the derogatory term for a non-jump qualified soldier).[3]

Up to this point in the war, the 82nd had been kept as a strategic reserve in case major combat operations commenced with the Soviet Union. However, following the Tet Offensive crisis of early 1968, Westmoreland pleaded with the Joint Chiefs of Staff and the president for more troops. As the enemy's attacks petered out, he desired one brigade from the 82nd and one Marine Corps regiment to "exploit the enemy's failures" and "capitalize on opportunities available to him".[4] His wish granted, the 3rd Brigade from the 82nd was hastily sent to Vietnam, with its duty status changed from airborne to light infantry. Knowing it would be short personnel, especially officers, the plan was to reconstitute it via the normal replacement process once in country.[5] Hence how my father became an enigma: an All American without jump wings.

With all of that in the past and way above his pay grade anyway, 2LT Naughton needed to focus on more practical things, such as his uniforms, understanding Vietnam, and his upcoming move to Phú Lợi, which was the main base camp for the 82nd located about 20 kilometers north of Saigon in the Bình Dương province.

Still in his short-sleeved khaki dress uniform, he was finally issued jungle olive green 107s (the Army's actual functional utility uniform for war versus the Velcro pajama monstrosity I wore). He was given several sets, only one of which he kept for garrison wear with all its required patches, nametapes, and ranks—to appease the senior ranking Rear Area Mother Fuckers (RAMF) when they visited, also known as pogues. The rest were strictly for field use and eventually looked it; permanently ringed with salt-crusted sweat stains and rips haphazardly sewn closed by Frankenstein's seamstress. Reissues consisted of a box of random uniforms stored in supply that the men could riffle through as they needed a new pair; size, rank, or nametapes be damned. At first my father wore the issued underwear, t-shirts, and socks; however, as in Panama, those were quickly discarded as he learnt how to avoid prickly heat, crotch rot, and trench foot.[6] "I'm beginning to look like a Vietnamese 8 deuce soldier—jungle fatigues, jungle boots, and jungle hat," he naively wrote home in his newly issued gear before eventually tossing all the extra shit.[7]

Besides his uniforms, he also received his Table of Allowances 50 (Army-issued individual equipment), the official designation for one's field gear issued by the Army. It was known as TA-50, a slang term still in use, and consisted of a host of items including a helmet, web belt, ammo pouches, canteens, first aid kit, suspenders, gas mask, rucksack, poncho with liner, sleeping bag, flak vest, bayonet, and other assorted items. Like his uniform, he quickly learned what was really needed in the field. Most times, he just shoved his pants cargo pockets full of supplies and left the rucksack and the rest behind. Another field-expedient way to carry gear was to fill an empty sock with essentials and drape it around your neck or tie it to your belt. Whatever you could do to cut down on weight was the way to go.[8] The infantry still does this today. It is interesting how fast a callus will form under your cargo pockets on the outside of your thighs from being rubbed against repeatedly while marching.

In contrast to some previous conflicts, the American taxpayer spared no pennies in making sure we had the gear we needed for my generation's wars. Still, I was issued a host of nonsense before going to Iraq, including the Extended Cold Weather Clothing System. This was a seven-layered system of clothing meant to allow us to survive in and up to Arctic conditions. The final layer was a gray monstrosity we all called the Pillsbury Doughboy suit. I'm not sure why we needed that for Iraq but it, along with all the chemical defense gear I was issued, lay shoved under my bunk for a year collecting dust. Of course, many were unsatisfied with what we were issued, and would shop the various Ranger Joe type stores to purchase all kinds of extra nonsense to strap on to their body armor. After all, they had to match what the movies said a global war on terror soldier should look like for their social media pages. I proudly stick by the mantra that if the Army does not issue it, then you probably do not need it.

One final interesting note about TA-50. It does not matter what conflict it is from, be it the Civil War, World War II, Vietnam, or even today. When you crack open that bag of gear, it all smells the same: mildewy canvas combined with rusty metal. Unmistakable and almost comforting to a soldier, it instantly triggers memories when encountered. Even when brand new and still sealed in a plastic bag, it smells like that. I've often wondered if inserting that aroma is a mandatory part of the contract for those who produce field items for the military.

As he squared away his gear and shaved his head to avoid lice and make it easier to stay clean, my father next needed to understand just what it was the US was trying to achieve. A host of additional GTAs were dumped on him at Long Binh: *Code of Conduct for Members of the Armed Forces of the US, Nine Rules for Personnel of US Military Assistance Command Vietnam*, his Geneva Convention Identification Card, and a GTA on how to properly handle prisoners of war, to name a few. He later sent these on to me with an attached sticky note, "supposed to carry in the field but didn't"; a fact made painfully obvious by their still near-mint condition.

More importantly, another informational pamphlet set to explain everything he needed for the conflict was given to him. Unlike *Pacification*, which was introduced earlier and outlined the US latest strategy to win the war (great reading, as we have already learned), the second aimed to teach him the basics. This was achieved via the snazzy *Pocket Guide to Vietnam*. Its main message? "Vietnam is a major testing ground for Communists' theories of 'wars of national liberation'." As such, continued the guidebook, "your exemplary conduct … will do a lot toward bridging the gap between East and West." It further called it essential that US forces build a good relationship with the South Vietnamese people. "This can be done only through day-to-day association with them on terms of mutual confidence and respect," it instructed, "both while doing your military job and in your off-duty hours."[9] These overarching themes, combined with practical necessities such as greetings, phrases, and instructions on how to buy souvenirs, made for a true tourist-cum-war-junkie pocket-sized guide that fit all needs.

Armed with this new information, it was finally off to Phú Lợi; a nervous ride in the back of an open army truck packed with cherries and not a weapon in sight—let's get our fucking war on. "Am looking forward to starting," as he more eloquently told the family, "I don't like this sitting around."[10]

Phú Lợi, Vietnam; May 1969: An explosion ripped through the air as a torrent of burning liquid lit up the night sky and the entire compound. A fougasse mine—a field-expedient creation consisting of a barrel of flammable liquid directed onto a target via explosive charges—had been detonated on the Phú Lợi perimeter. Like Long Binh, the base was surrounded by a strip of barbed wire laced with mines, claymores, and firebombs, all covered by a series of interconnected reinforced bunkers with machine guns. "Shit," thought my father, who was so close that he tasted the gas on his tongue and felt the petrol bomb suck the air from around him as he hit the ground, "we're under attack." Scrambling back to his quarters, he soon found that some asshole had just mistakenly sat on the detonator while on guard duty.[11] Welcome to Vietnam.

Arriving in Phú Lợi, the main base camp of the 82nd, my father noticed two things. First, everything outside the wire was green and lush, like a tropical paradise. It was not quite like what I saw in Iraq, but the unmistakable signs of everyday life existed beyond the military borders for both—while everything inside was dusty, dead, and brown. Second, the wire perimeter was far too narrow and in no way adequate for keeping the enemy out.[12] Still, it was much better than the porous one I saw in Iraq, even though the internal view appeared the same. Be that as it may, this was his new home for a brief period while he completed the five-day proficiency field training (P-Training) course that all new soldiers assigned to the brigade went through before joining their unit. It was almost a mini jungle school all over again to teach basic tactics and field craft for the unit—this time executed in an actual combat zone.

P-Training went smoothly aside from three incidents, two of which involved a field hospital. The first involved an M-16 and a common issue for the weapon. When at the range, practicing firing on fully automatic—rock and roll as it was known—a spent shell ejected right back into my father's face, shattering the lens and pushing glass into his right eye. This problem was fixed by my day with the simple addition of a brass deflector. Luckily, after a thorough eye wash at the hospital, the only casualty was a pair of glasses.

Second, while traversing a combat reaction course on a scorching 115-degree day, he found himself staring up at the sky wondering what had happened as the medics worked to frantically pump sodium chloride solution into his arm. Now a repeat offender at the field hospital over a two-day period, the doctors sent him on his way, chalking it up to the heat combined with the severe weight loss he experienced, starting in Panama.[13] Maybe he just really wanted to see the nurses.

Lastly, his fears about the perimeter became true. In the largest attack since the Tet Offensive, communist forces shelled and attacked over 150 civilian and military sites in South Vietnam, including five of the nine US divisions in country.[14] As part of this offensive, five enemy rockets exploded within the Phú Lợi compound, instantly turning the training unit into a combat one. As the trainees streamed out of their wooden sandbag-packed huts, they were handed weapons and live ammunition and cajoled noisily into some semblance of a defensive perimeter by their instructors around their section of the base. During the commotion of the rocket attack, as some American guards slept in one of the reinforced concrete bunkers, five VC easily infiltrated the perimeter. Hunting for easy prey, the enemy would have graduated an entire P-Training class posthumously had they run into them. Luckily, the VC were quickly killed by the base's reaction force before that could happen. The compound then stayed on grey alert (just below red) for the rest of his training: no lights at night and a weapon with ammo. At least Vietnam was not boring.[15]

Camp Red Ball, Vietnam; May 1969: Out of an envelope mailed home fell an army patch; a centered blue circle with the white capital letters AA, framed by a red square. Above it, in blue with white letters, was the word "Airborne." "Funny thing is," my father mentioned, "back in the states the boys at Bragg wear blackened patches while over here we use these colorful types. You can't see them at night, but they are bright enough in the day to let Charlie know who they are dealing with," he wrote with pride.[16]

Now a graduate of P-Training and after a thorough scrubbing of his teeth with fluoride to prevent cavities (called a brush in), he was fully qualified to join the All Americans.[17] Reading this in his letter made me think back to the 1987 movie *Hamburger Hill*. "Brush your teeth in a rapid vertical motion, troooop," screamed the combat medic to a bunch of cherries, in a scene that depicted this exact act.[18] Nice to know that from all the movies I watched as a kid, at least one contained a kernel of truth.

My father and another newly assigned officer piled into a jeep and were driven to Camp Red Ball, the Brigade's Tactical Command Post next to Tân Sơn Nhứt, to meet the commander, Brigadier General Dickerson. Along the way, he noted the lack of any grass along the sides of all the roads, which had been either stripped for animal feed by the Vietnamese or by US bulldozers (called Rome plows after where they were made in Georgia) to destroy any possible ambush concealment locations.[19] We tried to do the same on our well-traveled routes in Iraq and Afghanistan.

"Let's remember that we are the men of the All American brigade and just what that means," Dickerson began in his starched fatigues and shiny jump boots as he laid on the party line thick to his new officers. "We are operating in a densely populated area, in daily contact with the Vietnamese people," he continued, describing the mission of the 82nd in the Saigon region. "To the housewife in the marketplace, to the child who pesters you for candy, you are America," he confidently stated, the stars on his starched collar making them pop as he spoke. "By what you do, by how you act, America is judged in the eyes of the Vietnamese. Let's behave toward these people in a way that will make the notion of 'the ugly American' nothing but an empty, worn-out idea."[20] As the air conditioner in his office hummed in the background, the general concluded the speech with a nod and an assured look that his lieutenants understood his lecture.

Unsure what to make of this imparted wisdom just yet, except to know that it matched the verbiage in the war-tourist guidebook tucked away in his cargo pocket, my father responded affirmatively with the required "All the way, Sir." This was the motto for the 82nd; senior Army leaders love that cheesy shit. Secretly, the rank and file adore it too. My favorite is to say "Air Assault" and keep it moving. With that out of the way, he was then dumped at the doorstep of S1 Personnel Section to get his unit assignment.[21]

Originally slated to go to the 1st of the 508th Infantry Regiment, he was told he was being redirected to the 1st of the 505th, which was then protecting the western flank of Saigon. Put in another jeep, still unarmed, he was driven directly to the field to meet the battalion commander, Lieutenant Colonel (LTC) Grace Thomas. Sizing up his new six-foot-one lieutenant, Thomas thought back to several weeks ago when one of his companies had spent 10 hours in a firefight in an enemy bunker complex situated along the banks of a canal. There, the men slithered on their bellies through sticky mud bunker-to-bunker, dropping hand grenades into each as they went. Thomas himself joined in the fracas; ordering the Light Observation Helicopter (known as a Loach, a play on its LOH acronym), he was sent in to hover over a particularly vexing bunker, deftly slam-dunking a grenade through its entrance.[22]

Delta Company, 1/505th Infantry—the Delta Dragons, the bunker busters of the regiment. "Hmm, that's where this lieutenant will go," determined Thomas.[23] With that decided, my father declared "Only 49 more weeks to go" to his family.[24]

"To be truthful, I wasn't upset," said my father years later when I asked him about my deployment to Iraq. "Every generation has its war, and this was yours." He shrugged, as though this was a normal part of growing up that all families went through, like puberty or high school graduation.[25] I remember when I sent him pictures of Iraq the first time I skimmed over it in a low-flying helicopter. "Huh," he noted, "looks like Vietnam."

Chapter 10

"My men are a strange group ..."

PATRICK W. NAUGHTON SR.

Time creeps by at the 30th Adjutant General (Reception) Battalion, the starting point for all enlisted infantry soldiers before being sent to begin their basic training. In between the mandatory briefings, medical shots, and uniform issuance, there is nothing to do for hours but sit and wonder why in the world I joined the Army. During one of these lulls, I can still remember lying on my metal-framed bunk, with fingers intertwined behind my head, staring at the bottom of the bunk above me. I noticed some small writing tucked away near one of the corner joints. Scrawled in permanent marker were the words "Private Jones killed himself in this bunk," with a date I now no longer remember. Unfortunately, the 30th can be a lonely and scary place for some.

The only other activity to help pass the time and cure homesickness is to get to know your fellow enlistees who have joined from all around the world. "For fun I like to slip my dick through a padlock and do jumping jacks," blurted out one young soldier with a deep Kentucky drawl to a group of us socializing. Everyone stopped and stared, no idea how to respond. One brave trainee finally did, looking around at the group for approval before quickly whispering, "Prove it." Sure enough, the Kentuckian snatched a padlock off his footlocker, pulled off his army-issued physical fitness shorts, slipped his dick through the shackle, and began a vigorous side straddle hop session (the army's name for jumping jacks). Shocked and wide-eyed, we soon rolled over laughing as he continued his exercise with a focused scowl on his face.

The army attracts some interesting characters. I have often wondered how some of the soldiers I have known ever survived to adulthood. All who serve have their own collection of dick-hopping-knucklehead stories to share. On the flip side, the military also contains some of the best human beings I have ever met. Dedicated, hardworking, brave individuals who want to be part of something larger than themselves; who want to give back to their country and truly be part of a brother and sisterhood forever. Black, White, Hispanic, Asian; whatever one's race or sexual orientation, for many it no longer matters. Throw them all in a blender, add a little Army green, and some drill sergeant love, and out comes a soldier. I am not so naïve as to say that racism, sexism, or prejudices do not exist in the army; however, wearing the green certainly goes a long way in pushing some of that nonsense to the background. That is the best part of service.

Unfortunately, I was not able to find many men still alive who had served with my father in the 82nd. Line units like this were primarily made up of enlisted soldiers, many of whom were drafted. Once they completed their stint with the Army it seemed they went back to whatever small town or inner-city neighborhood they came from. Absorbed back into their daily life. Their one exposure to the wider world outside of their small confines complete, they went on living. The few I did find were of course shocked by my interest in their small contribution to history.

As I delved further into my father's war, I remained surprised how similar our military experiences were. It seemed his platoon in the 82nd mirrored the same cast of motley characters I would encounter during my career—minus helmets decorated with motifs and derogatory remarks written in black permanent marker. That was a sight synonymous with the war; we were never allowed to do anything remotely like that.

Every officer makes it solely by relying on his NCO to show them the way. Like SFC Boorn and 1SG Watson would later do for me, his first real NCO taught my father how to survive in Vietnam. Lessons like the one about children and war. Just as we learned in Iraq and Afghanistan, children are direct intelligence assets used by both sides. Any time US troops approached a populated area in the Middle East and zero kids were playing or walking the streets, we knew it was about to be on. He also kept him alive by educating him on one of Vietnam's ugliest dangers—booby traps and how to avoid them. Among my father's leftovers from the war sits a small piece of wood with a crude skull and crossbones symbol drawn on it. As I handle that sign now, I am thankful that some VC did not rig it to blow, betting that a curious American would snatch it up as a souvenir and get a deadly surprise. He also learned what it meant to be a true field soldier.

Vietnam, as was Iraq, was like being on Mars. Just as I struggled to understand the culture I had entered, I found that my father experienced the same. Once, in a demonstration of his cultural ignorance, he waved hello to an old man plowing his rice field. The man immediately ceased what he was doing, tied down his water buffalo, and walked over to him. Surprised by this, he stuttered out something about seeing any VC in the area. Turns out that the Western way to wave means "Come here" to the Vietnamese.[1] Whatever you do, don't call an Arabic man to you with your palm up and fingers beckoning as we do in the West—nothing more offensive than that. Well, except for throwing your shoes at George W. Bush during a press conference.

Lastly, my father understood the human side of being away from home which has since been destroyed by technology. Today, handwritten letters have been replaced by video calls and emails. My father, with his memory of Vietnam, still writes to me voraciously whether I am deployed or not. I still remember getting his first letter in the field one dark night. It was like something magic. I eagerly snatched it out of the drill sergeant's hand and quietly scurried to a secluded part of the forest. I excitedly ripped it open and with my red lens flashlight (must have light discipline) I reread it for hours. People often ask me what they can send deployed soldiers. With the robust MWR support, I tell them there is nothing material that we really need. They walk away disappointed as they were hoping for some grand wisdom on what to ship. So here it is and long overdue—what to send to soldiers overseas—how about a handwritten letter? And ladies, be generous with the perfume if sending to your significant other.

Firebase All American I, Vietnam; May 1969: "My men are a strange group," my father informed the family.[2] They consisted of a measly 12 soldiers (a normal platoon is roughly 30) and one Vietnamese Kit Carson Scout, a former enemy combatant flipped to support the allies.[3] His scout was a young teenager who spent much of his time chasing girls. That and stealing anything not nailed down from US soldiers were his preferred activities.[4]

My father struggled at first with understanding the foreign culture he found himself in. Seeing men walking around holding hands or with their arms around each other's necks, looking like high schoolers in love, made him think the entire nation consisted of homosexuals. He soon learned this was a sign of respect between male friends. One usually only saw men with men and women with women; rarely did the two demonstrate public displays of affection. "A woman always moves out of the way of a man walking on the sidewalk," he further observed about the fairer sex and their submissiveness; "quite funny when the GIs step off into the street to let a gal pass and she does the same thing."[5]

His first platoon sergeant only had a week left in country and spent little time positively mentoring his new lieutenant on the culture. On his first patrol, my father was waylaid by an old sickly-looking mama-san who manifested seemingly out of nowhere and offered him a free boom-boom (slang for sex) as a welcome souvenir to Vietnam. Anyone else after him would be charged 500 piasters (about $5 US) for a turn. Physically pushing her away with a hard no, he was shocked when his platoon sergeant eagerly took her up on the offer. Instead of hunting VC, my father's first mission was spent standing around waiting for some of his soldiers, who were lined up outside mama-san's shack with 500 piasters in hand.[6]

Boom-boom girls weren't the only ones who accosted him and his men whenever they operated in populated areas. Children constantly reacted to them in one of four ways as they moved about. One, they just gestured wildly and generally yelled; two, they would stick their hands out and say "chop-chop" for food, candy, or cigarettes; three, they would yell "Fuck you GI" and flick the bird; or four, they would just observe them silently from a distance. Understandably, my father especially liked the kids who were shy and did not yell anything. He would always wave at them and return a salute to those who gave him one.[7] Children would also constantly harass them, trying to sell mainly sodas. Anything to break the monotony of iodine-treated canteens; of course, they could only buy the canned ones after a thorough inspection to make sure they had not been tampered with. Anything bottled may contain poison or ground-up glass.[8] His new platoon sergeant taught him this first lesson.

Sergeant (SGT) Kurtz was only one month older than my father's baby sister Momi, but he was very good and highly experienced.[9] A definite boon for a cherry lieutenant. Due to the shortage of NCOs in Vietnam, some enlisted men were able to take advantage of a new Army promotion program. Selected initial entry soldiers who showed leadership potential could graduate straight from AIT into an accelerated NCO training pipeline which would quickly pump out sergeants. This sought to both maximize a draftee's time in the Army and fill NCO shortages in Vietnam. Because of the swiftness of the promotion, they earned the derogatory nickname of "Shake'n'Bake Sergeants," named after the tasty seasoning introduced in 1965 that could quickly turn bland chicken into something more.[10]

Another Shake'n'Bake arrived at the exact same time as my father, and even though he ended up in a different platoon, he was one of the few I was able to connect with to learn more about my dad's time with the 82nd. SGT Larry Lockeby from England, Arkansas was drafted in 1968. After basic training, Airborne School, and time as a drill sergeant, he found himself standing next to my father during both of their first days in Vietnam. Lockeby remembers some of the hatred those from the old Army had for the Shake'n'Bakes. Every morning at Airborne School the jumpmasters would rush the formation screaming, "All E-5s and above with less than two years' time and grade get on down!" They would make them do pushups until they got tired.[11]

After replacing Mr. Boom-boom, Kurtz, quickly shaken then baked or not, was also the only NCO in the entire platoon.[12] His second lesson? Do not pick up items you think would make great souvenirs. More than likely, they are booby trapped. My father paled as he thought of the cool sign he just swiped from a village stashed in his pack, the same one I have described at the start of this chapter. Hand painted in red on the small rectangular piece of wood under the crude skull and crossbones are the words *nguy hiểm*—danger in Vietnamese.

Besides the souvenirs and tainted soda cans, my father also learned from Kurtz that some of the children darting in and out of their formations selling soft drinks were reporting troop counts and movements to the VC—as were the boom-boom girls from their backs.[13]

Nontraditional intelligence gathering aside, as for the men in my father's platoon, only one was older than him; at the ripe old age of 30 he enlisted six months before being shipped to Vietnam. No one ever quite figured out why he joined. Most of his men were born in 1948, with the youngest being born in 1950.[14] They were White, Black, and Hispanic, and were a mix of volunteers and draftees.[15] Just a bunch of 18- or 19-year-old kids with varying degrees of comprehension, united by the green, fighting to protect a foreign nation's capital from the dreaded communists.[16]

What was the difference between a draftee and a volunteer? Not much, it seemed. It depended more on the person versus how they entered the service. At least that is the response I got from most I asked who knew my father from the war. Some draftees did have drug issues that when discovered often resulted in the worst punishment being a transfer to another unit to be someone else's problem. An officer my dad served with figured out a unique solution to this. Do not take their drugs or even say that you found them. Rather, dip their needle in dog shit and then wipe it clean. Next time they shot up they would get an infection and would be evacuated out of country. Problem solved.[17]

If not doing drugs and as noted earlier, the men in Vietnam graffitied up their helmet covers with permanent markers. Some drew peace symbols, while others scribbled out their girl's name or wrote the date they were supposed to rotate out of Vietnam; some were bolder and wrote Fuck the Army (FTA) and other derogatory comments on their steel. They would have done the same to their issued flak vests but they never wore them (too hot), so those remained safe from their eager sharpies. The only rule was that anything written had to be in black—no color. If they stayed within that guidance, no-one said anything. However, each company had on hand enough clean covers to hand out to the men for official ceremonies or visits to the rear. Only in the field was that scrawl allowed.[18]

"They bitch like anybody would in similar surroundings but are generally in good spirit," my father stated about his men.[19] He also noticed how many of them suddenly found God. "This is the first place I have seen soldiers go to 'chapel-in-the-open' readily," he observed to the family. "It seems to mean more out here."[20] This proves the age-old saying: there are no atheists in foxholes.

Similar to seeing the chaplain, my father quickly realized another thing that kept his men going: mail. "You know what I do at breakfast and supper first? Look for mail," he sadly wrote home. The Army had lost track of him during his travels between Fort Benning, Panama, and now Vietnam. This meant that his mail was still trying to find him and would not do so for several more weeks.[21] "Please send a care package, like a can of cookies or date nut bars," he implored.[22] To make sure the family clearly understood, he clipped and sent the Army's official instructions on the difference between sending packages Space Available Mail and Parcel Air Lift.[23] But whatever was sent, as the leader you must share, so: "Please send plenty—got to feed 20 people."[24]

Unfortunately, mail was not always a blessing—sometimes it brought bad news. "Had my first real personal problem from one of my men," he sadly wrote, "he got a letter (Dear John type) from his girl." Ah, the timeless Dear John; you are not a real soldier until you get at least one under your belt. This was not a small one either—she wrote to him the exact same day she got married to another! "A Dear John can be mighty destructive out here," he correctly predicted. It was time to get some beers in the man and get the chaplain; the perfect combination to cure any life trauma.[25]

As he got to know his men, the monsoon rains came with a vengeance. The days grew shorter and somehow it was simultaneously hot, humid, cold, windy, and wet during the deluges. This spelled misery for the soldiers in base camps and in the field.[26] One night during perimeter guard on the firebase, it rained so hard my father thought the bunker would collapse. "I was so tired I just lay there on the ground and got soaked," he recalled. Meanwhile in the field he remembers patrolling in wet sticky mud up to his knees through rice paddies, corn, bean, and tobacco fields as the water rushed over him.[27] One more thing about the field which all infantrymen quickly became adept at: "One of the new things I've learned since coming to the field is that the squatting position is very natural."[28] Nothing like taking a dump while avoiding both the enemy and bamboo viper snakes.[29]

Base camp offered little respite or comfort from field conditions. "Since I joined the company, I have slept on a cot twice, on an air mattress once, sat on six chairs, and eaten with silverware once," my father groaned in a letter home.[30] His current living quarters consisted of a sandbagged bunker where the sand was constantly leaking, which formed into mud on the floor of the bunker. Cot frames without mattresses and hammocks made up the sleeping arrangements, with a hole in the ground for a toilet. "All in all, not a very comfortable place," he noted.[31]

"Oh, I failed to mention," he wrote home about a further torment brought by the rains, "the local VC mosquitos are the worst I've seen."[32] His hands, arms, and neck soon became covered in bumps. That is one thing war movies never show you, the torment of constant bites from insects on one's body. They often carry with them numerous illnesses like the scourge of Vietnam: malaria and typhus. When the US was contemplating committing troops, the Army surgeon general Leonard D. Heaton cautioned against it, presenting a "gloomy picture of an environment in Vietnam so replete with vermin, reptiles, heat, and disease that westerners would be unable to survive."[33] It was somewhat of an exaggeration but still a heck of an ordeal for the grunts on the ground.

Interestingly enough, the bites on my father were almost invisible due to the amount of dirt covering his body and uniform.[34] His last bath had been from a dirty well via a bucket for which he traded some macaroni noodles with an old woman.[35] Before that, his last real wash had been way back in Honolulu.[36] "I'm glad that we perspire for one reason," he joked, "it keeps the dirt in motion."[37] Being in the infantry is like being homeless. They know to eat whatever food is available, sleep whenever and wherever it's safe, never pass up the opportunity to use a real toilet, and never turn down a bath if offered. It is the same for a field soldier.

Village of Ap Thung, Vietnam; May 1969: A small American element of troopers from 2nd Platoon, Delta Company of the 1/505th snooped around the perimeter of the VC-controlled village of Ap Thung, in the Hóc Môn district, just northwest of Saigon. Their mission? Determine the best places to set up three evening ambush sites in the hopes of surprising the enemy. The east side of the village was chosen; just as directed, travel light and fight them by night.

Led by their brand-new lieutenant, the troopers set in their positions and hunkered down for a long night of waiting. With the Americans so close, in the early morning hours the VC tried to sneak out the west side of the village, straight into preset artillery coordinates. My father, young and eager, watched them go and grinned as he keyed his radio hand mic and called for fire through the commander to the forward observer (FO): "Dragon 6, Dragon 6, fire mission over." The 105-millimeter howitzer shells streaked overhead with a swoosh, momentarily blocking out the stars behind them as they soared. Impacting with an air-sucking explosion, they tore through the VC element trying to flee. Finally—my father's first contribution to pacification in Vietnam that did not involve keeping his men away from boom-boom girls.[38]

Chapter 11

"No VC here …"

VIETNAMESE CIVILIAN

In the cave behind my couch, tucked among the old medals and aged texts, sat another book whose title made little sense to a nine-year-old boy: *The Tunnels of Củ Chi* by Tom Mangold and John Penycate. As I continued to play soldier, I would slowly learn from cheesy 1980s war-action movies about the tunnels in Vietnam and the famed "tunnel rats" who tried to counter them. *Rambo* and *Missing in Action* were historical masterpieces to a young boy like myself. Years later, once my father understood that I was trying to learn more about Vietnam, he mailed me this exact book, missing its dust cover and with the text on the spine now barely legible. I cracked open its browning pages, finally learning what it contained.

"There were hundreds of kilometers of tunnels connecting villages, districts, and even provinces," explained the book, describing in detail the vast subterranean passageways that stretched from the outskirts of Saigon to the Cambodian border. "They held living areas, storage depots, ordnance factories, hospitals, headquarters, and almost every other facility that was necessary to the pursuit of the war," it continued.[1] Củ Chi and its underground complexes were where the Tet Offensive against Saigon was launched. It was still a region in which the enemy could effectively and secretly muster and train forces before an attack or infiltration into the capital. Despite repeated attempts, no amount of US bombing could ever destroy the complexes. "A stork can't shit into a bottle," supposedly said the enemy's celebrated leader Hồ Chí Minh, known as Uncle Ho on both sides of the war, "so with our tunnels we shouldn't be scared of American bombers."[2]

Due to the inability to clear them from the air, Củ Chi was the site of repeated US operations, to include the 82nd. Insurgents in Iraq were just as hard to ferret out as the VC were; however, besides the use of some already-built sewer and drainage tunnels, I cannot imagine how effective and elusive they would have been if they had dug at the rate of the Vietnamese.

Today, among the tunnels that have been widened to accommodate Western tourists, caged monkeys, souvenir vendors, and a shooting range of US weapons, it is easy to overlook the sheer dedication and willpower it took the Vietnamese to build these structures of war. "No one has ever demonstrated more ability to hide his installations than the Viet Cong," noted General Westmoreland on the enemy's efforts to conceal and move their forces. "They were human moles."[3]

Tunnels aside, throughout my life my father only told me a spattering of stories from Vietnam, often at unexpected times and spurred by random unrelated events. The drill instructor (DI) scene from the 2005 movie *Jarhead* really resonated with me when I saw it on the big screen. "You—the maggot whose father served in Vietnam?" the DI piercingly questioned the recruit. After the recruit answered in the affirmative and added that his father only spoke about it once: "Good!" the DI screamed. "Then he wasn't lying."[4]

As I continued to read my father's letters and diary from the war, I stumbled across one of the stories he had told me as a child: about how he and his men had unloaded, on fully automatic, four M-16s and one M-60 against a VC right in front of them. I still remember running in and telling him about a peculiar miss I just had with my pellet gun. He looked up from his book and quickly described to his now-shocked child how once, he and four of his men were all firing at a VC not 10 feet away and missed. "Sometimes bullets zig when they should have zagged," he shrugged, before going back to his book.

In today's military, we often have ethical and leadership discussions using historical examples. We debate whether the actions taken by the leader were right or wrong. During these deliberations, I always bring up another one of the stories my father told me from the war about striking the balance between obeying orders and trying not to recklessly get his men killed. During these debates, not everyone agrees with his perspective, but I always do. My father repeatedly asked his company commander why they dangled his men out there in small ambush teams like worms on a hook to be snatched up by the enemy. He was told to "shut up and carry out his orders."[5] Sometimes military leaders are so focused on the assigned mission and achieving results that they do not stop to ask what the repercussions of their directives at the ground level are; this is a lesson I have absorbed from his time at war.

Most of all, from his writings I could tell he was changing. I could almost sense him becoming hardened.

Hóc Môn District, Vietnam; June 1969: "I am getting quite bored with these operations," my father irately complained about his time in Vietnam so far. Patrolling and setting ambushes in horrendous rainy conditions with no action made him weary.[6] But where to conduct patrols and set ambushes to best protect the capital from rockets was the burning question. Soon after assuming the mission, the 82nd studied the history of enemy attacks and created a set of metrics to determine possible future actions. The data points were compiled: timing of attacks, maximum ranges of 107- and 122-meter rockets, common launch sites, and the enemy's exploitation of electronic surveillance gaps and unit boundaries. This basic time, location, and weapon range formula enabled intelligence estimates to map out potential land and water infiltration and supply routes, civilian areas that the enemy might leverage to conduct attacks or stash insurgents, and possible rocket caches.[7] This, in turn, determined what areas to patrol or set ambushes.

Despite these calculations, things remained quiet. Intelligence believed this lack of activity could be due to one of two reasons. One, that the enemy was keeping silent because of the current peace conference in Paris; or two, they were building combat power to conduct another push on Saigon.[8] My father hoped for the latter as time crept by with nothing to do.[9]

Although he desired to contribute to the war effort, my father was also not stupid. To prevent rocket attacks with his 12 men, he was supposed to set out three unsupported ambush sites per night. This equated to only three to four men at each location. Ambushes were one of the most common and dangerous operations in Vietnam—setting in positions in the pitch dark of night was serious business. Making too much noise when establishing a location or putting it in the wrong place could invite an enemy ambush in return—or worse. US forces being fired upon by mistake for being at the wrong grid was a common occurrence. The whole point of an ambush was to engulf your adversary with overwhelming firepower when they entered the kill zone. How in the world could four men do this from non-mutually supported sites?

"We were all too scared to move from our positions," he later explained. "One of our greatest fears was that we might walk into the killing zone of another patrol."[10] General Abrams himself commented on the dangers of this around Saigon. "I'd hate like hell to drive down Route 4 [just outside of the city] at night—not for any fear of getting picked off by the VC, I don't think there's a chance of that," he told his staff in a meeting, "but you run an excellent chance of getting shot up by your own people out there."[11]

With this danger and the lack of manpower to overmatch anything he may encounter, my father would take his 12 men to their first designated ambush site and instead of pushing out his other two teams they would all stay together at the initial location. They would then conduct radio checks all night on the different sets as though they were emplaced at three different locations.[12] This led to the debate I have had years later with many on the fine line between obeying orders and needlessly endangering your soldiers. Regardless of when and how an ambush was set each evening, according to my father, they all had one thing in common: "The first thing you did was pray for it to be morning."[13]

His fears were not unfounded. In one of the sister battalions, B Co 2/505th had a squad-sized ambush position overrun by the enemy. Eight men were killed, one missing, one wounded, and the last fled smack into another US ambush site and was killed by them. "It is apparent that somebody wasn't where he was supposed to be and everyone was asleep," my father noted to himself.[14] The Army had a different story and claimed that the men were not resting but that it had been a coordinated and well-planned VC attack. To this day, my father still disagrees. "I've been on ambush and found everyone else went to sleep," he sadly noted. "It was hard to stay awake."[15] In his mind, this justified his actions as being the right thing to do. If a squad could not stay alive, how could three-to-four-man teams that he was expected to emplace do it?

This was a lesson he took to heart just before his unit was ordered to move. His destination? The Củ Chi area, tunnel city. "This is dink country," he excitedly noted, "maybe we will see some action."[16] Again, the Army is not a PC organization.

Ấp Bàu Sim, near Củ Chi, Vietnam; June 1969: "Avez-vous vu un VC ou NVA dans la région?" asked my father repeatedly in French, which he learned in school and via old records he used to listen to with Tutu. "No VC, no NVA here," was the only response he would get from surprised elders, who still spoke the language of their previous enemy.[17]

Although the opposing fighters were formally known as the National Front for the Liberation of South Vietnam, the official name given to the hodgepodge of fighters operating in the South to help unite them, their opponents just called them the Viet Cong, supposedly short for Vietnamese Communist. Was it an American bastardization of a term or a Vietnamese invention? This is something historians cannot even agree upon from this controversial conflict.[18] Regardless of the etymology of the moniker, throughout his time my father would encounter numerous Americans trained to speak Vietnamese only to discover they could not communicate once they got there. He got along much better than them with his broken French and pidgin Vietnamese.[19]

Despite the population constantly reassuring him of their innocence, it did not stop his men from frequently finding tunnel entrances. These underground complexes served several functions and were protected with an array of devious devices to thwart the discovery and entry of US forces. Not only were the entrances ingeniously concealed, but they could also be deadly. A series of twists, turns, and partitions were built to foil entry attempts and destruction efforts. The worst was known as a floating lid, a sharp U-turn in a tunnel that was filled with water. This forced an intruder to literally swim through it and could also stop gas from seeping further into the complex. "If the enemy dared to put their heads through the floating lids," noted one former VC fighter, "the civilian self-defense forces in the ground could stab them to death with bayonets, shoot at them with small arms, or blow them up with grenades."[20]

Not knowing any of this, what did most units do (including the 82nd) when they found a hole in the ground in Củ Chi? Drop a colored smoke grenade and watch for it to billow out of any other entrances. Then mark them all and report grids to higher for follow-on tunnel rat missions. Finally, deposit several fragmentary and concussion grenades down each opening as a departing stork-shit-like gift before leaving.[21] Thankfully, my father, at 6'1", could not enter a tunnel even if he wanted to.

It was in Củ Chi that my father saw his first enemy up close. "Last night I saw my first dink," he wrote home about the man he and his men had unloaded their magazines on from 10 feet away. "We didn't get him, but we sure scared the heebie-jeebies out of him," he relayed, indicating serious zigzagging at its worst, much like my pellet gun. Or, as he mused later, "the guy may have been a local farmer, but the people know that anyone out after 2000hrs [8:00pm] is declared fair game."[22] VC or farmer, rules were rules.

Another lesson he soon learned that he drilled into his men was that when leaving their positions, they had to stop leaving stuff behind that the enemy could use to supply their own efforts. "Apart from a few old rifles and light machine-guns of French make," reported one journalist who visited with the enemy during the war, "everything one saw—webbing belts and water canteens and even flourbag 'knapsacks'—along the jungle trails and at the base camps was 'Made in the U.S.A.' exclusively."[23] The amount of ammunition, grenades, and other usable objects left lying around once US forces left an area was a problem in Vietnam. Captured enemy soldiers were reporting that these items were becoming a main source of supply for local VC, who, of course, gave it right back with deadly vigor every chance they got.[24]

Even though they were hunting tunnels, now he and his men could not escape their supposed specialty, the night ambush. Just as the boss wanted, they kept the pressure on the enemy 24 hours a day, every day. Ambushes continued to be a deadly business in the 82nd. An additional sister battalion, the 1/508th, had another mishap. Imagine their surprise when into their kill zone one night strolled three VC without a care in the world. Butt stocks were quietly tucked into their shoulders and rifles leveled before an inferno was unleashed on the unsuspecting trio. As the smoke cleared and the high-fives ceased, to their surprise they discovered three dead South Vietnamese soldiers who had wandered into the wrong area. My father noted this latest tragedy and added to his list the need to triple-check US and allied ambush locations before setting in. "*C'est la guerre,*" he reasoned in French: "That is war."[25]

Chapter 12

"The grenade belonged to him ..."

FOUL-MOUTHED DOC

I had walked so far and for so long on my bum foot that it would no longer fit in my boot. What started as a minor stress fracture that probably would have healed quickly if I had let it had developed into a clean break. Because my right foot hurt so bad, I developed a heavy limp, which eventually wore off all the flesh on the ball of my left foot. On top of that, probably due to my injuries and weakened immune system, I caught pneumonia. Sitting on the floor next to my bunk with my feet elevated and hacking up a lung, I turned to my Bible—the only reading material we were allowed to have in basic training. I let the book open on its own in my hands and read the first passage that my eyes fell on: 2 Timothy 4:7. Shaken, I read it to myself several times: "I have fought the good fight, I have finished the race, I have kept the faith."[1] With my strong belief in omens, I finally went on sick call.

Lying in a hospital bed in a small room with three other sick trainees with one foot bandaged, the other in a cast, and pumped full of drugs for my illness, I thought my army career was over. I felt so sick, miserable, embarrassed, and sorry for myself that I literally wanted to die. Late one night, the elderly African American female nurse (the only one who was nice to us) came in and sat next to my bed. As she ran her hands through my hair, she sang a song my mom used to sing to me as a baby: "You're the Apple of my Eye / And I love you so and I want you to know / That I'll always be right here / And I love to sing sweet songs to you / Because you are so dear." As she softly sang, I cried. In the morning I apologized to the others in the room if we had woken them. They had no idea what I was talking about. When the nurse came to work, I quietly thanked her for the night before, wondering how she had known about that song. With a bewildered look on her face she said, "Honey, I only work days." Was it a dream or an angel? I like to think the latter; either way, I now knew I would be okay.

"Stand by for the doctor," said the orderly as he handed me a phone in the hospital room. Much to my surprise, my father was on the line. He had not heard from me for several weeks and had been calling all over Fort Benning trying to locate me. Finally, my basic training company admitted they had messed up by not letting the family know I was in the hospital and told him where I was. No problem—he knew the system, so he called with confidence pretending to be a doctor and got linked into bedside. Usually not emotionally expressive, like his father, he told me he loved me and was proud of me. Just as I learned he did in Vietnam, begging to be released from the hospital despite his foot ailments, he understood why I had pushed it so hard past where I should have with my injury. Most civilians do not understand that mindset—the warrior culture of not being able to show weakness or being thought of as someone who lets their buddies down.

As we spoke, he further reinforced my new belief that no matter what happened, I would be okay. As I explained my feet problems, he sighed and said, "Seems your career is starting out the same as mine." I had no idea what he meant at the time, but after reading his letters now I do. It was then that he passed on a mantra to me that he learned in Vietnam; one that no matter how tough it gets, I can repeat and know that everything will be okay. No matter how challenging life is, "This too shall pass."[2] It has helped more than he probably knows.

His letters also highlighted another peculiar occurrence in the military; the fact that egotistical tyrannical leaders are nothing new. It seems he also encountered them during his service. I have met these types myself countless times in the Army; the military seems to grow them for some reason. I have noticed that with each promotion, my jokes told to subordinates get funnier. Somehow, as an LT I was not that amusing; now as an LTC I am a riot. If I ever become a general, I may be able to take my act on the road. Rank can easily go to your head; the deferment offered is intoxicating and can feed a real monster. Although, in all fairness, the Army has recognized the problem and is doing its best to root out toxicity at all levels.

Lastly, it was amusing to see how much it meant to my dad to get homemade treats sent to him from his sister. During my initial basic training, Aunt Momi, thinking she was being supportive as she had done for her brother, attempted to send me baked items. "Whatever you do Auntie Momi, don't send chocolate chip cookies," I begged of her in a letter,[3] imagining with dread the joy the drill sergeants would have as they obliterated them under their boots in front of everyone. I amend my earlier guidance on letter writing—send some homemade sweets too.

Củ Chi, Vietnam; June 1969: An artillery barrage ripped apart a sparsely wooded section in Củ Chi. Inbound rockets from attack helicopters shrieked as they joined the salvo before machine-gun fire strafed the area and the unmistakable sound of inbound UH-1 Hueys (the workhorse of the war) became audible. These machines changed the face of combat forever—first truly tested in Vietnam. Now troops could be inserted almost anywhere, anytime, although the distinct *whop, whop, whop* sound they made as they approached often negated that element of surprise. The ever-present fear of a helicopter being shot down necessitated the blind preparatory fires on a landing zone. By the time my father arrived in Vietnam, the loss of Hueys to ground fire was at an all-time high for the war.[4]

Quite a show was put on for the incoming battalion commander, LTC Alfred Zamparelli. Before his departure, the outgoing commander wanted to demonstrate the proper execution of a helicopter insertion. The battalion S-2 (intelligence officer) picked an area devoid of any enemy activity for the display. Chosen to lead the expensive demonstration? My father's platoon.[5]

Even though the area was considered secure, it was no stranger to US attacks, as evidenced by the pockmarked terrain from previous bomb strikes which had now filled with water during the monsoon downpours. One journalist who visited the area before and after US operations in Củ Chi noted the difference in how the war had ravaged the region. "Not a trace remained," he wrote of the previous vibrant communities there, "not a tree, not a buffalo … where there had been lush stretches of rice, magnificent fields of cabbages, turnips, and pineapple, there were only overlapping craters."[6]

In combat formation supported by Cobra gunships, the Hueys flew low toward the now slightly more deforested stand of trees. Six hundred meters east of their target, they touched down briefly in a clearing before taking off again, hugging the earth to avoid enemy fire. Left behind was a platoon of troopers loaded down with enough firepower to overwhelm an enemy company. As the deafening wash created by the helicopters subsided and the sound faded off into the distance, nature came alive again. It is amazing how fast wildlife recovers after a barrage of munitions or an intrusive helicopter landing. It is like the machines of war are just a minor nuisance to them in the grander scheme of life.[7]

My father quickly got his men in line as the coolness of flying with the helicopter doors open and rotor wash was replaced by the oppressive humidity. With the platoon stretched out in a single parallel line as though they were about to do a police call to pick up trash, he signaled his men forward; they advanced confidently toward the square of trees. Along for the ride was the S-2 who had chosen the demonstration location. My father remembers that the guy "thought he was a hot shit Airborne Ranger very recently promoted Captain" who had seen little combat but somehow knew it all. Before he left for the mission, a fellow lieutenant warned him that the men the S-2 led in his old company hated him so much they almost fragged his ass.[8] This is a type I know well.

Regardless, bored with crunching enemy intel back in the rear, the S-2 wanted to get out of the office and stretch his legs, in a safe space of course. The line moved forward, each man ready to support his buddy; close enough that if one was attacked, they could all return fire, but not so close so that an enemy machine gun or single booby trap could take out multiple men. Just as they entered the tree line, the S-2 heard a familiar ping. Instantly recognizing it for what it was—a grenade that has just had its pin removed and lever popped off—he threw his body behind a tree stump as the explosion ripped through the air around him.[9]

"Doooccc!" several of his soldiers yelled out in unison. The line medic—the lifeline that keeps a platoon healthy, who during Vietnam treated everything from venereal disease to combat wounds—was affectionately called Doc. This was a term of respect from grunts, who would scream it out over the din of bullets and shell when they needed help. To distinguish their medic from others with the same nickname, the platoon called theirs the "Foul-Mouthed Doc."[10] SGT Lockeby remembers him as being "one of the bravest men I've ever run across."[11] Steadily mouthing the famed expletives that he was known for, Doc sprinted across water-filled craters and pushed through thick brush with no concern for his safety and made it to the casualty's side while my father watched in amazement. After patching up wounds on each arm, left chest, and above the left eye, the S-2 was evacuated to a field hospital.[12]

Chalk up one Purple Heart for the S-2. Wounded by an enemy booby trap, he could wear it with pride. "Only one thing though, Sir," whispered the Foul-Mouthed Doc to my father, "the grenade belonged to him." Looks like the wounding was due to the S-2's own carelessness. As he entered the tree line, the pin from a grenade hanging off his web gear snagged on some branches. His heroic leap behind the stump was necessitated by his own sloppiness. None of that made it into the after-action report, though. The only results of the mission were that one leader was humbled, and my father made it into the unit's yearbook. On page 11 you can see his back as he and his radio operator watch three Hueys (also known in his war as slicks for their sleek look when not carrying any weapons) land to pick his men up.[13] Besides the wounding and photo op, nothing else was achieved, and yet they somehow still walked away with a casualty.

In a letter home after this event, the stationery used had a map of Vietnam printed in the lower left corner. To help the family understand the war, my father penned in "Bad Guys" in the north of the country and "Good Guys" in the south; if only it were that simple.[14]

Tân Sơn Nhứt, Vietnam; June 1969: My father finished another chocolate chip cookie as he thought about his upcoming promotion to first lieutenant (1LT) and looked down at his feet with growing concern. Aunt Momi had sent a batch of homemade brownies and cookies, which he shared among his men. They served as the morning's breakfast and as dinner the night before.[15] Homemade sweets beat army chow any day. As Momi later explained about this show of support, "One of those ironies of war is being against the premise of the war, but not the guys who went."[16]

Treats withstanding, his feet were still a problem. "I seem to be suffering from an old Hawaiian malady," my father described to the family, "luau feet."[17] This was the Hawaiian term for flat feet—the result of growing up as a child running around for years barefoot or with just slippers on. He started with size 10W for boots, went to 11R, and soon ended with 11W until he got the correct fit. It sounds trivial, but an infantryman with ill-fitting boots and blistered feet is completely combat ineffective. As we both learned, the Army is just not equipped to handle feet born from years of beach time. Soon luau feet would be the least of his worries, though.[18]

Waking up the next morning, he went to sick call. His feet had swollen to the point they could no longer fit in his boots. This was a centuries-old problem that has impacted all foot soldiers throughout time—trench foot, the crud, then known as jungle rot. Blisters and a growing fungus covered his heel and ankles and were causing his legs to swell. Admitted to the field hospital and placed on antibiotics, the doctors told him it would be at least several days until he could be released. However, after two days of RAMFing—RA meant rear area with MF being a "no-no" word, as he explained to the family—he pleaded with the doctors to release him.[19]

They obliged, with the understanding that he would not wear any boots or have any field time for three days. When he returned to his unit, his commander, shaking his head over what was he supposed to do with a bootless LT, immediately sent him to the rest and relaxation (R&R) spot in country, the beach haven of Vũng Tàu.[20]

Chapter 13

"Must get some rest now ..."

PATRICK W. NAUGHTON SR.

Wrapped in yellowing tissue paper, a small, silver-colored peace symbol attached to a dog tag chain fell out of a manila envelope with a thud onto my desk. "I do have something I've been meaning to send to you," my Aunt Momi had written during one of our many exchanges about the war days before it arrived.[1] About 2¼" across and probably made of melted aluminum cans, it had not lost its luster even after all these years. She recalled that my father told her it was made by soldiers out of used bullet casings.[2] In turn, he remembered that he purchased it from a Vietnamese street vendor during an R&R at Vũng Tàu for his "peace-nik" sister.[3] Time definitely blurs the memory some.

When he sent her the symbol, he also noted how many of his men wore that same necklace and that it was even drawn or painted on some soldiers' gear and helicopters. "Hard to tell what is on the minds of most over here," he told her."[4] I posted a photo of the peace symbol on several Vietnam veteran Facebook pages, hoping to get more information on it. Most of the replies stated they were cheap, coated aluminum items sold by souvenir merchants all over the country. That and a heated thread on whether or not the symbol was called "the footprint of an American chicken" is the only feedback I got.[5] The peace movement during the war is still an open wound for many veterans.

My father got a break at Vũng Tàu. This time allowed him to observe his surroundings more. His letters are full of small pop cultural tidbits from the war that have been lost to history; details drowned out by the historical Vietnam studies on grand strategy, operational troop movements, and tactical firefights. Music, comic strips, and programs played on the Armed Forces Video Network (AFVN) were his entertainment for the several days that he was there. I know we had the same *Stars and Stripes* newspaper in Iraq that he had in Vietnam, but I am embarrassed to say I never picked one up. I never watched Armed Forces Network-Iraq either. I was too busy watching pirated movies.

Like Vũng Tàu, Freedom Rest in Iraq was our temporary R&R oasis in the middle of a war zone, built to allow soldiers to take small breaks and recharge without having to leave the country. It contained a small hotel, movie rooms, a gym, wifi, and, most importantly, an outdoor pool. Most who stayed there just ended up purchasing bootleg movies and television shows from the local Iraqis. Their sale was heavily frowned on by the US government, but how could you prevent it when generals were in the same souks as the privates buying the pirated shows by the dozens? The soldiers on pass would then lock themselves in their air-conditioned rooms and forget about the war for a few hours. Nothing like watching a movie recorded in a theater on a home camera with heads bobbing across the bottom of the screen.

My girlfriend and I watched many an illegally copied digital video disc, but our favorite location to meet up was on Sundays at Freedom Rest's pool. Another oddity about the American way of war: towards the start of the second decade, sometimes duties seemed lighter on the weekends. I'm unsure if that was designed internally by the actions of staff and leaders or if the enemy mutually agreed that we needed a weekly break.

I would allow myself Sundays to eat junk food and would fill up on pancakes at the chow hall before heading to the pool. With her in a one-piece swimsuit (so as not to offend the Iraqi sensibilities) and me in my Army fitness shorts, ignoring the licentious and jealous stares of the other soldiers on break, we would while away the day in 115-degree weather as though we were back in the US. Besides a helicopter pad astride the pool that would drown out the area with noise and dust with each landing, it was bliss. Pancakes, bikinis, lust, and war—what else could a young man want?

Vũng Tàu, Vietnam; June 1969: "Welcome to the R&R Center" at Vũng Tàu, noted the stationary header that my father used to write home. The heading included a fancy logo with a sketch of a girl in a bikini under a beach umbrella, with a man jet skiing in the background.[6] Like Freedom Rest, this area served as a place for troops to get some down time without having to leave the country.[7] From watching old archive clips of the bars and clubs there, it looked like a total sausage fest, a far cry from the idyllic sketch on its stationary.

While there, my father managed to find a postcard that showed the type of terrain he had been operating in recently. A door gunner on a helicopter overlooked rice paddies as far as the eye could see, broken up only by earthen dykes and small islands of tree-lined squares.[8] When most think of Vietnam, they picture lush, thick jungles that concealed hordes of enemy soldiers. Not flat agricultural areas where the VC hid in plain sight in the various local communities and in tunnels under the ground.

In between buying cheap souvenirs, Vũng Tàu also gave him free time for other things in Vietnam, namely entertainment and healing his feet. Instead of the bootleg movies of my war, he had to settle for comic strips and voice radio. Vũng Tàu was the first place in which he started saving the Nguyen Charlie cartoon strips by Corky Trinidad from the daily *Stars and Stripes* newspaper.

World War II had Beetle Bailey; Vietnam had the blundering and buffoonish guerrilla named Nguyen Charlie. Each day, his strip featured a cast of characters which included his fellow insurgents, his boss Comrade Commander, and his archrivals, a US infantry platoon led by a young lieutenant and grizzled old sergeant who were constantly harangued by their mama-san maid. Each time a strip reminded him of something he was experiencing in Vietnam, he would rip it out and send it home. Often, he would scribble across the top of each torn-out strip on how it pertained to him. He acknowledged that the cartoon "only has real meaning for the boys over here," but it was nonetheless a way for him to cope and share his experiences with the family through humor.[9]

He was also able to catch up on the latest Charlie Brown cartoons by Charles Schulz, an artist and World War II veteran who was growing steadily more critical of the war. This week's comic featured Lucy barking at poor Snoopy that he was her dog while Brown was on vacation and to jump when ordered. Linus then gloomily commented to the poor bouncing dog, "I see you've met our First Sergeant."[10] "Everyone is getting a big kick out of Peanuts right now!" he amusingly wrote home.[11] Interestingly enough, his call sign was actually "Snoopy 6."[12]

In addition to comic strips, he was able to catch up on the latest Chicken Man radio series on AFVN. The comic-book hero radio spoof was widely broadcasted during the war. Every so often they would randomly play his theme song over the loudspeakers in Vũng Tàu. My father didn't really understand why this occurred. "It's sort of the theme of the rear area types—I guess," he reasoned.[13] I listened to several episodes from that time period and found them hilarious—not sure what that says about me.

Finally, besides enjoying the time off and catching up on the latest funnies, he was also able to heal using an age-old trick learned in Hawai'i. "Salt water really good for feet," he relayed, "better than foot soaking at hospital."[14]

Tân Sơn Nhứt, Vietnam; June 1969: After a short ride on a Wallaby Flight, courtesy of a Royal Australian Air Force twin-engine DHC-4 Caribou, he was back in the war. The only difference now was that he was no longer a butter bar but officially a 1LT. He was promoted without fanfare or family members present, but at least it put him one step closer to losing his cherry status. The doctors still had him on three more days with no boots, so he didn't immediately return to the field. Instead, he was directed to cover down for the executive officer (XO) who was out on R&R.[15]

While he was gone, the battalion lost an officer—one who joined the 82nd only a week before my father did. 1LT Johnny F. Davis from Bravo Company was killed while entering a VC village with only his Kit Carson Scout as a guide. Incredibly brave, he was hoping to catch the enemy sleeping but instead found them wide awake and ready to greet him. "The only times Americans get hurt is when they make mistakes," mused my father. "This incident just reinforces my own theories on fighting this war—stay as a unit."[16] Thirty-six years later, buried deep in an obscure website on the dead from Vietnam, rests a sad note: "Johnny was my hero," wrote his sister Karen. "I miss him more now than I ever have."[17]

In a few days, the Delta Dragons were set to move out to an area known as the Pineapple, which stretched southwest of Saigon to the Vam Gò Đống river. It was an old French pineapple plantation between Củ Chi and Đức Hòa, 8,000 meters from the Cambodian border. The area was known as a hotbed for enemy activity. "I'll have to be on my toes," my father excitedly wrote home, "maybe see a little action hopefully before the action sees me."[18] Or, as one of my previous bosses repeatedly said, "You have to get them before they get you." Indeed, yes you do. "Enjoy the peace at home," he closed his last letter before moving out.[19]

Chapter 14

"Charlie's shit is weak ..."

PATRICK W. NAUGHTON SR.

Once, as a normal curious young boy who loved to try to sneak up on their parents anytime they were having a conversation, I overheard something strange. In a hushed voice, my father told a fellow veteran friend of his about a recurring nightmare he kept having. Something about a footprint filling up with water. What was so scary about that? I thought to myself at the time. Imagine my surprise when I discovered the reason for his fright in a letter from his time in the Pineapple.

The Pineapple was an ugly and unforgiving place; from his letters it quickly became obvious that it was where my father became an effective infantry leader. It was also interesting to read between the lines about his leadership style, including some old-school Army butt-chewings that still existed, at least up until the late 1990s when I was in. For better or worse, those have since gone out of style. I won't get into the debate on whether the military is now a petri dish for "wokeness" being cooked up by certain politicians who believe the Army is not inclusive and is too tough on its soldiers; however, I will say if I said some of the things my father did in Vietnam, or that my NCOs used to say to me, I would be quickly fired. It is a much nicer Army now.

Despite some hurt feelings, for my father the Pineapple was a defining moment. He had performed well and gained confidence in his platoon; best of all, he was no longer a cherry. It is intoxicating when you cross that undefined and invisible line from being a useless tub of lard to an old hand. No one tells you when that happens, you just wake up one day and realize that you know what is going on and no one has called you a "fucking cherry" in a long time. My father had also met the elusive enemy and bloodied them. Later, he admitted that he had been shooting to kill but was secretly relieved that he did not. Lastly, he also earned the only award he desired—the Combat Infantryman's Badge (CIB).[1]

The Model 1795 Springfield Arsenal Musket, framed by a silver rectangle with an infantry blue background surrounded by a wreath, made up the coveted badge I remember seeing as a child. I own his CIB now: the paper certificate has browned, the edges have cracked some, and the shiny chrome badge itself has tarnished with the years. I even have the cloth olive drab insignia that he wore sewn on his field uniform. It too has faded, but amazingly it still has the sweet smell of excessive sweat.

All still have a glow about them that demand respect. When I earned my Expert Infantry Badge, which is just the musket in a rectangle, I set it next to my bunk and stared at it for several days. The striking blue color made me think, "Wow, I am halfway to catching up to my father." I never earned a CIB. However, that little badge I held in my child-hands before carefully placing it back into his old army-stuff-box had a big influence on why I joined. Who knew such a tiny little piece of metal could do that?

The Pineapple, Vietnam; June 1969: Previously a large French pineapple plantation, the once heavily managed fields had been taken over by low-growing foliage and eye-height elephant grass. Much like the area my father just left that was flat, wet, and full of rice paddies, the Pineapple was flat, wet, and full of thick undergrowth, with the errant, prickly fruit gone wild sprinkled throughout. The only dry parts were the old narrow raised dirt roads and earthen dikes that crisscrossed the region, as explained to me by Private First Class (PFC) Doyle Wilkins[2]—another one of the men I was able to track down from my father's time with Delta Company.

The 82nd Airborne's official history of the war called dry land a luxury and depicted men immersed in standing water up to their waist while on operations. Due to its unforgiving terrain, the enemy used the region to infiltrate forces into Saigon and access the Vàm Dam Cống river water supply route. Because they understood that the Americans realized the area's importance, it was riddled with booby traps.[3] Or, as Lockeby more eloquently remembers, the Pineapple was "booby trapped out the ass along the dry places."[4]

On patrol on June 30, 1969, LT James Rogers and his radio operator (RTO) Corporal George Gibner (who all called Tex) from 1st Platoon slogged through the rough terrain. Back slaps and handshakes preceded the patrol as Tex had just turned 21 the day before. "Last night I dreamed I got blown away," Tex quietly responded with a stoic expression to a friend's well wishes just before stepping off.[5]

Signs of enemy activity were everywhere, including fresh human feces. Mainly because of these turd-signs, Rogers decided to continue the patrol rather than return to their new home Firebase Claudette as originally planned. Coming across a dry open area, the platoon quickly fanned out to further search for possible tunnels or further signs of the enemy. Wilkins, with water sloshing out from the tops of his jungle boots and dripping off his web gear, joined the men as they excitedly swarmed the clearing, hoping to finally find the enemy.[6]

Next to a small stream on the edge of the clearing, Tex triggered one of the numerous surprises left by the VC, the largest the unit had yet encountered in

Vietnam. A geyser of water and dirt flew high into the air as the shockwave and sound hit the rest of the platoon. Wilkins watched shocked as Rogers stumbled from the blast, bloodied and shaken but still standing. Left behind, crumpled and unconscious in the now steaming churned-up mud, was Tex. Doc got to work on the pair, Rogers with his legs bleeding profusely from various punctures and Tex with multiple gaping wounds. He called in a medical evacuation helicopter for them both.[7]

The acrid smell of the explosion dissipated as several men hastily hacked down some small trees, stripped them of their branches and created a field-expedient stretcher for Tex. As the bird landed in the clearing, his buddies shielded Tex's face from the stinging debris kicked up by the rotor wash. They then carried his pale limp body to the chopper before helping Rogers aboard. The lieutenant recovered from his wounds but never returned to the platoon. Tex died at the field hospital; his premonition came true.[8]

"Booby traps were not uncommon in the Pineapple," said Wilkins about this patrol. "They were not always deadly, but they did serve to slow us down." He emotionally recounted Tex's death for me before describing his brief interactions with my father. "I enjoyed reading your father's notes about those days," he shakily told me after I shared with him his accounts of the Pineapple. "He [Rogers] was a pretty good platoon leader and I hate we lost him so soon."[9]

Firebase Claudette, The Pineapple, Vietnam; June 1969: My father and his 2nd Platoon entered the Pineapple from the northeastern end of the region the day before Rogers and Tex hit the booby trap. The region was peppered with PPS-5 ground surveillance radars, high-tech gadgets for that era designed to pick up any movement on the ground. In addition, firefly missions were flown all night—Hueys rigged with powerful spotlights that hoped to illuminate enemy units or sampans that could be hit by the accompanying gunships. Despite these efforts, the only way to truly find the enemy was still boots on the ground[10]—hence why the 82nd had to wade their way through the tough terrain.

Like 1st Platoon, my father's troopers spent the day finding numerous signs of the enemy, including tunnel openings and booby traps; luckily, no one was hurt. As the day wore on and the cruel heat set in, pack straps dug into shoulders as the first signs of prickly heat started to appear. As the men patrolled, some were more attentive than others. The veterans scanned the terrain looking for signs while the cherries hung their heads and plodded along just trying to keep up; both spent each brief halt bent over at the waist trying to relieve the load of their packs just for a second. Each man fought his own personal battle of wills to keep moving as the patrol advanced when suddenly, two armed VC materialized before them.[11]

Energized by the sight, each man within view raised their M-16 and unleashed everything they had against them—the sound was deafening. Completely startled but with only one slightly wounded, the VC quickly disappeared into the underbrush. "Fuck," my father screamed internally, "how did we miss them?" He quickly got the platoon on line and began to follow the blood trail of the wounded enemy.[12] He and his men spread out and eagerly thrashed the bush for about 30 minutes, hoping to shake their prey loose, rapidly losing sight of each other as they did. As my father brushed aside some tall grass, he glanced down and saw a sandalled footprint filling up with water—the same story I overheard all those years later. The VC had literally been right in front of him milliseconds before. Coming face to face with a desperate and wounded VC was not something he wanted to experience alone, nor did he want one of his men to. Startled by this, he reined in his platoon.[13]

Soon after, one of his men thought they saw the wounded VC running in the opposite direction. Keen to get him, they went back on line and moved forward. Two Cobra gunships with giant shark teeth set in a gaping mouth repeatedly dived and strafed the area his men had cordoned off with their miniguns and rockets. My father empathized with the poor guy: "I wonder what the VC felt in seeing the Cobra with their painted-on open shark mouths diving on them," he mused.[14] I once witnessed an Apache helicopter dust a tree line to try to shake an enemy loose and thought the same—what do they think of this flying tank hunting them? The Nguyen Charlie clip sent home that week featured the bucktoothed guerrilla running from incoming US aircraft which later turned out to be geese—illustrating to the family this concept in a lighter tone. It was an amusing thought, but now the platoon had to find his body to add to the count demanded by the war. Unfortunately, it grew dark, and the enemy was never found.

Before he set into another ambush position that night, my father called over his squad leaders. His men had initially fired on the VC earlier that day on fully automatic, sending all their rounds soaring over their heads. Hence why, with all that firepower, they failed to hit anything. Getting in their faces, he snarled that the next time he saw that he would "personally shoot the man firing automatic."[15] I'm not sure if that threat would fly today. Regardless of any hurt feelings, as he lay in his ambush position that night, he fought to stay awake. He thought to himself, "Man, what a day."

"The war has come much closer the last few days down here in the Pineapple," my father wrote home about the recent events.[16] He closed out June with more signs of the enemy and another night ambush. He had just got word of the booby trap from 2nd Platoon. He was red hot and out for blood over the killing of Tex and wounding of Rogers. Rogers arrived in Vietnam two weeks after he did, and my father considered him a friend. Unlike the previous ambushes, he lay wide awake fuming, trying to manifest the enemy walking through his kill zone; no one materialized. "We've been wet and miserable and on our toes," he wrote home, "keeping me eyes open."[17]

The Pineapple, Vietnam; July 1969: My father soon humped (the infantry soldiers' term for walking) every inch of the Pineapple. Hump all day and ambush all night became the new norm. Some evenings, to surprise the enemy, they would change their ambush sites in the middle of the night. He and his men would stealthily rise from their positions and slither through the water as they crawled and sometimes swam through the marshes, with only two-foot-high earthen dikes to shield their movements.[18]

Helicopter rides, followed by pulling one leg out at a time from knee-deep sucking mud on patrol, became the daily routine. Lots of old bunkers, booby traps, and other signs of the enemy were encountered—but no more contact. They encountered so many devices that it no longer fazed them. Once they found a live grenade with its tripwire cut but still in place. "Never mind," said the commander over the radio—there was no need to disarm it, they just had to keep moving. "Just a miserable wet feeling," he wrote about this time, adding, "to give you a better description of this war … the mud in the rice paddies smells like *kukai* [Hawaiian for feces]."[19]

All that water immersion was, of course, horrible for his feet. After 10 days in the field, he was medically evacuated again. The commander ordered him out on the next resupply chopper, but he conveniently missed it by taking his men out on patrol. Unfortunately, that only worked once and the next day the commander made sure he was on it. "I'm sure it sounds strange to you to think that I wanted to stay in the field," he told the family; "I enjoy the camaraderie and the command, I think these factors just tip the scale in favor of the field over the rear." As I noted earlier, you just can't miss out or run the risk of being called a shirker. As the water from the shower in the rear washed away the dirt and grime—his first in weeks—he thought, "Hmm, maybe this is not so bad."[20]

The guilt of being gone quickly overrode the hot showers though. Two days later, he talked his way out of the field hospital again and was back in the Pineapple, staring silently at a gruesome sight. Days earlier, another platoon had killed two VC soldiers and marked them. Using the dead soldiers' blood, they drew the patch of the 82nd on them and other derogatory pictures—just so the enemy would know who had done this. Imagine drawing a penis on your passed-out drunk friend's forehead with a permanent marker, but much, much worse. My father hated this barbaric tradition and would only allow his men to tear a patch off their uniform to leave with the enemy's dead.[21] After the sister platoon searched them for intelligence and marked them with their graffiti, rather than remove the bodies it was decided to leave them, post an overwatch, and ambush anyone who collected them. A ghastly twist on their data collection efforts: count them and then use them as bait. With the flies multiplying and the stench of decay spreading, my father and his team stared at the bloated and desecrated bodies. No one ever showed up to join them.[22]

"We have been through hell since last I've written," he told the family. Besides ghoul-duty, since he returned to Delta Company he had killed four enemy and his platoon had wounded eight—two of them by his own rifle.[23] But back to the firefights.

4,000 Meters Northwest of Bến Lức, The Pineapple, Vietnam; July 1969: The point man on an eight-soldier patrol could not believe his eyes. He wiped the sweat away and shook his head to be certain: yup, still there. Four enemy combatants sauntered along about 200 meters in front of him. No way these guys were farmers—one even had a rocket-propelled grenade (RPG) over his shoulder and another was in uniform. Finally, they had found the enemy again—hump enough and sooner or later you will find what you are looking for. He slowly threw up the hand to signal for freeze and waved up his LT. My father could not believe his eyes either. The plan was clear: quickly get the men on line and set up a hasty ambush. Textbook Fort Benning training.[24]

The four men continued to advance, unaware of the American presence. They got within 150 meters of the ambush when my father fired to signal the attack, hitting and knocking the uniformed NVA soldier down. All eight men unleashed an inferno on the rest. They all started to run; the wounded enemy solider tried to crawl away but one of my father's men rushed out and clubbed him unconscious. Known as Chief Wetback for his Hispanic-Native American background (beware of reading on, PC police) the group chided him later that he was trying to take a scalp.[25] Unfortunately, days later in the Pineapple the Chief would lose it on a night ambush and have to be gagged and restrained until he could be evacuated in the morning, less he give their position away. "If you mention the incident," my father asked me, "I would suggest not using his name."[26]

The bullets and beating were not enough for the foursome. Cobra gunships, artillery, and even a Spooky (Air Force C-47s mounted with mini guns) joined in the fracas. Ultimately, the hasty ambush resulted in one wounded, but alive, NVA sergeant who the commander proudly turned over to the battalion S-2 (Intelligence) for questioning. The other three continued their escape and ran smack into another element of Delta Company, following which one was killed and the remaining two captured, all local VC. It was a bad day for the RPG-wielding enemy quartet.[27]

In the dark of night, several days later in the same area, ten VC stealthily traversed an open area using one of the earthen dykes. My father could not believe his continued luck as he watched them all, illuminated by the light of the moon, lined up like duck-shaped silhouettes in a circus shooting gallery. It was rarely possible to sneak up on the VC once, much less twice in the same week. With unwashed bodies reeking (a helmet filled with rice paddy water and used as a wash basin only got you so clean) and week-old beard stubble, he and his men had worked their way to an ambush site for the evening when they stumbled upon this turkey shoot. Another halt and a hasty ambush was thrown together using hand and arm signals and silently mouthed instructions.[28]

A hollow bloop sound broke the silence as the 40-millimeter projectile fired from an M-79 grenade launcher arced towards the enemy.[29] Detonating with a sharp report in the middle of the column, it knocked six VC off their feet with its shrapnel and tossed them into the mud. At the same time, my father leveled his M-16 and sighted on one of the silhouettes. The recoil of his rifle bucked into his shoulder as the rounds ripped through the left leg of another VC. With ears ringing, his men moved into the kill zone; time to search them for intel and money.[30]

Standard procedure in Delta Company was that any money found was distributed amongst the platoon who found it. Recently, 3rd Platoon had got an NVA paymaster with over $68,000 piasters (the local currency). Each man got $250 while the platoon leader got $1,000. My father's men frantically searched their catch, some thinking "Five dollars make you holler"—but no luck. Still, seven wounded combatants, all now POWs. 2nd Platoon was on a roll.[31]

His last night in the Pineapple, my father witnessed the full might of the combined arms firepower the US could bring to bear in Vietnam. With several VC on the run, his men closed in on them on one side. On the other, two Cobra gunships pushed them towards the Vàm Dam Cống river. There, silently waiting for them with heavy machine-gun barrels yawing, was a Navy Swift Boat. "Charlie's shit is weak," he thought to himself.[32]

Reports from the 82nd were strangely quiet on what was accomplished in the Pineapple. The most I could find was that a month in, the 82nd's work in the region resulted in the prevention of more rocket attacks against Saigon.[33] One interesting piece of intelligence of note was that all the encounters were with uniformed NVA soldiers; a rare occurrence near the capital before 1968. The Tet Offensive had seriously weakened the local VC forces across the South, resulting in the northern People's Army of Vietnam (the actual name of their conventional army popularly called the NVA) having to directly prop the guerrillas up with more men and supplies. By late 1969, MACV intelligence reported that the NVA made up 72 percent of the enemy forces in the South—up 46 percent since the start of the war in 1965.[34]

These encounters with the white whales of the enemy would continue for the rest of my father's time in Vietnam. Just as in one of the most powerful scenes that I remember from my childhood Vietnam movie-watching days, *Hamburger Hill*, my father had transitioned from calling the NVA soldiers dinks, to Nathaniel Victor, to the now respectful Mr. Nathaniel Victor.[35]

My father left the Pineapple a little early; once again, due to his feet. On August 1, the rest of the 1/505th moved back into Firebase All American and resumed its mission set, immediately surrounding the capital. Like Iraq and Afghanistan, it looked like a game of whack-a-mole. Throw some troops at a problem area to squash activity; once smashed, move on to another zone that has flared up. Rinse, repeat, and then do all over again.

Chapter 15

"Luckily the beer arrived ..."

PATRICK W. NAUGHTON SR.

It's funny, when I was 18 and about to leave for basic training all I wanted to do was hang out with my friends. They were my world and I thought I would miss them the most. However, once I got there the only ones I truly missed were my family: my mom living in Las Vegas and my dad and sister still in Hawai'i. It was my sister that I missed the most. I still remember the day I shipped when the recruiting sergeant came and picked me up at 3:00am to take me to the processing station. My sister bawled her eyes out. I don't think I ever fully realized until now how much my leaving impacted her. Sixteen and still growing up, she needed her big brother to be there.

While soldiers serve, life goes on at home. It's almost like going to prison, especially when sent overseas. The incarcerated are put on hold while the families left behind continue to live their lives. Soldiers and prisoners are always shocked when they get home by what has changed. It was the same for my father during his time away, the only difference being that the war spilled over from Vietnam and fueled protests on the home front. Although not hit hard like the continental US (known as the mainland), Hawai'i still had its fair share of antiwar movements, much different than my generation's conflicts. Like most who went to Vietnam, this is something my father thought about and which came across in his letters.

I learned that between hiding an injury and conducting operations, my father had little time to focus on home. Being hurt in the Army and trying to disguise it is a full-time job. You literally evaluate every activity by measuring how it will aggravate your injury before doing it. If I can just sit here for two hours, I can then function for four more. Or if I can illegally get my hands on some muscle relaxers, I can last for at least two more days. It becomes a messed-up math game that always ends up bad. Some advice I have learned the hard way, and it seems he did as well: stow the macho stuff—just go to sick call, recover, and then come back ready to fight better than ever.

The last man I was able to find from my father's time with the 82nd, Specialist (SPC) Joseph Hindle, was able to fill me in more about this time with the unit. He had been good buddies with Lockeby during the war but they had not spoken for 20 years. It was nice to be able to reconnect the two.

In between reading about my father's injuries and attempts to "suck it up and drive on," the Army's unofficial mantra, it was interesting to learn more about some of the things he did there to pass the time outside of soldiering—like drinking. We definitely never got any type of alcohol in Iraq. The closest we got were the nonalcoholic beverages we affectionately called near-beer. We did, however, get tons of visits from celebrities across all mediums. I hope those who came truly know how much we appreciated them. I still remember watching my own B-movie projected onto a massive screen in Iraq; an action flick called the *Circle of Pain*. "Holy smokes is this movie horrible," I remember thinking as I watched it. However, all the main stars were there and met with us afterwards. For that, it will always be one of my favorites. After the showing, I got to take a picture with one of the actresses, Bai Ling, best known for playing the crime boss' lover/half-sister, Myca, in *The Crow*. Later when I looked at the pictures, I realized I had inadvertently got a shot down the front of her shirt as she bent over to sign an autograph—whoops.

I also never got the whole cigar-smoking thing during war, which my dad partook in as well. Maybe it's a weird homage to Patton, I don't know. Many in Iraq would sit around on the roofs of buildings and watch the war go by as they puffed away, scrambling down each time a rocket or mortar came in only to climb back up, imagining they weren't in a foreign land miles away from home. It just wasn't my thing; me, I would rather "borrow" vehicles to sneak across the base to see a girl or unintentionally take pics of movie star boobs.

Fire Base Barbara, The Pineapple, Vietnam; July 1969: As he answered his commander's summons, my father tried his best to hide the hobble caused by his wrecked feet as he walked to his hooch. A muddy hole in the ground, covered by sandbags perched on a ridgeline overlooking the Pineapple, made up the commander's abode. The current company XO had five days left in country. My father had taken his place briefly when he was on R&R the previous month and had done a decent job. So good that his commander Captain (CPT) Ronald Pettit (call sign Raider) did not chew his ass once.[1] That's how the Army works: the only way you know you are doing well is if no one tells you. Do a decent job and you get rewarded with more work, meanwhile the shit-birds continue to fly by under the radar. I suspect that's the same for most massive bureaucratic machines though.

The Army had offered the XO a deal. If you reenlisted and had been in Vietnam for more than 10 months, you could transfer to the 9th Infantry Division in Hawai'i. He was all over that arrangement.[2] Beware of the big green monster bearing gifts, that's what I always say. Regardless, the position was now vacant, and my father was going to fill it whether he wanted to or not. "When do I leave?" my father asked. Briefly looking up from his map, CPT Pettit replied, "Thirty minutes."[3]

Shouldering what little he had on his back, he prepared to depart. He grabbed a brownie and date nut bar, part of a new stash of sweets his sister Momi had sent, and left the rest for his men. Unfortunately, the cookies in the package had been reduced to mere crumbs during shipment. Still awesome though—just thrash your hand around in a rice paddy or puddle of water to wash it, thrust it into the plastic bag of crumbs, and then lick your fingers clean of the delicious morsels stuck to them.

The unforgiving wet world of the Pineapple, strewn with booby traps and occupied by an elusive enemy, was now behind him forever. That week in the latest comic strip, Nguyen Charlie joked with his comrades about the transferrable skills he learned during the war that would later help him find employment. The blundering VC declared to his bemused comrades that he had excelled in "Booby Trapology."[4] Another attempt by my father to make light of the deadly and efficient skills of the enemy. As for the sweets, "Please send more," he begged his sister before leaving his unit in the field.[5]

Tân Sơn Nhứt, Vietnam; July 1969: The worst had happened. My father had been turned into that breed of soldier most despised by front line troops. He had become a rear area motherfucker, a RAMF, a filthy dirty pogue. "I don't do much that is exciting," he informed the family about his new position, "my job is essentially the same as an Executive Officer back stateside excepting the few mortar attacks and the weather."[6] At least his feet would get a chance to heal now. Keeping the administrative functions of the company moving—personnel actions and logistics issues—primarily makes up the dull existence of an XO. Basically, as my father complained to the family, the job is for the birds.[7]

Munching on some cuttlefish sent from home (a Hawai'i treat of dried, shredded, and then seasoned squid) my father worked on his daily tasks as the new XO. The pungent, fishy smell of the cuttlefish had a way of keeping others not accustomed to it away. I always got disgusted looks when I ate it in the field as well. Anyway, back to the grind. The processing of awards, paperwork, and the looming deployment of the brigade back to Fort Bragg sucked up most of his time. Occasionally, this drudgery was broken up by something interesting, like, for example, leading an investigation into a private who shot himself in the leg to get out of country. Mainly, though, it involved working on all the behind-the-scenes, unappreciated details that make any organization function.[8]

The 82nd Airborne's time in Vietnam was winding down—soon they would be sent back stateside, leaving my father's fate up in the air. Would he go back as well, or would he be transferred to another unit to complete the rest of his year in Vietnam? He had no idea what the green machine had in store for him. In the meantime, he did his best to make the time fly by, which was an easy task for a RAMF.[9]

Stimulating activities—like lying around in his hooch drinking orange juice, reading anything with words, smoking cigars, writing letters, and watching cheesy B movies shown to the troops such as 1968's *Tarzan and the Jungle Boy*—filled up what little free time he had. That, combined with pop-up baseball games between all the RAMF entities, helped pass the time quickly. Luckily, as my father recalled, the beer always arrived in time to make the games bearable.[10]

Cầu Bông, Vietnam; August 1969: With his trademark big sunglasses, Elvis slicked-back hair, and light blue towel around his neck, CPT Pettit stood ready to hand over Delta Company to a new company commander.[11] The change of command ceremony is an event as old as armies themselves—a chance for the outgoing commander to thank their troops and for the incoming to set the stage for their tenure. Most importantly, it allows the soldiers to start judging them. This gauging will be brutally stark and will last quite some time. Which it should—soldiers must hold the commander to the highest standard.

A picture of this event survives in my father's files. CPT Pettit stands at the forefront; adorned with smoke grenades fastened to his web gear, a clutch of maps shoved into his right cargo pocket, and a goodbye gift in hand, he looks at the camera and smiles. It was almost as if the burden of command had been suddenly lifted off his shoulders and placed on another. In this case, it shifted to CPT Robert Wilkinson (call sign Jumper) who stands in the background with a straight face. Off to the right stands my father, the XO, the one who planned the whole event. He silently looks on, wondering what the new boss will be like. Stretching out behind them as far as the eye can see sits the terrain they have been fighting in. The timeless, flat, and ever-wet rice paddies.[12]

As he stood there, he reflected on his time under Pettit. A two-timer for the war, Pettit had already served one tour with the 1st Cavalry Division and, as such, was skilled at the business of war. "Men, I am here because I want to be here," he eagerly began most of his mission pre-briefs, "this is my second tour and there is nothing I would rather do than kill dinks." He was personally invested in the war. Once, out of nowhere, he showed up in a kill zone after one of his platoons had emptied a machine-gun burst into a VC point man that started at his ankles and hit every part of his body on its way up to taking off his head. He seemed to be everywhere at once. One time, Pettit even got a little too eager and was accused of burning down a village that, perhaps, was not supportive of the VC. He was turned in by the Foul-Mouthed Doc who was appalled by the action, although nothing much came of it.[13]

Pettit, regardless of his tenacity, did not push his men into dangerous terrain needlessly. When on patrol, he operated from the middle of the formation rather than the front. This allowed time for situations to develop fully before he committed his troops to combat. Because of this, his men loved him.[14] Wilkins remembers him as a "no-nonsense but competent commanding officer."[15] Joseph Hindle recalled that he was an excellent commander "who kept us on our toes and made sure to cross train us."[16]

Although the men liked Pettit because he did not squander their lives needlessly, he was strict with his officers; an unforgiving task master who demanded things be done his way, which funnily enough was the only way. As the company XO, my father had to be the go-between for Battalion staff and the commander. Because Pettit demanded things a certain way, he was in constant conflict with the staff who tried to rein him in. My father remembers continuously being between a rock and a hard place—that of Pettit saying what must happen and the battalion XO and staff telling him no, that can't happen. The perfect example of this was tent pegs.[17]

"I want more tent pegs," Pettit had demanded of my father. With only two pup tents allowed in the field, one for the commander and one for the RTO, why did they need so many? Turns out, Pettit was having the men use them to set up booby traps and trip flares, which were abandoned once they moved from that position. The battalion S-4 (logistics officer) refused to obtain more pegs, suggesting that before moving on, they should just be recovered along with the devices and flares. Pettit was not pleased with this answer and refused to budge. "Why don't you just send me back to the field if you are not happy with my performance?" repeatedly demanded my father. Pettit would just slowly shake his head at his fuming LT and slyly smile, "Can't do it, you're my only buffer between me and battalion."[18]

With the great tent peg debacle of 1969 behind him, it was time for a new commander, thought my father as the ceremony concluded. His first impression of Wilkinson was that he was "super Airborne." In 1965, as an enlisted soldier, he had served in Operation *Powerpack* in the Dominican Republic. As a result, he wore two 82nd patches, one on his left sleeve designating the unit he was assigned to, and one on his right, which displayed which unit he had deployed to combat with. Wilkinson had definitely drunk the Kool-Aid. With the company done in the Pineapple and set to enter another dangerous part of Vietnam, "Things could get interesting," thought my father.[19]

Church of the Crossroads, Honolulu, Hawai'i; August 1969: "Thanks so much for your picture," my father emotionally wrote home after they mailed him one of the family, "I almost cried when I first saw it."[20] Thoughts of home spurred by the photograph were disrupted by someone asking him about Hawai'i.

"Have you ever heard of such a lousy fucking church as the one in Hawai'i?" the unit chaplain angrily asked my father upon hearing he was from the fiftieth state. "Yes, I belong to it," he proudly replied as he showed what was inscribed on his dog tags as proof to the now shocked chaplain, who then sheepishly walked away.[21] His sister Momi even sang there from time to time.[22] Originally not heavily antiwar when my father had belonged to it, the Church of the Crossroads, a United Church of Christ member, had over the years hardened its stance against the war.[23] Initially run by Minister Delwyn Rayson, it shifted once he left and Mitsuo Aoki took over. Aoki took it to the next level, but most remember that it was Rayson who planted the seeds for what happened next.[24]

Since February, the Church had thrown open its doors as a self-titled sanctuary for "alienated persons," which included deserters and draft dodgers. It was a way for them to protest the war, military justice, and racism. Its intent, according to Aoki, was to offer "moral support to men who, for conscience sake, must resist what they believe to be the immoral activities of their own government." Some praised the Church's efforts to include other congregations, who followed suit and harbored men of their own. Others lambasted it, calling it "an amateur, naïve dilettante approach" to protesting the war and a "lesson in bumbling do-goodism." State officials described the sanctuary as a refugee center akin to "Haight-Ashbury during its flower-power days."[25]

Regardless of what one thought of their activities, the Church of the Crossroads and several of its copycats were raided by authorities in the early morning hours on September 13. All service members absent without leave (AWOL) were rounded up and turned over to military authorities. The Church declared that it would stand by the arrested men who "because of their conscience, found it impossible to carry out their miliary duties."[26] Not that it mattered now anyway—the sanctuaries were effectively over in Hawai'i.

My father watched these activities from afar and vented to his sister. He was proud that his church was still involved in the community, trying to do its best for social justice, but he felt the sanctuary was a shameful thing. "Why do they protest only now when they are in Hawai'i?" he asked Momi in frustration. "Why not when they were over here?" It seemed like a coward's move to him. Plus, Hawai'i was a choice R&R spot for those in Vietnam. Actions like this now made it impossible to go there. "Oh well, sorry for the dissertation from your warmongering brother," he sadly closed out his letter, "it is just that I feel strongly that these men's protest is at the wrong time and is of little use."[27]

Peace attempts, as desired by those protesting back home and with the Church, were occurring in Paris, just with little progress. Secretary of State William Rogers lambasted the North Vietnamese every chance he got on their lack of cooperation. "The only reaction we get from the other side is totally negative," he explained to the public, "they call us names and use phrases like 'swindle' and 'fraud,' which doesn't help the situation at all."[28] It seemed, stated media critical of the process, that the Paris peace talks had ceased to be productive and had "joined other Paris landmarks as a 1969 tourist attraction."[29]

Three American POWs were released during this same time by the North Vietnamese as a supposed gesture of goodwill during the talks. This soon backfired as the men outlined the brutal conditions they and their comrades were held under.

Back home in the US, the Tate–LaBianca murders had also occurred, which were eventually connected to Charles Manson and his motley crew. One detective, after viewing the bodies at Roman Polanski's house, shook his head in disgust and said the scene "looked like a battlefield."[30] The murders were initially thought to be possibly related to antiwar protesters; what was going on at home? Unsurprisingly, the war's unpopularity continued to accelerate.

Chapter 16

"Disgusted with the whole business ..."

PATRICK W. NAUGHTON SR.

We all watched unsurprised as our task force commander was summoned to see General (GEN) Raymond Odierno, commander of all US forces in Iraq. A towering 6'5" man who I used to see in the gym in Iraq daily, Odierno and I somehow usually ended up on treadmills next to each other. He always had a smile and kind words for the rank and file; however, he was a leader who did not suffer fools lightly. Some hours later, our commander wandered back into the CHU area head hanging, weaponless, with a shocked look on his face. He had been relieved of command by GEN Odierno, who took his pistol away until he could be sent home. Why had this happened? Simple. The highest commander in the land had lost faith in him to lead. I mean, he used to show up to GEN Odierno's briefings—where plans to fight the war were literally discussed—with a Sudoku puzzle book and an uninterested look on his face. What did he think was going to happen?

His replacement ended up being one of the best commanders I have ever served under. Like the Pettit/Wilkinson dichotomy my father encountered, the air of change that wafted in was palatable. A military commander has an awesome power bestowed upon them that does not have a civilian equivalent. What they choose to do with that power has a direct impact on soldiers' quality of life. Huge egos, demeaning attitudes, and favoritism can often accompany military leaders, especially senior ones. These types of bosses are now known by the latest buzzword—toxic leaders. I always thought this was a myth created by the lazy who finally got a superior that made them work. That was until I experienced it myself. It is all consuming when you have a toxic boss whose actions spill over into every facet of your life. The negativity is omnipresent, as is the growing feeling of helplessness as you watch other senior leaders do nothing to address it; either clueless as to what is happening or ignoring it all together.

Not only does toxicity break an organization, but the same effect can also be achieved by great leaders with good intentions. When an officer assumes command, enormous pressure is placed on them to achieve results. They jump in the saddle and ride that horse for the next few years until it collapses near death on the finish line. They then hand the reins of the sickly and broken nag off to the next commander and walk off into the sunset. Instead of nurturing the steed they receive back to health and turning it into a marathon runner, most new commanders mount, roughly jab their spurs into the unit, and off it goes again.

Each time a change of command occurs in the military, a unit goes one of three ways—it becomes a toxic wasteland, it is ridden until broken, or through deliberate and caring actions it is developed into a powerful beast. Unfortunately, the third option is rarely exercised. There is absolutely a time and place to push a unit to its limit, but—I'm sorry—that time can't be 24 hours a day, seven days a week.

Vietnam was interesting in that commanders at the tactical levels usually only served six months to a year. For officers, it was seen as a quick stepping stone to complete before moving on to bigger and better things. The mandatory short combat deployment was all one needed to advance in their career. It was brief because, as some accused, the Army wanted to get as many officers as possible some combat time.[1] "There were too many battalion and brigade commanders getting their tickets punched," wrote one infuriated general after the war, "rather than trying to really lead."[2] Another noted that the common desire during Vietnam was to assume command for six months and then "get out with a clean slate" as soon as possible.[3]

Anyway, the biggest lesson learned from all of this? Do not do puzzle books while the boss is talking. Back to the suck and the new commander of the Delta Dragons.

Near Ben Cat, The Iron Triangle, Vietnam; September 1969: Early one morning, the soldiers of Delta Company stared through the sights of their weapons out into the tall elephant grass surrounding their patrol base, anxiously awaiting an order. "Now," shouted the commander, just before the entire unit fired every weapon system they had into the undergrowth for one minute. This achieved nothing in the way of enemy killed, but at least these mad-minutes—as they are known—relieved the tension for some of the men, remembered Wilkins.[4] This new commander was a trip.

By mid-September, the 82nd had turned over its mission of protecting the western flanks of Saigon to the Army of the Republic of Vietnam (ARVN) forces. The success of their pacification efforts that had allowed them to achieve this, proud of the fact that while they controlled the area of operation, not one enemy rocket hit a high-priority target and not a single successful ground attack was perpetrated against the capital.[5] From their new Firebase All American II, bordered by the Saigon and Thị Tính rivers and located atop a small hill 3 kilometers south of Bến Cát, they now overlooked the forbidding and notorious Iron Triangle. This was a flat area with dense brush and undergrowth dotted with patches of elephant grass, some taller than a man's head.[6]

Infamous for being a staging, cache, and resting area for NVA and VC forces, it was the scene of multiple US combat actions and heavy fighting. Even following massive operations such as Attleboro, Cedar Falls, and Junction City earlier in the war, the area was never cleared. Along with boots on the ground, the US tried to pacify the triangle with herbicide spraying and Rome plows, both aimed at deforesting the region. After the war, one communist party secretary remembered how the US tried to strip every living plant away, thinking that would make it easier to see the enemy. So effective was the effort that he noted it was not until 1972 that the flora began to fully grow back.[7] "They used giant bulldozers to uproot and crush everything that lived and grew," remembered another cadre member on the attempts to scrape away what herbicides could not; "1969 was the peak year in this war against nature."[8]

Despite the attempts to strip away the foliage, 8-foot-tall elephant grass soon replaced the trees. Without a continuous US presence, the enemy was able to honeycomb the province with tunnels and reconstitute itself among a supportive civilian population. Before redeploying to Fort Bragg, the 82nd decided it would take a crack at the area and conduct one more sortie. Into the Iron Triangle it went.[9]

Under operational control of the 1st Infantry Division (ID) and partnered with ARVN forces, after a short delay due to Hồ Chí Minh's death and the subsequent ceasefire, the 1/505th embarked on Operation *Yorktown Victor* in direct support of the 1st ID's own operation, codenamed *Strangle*. After an extensive barrage on September 12, Bravo Company air assaulted into the Iron Triangle to secure the landing zone for follow-on forces. Meanwhile, Charlie Company moved by ground convoy, clearing a supply route to link up with them. Once secured, Delta Company joined the fight via five CH-47 Chinook lifts.[10] "The great exhortation—fight and die for Uncle Ho—won't carry much weight now," excitedly believed some at the higher echelons of command, claiming that the fighting would slack off now.[11] As for Uncle Ho's death and the actual impact on the war? There would be none; "Some other bastard will take charge" was the general belief at the soldier level.[12]

BG Dickerson picked the 82nd operation's name; *Yorktown Victor* was a reference to the American battle of Yorktown in 1781, where US forces were victorious only with the help of foreign troops. He thought it fitting to tie the last operation of the 82nd to South Vietnam's quest to achieve their freedom. Another boon to the brigade was that the Iron Triangle was home to the elusive 83rd Rear Service Group—the element that had been supplying all the enemy forces they had encountered thus far. Successfully destroying this unit would reverberate across the region.[13] Where was my father in all this? Pissed off and still back in the rear with the gear.

While he was at the base camp of Phú Lợi coordinating the unit's resupply and redeployment back to Fort Bragg, Delta Company was getting their shit pushed in. Booby traps were stacking up wounded in the company. The operations officer's daily staff logs from the time are riddled with references to these woundings. Most were caused by stolen or captured US ordnance repurposed into deadly traps. US forces were still leaving stuff around or unguarded for the VC to steal.[14]

Unlike my war, where technology helped to counter IEDs, there was little the troops in Vietnam could do to defeat booby traps. Soldiers had to revert to homegrown inventions, such as a 6-foot-long fishing pole with a 5.56 round hanging from a piece of string attached to it. The point man would walk with this contraption dangling out in front of them. If a trip wire was encountered, it would bend the string without detonating the device.[15] Efforts like this, combined with good old-fashioned luck and a sixth sense, were often the only thing standing between surviving an encounter with a booby trap and a horrific explosion.

Interestingly, most of the injured now seemed to be in leadership positions, including one forward observer who was in the unit for only 14 hours. As the 82nd stood down its formations to redeploy, the 1/505th would be the last, as such men from the other battalions who desired more combat experience flocked to the unit. For the first time the battalion was at full strength but was hemorrhaging leaders due to combat actions.[16]

Due to the steady stream of the wounded, morale was low. Compared to Pettit, the new commander did not seem to know what he was doing. It was, my father concluded, one big cluster fuck: "Needless to say," he wrote home, "I am very disgusted with the whole business." He quietly fumed and pined for the "good old days when I got my butt chewed by somebody who knew what he was doing."[17] Lockeby had a different perspective on him. Wilkinson was "scared of his shadow," he claimed. "He wasn't trained very well."[18]

Wilkinson was not bad, he just did things differently than Pettit. The new commander was much more aggressive and led on patrol from directly behind the point man. This allowed him to experience the initial enemy contact himself and quickly and violently commit his troops to action. This was in contrast to Pettit, who was more cautious and deliberate. Wilkinson wanted results and he would push his company wherever it needed to go to achieve that, despite the risk. Another change implemented by the new commander was the use of CS riot gas instead of smoke grenades on caches and bunker systems. He reported to higher that the use of this persistent agent underground had proven to be "very effective."[19] Although the floating lids contained in the tunnels described earlier probably negated some of the perceived effectiveness, it still briefed well.

Gas or no gas, as the XO my father never knew what Wilkinson wanted. Pettit micromanaged down to the team level, and there was never any question about what he desired. The new commander, on the other hand, allowed his NCOs and officers to operate more independently and then became angry when his men did not meet his uncommunicated expectations.[20] It was night and day between the two leadership styles that the company now had to adjust to. Neither was right or wrong, just different. Every time the mantle is changed, it offers an interesting case study in leadership; one that has played out countless times since the beginning of organized conflict.

The Iron Triangle, Vietnam; October 1969: In the early morning hours, the Shadow, moving stealthily as his reputation and nickname suggested, led 3rd Platoon back to the Delta Company patrol base after several days of hunting for the enemy. The La Grange, GA native, who his comrades remember as an "easy to like kind of guy," moved cautiously while on point, thinking about the day before where the platoon had encountered a lone VC in broad daylight—the score, one man paralyzed from the waist down by a gunshot wound and the enemy escaped unharmed. This event caused Wilkinson to flood the area with more patrols; however, besides finding some bunkers, no more contact was made. Despite the lull in contact, as relayed to me years later by Hindle, one of the men in the platoon, PFC Alton Ellison, knew this meant that the area was hot.[21]

As he led the platoon, Ellison noticed something suspicious in the bottom of a bomb crater. He halted the formation to investigate; funny, it looked like some ammo boxes were hastily buried in the bottom of the depression. As he moved closer to get a better look, Ellison noticed with the rising sun that something directly in his path was seemingly out of place, a black wire lying on the ground was now illuminated by the light. Pushing his helmet back from his brow to see better, he quietly followed the wire until he came upon what appeared to be a strange-looking circular frying pan supported by four small legs. Unfortunately, Ellison had followed the detonator wire to the wrong side. Instead of finding a man with a clacker, he found a deadly Chinese communist (CHICOM) claymore mine.[22]

Patiently watching this all play out with the ability to command detonate the device was the enemy. Before Ellison could react, a huge explosion tore through the morning air, shredding his body with cylindrical steel rods. The soldiers in 3rd Platoon, including Hindle, who up until this time were just itching to get back to the company area and some much-needed sleep, suddenly came under fire. Several men tried to advance to reach Ellison but were met by a hail of grenades. As these projectiles landed and exploded among the men hugging the ground to avoid the shrapnel, a strange and deadly game of hot potato ensued.[23] One man used his body to shield his comrades from a blast and was considered for a Silver Star. However, when my father went to interview him and witnesses, it could not be determined if he had covered an enemy grenade or if he had accidentally pulled the pin on his own grenade while it was still secured to his web gear—thereby actually shielding the men around him from his own mistake.[24]

Regardless of who threw what, as recounted by Hindle, live grenades were being tossed back and forth between the opposing sides until Ellison could be dragged to safety. It was no use though; 10 days before his 20th birthday, amid a thunderstorm of explosions, Ellison had been killed in Vietnam, Republic of.[25]

Medical evacuation helicopters were called as soon as the claymore went off, but they were driven off by enemy fire. All of this activity alerted the battalion commander, LTC Alfred Zamparelli, who quickly flew to the area in his Loach where he was immediately shot down, wounding the pilot, the S-3 (operations officer), and Zamparelli. What started as a platoon movement back to the company area morphed into a rescue mission, with Delta Company in the lead. Wilkinson had his men strip to just their combat gear and rush out to reinforce 3rd Platoon and rescue the battalion commander. As the men hurried to their aid, artillery fire and jets heavily pounded the area. No one in Delta had any idea what their purpose was or who was directing them as they were not hitting anywhere near where the enemy reportedly was.

The crash site was soon secured—the S-3 with wounds throughout his lower extremities was evacuated out of country never to return, as was the pilot, who was hit in both feet. Zamparelli, with only a minor flesh wound, was quickly returned to duty. With the trio safely evacuated, it was on to rescue the 3rd.[26]

The besieged platoon had found refuge in a partially abandoned enemy bunker complex. Delta Company spent the rest of the day in a hectic game of find-a-tunnel. Working in squad-size elements, each would engage the enemy at one tunnel opening, only to have them appear behind them in another. Fuck it, it was time to call in the engineers to CS gas the tunnel complex—but they still had no luck in driving the enemy from their subterranean refuge. Besieged by the heat, thick bush, and elusive enemy, one man remembered it being a brutal day for the company. Exhausted, the unit returned to their company area. The results: one US killed and several wounded. Later, the brigade newspaper reported 12 enemy dead recovered—the unit's official history said 15. How many dead did the men of Delta Company see themselves, according to Hindle? Zero.[27]

What initiated all of this was a new tactic by Wilkinson. Knowing the enemy was watching them, instead of patrolling he had his platoons set up dummy ambushes during the day. The unit would quietly lie there all day, soaked by rain, heated by the sun, and besieged by insects. Once it got dark, they stealthily moved to their real ambush location. This seemed to throw off the enemy, which resulted in a higher contact rate. As the XO, my father had to deal with the results of this; in this case, Ellison's remains and personal effects. "I've gotten use to looking at dead bodies as well as wounded GIs," he sadly wrote home.[28] His feelings about the whole affair? "I guess if one plays in Charlie's backyard you occasionally get your fingers burned."[29]

Company Patrol Base, The Iron Triangle, Vietnam; October 1969: "Take two squads and conduct a sweep around the perimeter," barked Wilkinson to my father as he got off the resupply helicopter days later. As the XO, once a day he would land within the company's patrol base in a Chinook CH-47 to drop off supplies and backhaul any dead soldiers or those who needed to go to the rear. He nervously fingered the

.45 caliber pistol on his hip as he got the squads ready to go. No longer expecting to be part of any combat patrol, this was the only weapon he now carried. He idly wondered what the emergency was.[30]

Earlier in the day, Delta Company had established a new patrol base in an area secured by a scouting party. All seemed fine until suddenly someone realized that they were set up over a large tunnel complex. Delta sprang into action and began trying to extract the underground enemy. My father landed in the middle of this and was ordered to secure the perimeter as the rest of the company focused on the tunnels.[31] Talk about luck—Delta had hit the mother lode. After one tunnel rat was wounded along with several other troopers, they dug out a full field medical hospital, nine AK-47 automatic rifles (Chinese), one old M-16 American rifle, VC radios, poems, intelligence documents, and political literature.[32] Most importantly, they discovered over two tons of unpolished rice.[33] "Just oodles of things," my father excitedly reported.[34] They also killed two VC soldiers. More patches and expletives were written on the bodies as the company celebrated their success.[35]

By the time Operation *Yorktown Victor* culminated in the beginning of November, my father now had a nephew. Sean Naughton was born to his brother as Delta slugged it out in the triangle.[36] Meanwhile, Dickerson ceremoniously pulled the lanyard on the last howitzer to be fired by the brigade in Vietnam.[37] And the 82nd was going home. "Old Charlie was up to his usual tricks and we handed out the treats," my father wrote home in his best macho prose about this final Halloween month with the brigade, "beaucoup M-16, M-60 M Gun, Mortar, and Artillery."[38] Nguyen Charlie joked in the latest cartoon strip that with the departure of the Yang Khi, they would not be able to sleep without the sounds of circling gunships. Meanwhile, his comrade commented on how the recruits being sent down from up north were so scarce that even the officers were young boys now—although it seemed their age had not hindered their deadliness.[39]

Officially, the mission in the Iron Triangle had been to operate within the region to "interdict enemy movement in the area and to seek out and destroy his base areas and supplies."[40] The real result of this nonstop aggressiveness? Multiple casualties and only a temporary halt to enemy activity in the triangle. "More people were killed there," recalled Lockeby about their time in the triangle, "than all the other operations put together."[41] Another game of whack-a-mole.

Chapter 17

"The majority of the company has gone ..."

PATRICK W. NAUGHTON SR.

The large room in the Iraqi government building had no air conditioning and only one door open to the outside. The heat in July was already unbearable before I walked into the dark and dusty chamber. As I entered, a young Iraqi girl of about six looked up at me and smiled. As I smiled back, she walked from the corner she was in and handed me a little Iraqi flag mounted on a small pole, the type one would wave in a parade.

As my eyes adjusted to the dimly lit room, I noticed two large Iraqi flags tacked to the wall behind a government official who was prepping for a speech. Next to him stood Brad Blauser, a 2009 CNN Top Ten Hero for his work obtaining wheelchairs for kids in Iraq with disabilities. He had heard from an Army surgeon about "heartbreaking accounts of helpless children pulling themselves along the ground, or living motionless in back rooms, too big to be moved long distances very often," and decided to do something about it.[1]

Arrayed at these two men's feet were various pieces to assemble about 20 wheelchairs. As the room slowly filled with US soldiers and Iraqi families cradling their disabled children in their arms, the room became excruciatingly hot and soon smelled of sweating bodies. Witnessing the procession of families, one right after the other, carrying their young children with crippling disabilities in their arms broke my heart and quickly made me forget about my discomfort. It became even more upsetting when a US doctor in attendance whispered in my ear that many of their ailments probably could have been avoided or averted had they been born in the States.

After the Iraqi government official gave a long speech that I did not understand, everyone descended on the wheelchair parts and attached themselves to a family to assist with assembly and the exact fitting of a chair. I scanned the crowd for the little girl and worked my way to her as a small Iraqi band played traditional music in the corner. She turned out to be the older sister of a young boy with a severe disability, who was obviously in desperate need of the device. As I did my best to help, I affixed the flag to my beltline so that she could see it. Once assembled, I retrieved it from my waist and waved at her with a smile as though we were at a parade back home. Her beaming return smile more than made up for the heat.

Once complete, the wheelchairs were marked with a tag and lined up outside the building. By now literally soaking wet with sweat, I headed for the door. When I exited it felt like I had emerged from Hades—the once oppressive Iraqi sun now felt amazing; the scorching air now cool, the smell wonderful. As I took deep breaths, I noticed an Asian US sergeant with a recognizable accent talking to someone. Could it be? Could it happen again? "Hey sergeant, where you from?" I asked. "Hawai'i, Sir," came the expected answer. We immediately began comparing where we were from and who we knew—this is something that must always happen when two Hawai'i people meet each other off the island, and remarkably, it is always the case that we will at least have someone we know in common. Turns out this sergeant was the brother of my sister's best friend growing up. Imagine the surprise when we sent a picture back home to them. Like I said, somehow, we always seem to find one another.

As we reminisced in a war zone thousands of miles away from our paradise home, a small brown pickup truck pulled up. The 20 wheelchairs lined up outside were quickly piled into the bed of the truck, and I mean piled. By the end the heap of haphazardly stacked chairs extended about 4 feet above the rim of the bed. I watched incredulously as the vehicle drove off, looking like a clown car filled with props, and thought, "Well, there went the precision fitting we did." I still hope that the chairs were reunited with the proper families and not sold on the black market. They had to have made it, right?

This was an Iraqi version of a Medical Civic Action Program (MEDCAP), like the ones that Dickerson bragged about. His units were not only executing combat operations in Vietnam but they were also pacifying the people through MEDCAPs as well. The official histories published by the 82nd rave about these actions and how they impacted the operational environment. My mind instantly filled with a picture of the grizzled sergeant under trial for war crimes played by Sean Pean in *Casualties of War* who defended his actions by lecturing on his humanitarian accomplishments. "That just shows you we ain't all combat over here," he bragged about his civic achievements.[2] My father seemed surprised when I asked him what MEDCAPs he was a part of. "No, we never did those things," he replied to my inquiry, "the closest we came was throwing candy or cigarettes at kids."[3]

With my Penn-like MEDCAP behind me I realized, just as my father did as his time wound down, that I needed to get some souvenirs to take home. I searched for the perfect item in one of the many bazaars thrown up by the Iraqis for US troops, looking among the rows and rows of fake antiques made to look like medieval, Ottoman, or Roman artifacts. One thing foreign-occupied lands quickly learn about Americans—we love us some souvenirs. Behind the fake helmets marked as Ottoman Empire relics lay a small item wrapped in wax paper. I brushed off the dust and cobwebs and opened the packet. In it was a stack of still crisp Iraqi money with Saddam Hussein's face on the notes. "Awesome, found my first war memento," I thought. It was definitely obtained the easy way, at least compared to my father's war where you had to take money off of dead enemy combatants to buy things.

Looking at the Saddam funny money, my young, single mind formulated a plan on what to do with the 250 or so bills. I thought of my rotation back to the world and how they could serve as the perfect icebreaker to pick up girls. Yes, I had a plan and couldn't wait to test it! Back in the US and after years of failed attempts, I believe I may have five or six bills left. Come to think of it, I met the love of my life, my wife, without help from the deposed dictator. A stupid plan, then, but man did it sound good at that time.

I also got several pieces of art which reminded me of my father's two "gorgeous" Vietnamese paintings, as he described them to family in a letter, which he would purchase. Those two pieces now sit on my walls and have followed me across multiple military moves. A frame replacement aside, the Saigon customs clearing stamps are still visible on the back and the colors remain vivid. The velvet pictures depicting a peaceful Vietnamese village scene and a roaring tiger stealthily emerging from the jungle look like something a stoner would have in their room, but I still love them. This affection has not been shared by all. Besides my wife, who allows them to be displayed prominently, past girlfriends always turned their nose up at them for being tacky. I did not care, I hung them anyway.

Over the years I have shed all surplus artwork across numerous moves, including most of my Iraq items. The only one I have left is a beautifully framed golden Assyrian deity called a Lamassu. This ancient celestial being from Mesopotamia has a bearded human head, a bull's body, and is adorned with wings. I first saw this protective totem behind the desk of one of our Iraqi interpreters. I remarked to her on the beauty of the object before she explained to me what it meant. The next day the very same piece that she owned was now sitting on my desk; a gift from her that I still cherish to this day. Every time I look at it, I think of Nori; I hope she is okay. I also wonder what my son will think of the two generations of war art that he will inherit.

Phú Lợi, Vietnam; November 1969: After serving nearly 22 months in Vietnam, the 82nd Airborne was going home—a far cry from the "six-month loan" of the unit that General Westmoreland had begged for after the Tet Offensive.[4] The reason for sending such a storied and effective unit back to Fort Bragg was simply a shell game, explained Chairman Wheeler to Abrams and his staff. Some members of Congress had grown tired of the war and had begun to tighten the purse strings on the military to force it to a conclusion. "The cost of the division is cut in half," he explained about the rationale behind sending their third brigade home, which would free up money to be used elsewhere, such as paying for their commitments to NATO in Europe.[5] "In my more cynical moments, I even suspect that some of these expenditure limitations are designed basically to force a reduction in our efforts here in Vietnam," he further decried.[6]

As pawns in this sleight-of-hand trick to shake loose some money, all brigade staff and headquarters had collapsed to Phú Lợi by early October. They were followed every 15 days by a battalion and battery until the last unit, the 1/505th—my father's—stood down on November 15.[7] The colors were going home, but not most of the men. Of the 5,000 or so soldiers in the brigade, only those with 10 months or more in Vietnam went back with the unit, which ultimately equaled about 1,000 soldiers. The rest had to submit three choices on where they wanted to be transferred to in Vietnam.[8] It's dangerous territory when the Army asks you what you want. Now the fun part began—executing the personnel and logistical plans to make all of this happen. As he lay in his bunk at Phú Lợi under a mosquito net, with the buzzing hordes surrounding him, my father thought, "Shit, I have a lot to do."[9]

Now that the rains had begun to subside and Delta was in the rear, it was overwhelmed by the curse that strikes all units with listless soldiers; they start getting in trouble. My father spent the next few weeks chasing down AWOLs in Saigon, curfew violators, men who resisted arrest for minor infractions, and those being sought for illegal possession of drugs.[10] Meanwhile, Nguyen Charlie poked fun at his US nemesis in the funnies, the grizzled old Sarge, who instead of enjoying his time in the rear at bars chasing girls, spent most of his time wrapped in a mattress huddled fearfully under his bunk, hiding from incoming fire.[11]

Even with the safety of the rear, one of the AWOL men put my father at great risk. A Post Exchange (PX) Ranger—someone who buys and wears badges, patches, and tabs that they did not earn—disappeared from the company twice. I myself have encountered this breed of soldier. When they are confronted with the truth, it is shocking how they swear until the end that the Special Forces tab they are wearing was legitimately earned. Eventually caught in Saigon, Dickerson had had enough of his this PX Ranger's antics and sentenced the soldier to three months in Long Binh jail. My father was charged with delivering the prisoner.

Armed with his .45, he jumped in a jeep with a driver and another man with an M-16. They drove the shackled man to Long Binh. Once there, he was told he had been given the wrong paperwork and was sent back to Phú Lợi. Incensed, he and his crew braved the dead of night to drive back to base; you did not drive at night in Vietnam in one vehicle with no support. Eventually it all worked out though and the man was delivered to serve his time. There my father had to witness his strip search as the Military Police emptied his pockets of all the unearned airborne, rank, and CIB badges that the man had been illegally wearing.[12]

On November 24, my father took command of what was left of Delta Company. By then, most of the men staying in country had already been transferred to their new assignments.[13] Before the enlisted soldiers left to join their new units, my father did his best to take care of them. Every man worth anything was promoted to SGT (or higher if possible) before they departed. "Nobody at battalion or brigade cared," he recalled, "they just wanted me to use the promotions up."[14] Besides nine men left behind to escort the battalion and brigade colors home, only himself and three others were left to close the company.[15] The smallest and shortest infantry command ever.

He was charged with finding three missing M-16s and various other items before he could close the unit out. Luckily, the left-behind supply soldiers scrounged up all that was missing and then some.[16] A good supply section is worth their weight in gold, that's for sure.

As Apollo 12 rocketed towards the moon, the first stories of the My Lai massacre were being made public by investigative journalist Seymour Hersh, and the Vietnam Moratorium Committee staged a massive antiwar protest in Washington, DC as the 82nd went home.

At the same time, Nixon's war strategy was also beginning to show cracks. After a slew of previous supportive stories, *Newsweek Magazine* unfavorably reported on the recent performance of the president: "The conclusion seemed inescapable that the machinery of the Nixon Administration had shown itself inadequate to cope with the complexities of the Vietnam war."[17] Senator Eugune McCarthy, a prominent anti-Vietnam politician, commented in disgust that it seemed like Nixon's plan for the war was "almost like we were back in 1966," ramping up the war again instead of disengaging.[18] In an attempt to assuage this waning support, Nixon visited both the House and Senate in person, where he beseeched both chambers and parties to believe that a just peace was achievable if they could only come together and act "not as Democrats or Republicans but as Americans."[19]

Despite these attempts, unfortunately, the Paris peace talks lumbered on with no results. Vice President Agnew called the communists "intransigent, totally intransigent" during the process.[20] In other words, the North Vietnamese were stubborn and uncompromising negotiators. Fancy terms aside and oblivious to these events, my father prepared to move on to his next unit. "I guess this will be my last letter from the 82d Abn Div," he wrote home. To commemorate it, he purchased the two Vietnamese block velvet paintings mentioned earlier, which hang still on my wall.[21]

My father's next assignment? To be an ARVN advisor under MACV. Up to this point, he did not have a positive opinion of the South Vietnamese Army,[22] complaining that if the US planned to pull out before 1984 then the country would quickly be lost. "I don't know how the ARVN troops plan to win this war," he griped, "they rarely leave their compounds—and only conduct operations when the Americans are with them and providing supporting fires." On a personal note, he thought that "most of them look like dandies, all dressed up in fancy jungle fatigues, tailored to skin tightness, colorful berets and tabs … I would hate to have to live in Vietnam knowing the Yang Khis are pulling out."[23] His opinions were about to be put to the test.

Chapter 18

"The best part was the hot water ..."

PATRICK W. NAUGHTON SR.

As the 82nd completed its operations and cleared out of country and my father reported to his new unit, it was clear the war had changed. When I attended the Command and General Staff College (CGSC) at Fort Leavenworth, Kansas, I had the pleasure of briefly meeting Doctor James Willbanks, a renowned Vietnam War historian, as he prepared to give a lecture. I mentioned to him that my father had been in Vietnam, and he smiled and asked what years he had served. When I replied with 1969–70, he contemplatively looked up from his lectern and quickly said, almost to himself, "That means he fought in two wars then," before going back to shuffling his notes.

In Willbanks's published landmark almanac on the conflict, he divides US involvement in the war into five phases, the last two being large-unit offensive combat operations or pacification (1967–69); and then Vietnamization (1969–73). By the time my father joined the 82nd, US forces were still taking it directly to the VC and NVA in various operations designed to find and kill enemy forces. As Willbanks noted, the main result of these efforts "was a bloody war of attrition that caused heavy casualties on both sides." After the failure of the Tet Offensive, Richard Nixon was elected president and reread the tea leaves. "American objectives shifted," noted Willbanks on the change, "from winning the war to a prolonged disengagement." As US forces conducted a gradual troop withdrawal, efforts were to be shifted to the South Vietnamese government and military forces—hence the name, Vietnamization.[1] Pacification was still occurring, it was just that turning over the fight to the South Vietnamese was now the main effort, with pacification merely in the supporting role. My father waded right through the middle of these two phases.

By Nixon's first year in office, he had steadily developed a strategy for Vietnam which would allow for the withdrawal of American troops. Like pacification, the Vietnamization concept was not new and had been discussed at the highest levels since at least 1963. The secretary of state once even asked the MACV commander, "Isn't there some way we can do this where we don't get Americans killed?"[2] Ambassador to Vietnam Ellsworth Bunker was once embarrassingly quoted as saying that the new policy essentially sought to change "the color of the corpses."[3] Despite these insensitive comments, Vietnamization was the first time a plan to reduce US involvement in direct combat was made into policy and codified into a guiding strategy by the administration.[4]

It was newly appointed Secretary of Defense (SECDEF) Melvin R. Laird who would coin the phrase for the new strategy at a March 28, 1969 National Security Council (NSC) meeting. We are close to "de-Americanizing" the war, claimed one military general during the meeting. "I agree, but not with your term," harrumphed the new SECDEF. "What we need is a term like 'Vietnamization' to put the emphasis on the right issues." Nixon concurred—and there the strategy was born and soon directed in National Security Study Memorandum Number 36, titled "Vietnamizing the War."[5] Laird was known for his knack for coining buzz terms.[6] It's always amazing how an offhand comment can suddenly become guiding policy.

Shortly after the NSC meeting and published top secret memorandum, Laird reported to the US public that he was "for Vietnamizing the war … as soon as we possibly can."[7] Nixon followed suit in June at a conference with the South Vietnamese President Nguyễn Văn Thiệu at Midway Atoll. There he announced that he felt confident enough in the progress of the country's forces that 25,000 US troops could be withdrawn shortly.[8] In October, US newspapers reported that military planners had told them that their efforts had shifted from "battlefield support to military and technical training" of the South Vietnamese military. One officer unofficially declared that the "babying" of the South Vietnamese armed forces was over.[9]

In November, Nixon publicly confirmed the shift in MACV priorities in an address to the nation on the war. "Under the new orders," he informed the public, "the primary mission of our troops is to enable the South Vietnamese forces to assume the full responsibility for the security of South Vietnam."[10] By the time my father started advising ARVN troops, the policy of Vietnamization was "irreversible"; so stated Nixon when pressed by reporters on the strategy in January 1970.[11] Along with this came another unwritten rule for the war, that of "protective reaction." Laird was no longer interested in kill ratios or other metrics—as one US official noted, "he keeps pounding on the theme that Vietnamization of the war has first priority, not combat operations."[12]

Abrams, the commander on the ground in Vietnam, was initially surprised by this new strategic shift. After obtaining copies of various speeches and Laird's testimony before the Senate Foreign Relations Committee, he gathered his staff to try to find out just "what they're after," those politicians in Washington, regarding this thing called Vietnamization.[13]

By January 1970, however, Abrams had quickly realized just what they were seeking; "there's more involved in this war, goddamn it, than US brigades and battalions and divisions," he fumed after a recent visit to a field force headquarters about their lack of knowledge on anything the ARVN were doing in the area. "If the war is going to turn out right," he scolded his staff, the ARVN must be placed in the lead for combat operations so that the conflict could end with the "Vietnamese on top and the VC underneath."[14]

Pacification, on reflection, "probably was really good for this war," noted the MACV commander, but Vietnamization was his guiding strategy now. A cascading snowball had started which could not be stopped. A tit-for-tat game between the White House and the Democrats in Congress began on who could accelerate the withdrawal faster. Driven by political and domestic pressures rather than military realities, it soon took on an unstoppable life of its own.[15] Henry Kissinger, when advising the president on this, called it salted peanuts: "The more you offered, the more you would want to eat."[16] The train to get the US out of Vietnam was screaming down the tracks.

"There are just a hell of a lot of ideas that have been tried on over here," Abrams said half-jokingly about Vietnamization, "that haven't been worth a shit." Clearly, he was just a little frustrated by the slew of concepts introduced and attempted over the years.[17]

Tân Sơn Nhứt, Vietnam; December 1969: The days grew longer, and the monsoon rains let up, finally drying out Vietnam. Among the swirl of kicked-up dirt, a slick with the All-American logo painted on its nose touched down in Tân Sơn Nhứt. Catching this helicopter flight—nicknamed the Pony Express due to its daily delivery of messages between the various units—was my father's last official activity with the brigade. As he walked away from the landing pad, the rotor wash and noise from the blades subsided and he put the 82nd behind him forever. He then boarded another chain-link window-covered bus to the MACV headquarters to get cleaned up and find out his new assignment.[18]

As he stood under a hot shower, his first since Vũng Tàu months earlier, he tried to wash away embedded layers of grime. He stared at the brown water as it swirled down the drain, scrubbing funk away from places he didn't even know it could accumulate. He stood there for hours until the water off his body finally ran clean.[19] I don't care what anyone says, every hot shower I ever took after only weeks in the field was better than sex. Taking one after months must have been orgasmic.

Because he was an in-country transfer, he did not need to in-process and go through the series of classes and inoculations that he did the first time around.[20] Since he had spent so long protecting the capital, he asked for a preferential assignment, hoping to actually see it and be assigned to Team 43 or 70 serving in Saigon. Of course, he knew that it would probably do no good to ask but he thought he may as well try.[21] Make people tell you no, that is the advice I always give young lieutenants. The Army's decision? Since he had already served in the ARVN III Corps area, it was back to the 82nd's area of operation he would go—so on a chopper to Biên Hòa he duly went.[22]

III Corps had three ARVN units under it: the 5th, 18th, and 25th Infantry divisions. Once my father got to the headquarters of III Corps in the northern outskirts of Saigon, he was shuffled off to another helicopter immediately departing for Đức Hòa. The ARVN 25th Infantry Division would be his new daddy. As he flew west away from the city, he began to see familiar terrain—dirt that he had already chewed before.[23] In Đức Hòa, a jeep picked him up and took him to the 25th headquarters, where he spent the next several days squaring his gear away before reporting to Team 99, working out of a hamlet called Trung Lập.[24] It was probably best he got away from the land of hot showers as it was making him soft. "I can't get use to this air conditioning," he wrote home about his short stay in the rear before moving back into the field, "gives me a sore throat."[25]

Another patch was mailed home. This one was in the shape of an elongated shield, with an upward-pointing sword piercing through a fortified wall. In color it was yellow and red; however, unlike the 82nd, in Vietnam the MACV patch was worn subdued in black and olive drab. It was supposed to represent fighting off communism by forcing it back behind its iron curtain with a sword.[26]

My father had some gear issuing and uniform reorganizing to do before he reported to his unit—colloquially known in the Army as one's "shit." The catch-all phrase for everything to be accomplished at any given time. Get my shit together, clean up my shit, pack my shit; all basically mean the same thing—preparing yourself for the next phase of an activity. Really shitting or not, he still had to prepare his gear and uniform. The MACV patch replaced the 82nd, which was moved to his right shoulder. A subdued Vietnamese *trung úy* rank (two small chrysanthemum flowers, their rank insignia for 1LT) was sewn on his chest. This was so the ARVN soldiers he advised would know his rank. A colored 25th ARVN division patch was added to his right chest pocket.[27] Another shield, this one with a green background and red sun, with a yellow lightning bolt struck through it. With his subdued *trung úy* and MACV patch, combined with his color ARVN and 82nd combat patch, he looked like a fighting kaleidoscope. At least he was eye-catching.

The passage of time has blurred my father's memory some on the types of gear he needed to prepare. Luckily, he saved an issue of *Infantry*, the professional magazine for soldiers published by the Army at that time. In it, an article titled *Battalion Advisor—Vietnam: Ambassador in the Boondocks* outlined what to expect from this duty, including a packing list. Fifty years later, the checkmarks made next to each item in blue pen still survive. All the traditional field items were there: poncho liner, canteens, flashlight, extra clothes, shaving kit, and a knife. Items listed with no blue tick? Field jacket, hammock, and a mosquito net. Comfort items for pogues and rear area motherfuckers that he could not enjoy.[28]

What else was in this professional publication for all the troops to read? Opinions on the ARVN. "While tactically sound," the piece criticized ARVN leadership, "they lack the aggressiveness and swift reaction which characterizes a US unit." Concerning the *binh sĩ* (soldier), three main topics were highlighted in the editorial: their easygoing, curious, and good-natured will; the fact that they would steal anything not locked down; and, most importantly, that they lacked the "aggressive nature of [their] American counterpart" both on and off the battlefield.[29]

But back to his new assignment. After my father's shit was squared, a jeep with a South Vietnamese driver and American advisor picked him up and drove him through much of central Hậu Nghĩa province before arriving at his new home for the next six months, Trung Lập.[30] "It now amazes me that we used to drive around in a jeep all the time," remembered my father. "I guess I was just lucky."[31] Moving around unarmored with no escort and maybe one rifle between us was virtually impossible in my generation's wars, although my girl and I almost accidentally drove off VBC and into Baghdad a couple of times in our borrowed vehicle.

Later, in a counterinsurgency history published by the Army, the assessment outlined in the *Infantry* journal of his day was supported, and the ARVN are remembered poorly. "They generally did not feel inclined to embrace calls for vigorous, offensive action," stated the Center for Military History publication, which touted their passivity, "preferring instead the relative safety of their cantonments."[32] After all, who can forget the classic line from *Full Metal Jacket*, when Cowboy attempted a trade for some number one fuckee? "Be glad to trade you some ARVN rifles. Never been fired and only dropped once," he offered.[33] As so many books have codified in history, all the movies I watched growing up also informed me that the ARVN sucked.

Chapter 19

"Killing people is the easiest thing in the world ..."

1LT ALIC TAHIR

My father was to advise the ARVN, but first an important question: what had all his efforts with the 82nd achieved for Saigon? "Between patrols on the outskirts of the city and almost 1,000 ambushes set up at night," noted CMAC's assistant operations officer in January 1970, "the enemy just can't build up his strength ... they build up a big cache and we find it." Due to heavy pressure from the 82nd and the ARVN once they assumed lead of the protection mission, the enemy could not rally enough combat power to seriously threaten the capital.[1] "Now you rarely run into a guerrilla unit that is even platoon size," excitedly echoed CMAC's deputy intelligence officer.[2]

In MACV's Office of Information's Monthly Summary released to the media for January 1970, it highlighted a report from an enemy prisoner captured just outside of Saigon. The man stated that normally his battalion planned at least one attack a month on the capital, but that since October 1969, when the 82nd began tightening the ring around the city, "no attacks were conducted because of a shortage of ammunition and Allied pre-emptive activity."[3]

In the brigade's self-published history, it gloated that not a single rocket had made it into Saigon during their time protecting the capital. A later declassified document tells a different story: "Only six rockets have been fired from within the brigade's boundaries," stated the report, before concluding that none of them hit anything important.[4] Zero, six, who's counting anyway? Regardless of the number, it appears the 82nd did a bang-up job throwing up a protective curtain around Saigon, a task being carried forward by the ARVN. A tangible success, unlike the efforts in the Pineapple and Iron Triangle.

Military efforts outside the city were buoyed by the South Vietnamese police within. Via citizen support and covert infiltration into the Viet Cong network, "we get reports about the enemy," gloated Police Chief Trang Sĩ Tấn, "often in advance."

In an average month, Tấn reported that his officers conducted 2,800 check points, searched 50,000 homes, checked 574,000 individuals for proper identification, and conducted 555,000 vehicle stops and searches.[5] Who can forget the peacocking US advisor who declared "We are winning the war through urbanization"?[6] "Christ," excitedly shouted Abrams during a meeting, as he pounded on the wooden table for luck, "we haven't had Saigon burning for over a year!"[7]

The enemy's view on all of this? "There were hundreds of ways of getting into Saigon," shrugged one former VC when asked how hard it was to infiltrate the capital. "Ordinarily, we would just take the bus along with other people," he elaborated.[8] Even though overt activities were no longer occurring, the enemy was still covertly building VCI infrastructure within the city.

Regardless of bad guys with bus passes, my father's time with the 82nd protecting the capital against indirect and ground attacks was over. Now he was off to a different war under a new guiding strategy, this time from the perspective of the Vietnamese. Being an advisor was a rare assignment that most US service members who served in Vietnam never experienced. The positions were selective as the Army only wanted mature and seasoned soldiers advising the Vietnamese. "In this game," Abrams once noted about these personnel, "the good works of a thousand can be negated by the bad works of ten."[9] It was important that the Army got the assignment of its advisors correct. "One guy that doesn't really think much of the Vietnamese floundering around down there in a small community," explained Abrams, "can really fuck things up for everybody."[10]

My father started keeping a diary upon assignment to this new position. It began as a vehicle to record grid locations of helicopter insertions so that he could earn an air medal, but it soon morphed into a way to record his most private thoughts. I tried to do the same in Iraq. I filled out about two pitiful pages of a yellow legal notepad before I lost interest. Unlike my pathetic attempt, he followed through with it each day, giving an insight into the war that was never shared with the family or meant to even see the light of day.

It was from this assignment to MACV that I met two people who knew my dad very well from his time in Vietnam. From the 82nd, I was only able to find soldiers still alive who had served under him but did not know him on a personal level. All the officers he knew from the 82nd have already passed, including his best friend, who was murdered later in life, most likely by his daughter's boyfriend; the case has never been fully solved.[11]

The first of his MACV associates was retired Lieutenant General (LTG) Richard Keller, who was his team lead as a major then. The second was his best friend during his time with the unit, 1LT Alic Tahir, who would retire as a lieutenant colonel. Born in Philadelphia to Albanian immigrants and orphaned at 12, Tahir had a rough upbringing attending all boys' schools but still landed on his feet, going to college at George Washington University. Tired of school, he took a break and was visiting a friend in Canada when he received his draft notice. Rather than staying there and dodging the war, Tahir dutifully reported to the induction center and went through the process, eventually becoming an officer through OCS and finding himself next to my father in Vietnam.[12]

"I'll just say this about your dad," he told me during one of our conversations, "that guy could always make me laugh. It didn't matter how bad things were. It didn't matter what was going on. He could make me laugh, man."[13] This struck me as odd; even though my father loves corny movies, he was always very stoic growing up. My friends would often comment on his serious demeanor and how strict he looked—rarely laughing in public or cracking jokes with anyone. Because the Vietnamese could not pronounce his first name, my dad told everyone that Tahir's name was actually Alric and not Alic. He thought this was hilarious and still does it to this day.

Tahir had a joke of his own when he reported. Being short like me, he often poked fun at my father, who towered over him, about the likelihood of him dying while advising the ARVN. He explained that the enemy knew that most Americans were much taller than the Vietnamese they advised. As such, they would string booby traps 6 feet in the air in the hopes a US advisor would trigger them. He witnessed this firsthand when he passed under a hidden strung-up 105mm round secreted in a tree, only to have another tall advisor just behind him walk right into it, killing him instantly. "You know, I always regretted being short," he often told my father, "but if I make it out of this mess, I'll never make that complaint again."[14] Nothing like trying to scare the new guy.

A colorful and outspoken character, Tahir certainly pulled no punches when I talked to him about Vietnam. It was he who called those who committed suicide upon returning from war "pretty goddamn dumb." He had another interesting comment to relay when we finally were able sit down and talk about the conflict. "Well, I'll tell you," he began about the war, "killing people is the easiest thing in the world." As I did my best to hide the shock on my face, he continued, "It's so easy. It's pathetic."[15]

Village of Trung Lập, Hậu Nghĩa Province, Vietnam; December 1969: Once called a "wretched settlement" by the *New York Times*, Trung Lập loosely translates as "neutrality."[16] Located in an area where the rain forest and the natural savannah meet, it was mainly an agricultural region. Rice paddies, peanuts and abandoned rubber plantations dominated the landscape, including one of the best-known examples of the latter owned by the Michelin Tire Company, which was all but destroyed by that time due to the past decades of conflict.

Despite such a neutral name, it had a strong military past dating back to World War II. The French established their training base for an elite colonial ranger unit there, where it gained its nickname, the French Fort, from among the locals. The

South Vietnamese forces who later occupied it were overrun by the NVA and VC during the Tet Offensive. It was then reoccupied thanks to some hard fighting by the ARVN.[17] It lay 30 miles north of Saigon and contained living accommodations for the soldiers as well as a short airfield that could fit five to seven Hueys packed in a close line. It was surrounded by areas well known to my father: Hobo Woods to the north, the Iron Triangle to the east, and Củ Chi to the southeast: his old stomping grounds with the 82nd.

Prior to mid-1969 Trung Lập, as recognized by the Saigon government, was a loosely associated group of various farming villages that mutually supported each other. It was in this area in 1966 that my father's ROTC buddy Thomas Blevins was killed. Military operations in late 1968 and early 1969 by the ARVN 25th and 5th divisions, combined with the US 1st, 25th, and 82nd proved that it was an area still rife with communist activity. As such, it was decided to relocate all civilians and collapse them into one hamlet near the old French Fort where the ARVN were based. By the summer of 1969, all civilians, either voluntarily or forcibly, were moved into a village that was originally called Ap Đời Mới, now relabeled as Trung Lập. Huntington's urbanization theory come to life.

The old communities scattered throughout the area were destroyed and any recyclable building materials were moved and used to build dwellings in the new centralized village. The civilians now only farmed in plots and paddies immediately surrounding the enclave and returned each night to live in the protected hamlet—or at least that was the desired intent. One journalist visiting the area noticed something different: "I saw the soil itself standing up after the passage of a flight of helicopters," wrote the reporter on how the Vietnamese were still farming in areas they were not supposed to. He described "stark naked men who rose up from the mud to haul and push plows and wield hoes," who would then "drop back into the mud when the helicopters returned."[18] They were of course risking their lives by doing this, as any farmland outside of what was designated was now declared a free-fire zone.[19]

Trung Lập was a large compound surrounded by layers of barbed wire, defensive sandbagged positions, and old minefields laid by the French in the 1950s. An occasional wild animal or dog would wander into the area and trigger an explosion, its carcass left to rot and its stench wafting over the compound—a constant reminder that the old mines still functioned. Over the years as the area changed hands a series of bunkers was built all over the compound. Once part of elaborate defensive postures, most were now long abandoned decrepit dwellings, only fit for nasty insects, snakes, and other biting creatures.[20] There were similar positions strewn all over the base I was on in Iraq—whether vestiges from the Iran-Iraq war or the early American invasion it did not matter; most were uninhabitable, filled with water, and home to who knows what.

Occupying this sprawling complex was a unit from the ARVN 25th Infantry Division which consisted of three regiments: the 46th, 49th, and 50th. Originally stationed in the Quảng Ngãi province located near the central coast of Vietnam, in 1964 the 25th was moved closer to the capital to help counter an increase in VC activity. "A full three years was to pass before the 25th Division recovered from the exercise and became fully proficient," Westmoreland later said about this move, which he called a mistake.[21] The 25th was plucked from their home territory where most of their soldiers were recruited from and dropped into an alien and hostile landscape where they were expected to perform. My father arrived just as they started to get their act together.

Because of this move, the reputation of the 25th was considered to be on the lower scale of an effective fighting unit. Moreover, some claimed that at least 25 percent of their formations consisted of VC sympathizers if not outright operatives. One unforgettable story quickly spread throughout the country about them. One night, in one of the now probably crumbling bunkers, four ARVN soldiers pulled perimeter guard. Only one would awake and then disappear into the early morning mist, leaving behind the three others with their throats slit.[22]

Needless to say, the forced consolidation of villages and the basic annihilation of their way of life did not align the inhabitants with the anti-communist cause. Normally, ARVN soldiers moved their families on to the compounds they served in. This allowed them to keep them safe and better provide for them. Trung Lập was one of the exceptions. Due to its heavy communist leanings, besides the senior officers and some local workers on the base, family members lived closer to Saigon. The team did what they could to help the families by donating personal hygiene items and even bribing local hospitals with American goods such as cases of soda to take care of ARVN family members.[23] They were given leave to visit their families and give them any extra toiletries kindly donated by their US advisors, but they had to be back before dark, less they be disappeared or were found on the side of the road with their own necks sliced.[24]

Each regiment under the 25th had four battalions with four companies each. Companies were designated by number and not by alphabet like the US system. In another difference from the American system, where a regiment and battalion are the same echelon, an ARVN regiment was the equivalent of a US brigade. My father was assigned to Team 99 as a battalion advisor to the 1st Battalion of the 49th Regiment (1/49th), which was based in Trung Lập.[25] He and two other Americans were tasked with advising the battalion during combat operations[26]—although mostly what advising consisted of was providing US military might, namely artillery, attack helicopters, and tactical air strikes.[27]

Not knowing what to expect, my father was pleasantly surprised to find the compound at Trung Lập to be a virtual paradise compared to US ones. American field camps were purposely kept austere for economic reasons and to allow for them to be moved quickly if needed.[28] This was in contrast to Vietnamese encampments, which were usually clean and orderly and built with a more permanent nature to support extended military operations. Luckily, they also shared the base with the Recon Company from the US 25th Infantry Division, which meant the chow was American and not primarily provided by the ARVN.[29]

Even the comfortable surroundings could not keep the enemy away, though. As he tried to settle into his new location, a steady stream of attack helicopters strafed the perimeter with deafening rockets and mini guns. Some VC had been spotted from one of the guard towers and everyone was in a frenzy trying to kill them, including one ARVN patrol, which was accidentally wounded by US artillery rounds called in to join the melee. "Lots of action around here," he wrote to the family about his first day with the ARVN.[30] It was another warm welcome to his new home in Vietnam, but at least he would be fed well.

With the perimeter now quiet, and by the light of a pale moon due to a generator malfunction, my father took some time to reflect on the Vietnamese he had met so far.[31] "Have noticed that Vietnamese people are a mixture of races, all small stature," he wrote in his diary, "some look Indian, Caucasoid, real Chinese but most are light skinned with a slight modification on the classical oriental frame." He also noted that most were stocky and strong, and those who had been around Americans spoke some type of pidgin English. Curiously, the ARVN troops were friendly and showed respect to US officers, "more so than to their own," he wrote.[32]

To his surprise, most of the officers in the 25th were from the north. Many had belonged to the primarily Catholic families who had fled the communists after the 1954 Geneva Conference which divided the north and the south. All spoke English exceptionally well. The commander and XO of the battalion he was advising had both attended the eight-month officer advanced course at Fort Benning. My father had to be careful not to fall into the trap that Westmoreland warned his advisors against, that of evaluating the ARVN officers by their ability to speak English and not their tactical competency.[33] Moreover, most of the enlisted could speak a few words or phrases at most. Overall, they were derisively described by US troops by a rhyme: Marvin the ARVN.[34]

His interpreter Đắt interrupted his contemplative expose several times, asking for food. With four years of high-school English, three years of Army English lessons, and one year learning American slang, he spoke excellently, "and even pronounces the swear words right."[35] Between Đắt's interruptions, an older sergeant who served under the French who loved to banter back and forth in the language with him, and their Vietnamese maid asking if he needed laundry done, he struggled to complete his thoughts and prepare for the next day's events.[36] Ba Chen, one of the few family members living and working in the base, was a war widow whose first husband had been killed by the VC during the Tet Offensive. Remarried to another soldier, she was now one of the richest women around, getting paid 20 US dollars per soldier to do their laundry and extra money to cook them meals.[37]

The next day, after a steaming hot breakfast of *phở* (Vietnamese noodles), my father was slated to go on a helicopter assault with one of the ARVN companies. He was one of the few Americans who ate meals with the ARVN, believing that the noodles were boiled so hot that no bacteria could survive.[38] "Old hat but new friends," he recorded about the next day's operations.[39] He would now find out for himself if the ARVN sucked. You may rarely run into guerrillas in Saigon, but you were not so lucky in the countryside, as my father would find out over the next several months.

A traditional Hawai'i sendoff to the Army at the Honolulu International Airport on July 27, 1968. The Vietnam War was raging as the family gathered at the airport and wished my father well. From left to right: Andrew Melchoir, Noreen Naughton, my father, Momilani Naughton (holding her son Tommy), Anne Marie Naughton, John Naughton, and Eleanor (Tutu) Naughton. (Patrick W. Naughton Sr.)

Momilani Naughton with Jan Doxey attending Senior Prom 1965, Roosevelt High School. Three years later he would be killed during the Tet Offensive by a new weapon unveiled by the communists, the Type 53 multiple rocket launcher, shattering the island community he grew up in and sadly extinguishing a true talent in music. (Momilani Naughton)

Following in my father's footsteps to the then-named Fort Benning, Georgia, home of the infantry since 1918. There, I literally marched on the same footpaths and parade fields that my father did as he prepared for Vietnam. I am in the front row, second from the left. (Patrick W. Naughton Jr.)

The infantry of the late 1990s was a mere shell of its once great self, racked by insufficient funding and manning. Many theorized that the day of the grunt had passed, and that strategic airpower and technology would be the answer to all future conflicts. Here the author and the infantrymen of Charlie Company, 2nd of the 502nd Infantry, 101st Airborne Division stand around dejectedly as we are told we have no money to fuel the trucks in the background which were supposed to mimic the also now unfunded helicopters we normally rode into battle. (Patrick W. Naughton Jr.)

Popular culture has led many to believe that Vietnam was a war fought primarily in deep, dank jungles. However, much of the conflict took place in the agricultural countryside surrounding major population centers. Here, rice paddies stretch for miles just outside of Saigon: terrain which my father learned well both with both the 82nd Airborne and as an ARVN Advisor with Military Assistance Command Vietnam, Team 99. (Patrick W. Naughton Sr.)

Small villages and hamlets dotted the agricultural fields that my father fought in. Here the Viet Cong, South Vietnamese government, and the US battled for the hearts and minds of the inhabitants. Most villagers were oblivious to the geopolitical communist struggle occurring around them and were just trying to stay alive. (Patrick W. Naughton Sr.)

Officers and senior NCOs of Delta Company, 1st of the 505th Infantry, 3rd Brigade, 82nd Airborne plan their next operation in the agricultural areas surrounding Saigon. Protecting the capital from indirect fire and enemy infiltration was of vital importance to the war effort. From left to right: SFC Mendenhall, 2LT Kushner, SSG Jarrell, CPT Ronald Pettit, 1LT Martin Grisham. (Patrick W. Naughton Sr.)

Vietnamese children wave at my father as he travels along the road from Di An to Phu Loi, July 1969. Soldiers in every war quickly learn to utilize kids as an intelligence-gathering tool. If no kids are present waving, begging for candy, or asking for fist bumps and high fives it means that an attack is probably imminent. (Patrick W. Naughton Sr.)

The weather always presents a challenge for military operations. In Vietnam it was oppressive humidity and monsoons. Here, the nonstop rain turned the 82nd's rear area into a muddy swamp, July 1969. (Patrick W. Naughton Sr.)

In Iraq, excessive heat and blinding dust storms created challenging conditions for operations. The author stands next to a bunker near Baghdad, June 2010. The sand literally coated everything one owned. When it rained it turned into a muddy goop that was impossible to maneuver in. (Patrick W. Naughton Jr.)

The change of command ceremony, an act as old as organized warfare itself. Each changeover presents a unique case study in leadership and group dynamics. Here Delta Company gets a new commanding officer. The background is indicative of the constantly wet terrain that the company fought in. Cau Bong, August 30, 1969. From left to right: Unknown guidon bearer, LTC Alfred Zamparelli (BN CDR), CPT Ronald Pettit (outgoing CDR), CPT Robert Wilkinson (incoming CDR), my father (CO XO). (Patrick W. Naughton Sr.)

82nd Airborne operations in the Iron Triangle in October 1969 netted many captured weapons. Here my father poses with a US M-16 which the enemy took off an American or ARVN soldier somehow, two Chinese AK-47s, and one Chinese SKS. (Patrick W. Naughton Sr.)

Overview of the terrain in the Iron Triangle from a US Huey near firebase All American II, October 1969. War can seem so normal when buzzing over it from the air. (Patrick W. Naughton Sr.)

Unidentified men of Delta Company, 1st of the 505th, 3rd Brigade, 82nd Airborne pose with weapons, equipment, and supplies found in a Viet Cong cache during operations in the Iron Triangle, October 1969. Delta Company Commander CPT Ronald Pettit stands in the center with hands on hips. (Patrick W. Naughton Sr.)

With the monsoon season over, an 82nd Airborne resupply helicopter kicks up a cloud of choking dust as it lands in Delta Company's patrol base in the Iron Triangle, October 1969. As in Iraq, helicopters were indispensable for operations and sustainment activities. (Patrick W. Naughton Sr.)

Flying over Iraq in October 2010. When I sent my father these pics, he found them eerily similar to his war. "Huh, looks like Vietnam," was his response. In the global war on terror, one could puddle jump from each American Forward Operating Base and never actually set foot in an unsecured area. (Patrick W. Naughton Jr.)

Traveling in aircraft of all types quickly became the norm in Iraq, as seen here in a C-130, January 2011. (Patrick W. Naughton Jr.)

White phosphorus and high explosive artillery rounds are lobbed against the enemy in the Iron Triangle, November 1969. In the foreground is Delta Company's patrol base. Men lived in holes under ponchos hung from string for days on end while they hunted for an elusive enemy. (Patrick W. Naughton Sr.)

Patrol Base Hunsley, December 1969. It was named after 1LT David Hunsley, killed in Vietnam while dragging five wounded men to safety. My father's ARVN unit tore down the base, closing it forever: one of many dedicated to a hero that is now lost to time. Sadly, the same thing has happened to the global war on terror's outposts and bases. (Patrick W. Naughton Sr.)

Since the ARVN looked like any other Vietnamese, the American advisors had to work hard to ensure they did not become victims of friendly fire. Here in January 1970 my father pops colored smoke grenades to mark his positions as a jet conducts an air strike in the distance. Guided by his radio coordinates, the jet can be seen pulling up after a run in the middle of the picture with a burning target beneath it. (Patrick W. Naughton Sr.)

A captured communist flag that was given to MAJ Richard Keller, Team 99 leader, by the ARVN. Later he would present it to an Air Force Cessna O-1 Bird Dog pilot for saving him when his unit was surrounded by the enemy. (Richard Keller)

Vice President Spiro Agnew visits the troops at Firebase Patton on New Year's Day, 1970. (Patrick W. Naughton Sr.)

MAJ Richard Keller, Team 99 leader, poses with a mangled captured communist flag in January 1970. A retired lieutenant general, his mentorship has been invaluable to me over the years, as it was to my father. Each year, he continues to share his strategic perspective on Vietnam, the global war on terror, and leadership with the students at the Army's Command and General Staff College in Fort Leavenworth, Kansas. (Patrick W. Naughton Sr.)

There were zero women in combat units when I first joined the Army. Now they are everywhere, serving with honor and distinction in all capacities. Diversity gives the Army strength. Some of my greatest mentors have been women and soldiers of every race and ethnicity. Here I am seen with one of my closest friends who helped me get through Iraq, Dawna Allen. (Patrick W. Naughton Jr.)

My father poses with the same communist flag. Trung Lap is in the background. (Richard Keller)

My father with his best friend in Vietnam, Alic Tahir in April 1970. I would track down Tahir, a retired lieutenant colonel, and spend hours learning much about the Vietnam War and my father. His unfiltered comments on the conflict changed my perspective on a war I thought I knew. (Patrick W. Naughton Sr.)

My father receiving the South Vietnamese Cross of Gallantry, January 1970. He still suspects that he was awarded this medal to silence him over an illegal killing of a prisoner by the ARVN that he witnessed. (Richard Keller)

Secretary of Defense Melvin Laird visits Trung Lap, February 1970. It was during this visit that MAJ Richard Keller tried to explain to Laird about the discrepancies between the reports he was receiving compared to what was happening on the ground. Keller's words fell on deaf ears. Vietnamization was the way forward in Washington and had already been predetermined to be a success. (Richard Keller)

Although often labeled as an overall failure, ARVN-led 25th Division operations into Cambodia were extremely successful, evidenced by the amounts of weaponry that was captured during forays across the border. April 1970. (Patrick W. Naughton Sr.)

My father before heading out on an operation advising the ARVN. The South Vietnamese flag is displayed in the background over Trung Lap, March 1970. He wears a subdued MACV patch on his left shoulder with a color 82nd Airborne patch on his right and the ARVN 25th Infantry Division on his chest, identifying him as an advisor. (Patrick W. Naughton Sr.)

My father after operations covered in sweat. I can remember riding in vehicles in Iraq with full body armor and sweat literally pouring off my brow, looking much like my father did here in March 1970. (Patrick W. Naughton Sr.)

After spending hours in the dismal Iraqi heat fitting wheelchairs to disabled children, they were piled high into one pickup truck and driven away. The precision fitting we achieved wrecked, we all just hoped the chairs were reunited with the children who needed them. Baghdad, August 2010. (Patrick W. Naughton Jr.)

A young Iraqi girl handed me this flag during an event to help her disabled younger brother obtain a wheelchair from an American charity at a Medical Civic Actions Program (MEDCAP), Baghdad, August 2010. (Patrick W. Naughton Jr.)

With map board in the foreground, from the air MAJ Richard Keller oversees the rescue mission my father led to recover the body of SGT Gary Brown, April 9, 1970. The location where Brown was killed is halfway between the wristwatch and top of the picture. My father called this his "toughest day in Vietnam." (Patrick W. Naughton Sr.)

A Cobra gunship (seen in the distance, center shot) lines up for a gun run, providing close air support to my father as he battles back the enemy to recover SGT Gary Brown's body. April 9, 1970. (Patrick W. Naughton Sr.)

Artillery rounds land as a Cobra gunship continues its run and three Hueys prepare to land, delivering more ARVN reinforcements to the fight. April 9, 1970. (Patrick W. Naughton Sr.)

Colonel Nguyễn Văn Chuyền, the ARVN 25th Infantry Division, 49th regimental commander, examines an enemy recoilless rifle and mortars captured during the unit's attack into Cambodia, April 1970. His fate after the fall of South Vietnam is unknown. Due to his high rank, he was most likely killed by the communists. (Patrick W. Naughton Sr.)

Major Liem, battalion commander and Captain Koa, the executive officer of the 1st of the 49th Regiment, ARVN 25th Infantry Division, pose for the camera. Like their commander, their fates are unknown. (Patrick W. Naughton Sr.)

Seven Hueys prepare to land at Trung Lap to pick up a lift of ARVN soldiers before an operation, early 1970. (Richard Keller)

Much of the countryside in South Vietnam was littered with bomb craters and the leftovers of war, leading one South Vietnamese man to call it a "nightmare that never seemed to end." (Richard Keller)

In the areas my father operated in the soldiers stayed permanently wet during the monsoon season. Here a squad of ARVN attempt to maneuver through flooded rice paddies. It is easy to see how an American advisor would have stood out. Most would have towered over their Vietnamese counterparts while on patrol, easily discernable by enemy snipers. (Richard Keller)

The feared Cobra gunship up close, early 1970. Once as he witnessed a gun run my father wondered what the enemy thought of this beast with white teeth and gaping mouth who spat fire. I often pondered the same question about the modern Apache gunships in Iraq. (Richard Keller)

American made and supplied ARVN armored personnel carrier stuck in the rice paddies while out on operations, early 1970. Critics claim that armor has no place in counterinsurgency operations. In Iraq I once heard a general make a valid argument for the use of tanks as moveable pillboxes that can be used to control terrain and populations when needed. (Richard Keller)

MACV Team 99 advisors, May 1970. From left to right: 1LT Alic Tahir, Unknown, SSG Hodge, MAJ Richard Keller. (Richard Keller)

Leadership from the 1st of the 49th Regiment, ARVN 25th Infantry Division, intensely plan for an upcoming operation, early 1970. The indistinguishable American advisor from Team 99 is sitting very bottom left. (Richard Keller)

A typical ARVN soldier and his family, early 1970. Originally, my father thought that most of the ARVN looked "like dandies, all dressed up in fancy jungle fatigues, tailored to skin tightness, colorful berets and tabs." As an advisor his preconceived notions were shattered as he witnessed firsthand what tigers they were on the battlefield. (Richard Keller)

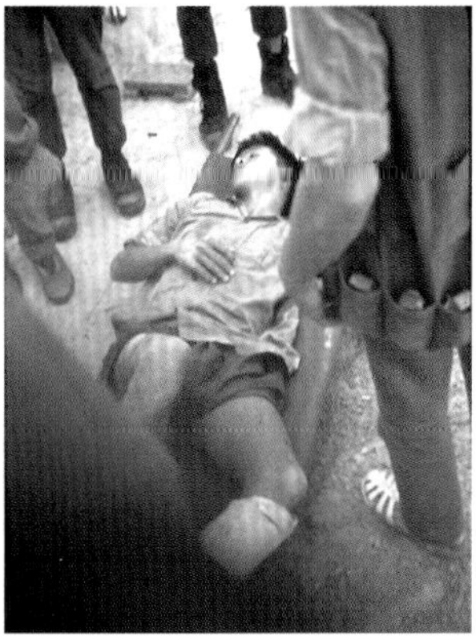

Captured wounded Viet Cong, early 1970. Becoming a prisoner on either side was often an ugly and brutal experience where torture was a common occurrence. (Richard Keller)

Major Keller and Captain Koa, 1st of the 49th Regiment Executive Officer, oversee an operation from the air. Captain Koa is in charge; MAJ Richard Keller is in an advisor role. The most valuable thing he brings to the fight though is not his advice, rather it is his radio. With it, Keller can coordinate for reinforcements, deliver artillery, and close air support at any time. (Richard Keller)

Captured enemy World War I and World War II era machine guns, early 1970. The capture of enemy weapons increased as the war progressed. Since they no longer fought so hard to recover their gear after a fight, many intelligence analysts theorized that this signaled a weakening of the enemy's resolve. What they failed to realize is that the enemy was so well supplied with modern weapons that they no longer needed to hang on to these antiques. (Richard Keller)

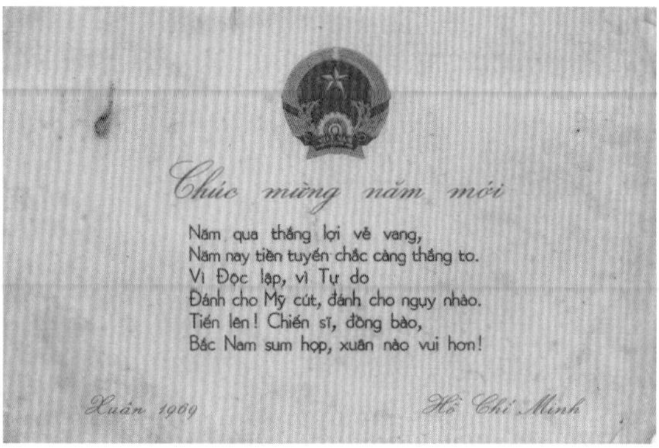

My father took this card off a captured Viet Cong. It is a Happy New Year card from spring 1969. Issued to the troops by Hồ Chí Minh, it reads: "Last year was a great success. / This year the frontline will win even more / For Independence, For Freedom / Fighting until the Americans and their puppets get out / Let's go! [My] soldiers, [my] compatriots / No spring is better than North and South reunion!" (Patrick W. Naughton Sr.)

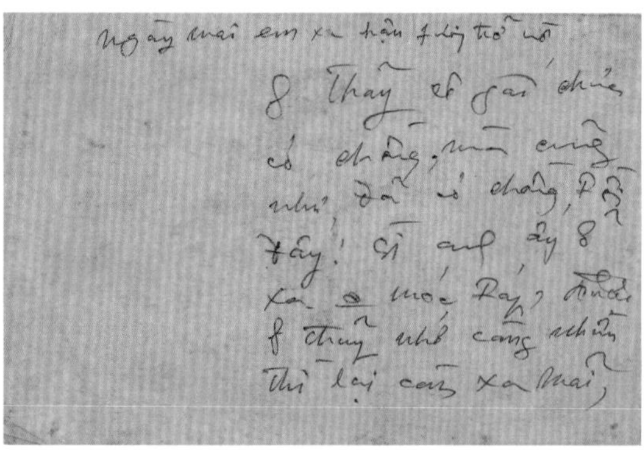

What makes this captured Happy New Year card so unique is what is written on the back. My father never knew what it said until I had it translated. It is a love poem from the Viet Cong's sweetheart; more than likely they never saw each other again. It reads: "Tomorrow from far away you return to the rear / I see [myself as] an unmarried girl, but no different than being married! / Since he is far away and unable to connect, / The more I miss him, the further away I will be." (Patrick W. Naughton Sr.)

It is amazing how fascinated we are with the leftovers of war. Here I pose before a bullet-riddled wall that I had nothing to do with. My young social media hungry self just could not resist. Tikrit, Iraq, October 2010. (Patrick W. Naughton Jr.)

Author in Iraq just before traveling by helicopter to yet another base camp, Baghdad, February 2011. (Patrick W. Naughton Jr.)

Dinner at retired Lieutenant General Richard Keller's house in 2018. He is sharing the pictures that he has of my father from their time together in Vietnam. From left to right: my wife Sheila Naughton, Richard Keller, the author. (Patrick W. Naughton Jr.)

My father's return from Vietnam, Honolulu International Airport, April 1970. Greeted with leis just as before he left, my father is holding the captured SKS rifle that he took home as a war trophy from Vietnam. It now belongs to the University of Hawai'i ROTC program. From left to right: Eleanor (Tutu) Naughton, my father, John (Jack) Naughton, my grandfather. (Patrick W. Naughton Sr.)

On my father's return from Vietnam, he dumped out his entire duffle bag onto the family's living room floor. Here Momilani Naughton's son, Tommy, stomps around in my father's combat boots. (Patrick W. Naughton Sr.)

My father with me as a newborn in May 1978. He of course had no idea what an influence his wartime experience would have on his baby boy. (Patrick W. Naughton Sr.)

My father and me at my promotion ceremony to lieutenant colonel, February 2023. (Patrick W. Naughton Jr.)

My son Thomas Patrick Naughton (age 1 year) and me at my promotion ceremony to lieutenant colonel, February 2023. He need not follow in our footsteps … unless he wants to. (Patrick W. Naughton Jr.)

Chapter 20

"The equal of the VC ..."

MACV COMBAT EXPERIENCES 5-69

Holidays in the Army can be lonely. Late one evening during the days leading up to Christmas, I lay in my barracks room in Fort Campbell, KY, listening to the dull boom of competing stereos blasting throughout the building. It was our unit's turn to be on a short-notice call in case anything happened in the world that would require the mighty 18th Airborne Corps to respond. Since we were on a six-hour mandatory recall, all this meant to us was that no one got to take leave for the holidays.

Soldiers getting drunk to forget home became, of course, the expected result of this policy—dueling piano style. All the hillbillies were packed into one room listening to country while the rockers and gangsters jammed in others, all trying to drown out the others' music. As I lay there, missing home, a sad sound seeped through lulls in the base and vied for my attention. Perplexed, I stood up and tried to figure out where it was coming from. The peculiar sound became louder as I went from room to room, eventually ending up outside on the second-floor stairwell. I stood there as a light snow fell which had blanketed everything in a thin layer of white.

Standing in a now snow-covered field in the middle of our cluster of barracks stood a tiny figure with a saxophone. In the dark of the night as the flakes continued to fall, he played the saddest version of "Have Yourself a Merry Little Christmas" that I have ever heard. One by one the stereos were shut off as the soldiers trying to drink their loneliness away paused and crowded every window and stairway surrounding the field, each listening to the melancholy tune as their own thoughts of home and loved ones flooded their memories.

The lone saxophone player finished his piece, lowered his instrument, and slowly ambled back to his room. It had grown so quiet that you could hear his footsteps crunch as he walked, shoulders hunched over from the now heavily falling snow, with only his tracks left as a reminder that he had been there. The somber moment was soon violently shattered by some asshole blaring Limp Bizkit and "I Did it All for the Nookie." Young men sluggishly turned away and went back to their cliques to drink their sorrows away, only momentarily touched by this emotional event.

I reflected on my holidays in the Army as I read about my father's December in Vietnam. With his shift to the ARVN, I tried to understand the operational environment my father had been in. As I did this, I could not help but reflect on the morass that my own generation waded into when we entered Iraq and Afghanistan. In the case of Iraq, this included Sunni, Shia, Kurds, Turkoman, Christians, and the multitude of indigenous insurgents that sprang from most of them; sprinkle some foreign fighters, tribal vendettas, and former Ba'athists into the mix and that described the operational environment there at its simplest. A whole hodgepodge of US and allied military and civilian organizations were shoveled into Iraq to counter the efforts of these enemy entities.

Years later, with time and some clarity, studying it from the comfort and safety of my own home, I still do not fully understand what we were trying to collectively achieve. With that, I soon realized that I also only vaguely recognized who the various military forces were that supported the government of South Vietnam to counter the VC and NVA during my father's war. Time, then, for a deep dive into that.

Up until late 1969, US and Free World Military Armed Forces (FWMAF)—which consisted of countries who actually sent troops to Vietnam—were mainly tasked with destroying VC and NVA elements and neutralizing their bases. These nations included Australia, New Zealand, Republic of (South) Korea, Thailand, the Philippines, and a tiny contingent from Spain. All were a part of Johnson's "more flags campaign," a pathetic attempt to build a coalition to give US efforts worldwide legitimacy in their desire to contain communism.[1] When Johnson asked for help from the US' allies early in the war, it is reported that the "ensuing silence" from many of its most trusted partners stunned the White House.[2]

They attempted to destroy the enemy via various tactical operations, the most famous of which was called search and destroy, the overarching controversial tactical term that came to define the whole war. Westmoreland considered this label nothing more than a phrase to describe the timeless traditional attack mission of the infantry conducted in every war since the beginning of time. However, "detractors of the war chose to distort it," as he explained, into an expression used to describe the entire conflict, which consisted of pointless searches followed by village-burning escapades.[3] One ambassador to Vietnam would later recall how this "very unhappy choice of words" made it seem that "you are out really to destroy the country which you were trying to save."[4] To counter the negative connotation, the term was changed to sweeping operations, reconnaissance in force, or clear and hold by my father's arrival.

Regardless of what tactical label was in vogue now, with the new strategy of Vietnamization, the government of South Vietnam and its military and police elements were now being asked to lead on these efforts. Knowing about the various

South Vietnamese organizations became even more critical to his war as my father transitioned from the 82nd to his advisory role, and as the conflict shifted from pacification to Vietnamization.

By early 1970, Marvin the ARVN was being forced to become the primary driver towards achieving territorial security in South Vietnam. Built on the bones of the Vietnamese National Army created by the French during their fight against the communists, its ranks were mainly filled by conscripts. Drafted soldiers represented about 65 percent of the army's total strength, making it one of the most heavily conscripted armies in history.[5] Regardless, by the time my father started working with them, the ARVN had more than one million men in arms, the largest army in the world at the time.[6]

From 1954 and the start of the American involvement in Vietnam, the ARVN were molded into what has become known as the Fort Benning model. With the Korean War fresh on the minds of US planners, it was thought that the ARVN should be able to fend off conventional large-scale threats until an international force could come to the rescue, hence why they were formed into corps, divisions, brigades, and battalions able to conduct large-scale combat operations against a peer competitor. They were heavily dependent on tanks, artillery, air cover, and a large logistical tail to survive and maneuver, which of course were available as long as the US was around. However, by 1970 and the beginning of the end of American involvement, the ARVN still struggled to replicate that support in their own formations.[7]

With Vietnamization, the ARVN were now taking it directly to the enemy. The theory was that as the ARVN secured and pushed out or destroyed VC and NVA elements, they would saturate the area with additional Vietnamese paramilitary and police entities, who would be more readily accepted by the local populace.[8] Before this could occur, however, South Vietnam had to gather intelligence which could feed and determine future operations. Thus, the Military Security Service (MSS), represented in all branches of the South Vietnamese military, were tasked with counterespionage, counter-sabotage, and rooting out sedition and disaffection within the ARVN.[9] With good intel, the ARVN could attempt to achieve that safety which was so desired.

Once an area was deemed secured, Regional Forces and Popular Forces (RF/PF) would then take over, thus freeing up the ARVN to resume major combat operations elsewhere.[10] Known informally as Ruff Puffs (due to their acronym RF/PF) they were similar to US National Guard troops when called to active duty to serve in their home state or town. Consisting of approximately half of the overall manpower in the Vietnamese Armed Forces, their contribution to security was crucial. After a brief training regime, RF/PF soldiers then served in their home province and helped provide security, mainly against VC, for the district they lived in. Some complained that the Ruff Puffs really served as a place for local VC insurgents to hide in plain sight. "If they're just recruiting the local VC squad," Abrams once fumed tongue-in-cheek about the lack of training for some RF/PF elements, "then maybe you don't need to send them to the training center!"[11]

Despite this accusation, RF/PF units, through local ambushes and small patrols, provided security for the hamlet in which they were based.[12] Although deficient in military skills due to their limited training, their strength lay elsewhere. "The RF/PF know the area like the back of their hands," stated a report by the 101st on how they were able to successfully secure a province, "and in this respect, are the equal of the VC."[13]

Intelligence sources believed that attacks orchestrated in the South by enemy forces followed a standard template. To augment insurgents already present, they would first infiltrate the region with personnel not local to the area. These additions would conduct recons, prepare caches, expand or dig tunnels, and complete other similar activities to assist with any follow-on attacks and the eventual withdrawal of that force. "Because of their knowledge of the people and the local area," noted a January 1970 MACV combat experiences circular, the Ruff Puffs "can be an invaluable asset in preventing acts of terrorism and sabotage by identifying infiltrators into populated areas and by simply being alert to and reporting unusual incidents."[14]

The Ruff Puffs' efforts were further augmented by the People's Self-Defense Force (PSDF) and the National Police (NP). These local self-defense volunteer PSDFs served as the eyes and ears of the community, who could report on VC activity when observed. When armed and properly trained, they could also support Ruff Puff or ARVN military efforts. The NP, or white shirts like the ones my father saw when he first entered Saigon, conducted basic law and order and other normal police functions. When called upon, they could also assist in civilian search operations and the suppression of VC activity.[15]

Through the Police Special Branch (PSB) of the NP, they collected and compiled biographical data on VC and communist cadre to create blacklists which could be used at checkpoints or to plan raids.[16] These lists were exploited by the paramilitary wings of the NP, the Provincial Reconnaissance Unit (PRU) and the National Police Field Force (NPFF). Both were used as security, searching elements, quick reaction forces, or to lead raids aimed at capturing VC personnel.[17]

At the local level there also existed a variety of other paramilitary groups with varied mission sets that could also collect and provide intelligence. These included the armed Revolutionary Development Cadre (RDC), 30-man teams tasked with linking the national government to the people via civic action programs aimed at political and economic improvement. While they assisted with these projects, they also gathered intel. The Static Census Grievance (SCG) did the same under the guise of compiling census data and addressing complaints at the local level. Finally, rounding out some of these bodies were Civilian Irregular Defense Groups (CIDG), combat paramilitary elements located in the border regions under the control of US and Vietnamese Special Forces. They conducted surveillance, interdiction and exploitation of enemy routes, and attacks against deep VC base areas.[18]

If they had had PowerPoint slides in Vietnam, all of this would have briefed extremely well. However, on the ground it was not so clear cut. Scattered throughout each of these organizations were actual VC or sympathizers to the cause. ARVN soldiers also deserted at alarming rates. Those forced back into the unit were made to go on operations without a weapon and used as mules to carry supplies and ammunition until they proved their reliability again. Due to all of this, many US advisors to these various organizations felt the need to exercise extreme caution. When bedding down for the night in the field, some felt it prudent to move to a different location after dark from where everyone saw them lay down—just in case anyone felt the need to kill or capture an advisor.[19] Nothing ruins a good brief like describing how the personnel in the organizations you are touting may or may not actually be accomplishing or fully supporting the mission.

Another South Vietnamese military effort was known as the Chiêu Hồi program. Abrams once commented to his staff about the "awful lot of strange fellows in that thing."[20] Loosely translated it means "a call to return" or "open arms." This was a government effort aimed at enticing VC and NVA soldiers to defect and rally to support the South Vietnamese government. Those who rallied were called *hồi chánh* (one who has returned to the path of the right) and would be offered a new beginning in life.[21]

Amongst my father's items from the war survive two propaganda leaflets which were distributed throughout the country, to include being dropped by air. One showed a smiling ARVN soldier embracing a uniformed NVA, pointing the way to freedom. This *giấy thông hành*, or safe conduct pass, signed by the president of South Vietnam, guaranteed the holder safe passage when presented to any government agency or allied force. There they would get a kind welcome, be secure and safe, and receive comparable treatment, or so stated the handout.[22] Another leaflet pleaded to those enemy forces serving in the South to not "fight any longer." Alongside a picture of dead civilians in a pool of water from supposed enemy activity and flanked by the Chiêu Hồi emblems, it entreated them to "come home to the love of the people of the South to rebuild the homeland together."[23]

Each province had a Chiêu Hồi center to receive, feed, billet, and then hopefully reindoctrinate defectors, converting them back into valuable South Vietnamese citizens.[24] Before that could happen, though, each rallier (as some also called them), had to be interrogated. "Hồi Chánh often possess much valuable information and/or intelligence," outlined an MACV "lessons learned" document from January 1970, "which can confirm/refute or add to existing information and be exploited for timely reaction operations."[25]

After a successful interrogation and re-indoctrination, some of these *hồi chánh* would then rejoin the fight, just from the other side—assisting US and FWMAF units in tactical operations as Kit Carson Scouts or in other specialized functions. Some even ended up joining the ARVN and serving in that capacity.[26] The program had mixed results and successes throughout the conflict due to the varying degrees of support and trust attributed to it by both the US and South Vietnamese governments. Who can forget the implications slung by Sergeant Frantz in the film *Hamburger Hill* on the Chiêu Hồi program's credibility? "This is Hân," he says, as he points at a *hồi chánh* defector. "After he fattens himself up on C-Rations," he will flip again and be back in the field, "hunting your young asses."[27]

Interestingly, there was a 1971 Research and Development (RAND) Corporation study on the effectiveness of the Chiêu Hồi program and what attracted many to join the VC insurgency instead of South Vietnamese forces. It noted, "The VC had good leadership, discipline, and a strong means of persuasion in their promise of personal advantage to uneducated and ambitious young men of humble origin who see little future in traditional Vietnamese society."[28] Replace VC and Vietnamese society with radical Islamic groups and Iraq or Afghanistan respectively, and this description perfectly fits the young men and women today who flock to the banner of violent extremist groups.

This description does not include all South Vietnamese and US government agencies and their efforts, very few of which were unified by agency or branch of service—much less any effective integration between the two countries. Wading into this morass was the US advisor. My father's boss of his advisory team would remark on this later in life. As part of a Library of Congress veteran project recorded in 2012, Richard Keller commented that "coordination was fragmented" when it came to synchronizing efforts between US and South Vietnamese military and government entities. "What they did I don't know," he frustratingly recalled about the Ruff Puffs and others in his area of responsibility, "and we were both walking on the same ground on any given day."[29] This was reminiscent of my experience in Iraq—I have no idea what we were trying to collectively achieve between the coalition, Iraqi forces, or the myriads of other agencies present.

Chapter 21

"Your dad did some really heroic stuff ..."

LTG (RET.) RICHARD KELLER

I can recall countless holidays in the Army, but none will ever beat Iraq on Christmas Eve. Walking back to my CHU from the chow hall on this cold dark night through an open area, I suddenly found myself flat on the ground. Shaking my head to clear it, I quickly realized that I was standing directly under the C-RAM as it fired a steady stream of rounds at incoming rockets and mortars. The sheer force of the blast from the 20-millimeter bullets erupting from its multiple barrels threw me to the ground. From the concussion of the detonations I heard in the distance and the ripple I felt through the ground as they slammed into the earth, I realized we were being inundated with enemy indirect fire—so much so that the C-RAM could not blast it all out of the sky.

With the night sky now illuminated by red tracer rounds as they arced towards their targets and the incoming siren blaring, I debated my next move: lie as flat as I can in the sand and pebble-covered field I was currently in or dash for a bunker. "Forget this," I thought as I regained my senses and sprinted towards the nearest bunker. Diving into it headfirst with a slide that would have made any umpire jealous, I crashed directly into a throng of people already stuffed into the tiny, sandbagged enclosure. Despite the smell of mildew and unwashed bodies, our group of newfound strangers all hugged each other close as the munitions rained down on us for 20 minutes. "Merry Christmas infidels," the Islamic extremists no doubt shouted with glee as they showered us with their version of Christmas presents. As the all clear eventually sounded, we shook it off and sheepishly looked at each other as we put back on our tough guy faces. No one had been scared, just a little indirect fire, no big deal.

As with every attack, the inevitable social media posts started right away. No matter what was done by leadership, there was no way to stop this. Glory hounds, PX Rangers, and pity-party junkies all had to get their fix. To this day, this Christmas attack has stood out to me the most, though not because of the occurrence. We were used to the sky falling—though not at that rate or intensity—but this was notable because of what it taught me. I distinctly remember one senior officer posting that it had been the scariest moment of his life. Every year on its anniversary, he still writes about that night and the PTSD he now has because of it.

"You wimp," I used to think, "the attack was not that bad." Dudes were out there getting shot and he was whining about some rockets. To me, indirect fire was not frightening to the point of sheer dread. However, for some, lying on the ground or huddled in a dank smelly bunker while praying that a rocket will not land on your head can be downright terrifying. That night taught me that everyone reacts to trauma differently, which needs to be considered when leading others. I now no longer look at that officer with contempt—the event taught me true empathy.

But back to the holiday season in Southeast Asia. "Your dad did some really heroic stuff," said Richard Keller, who led the ARVN Advisory Team 99 as a major, when I asked him about my father in 2018. He stood ramrod straight, lean, and with an air of confidence about him. Even after all these years he still looks like he could throw back on his uniform and lead soldiers—a real polished military leader who fits the Hollywood-enforced stereotype of what a general is supposed to look like. Tahir called him pedantic—I know, I had to look it up too. It basically means one who is unimaginative or who unduly emphasizes minutiae in the presentation or in the use of their own knowledge. You know, basically a general officer in the military.

I met Keller while I attended CGSC at Fort Leavenworth. His mention of my dad's heroism of course surprised me when I introduced myself with, "I think you knew my father in Vietnam." Retired in 1996, Keller was still mentoring officers in his free time by teaching classes at the college. It was a thrill to see him show pictures of him and my dad posing with captured VC weapons and an NVA communist flag to my classmates. "Wow, old-school killers right there," was the awed response I got just before he taught a class to my small group as part of the prestigious Art of War program.

Reading my father's letters and now diary, I stumbled across several more of the very few stories that he told me about the war growing up. For the first time, my father encountered a type of booby trap which has become synonymous with the Vietnam War—the dreaded punji pit. I read that he watched as a US lieutanent found one of them the hard way, falling into a hole that, thankfully, contained old rotting stakes. He crushed several under his feet while one remained and ended just before penetrating his groin. "Lucky son of a bitch," thought my father.[1] Traditionally used to hunt pigs, these dug holes studded with sharpened wood or bamboo dipped in animal dung or venom were greatly feared by US troops. I still remember sitting behind the couch as a child marveling in horror at the color illustrations of these various medieval traps shown in my father's books. When I asked my dad about them, it was the story of this LT that he told me.

Secondly, it was in December, with the ARVN, when the dinnertime story told all those years ago to his two teenage children occurred—that of seeing men blown apart by a booby trap right in front of him. While moving south along a stream, his ARVN point man hit a rigged 155-milimeter white phosphorus artillery round which, of course, decimated the man and those around him.[2] Interestingly, this was the only war story that he told my mother during their years of marriage. He told it to her on the day they met and then never told another. "People were being blown up right, left and center," he said about his time in Vietnam. "Once, some guy ahead of me stepped on a landmine and he just exploded," he described to this beautiful young woman he had just met, "and things spattered all over the people behind him, like flesh and all that kind of stuff."[3] A little more graphic description than the one he told my sister and I around the dinner table.

Patrol Base Hunsley, Vietnam; December 1969: "*Cảm ơn bạn nữ*," my father thanked an old mama-san as he traded a can of mandarin oranges for some rice, cucumbers, and spinach for lunch. He did not have the courage to try the fish that the ARVN soldiers had scrounged from a small peasant's hut near where the US was building Route 7A between Firebase Patton and Highway 1, but what he did get beat any issued rations. They were tasked with protecting the road as it was being constructed, a road littered with over 100 destroyed vehicles of all types and sizes. Swarmed by kids everywhere, begging for cigarettes and "chop-chop," he reflected on how easy his first several days as an advisor had been. There were missions every day, or ball games as they were colloquially known, but so far the only action had been the various mystery foods he was able to try. As he munched on another *bánh tiêu* (Vietnamese donut) on the latest walk back to Trung Lập, he wondered what his new boss—who was due soon—would be like.[4]

From Trung Lập, the 1/49th moved temporarily to Patrol Base Hunsley, also shared with the US 25th Infantry and named after 1LT Dennis Hunsley, Silver Star and Distinguished Service Cross winner. Asked by his battalion commander days earlier to be a "little less brave," he died while pulling five wounded platoon members to safety and was memorialized by the division.[5] Catching up on sleep as the ARVN solidified their part of the perimeter and sniffing out old friends from his UH ROTC now with the 25th, my father prepared for his first joint operation with US troops. That night, as he slept alone, a 107-millimeter rocket streaked over the patrol base and landed about 50 meters from the bunker he was in. As he was jolted from his slumber, "the whole world opened up on the poor little bastard that fired the rocket," he remembered.[6]

The next day, the joint Recon in Force (RIF—aka search and destroy) progressed slowly and quietly. The silence was soon interrupted by the sounds of a Huey as it conducted an unexpected landing next to a company from the US 25th Infantry, who were on the RIF with my father's ARVN company. Out jumped the battalion commander, who proceeded to ream out one of his company commanders to get on the right radio frequency and get his men moving. He then walked over to the ARVN unit my father was advising, where he asked if he could kindly slow his movement down as the Americans could not keep up. Shocked, my father of course agreed. "Funny thing was that we were in the bush while the US company was in dry rice paddies," he recalled.[7] Strange—I thought the ARVN sucked.

Overall, though, the mission was a success. Besides finding some wild boar tracks and tiger droppings, the patrol also found a cache of mortar parts, 10 CHICOM claymore mines, and 40 claymore stands, all buried at the bottom of a shell crater, and all of which was put to the torch by the South Vietnamese forces.[8]

More joint RIFs with few direct enemy encounters ensued over the next several days. Any tunnels or caches discovered received the usual treatment—smoke grenades followed by real ones, again probably with minimal impact due to the floating lids. Explosive booby traps and punji pits were also everywhere and remained a constant threat near Hunsley. Any discovered were immediately destroyed by C-4 plastic explosives or hand grenades.[9]

Tahir engineered a new way to counter the tunnels as the grenades were not working—one that US forces would have paled at due to the inhumane death it caused underground. Once a tunnel entrance was found, he would call in Chinook helicopters with 60-pound shaped explosive charges. "They come bigger," he explained, "but I mean, that makes a big bang." As the bird unloaded its payload, the ARVN knew what was coming. They would immediately start cutting 8-foot-long bamboo stakes to have at the ready. As the first massive charge was detonated in the tunnel entrance, puffs of smoke would be discharged from the other entrances and airholes all along the line. The ARVN would then take off with their stakes and mark each opening. Sixty-pound charges would then be dropped into each aperture along the entire tunnel and timed to explode all at once, collapsing the entire structure and burying its inhabitants alive underground. "That's how you kill people," he simply said about the process.[10]

Tunnels aside, in his first week with the ARVN "Charlie had two chances to get heep big MACV advisor," my father joked, "but blew them." One was the 107-milimeter rocket that landed next to his bunker, and the second was the booby trap detonated by his point man, where he was luckily protected by a few trees. "As long as Charlie keeps his marksmanship in the same order of lousiness," he wrote home, "I guess I have little to fear."[11]

The next five days were spent tearing down Hunsley and moving all troops back to Trung Lập.[12] Before they left, a USO show led by Johnny Grant accompanied by some Playboy bunnies came out to entertain the troops. The ARVN told my dad that the girls, wearing go-go boots, short skirts, and torpedo bras, were "too big and ugly" for their liking.[13] As the base was dismantled, any supplies left unguarded somehow ended up growing legs and being stolen by either the ARVN or VC agents. While this occurred, Keller showed up to be Team 99's new battalion advisor. Despite the hubbub in the media and among strategic leaders about Vietnamization, Keller remembers that he was never actually briefed on it as an official US program, either before or after his arrival. Rather, he was just told to assist the ARVN in conducting search and destroy operations as the US 25th Division prepared to leave.[14]

"He was a solid looking guy with a relaxed but professional manner," Keller told me when I asked about his first impression of my father. His Vietnamese counterparts quickly learned that they could count on him and even liked working with him. "He remained calm and effective in all things," Keller continued, "even in occasional intense firefights … I trusted him completely in all situations. He was a truly professional soldier."[15] It appears that he had the necessary qualities to be a good advisor that Abrams once outlined as being mandatory to his staff. It was not guys with CGSC, Ranger school, or War College under their belt who were needed but rather those who understood human relations, possessed a sensitivity to emotions, and demonstrated respect for the Vietnamese.[16]

Even though I had never been in a gun battle with my father, I felt Keller's description was spot-on. In contrast to Tahir's assessment on his humorous nature, Keller's description more matched the man I knew: stoic and strict while at the same time warm and generous to all who knew him. As I did decades later, my father got along tremendously with his new boss, so much so that he wrote home about him in glowing terms.[17]

With the new Team 99 leader in hand and their mission protecting Route 7A complete, just like that, Hunsley—territory won and secured in blood—was no more. As in Iraq and Afghanistan, places and buildings named after heroes of those wars have disappeared forever. When you think about it, it's heartbreaking for those who served there.

Before they left Hunsley, the ARVN went all Sherman's March to Sea on the area. The ARVN detonated explosives in every body of water that held fish, to deny the enemy the use of this food source. The bodies that floated to the service were gathered and either eaten or burned. Any containers that could hold fresh water were also destroyed. All caches found in bunkers or tunnels were bombed out and torched. Even a captured bamboo viper was burned alive on a small funeral pyre just in case it had VC leanings.[18] So many things were scorched that in his diary, my father adjusted the ARVN's nickname to "Marvin the Arsonists."[19]

It was Hard War, as made famous during America's own Civil War. "We are not only fighting hostile armies, but a hostile people," wrote Union General William Sherman towards the end of that conflict, "and [we] must make old and young, rich and poor, feel the hard hand of war, as well as their organized armies."[20] I, of course, understand the intent behind these actions. However, I am not sure if we could have gotten away with this approach in Iraq and Afghanistan to the level seen in Vietnam.

The next several days were uneventful. Several "ball games" filled up my father's time, including spending a night sleeping in a wet rice paddy (which remains the coldest my father has ever been in his life), one ARVN soldier being evacuated because of wood splinters blown into his eyes during a helicopter landing, and breaking in a new NCO into the unit. On one operation they uncovered three hastily buried enemy bodies whose graves had been blown open by a US airstrike. From among the remains, the bombing also blew open a small cache, where they recovered a signaling whistle, notebooks, extra clothing, five pounds of sugar, and 25 pounds of crude salt.[21] All in all, working with the ARVN had made for a pretty eventful holiday season so far. I wonder what Christmas would bring.

Eight Kilometers Northeast of Trung Lập, Hậu Nghĩa Province Vietnam; December 1969: The Chiêu Hồis led my father's ARVN company to a yuletide bonanza on Christmas Eve. In a secure cache were found eight antique Russian SKS rifles and four 55-gallon cans of high grade mogas, which were put to the torch. Four VC were also killed while fleeing from the hoard. Marking the spot was another ghoulish sight: two skeletons, one whose bones were scattered about, probably by animals, while the other was laid out perfectly, like a pirate sentinel of old guarding his booty.[22]

On their second air assault of the day on this culmination of the Advent season, the birds dropped them straight into a colony of hornets. As his ARVN company quickly organized and moved toward the objective, US forces fiddled around and took the full brunt of the insects' stings. Stopping 200 meters short of an unnamed village 8 klicks northeast of Trung Lập, the ARVN waited for the US company to get their shit together and catch up. As they did so, my father prepped his primary weapon system for the upcoming fight—his radio. With the click of his hand mic, he could materialize a host of options that the NVA or VC could never match: helicopter gunships, airstrikes, medical evacuations, reinforcements, and artillery.[23]

Tahir described the importance of the radio and how it worked. "We never chased anybody when the unit was with me and I was advising them," he explained. Often, the ARVN would glimpse the enemy in the distance and try to pursue them so they could engage them with direct fire. He would hold back the South Vietnamese and patiently try to get them to understand that the enemy wanted you to see them so that they could suck you into an ambush. "Now watch this," he would say to the ARVN officers before he radioed in gunships, jet-supplied napalm, and artillery fire on the enemy element. "And then they'd be flying," he described about the enemy's reaction, "they'd be running around all over the place trying to get away."[24] The ARVN quickly grew to respect the power of a US advisor with a radio.

As the US forces finally caught up and moved into an overwatch position, the ARVN descended on the village like an ancient plague. Informed by the Chiêu Hồi-supplied intelligence, they tore through the surprised hamlet, ransacking homes, killing four VC, seizing three AK-47s, and capturing seven prisoners, one of whom was the local VC company commander from Sub Region I.[25] A "real feather in our caps," as my father remembered.[26]

With the capture of the VC, the real medieval stuff began. The ARVN descended on them, punching and kicking, while shouting questions about further caches or enemy locations. As my father watched, shocked by what was happening, an

ARVN interrogator coolly walked up to one of the prisoners, leveled his weapon, and killed him. "What the actual fuck are you all doing?" demanded my father to the man. "But *Trung úy*," slyly responded the interrogator, "he try to escape." My father quickly regained his composure and remembered where he was. "I'm sitting there," he recalled years later, "one American by myself, what could I say or do?" The action did finally motivate the other prisoners to talk, though. Once back at Trung Lập, he complained about the action of the ARVN to US authorities, but nothing happened. After all, it was their war.[27]

"Yes, they did torture them," Tahir explained to me when I asked him about war crimes and captured prisoners. He described how the 1/49th S-2 NCO had a little leather case that contained a stainless-steel ball peen hammer among some other instruments. "When he showed up," Tahir exclaimed, "it meant get the hell out of the hooch because he's going to start breaking fingers and bones to extract whatever information." The advisors on the team learned quickly when it was time for them to walk away.[28] "I did not observe any actions during my tour that were war crimes," Keller answered when I asked him the same question. Being at the battalion level, "the few prisoners my ARVN battalion captured were not where I was located so I did not see them."[29] Wars look different depending on what echelon you are at.

For his actions supporting the attack, my father was presented with the Vietnamese Gallantry Medal, a foreign award for bravery. His translated citation declared he received it for being an officer, "who has demonstrated much fighting ability." For his heroic actions against hostile forces during Operation TT 845-847/A/49 (the ARVN had boring operational names compared to the US), he "showed self-control to communicate by radio and point out the enemy positions to the Helicopter Gunships who made accurate strikes on the target."[30] It was much appreciated, but he always wondered if he was awarded the medal to encourage him to keep quiet about the killing.[31]

After a good thrashing, the captured commander was eager to talk, reporting on other caches and VC in the area. Unfortunately, due to the upcoming Christmas truce his intel could not be acted on. As they headed back to Trung Lập, they squeezed in one more ambush, netting two VC killed, one more prisoner, and two AK-47s. Their loss? One ARVN soldier.[32]

As he walked back into the compound, he passed two female captives who glared at him through bloodshot eyes. Caught detonating a mine that killed three US soldiers and one civilian while they were gone, the Ruff Puffs had beat them to a pulp.[33] Due to their bad condition, my father knew that they had not talked.[34] Unfortunately, this was a sight he grew used to quickly. Unlike US forces, torture, beatings, and killing were common treatment for anyone captured, whether they were fighting for the North or South.[35]

Trung Lập, Hậu Nghĩa Province, Vietnam; December 1969: With the 24-hour Christmas truce in place Team 99 settled into a holiday dinner that included wine flown in from Đức Hòa. We always had a saying while in the infantry: beware of good chow in the field because it meant you were about to be screwed.

As he ate, my father inspected what he thought was a memorial card for Hồ Chí Minh's recent death that he had taken off the captured VC commander.[36] Not knowing what it actually said, he tucked it away with his items from Vietnam until I uncovered it. Years later, I had it translated and discovered that it is not a memorial card. Rather, it is a Happy New Year's card from the spring of 1969 issued by Hồ Chí Minh to those fighting. It declared that "last year was a great success," and that this year would be even better—they would fight "until the Americans and their puppets get out."[37]

The card from Uncle Ho was not kept out of love for his leader; rather, it was treasured for the handwritten note scrawled across the back in blue pen. "I see myself as an unmarried girl, but no different than being married," stated the love poem penned by the VC commander's sweetheart. "Since he is far away and unable to connect," she longingly wrote, "the more I miss him, the further away I will be."[38] Who knows when he had last seen his sweetheart, and who knows if he ever saw her again. Hopefully her memory kept him going during whatever happened to him next.

After almost a month in his new role, my father's initial uninformed opinion of the ARVN had been dumped on its head. He noticed three main things that differentiated them from the way the US fought the war. First, in contrast to the 82nd, where the emphasis was on killing the enemy to feed a body count metric, "dead VC don't talk" was the general opinion of the ARVN's senior leaders.[39]

Second, the ARVN moved differently on the tactical level. US units tended to maneuver on line, which slowed their movement and often caused them to lose their bearing in dense terrain. It also left those soldiers on the left and right flanks alone and afraid. The ARVN moved in a single file, with the commander and his radio operator directly behind the point man. This enabled them to move quickly and quietly though forbidding geography and allowed soldiers in the formation to feel safe and supported.[40] They knew the land and could live off it easily, often picking food directly from trees and bushes that grew in the area.[41]

Finally, the war on the Vietnamese side had fewer rules than what he was used to operating under.

Overall, it was a pretty good Christmas for the war effort. After meeting the ball peen hammer-wielding S-2, the now cooperative VC commander volunteered to lead them to several more VC hiding places after the ceasefire.[42] Maybe the ARVN weren't a bunch of dandies after all. "The battalion became very proficient," Keller reported to me decades later in a more dignified manner when asked about the ARVN's will to fight, "at all aspects of air/ground search and destroy operations."[43]

Chapter 22

"The days are still long …"

PATRICK W. NAUGHTON SR.

The purple smoke billowed into the air. First Lieutenant Pat Hiu, a 1966 UH ROTC graduate, maneuvered his medical evacuation helicopter towards the rapidly growing colored cloud that marked a clearing that had been secured by ARVN forces. Flying low to the ground to make it difficult for the enemy to track him, or nap of the earth in aviation parlay, he confirmed the color of the smoke and tactical situation with the requesting unit before landing. Even though his helicopter was unarmed and bore the proper red cross Geneva markings, he still occasionally drew enemy fire.[1]

With the monsoon behind them, Vietnam was cooked nice and dry now. As Hiu touched down, the draft from the rotor blades kicked up dust and debris which choked all nearby and temporarily obstructed their view. It was always a hot load (meaning the rotor blades were not shut down to load or unload) in Vietnam as a sitting aircraft made for an inviting target. As the dirt cloud dissipated, his crew chief tossed out a couple of litters to the approaching ARVN. As the soldiers strapped the wounded—including a VC POW—to the olive drab canvas gurneys, a tall shirtless American materialized through the debris and caught Hiu's attention. "I think I know that haole guy," he thought to himself. As the dust further cleared, the mystery man's facial features became recognizable. "A lot of years have passed between now and 1970," Hiu told me when we talked about this encounter, "but I remember seeing your dad in Vietnam as if it was yesterday."[2]

Hiu stuck his arm out of the cockpit and frantically waved to my now confused father, beckoning him to come over. He came, shielding his face from the rotor blast which subsided some once he got right next to the cockpit, where the mystery pilot lifted his blackened helmet visor and, with a huge smile, greeted my dad. "And there we were, in the middle of a tactical landing zone," Hiu fondly remembered, "laughing and smiling, [all] because of the recognition of a familiar face from

Hawai'i." It still brought on an incredible warm feeling for him when he described it to me decades later.[3]

This encounter, which as a child I overheard being told between my uncle and my dad when talking about old school buddies, reminded me of how important helicopters were to the Vietnam War. When you look up the conflict online, almost every picture includes a chopper of some sort in the background. One of my earliest memories of this aircraft is watching with my father the 1984 movie *The Killing Fields*, about the Khmer Rouge in Cambodia. The evacuation of the US Embassy in Phnom Penh, with its surreal music score, left an incredible lasting impact on a six-year-old. I'm not sure if I would allow my son to watch this movie at that age, but my parents never tried to shield me from the ugliness in the world. I watched in a trance as those who assisted the Westerners scrambled to escape on helicopters from what they knew was certain doom.

Similarly, my own generation's conflicts could not have been fought without these machines of war. I cannot count the number of times I flew in a chopper in Iraq or for training. None of them will ever beat my first ride though. A storm was brewing at the Joint Readiness Training Center at Fort Polk as my squad loaded into a Blackhawk helicopter to conduct an Air Assault on a mock enemy force. The bird took off smoothly enough—it reminded me of being in a fast-moving elevator as it gained elevation. Suddenly the aircraft swerved to the right and then left repeatedly for several minutes, gaining and dropping altitude as it did so. "This can't be right," I thought to myself as I fought to keep my lunch down. I searched the faces of the veterans in the belly of the machine for any sign of panic; they all seemed calm. "I guess this is just what it feels like to be in a helicopter," I reasoned. As a cherry, I tried to keep calm lest I incur even more teasing for my actions.

After about five minutes of this, followed by a rough landing that included one bounce, the doors were thrown open. Remembering my training, I leaped out of the bird, sprinted past the reach of the rotor blades, and threw myself down behind my weapon. I sat there for a minute before I realized that we were in the same landing zone that we had taken off from and that no one had joined me in the half-moon defensive posture that a squad assumes once they exit the aircraft. I glanced behind me and noticed everyone else slowly exiting the chopper as they ambled towards me. I sat up with a perplexed look on my face as I overhead one NCO talking to another. "Holy shit, did you see that," he yelled, gesturing wildly, "we almost got blown out of the sky by a tornado and died, did you see that thing!" It was an interesting first introduction to the workhorse of the army and limousine for the infantry, shuttling soldiers to war since 1958.

Besides near wrecks and trancelike background music, as I digested my father's letters and diary I learned more about his war. It was fascinating to read that even though Vietnam is remembered for not having a front line, it still had a clear division between those in the field and those serving in secure base areas, just as my generation's conflicts did. The only difference was the army slang: pogues and RAMFs were replaced with what became known as fobbits—a play on the hobbit characters from the *Lord of the Rings* movie and book franchise. Those who never left the secure Forward Operating Bases (FOB—hence *fobbit*) were now associated with hairy little fantasy creatures with big feet.

Every so often my father got to go to the rear for resupply or reporting requirements. Going from the field to a rear area is always a jarring experience. You suddenly become conscious of your tattered uniform and the stench coming off your body. It's best to keep your mouth shut and not smile the entire time, less someone sees the plaque buildup between your teeth and catches a whiff of your foul breath. Generally, it's just an uncomfortable feeling until you get cleaned up and recall the decorum and manners of civilized society.

My father felt this every time he went back. Once, he excitedly entered the officers' mess hoping for a good meal, to embarrassingly discover he only had 45 cents in US military script. In the ARVN areas American script was useless, so all he had was Vietnamese piasters on hand. Sent away, he ended up eating at the nearest local restaurant. Best to probably just stay in the field, he thought to himself, where everything makes sense.[4] In the field the only luxury was the constant stream of cookies still being sent by my Aunt Momi: rinse your hand in a rice paddy, dip it into the can of crumbs, and repeat.[5]

Hậu Nghĩa Province, Vietnam; January 1970: One of the most controversial decades in the nation's history was over. The 1960s were a doozy. The advent of the New Year was celebrated in style, in a bunker with booze and field chow, followed by a visit to Fire Base Patton, where my dad witnessed the visit of Vice President Spiro Agnew and Ambassador Ellsworth Bunker. However, 1970 brought with it new revelations about the ARVN.[6] For reasons outlined earlier, historically, the 25th ARVN Division is remembered as one of the lesser performing units from the war. My father recalled their "terrible reputation" but stands by the assertion that except for one bad apple, the rest of the companies in the 1/49th were superb.[7]

Company 3 was all kinds of jacked up and was the problem child of the battalion. The old adage that there are no bad soldiers, just bad leaders, was true in the case of 3rd Company. Every operation was a challenge. The men would patrol with no flank security and would not actively seek out the enemy or caches. My father argued with the company commander that he needed to be on the first lift for all helicopter assaults. When finally on ground in the landing zone, he struggled to get them to even start operations. Once they did begin to move, they would often get lost and foul up the entire operation with the adjutant units. The company once refused to move off the landing zone and the commander begged my father to report back to higher as though they were conducting the mission. He refused but nothing happened to the leader; a soldier today who would be known as a shit-bird.[8]

Besides this one company, the battalion was performing well. My father was now into his second month of advising the ARVN. A lot had passed since the day after Christmas when a mollified VC commander led them to a spider hole, where he coaxed out three of his brethren. They were then immediately taken into captivity for their own beatings, starting the process again.[9] My father had also traded in his M-16 for a 45-caliber pistol. His main weapon as an advisor was the radio now; the rifle just got in the way. There was also the unspoken theory that the 45 could be used to commit suicide rather than be captured.[10]

Countless helicopter insertions and armored personnel carrier (APC) rides followed by "de bo" RIFs (*đi bộ* meaning to walk on foot) made up most of January. His ARVN soldiers loved Johnny Walker whiskey, which they called Johnny De Bo. He would reward his men with a bottle from the PX whenever he could.[11] The Army loves its slang—de bo, ball game, hump. Whatever, they all mean the same thing in the infantry: dirt, heat, sweat, bugs, constant exertion, and just being generally miserable.

Speaking of insects, ARVN advisors could not wear repellent, also known as bug juice. "Mosquitoes were terrible," said my father, "and you can't wear repellent, or the enemy could smell you." Unlike with the 82nd, where the unique stench of large groups of American troops could be smelt a mile away, when with the ARVN, who did not use repellent and whose body odor blended in with the rest of the population, the unmistakable scent could carry for miles.[12] "I didn't know who was friendly and who was enemy," remembered Keller about another sinister reason why advisors did not use bug juice. In case of infiltration or a Chiêu Hồi counter flip, he was very careful to disguise his location. "They could smell where you were and take you out," he recalled before explaining his trick of lying down in one spot at the onset of darkness for all to see before moving to several others throughout the night. "You were very careful about where you stayed and what you wore," he remembered.[13]

Regardless of whose side the Vietnamese were on, sometimes US units could not differentiate a friendly from an enemy and would fire on his unit. On one particularly tough day for US troops, a company of the 25th Infantry "got the shit kicked out of them," as my father recorded in his diary.[14] On the verge of being overrun, my father saddled up a company of ARVN soldiers and rode by helicopter to the rescue. Once on the ground, they moved quickly towards the besieged US unit to try to break the attacking enemy force. Circling menacingly overhead were several Hueys, just itching for a target and payback.[15]

My father watched in horror as, one by one, the helicopters lined up for a run and they started taking machine-gun rounds on their positions. To add to the mayhem, US 105-millimeter artillery rounds started slowly walking towards them. With a "fire for effect" call imminent, my father frantically waved and popped smoke grenades to try to divert the incoming rounds and choppers. Finally, my father got in contact with Keller, who was able to connect the dots via the ARVN radios to the US battalion net, then to the supporting artillery and helicopters. "It was a hair-raising moment not being able to communicate directly with the US troops," he remembered about this near fratricidal kill by his own forces.[16]

The RIFs through the free-fire zones, however, produced more than a wicked Johnny Walker hangover, bug bites, and occasional fratricide close calls. Led by intelligence provided by Chiêu Hồi and a bloodied captured VC, my father and the 1/49th took the enemy to the mat. Two M-16s, six AK-47s, two AK-50s, five rifle grenades, and 17 B-40 rockets were captured. Along with the enemy weaponry, various irreplaceable supplies were put to the torch. The haul included medical supplies, sandals, clothing, water containers, cooking items, salt, explosives for booby traps, and about six tons of rice. Also liberated were three red communist flags—the same ones in the picture that I later wowed my classmates with at CGSC.[17]

Overall, for the month, 21 VC and NVA soldiers were also killed. More importantly, though, 13 VC and one NVA were captured alive, including one old man who, despite having a wooden stump in place of a leg, still fought on. The friendly body count for the month? One ARVN and Chiêu Hồi killed, and eight wounded, most from mines and booby traps that the APCs hit.[18]

Everywhere they went, whether engaging the enemy or incinerating caches, my father also continued to make macabre discoveries. It seemed that every time an air strike or artillery salvo occurred, it would toss up old remains buried under the ground. Mangled corpses and body parts poking through the soil, some smoldering after being struck, were constant reminders of the decades of war in the region.[19] Years later, a former VC would comment on this and how challenging it was to recover the remains of those Vietnamese killed during the war, noting how the land where graves were marked constantly changed hands between both sides during the conflict. "American tanks sometimes rolled through and flattened the markers we had left," he sadly recalled. Those not churned into the soil, he remembered, "were blasted to shreds by the bombs and will never be found."[20]

Another interesting observation was the same as noted by my father's friend LT Rogers and his team all that time ago in the Pineapple. VC poop piles were everywhere—when spotted they almost always guaranteed some type of contact would occur.[21] Excrement notwithstanding, during the month of January the ARVN's efforts produced more than found on most operations while he was with the 82nd. Again, I thought the ARVN sucked. Reluctantly, even some in the media were grudgingly stepping back from their usual ARVN-bashing stories. "They just might make it," wrote one *Newsweek* reporter after a recent trip witnessing the ARVN perform in their "pretty, dirty, sad little country."[22]

As 1LT William Calley started his trial for what became known as the My Lai episode, and the US government stated that they had no "immediate prospect of a negotiated settlement" at the Paris peace talks, my father became a "double-digit midget."[23] This meant that only two numbers made up the amount of days he had left in Vietnam. "My but the months go fast," he longingly wrote home, though "the days are still long."[24] He was getting short, as the slang of the time labeled those who were getting close to completing their year in Vietnam. I am not sure why my generation never came up with any catchphrases to mark our time left on deployments. While my father was working to rid the province of enemy activity, Noreen had a baby girl, my cousin Christina—making him a double-digit uncle now as well. "Do you know if Christina received the letter and present I sent her?" my father asked as he begged for a picture.[25]

Chapter 23

"Arrived down under ..."

PATRICK W. NAUGHTON SR.

I had the perfect plan. Or so thought my young, single mind, which spent an inordinate amount of time thinking about only one thing—women. During the height of Iraq and Afghanistan, if you deployed for a year, you got one 15-day block of leave to go anywhere in the world. Most went home. My grand strategy? I would go to Sweden, Finland, and Estonia.

But why start in Sweden? It was not because of the hit book and movie *The Girl with the Dragon Tattoo* that was all the rage then—although I was reading the book at the time, and it was interesting to see some of the street names in Stockholm mentioned in it. Rather, my cousin lived there and was a well-known concierge who knew the city well. I had sent him an Iraqi hookah as a souvenir before my arrival, and he was going to show me all the hot spots in return. Born while my father was in the Iron Triangle, little did he know that he was mentioned in numerous letters home from my dad, who treasured any baby pics sent of him.[1]

After spending a day in the sprawling tent city of Camp Arifjan to turn in my gear for temporary storage, I was off. Soldiers often hid out for weeks in these tents as they transited between theaters. Olive drab green or sand tan, with only metal bunkbeds and plastic-wrapped mattresses for furniture, they were poorly lit and just about us unwelcoming as you can imagine. One urban myth describes forgotten soldiers living there for years, dodging any duty or responsibilities while still getting combat pay. True or not, I did not care as I was going on leave. With just a small backpack and wearing a wrinkled t-shirt and a pair of jeans, both of which had sat stuffed at the bottom of my duffel bag for the last six months, I was dropped off 10 hours early at the gleaming Kuwait International Airport.

Like my father at the officers' mess at Tân Sơn Nhứt, a disorientating feeling among all that cleanliness set in. Planted at the Cinnabon outside security, I was told that due to the current threat level I was not to leave the vendor's area until my flight departed. "Then why the fuck am I here ten hours early?" I asked myself. Oh well, back to my fourth sweet and tasty roll as I ignored the stares from long white thobe-enshrouded Kuwaiti men, who were upset in their man dresses (as we called them) about me taking up an entire table to myself for hours on end as I contemplated my current conundrum and military logic.

Most soldiers spent an average of two days of flying on each end to get home—my grand plan, consisting of three steps, had me in my hotel in Stockholm in about six hours. The first step in my three-pronged strategy? Civilian clothes shopping. Fashion tip: do not try to buy a simple pair of comfortable jeans in Europe. There they are designer items versus utility like in the US and fit like skinny jeans before they were a thing.

Second step? Get a real meal. I quickly found a restaurant that advertised itself as a burger joint and ordered the biggest one on the menu. Chomping into the monster, I savored each greasy bite until I noticed that everyone was staring at me. Another culture snag—in Sweden, burgers are gourmet treats and eaten slowly with a knife and fork. Not that it mattered as by now all that grease had my head spinning. A glorious head rush subsided as I went back to shoving chow into my mouth in the most uncouth American way possible.

Dressed and fed, it was time to initiate the third and final step of my well-planned scheme. Armed with my Saddam funny money, it was time to hit up the bars and clubs to meet some foreign girls. I had a lot of fun in Sweden with my cousin, but I think the girls there were too tall for me, or at least that is how I consoled myself. On to Finland, where I heard they were shorter. "If you can't get laid on the ferry from Stockholm to Helsinki," my cousin confidently informed me, "then you can't get laid anywhere." Boarding the lauded booze cruise to cross the Baltic Sea, I kept an eye out for the crowds of partygoers who supposedly made up the usual passenger list. The result? A nearly empty boat with only a handful of drunk and belligerent Russians.

Everyone was definitely short in Finland, but still no luck. Fricking Saddam was getting me nowhere. I partied hard, but the only women I met were the ones in saunas. I joined in on the Finnish national pastime and met some interesting and naked characters while sweating myself sober each day. Once, an absolutely gorgeous woman entered the sauna, took off her towel, and lay completely naked right in front me. Shocked, I tried not to stare as everyone else was oblivious to her. As I would have had to step over her to get out, I sat there sweating for a lot longer than I wanted to. There were no sights like that in Iraq, so I was okay with the extended hotbox.

The next adventure was a short ferry-ride to cross the Gulf of Finland to the small country of Estonia. It restored its independence from the Soviet Union in 1991 and since then had become a tourist mecca. I went to a bank machine and pulled out 300 kroon, which at the time equated to about 50 US dollars. Startled by the awesome exchange rate, I got a good feeling about the enchanting medieval city of Tallinn. It was there that I encountered every young man's dream, an urban myth that only exists in exaggerated stories swapped among friends that grow with each telling … a nightclub where the women outnumbered the men 10 to one.

I arrived at the club early to reserve a good spot. I sat there wide-eyed as I watched group after group of girls walk in. Later, I would find out that Estonian men would rather save money and sit at home getting obliterated off vodka. After about an hour of watching the club fill up with beautiful women and building up my liquid courage, I finally talked to one of them. My pickup line? "Hi, do you speak English?" Luckily, she did, and she spent the next two days showing me the town. It was awesome closure to my leave from Iraq. Turns out that Saddam was useless after all.

On my last night in Estonia, I met three young merchant marines who were also on their final day of shore leave. Being the only Americans there, we decided to team up for a night of heavy partying. Sloshed by midnight, somehow, we got talked into going to a nightclub we had never heard of by some Russians. As we descended into a dark basement and the door closed behind us, guarded by four huge Russkis, we knew we had messed up. A row of young girls in lingerie filed out from a back room and lined up in front of us as the hulks demanded that we buy an overpriced drink from the tiny bar and pick which girl we wanted. We just stared openmouthed as it took our alcohol-numbed brains a minute to figure out what was going on.

As many an Army safety briefing had warned against, we had wandered smack dab into the middle of a brothel stocked by human trafficked victims. Without saying anything to each other, we immediately circled together back-to-back and demanded that they move away from the door so we could leave. After some tense back and forth in broken English, laced with globally recognized swear words (by which time we had armed ourselves with some beer bottles that had been lying around) they decided to let us leave. Even after being in Iraq and the merchants on a boat for six months, there was still no way we were going to partake in that. Made me proud to be an American—even though we did leave the poor girls behind.

Having survived the depravity of the Russians, it was back to Sweden. After another heavily promoted overnight party boat, which was also a dud, I landed in Stockholm to start my return trip. I mailed the civilian clothes I purchased to my sister in San Diego and then transited back through Germany, Kuwait, the abysmal tents of Camp Arifjan, and then Iraq. As I sat in my tiny, dusty CHU I thought back on my whirlwind leave. Surely its memory would keep me going. Five more months to go.

It was interesting to read about my father's leave from Vietnam. It occurred just past the halfway point of his year overseas, just as mine did. He was also young and single, and we shared the same preoccupation with the opposite sex, it seems.

Reading his letters and diary about his time away from the war reminded me how often we forget that our parents once had their own lives that had nothing to do with us. They had different priorities, hopes, and dreams, and made a lot of the same stupid mistakes that they tried to keep us from making. And, as we both learned, there is nothing like a break from war, regardless of which one.

Sydney, Australia; February 1970: My father's leave was a little different than mine. He only got seven days instead of 15 to visit one of the places approved by the US government. Thailand, Hong Kong, Japan, Australia, Taiwan, and Singapore were on the list by 1970. Hawai'i was as well, but it was mainly only open to married soldiers. It was highly discouraged for single men as too many had gone AWOL there, some because of the church my father had once frequented. Troops had to sign up for their desired destination and hope they got what they wanted. My father got lucky—he was on his way to Sydney, Australia, land of the round-eyes, the slang for Caucasian women (again, not a PC atmosphere).[2]

My dad was leaving Vietnam just in time. The year of the dog had begun; based on the 1970 lunar calendar, the Tet holiday was 5–7 February, right as he was scheduled to be gone.[3] A time of apprehension since the Tet Offensive of 1968—after all it was this event that spurred the deployment of the 82nd Airborne to Vietnam in the first place—the persistent fear from FWMAF was that the enemy would use the holiday to launch another attack. But what was Tet anyway? How to explain it to those from the West who had never heard of it? The Army's answer: the Graphic Training Pamphlet.

"Tet is Vietnam's biggest celebration of the year," described another stylized black-and-white covered training aid, which depicted an old Vietnamese scholar creating a traditional Tet calligraphy sign. "It corresponds to America's Christmas, New Year, Easter, All Souls' Day and Fourth of July combined," it explained.[4] It is a reunion with present family and past ancestors, a spring festival, a celebratory national holiday, a time to revisit traditional ceremonies and taboos, and everyone's birthday all rolled into one three-day extravaganza.[5] "This is the time when the Vietnamese people look back to the past, enjoy the present and look forward to the future," noted the pamphlet. "It is truly a comprehensive holiday, and all Vietnamese give it full observance."[6] Everywhere would be decorated with *cây nêu* (bamboo poles), wrapped in red paper for good luck, and blooming yellow apricot blossoms, all accompanied by sounds of the colorful and loud unicorn dance.

In 1968, the US overestimated the Tet's importance and underestimated the willingness of the enemy to violate this normally sacred time, with catastrophic results. "The enemy had achieved in South Vietnam neither military nor psychological victory," remembered Westmoreland about this offensive; "unfortunately, the enemy scored in the United States the psychological victory that eluded him in Vietnam," he regretfully recalled.[7] A repeat of Tet 1968 would be another disaster from a civilian support standpoint for the Vietnamization effort, but regardless of whether the enemy tried to exploit this holiday again in 1970, it did not matter to my father as he would not be there.

Out on a joint operation with the ARVN and a US mechanized unit, my father got the word from Keller that he needed to leave now. A Loach landed and picked him up to transport him to the rear so he would have enough time to meet the flight to Australia. After a short stay at Tân Sơn Nhứt, which consisted of safety briefings about loose women and the diseases they carry, a thorough search for weapons and drugs, and, of course, another training pamphlet, he was off.[8]

He flipped through the booklet as he caught the chartered flight to Sydney. The front cover depicted a trio of sailboats cutting through the crystal blue waters of Sydney Harbor. The back cover was even more appealing, though: a beautiful blonde woman in a tiny white bikini lay enticingly splayed out in the crashing waves of a white sandy beach.[9] From its advertised US-sponsored mixer, where 200 young ladies from in and around Sydney were reportedly invited to enjoy the evening with visiting servicemen, to a floating disco party that promised "magic groovy music, way out electronic lighting, sizzling steaks, and a whole raft of beautiful 'birds'," things were looking up for him.[10]

The Army met the chartered flight on the tarmac in Sydney and bussed the men to the main R&R Center for more safety briefings before they could be released on the town. There they strongly suggested that the men should not rent a car—not because Australians drive on the opposite side of the road, but because the women there are so beautiful that they "might be distracted and have an accident." Before leaving the center, he was able to rent some civilian clothes for $16 (plus a refundable $20 deposit) which got him one suit, one sports coat, a pair of trousers, four shirts, two ties, and one belt.[11] This supplemented his only outfit that, like me, he had squirreled away in the bottom of one of his duffels—a pair of slacks and an aloha shirt. Finally, he opted not to get a car and rode a shuttle (to avoid running over any women in a rental), which took him to his hotel.[12]

Splurging by staying at the now closed Menzies Hotel for $12.50 a night, he was introduced to a local girl by a friend he knew from his time in Canada. They had met as passengers on a transportation freighter through the Pacific Ocean—a very bohemian Sixties way to travel at the time. The first order of business once in his room (even before calling the girl) was to order a large glass of milk via room service. All they had in Vietnam was powdered milk, and he missed the real thing.[13] A flurry of postcards to the family, depicting kangaroos, kookaburra birds, and high-tech Sydney Harbor hydrofoils soon flowed home as he enjoyed his leave.[14]

My father, ever the consummate gentlemen, refused to tell me the juicy details that occurred over the next seven days, preferring to keep those memories to himself. However, from what I can tell from his correspondence home, he had quite the time. "I think I'd fall for this gal," mentioned one postcard about the dangers of remaining in Australia, followed by a later letter where he declared that it was "a good thing I didn't stay any longer or I would have gotten married."[15] Besides sending some roses to arrive at her work the Monday after he left and a few random letters, they never spoke again,[16] the last correspondence being when their mutual friend died from cancer in 1975; she in turn kindly sent letters of condolence to the family.[17] As often happens in life, they were ships passing in the night.

Armed with a stack of books purchased on leave to help pass the time at Trung Lập, he headed back to Vietnam.[18] Even though I never got the juicy details of his leave, if he was of the same frame of mind I was in during my vacation from war, I am sure he had a blast. I think his simple diary entry covering the time away probably sums it up best. Only two words were written which covered the entries from the first to the seventh of February: "Sydney—heaven."[19]

But back to Vietnam and the struggle against communism. While he was gone, congressional investigators from the Senate Foreign Relations Committee visited Vietnam and returned with a scathing report, writing that "despite statistical progress" in pacification efforts, the gains were fragile. Furthermore, Vietnamization was also progressing, but the ARVN were far from able to defend the country on their own, even with US artillery and air support. This was in stark contrast to the positive stories that the US military leaders were selling. However, conceded the investigators about this disconnect, "a visitor can easily find evidence to support any case he wishes to make."[20] My father could care less about all of this. Only "91 to go and counting," he informed the family.[21]

Chapter 24

"Is your battalion Vietnamized ..."

RICH KELLER

My hair was the longest it had been in over a decade. Normally kept short, 18 days without a haircut had caused me to look like a different person. My friends accused me of dyeing my hair black and would not believe that its length made it look darker. It was nothing that couldn't be fixed by a visit to the barbershop staffed by third country nationals (known as TCNs), though.

This virtual army of about 70,000 TCNs completed all the thankless tasks that needed to be accomplished to support the American way of war. This included everything from launderers, truck drivers, cooks, construction, fast food providers, and, of course, barbers. Just about anything you can think of was most likely supported by a contracted TCN, an often dubiously duped worker from a poor country lured to work in a war zone with promises of wealth and advancement.[1] Why send a soldier into harm's way to clean latrines when you can pay a contractor to execute the job cheaper?

Often the young females recruited would be preyed upon by their employers, and even soldiers. One soldier I knew of, via promises to help them get to the US, would get blowjobs from the Filipino janitors. Once, he caught a young girl slyly spitting his semen into a Ziploc bag in the hope of trapping him by trying to impregnate herself with it later. A commonly repeated soldier's yarn claimed that once a contract was terminated, or if a TCN failed to work hard, they would be let out the front gate of whatever base they were on and left to fend for themselves. I am not sure of the validity of this tale, but I would not be surprised if it was true.

Filipinos did the laundry. Nigerians guarded the chow hall. Indians prepared the food we ate. Irishmen even sold cars. And, I think, either men from Myanmar, Nepal, or Bangladeshi cut my hair—I was never actually able to clarify which. They all dressed immaculately as if they were in a fashion show, had perfect hair, wore eyeliner, and must have drenched themselves each day with five different types of cologne. With no sense of personal space as they cut my hair, the sweet stench coming off them caused my eyes to water, throat to hurt, and brought on sneezing fits.

In Vietnam, they used the local civilians to support these mundane tasks—not so much in the global war on terror. After a fresh high and tight haircut and the mandatory meeting with a psychiatrist to make sure leave had not messed me up, it was back to the war. Not everyone was welcomed with open arms when they went home. Some went back to cheating spouses or empty homes. Tired of repeated deployments, spouses sometimes took the kids and ran, leaving the soldier staring at empty walls for 15 days—messing them up good before they were sent back to war. Who can forget SFC Worcester's leave from Vietnam in *Hamburger Hill*, where he finds his kids running around barefoot and his wife shacked up with a "hair head taking a leak in the john."[2]

I especially remember one NCO who talked a tough game on how many times he deployed and how much combat he saw. His wife used to email him graphic sexual pictures of her in various poses which, for some reason, he felt the need to share with everyone. When he went on leave, he soon discovered that she was not using a tripod with an auto timer to take those pics. Rather, she was sleeping with just about everyone in their small town and doing a photoshoot after each. He had a mental breakdown and tried to commit suicide, so, of course, he did not come back to Iraq. For some, home was not always sunshine and rainbows. Hence the need for the mandatory head shrink check upon return to make sure the soldier was not about to hurt themselves or someone else.

Trung Lập, Vietnam; February 1970: "R&R should really be called a dream and daze (D&D)," my father firmly informed the family.[3] The return trip to Vietnam seemed, just as mine did to Iraq, to go by too quickly. I was back at the Cinnabon all too soon; for my father, the airport shuttle, charter plane to Tân Sơn Nhứt, followed by a helicopter ride to Đức Hòa, flew by. Leaning on a jeep with a smile was Keller, waiting to give him a ride back to Trung Lập.[4] "What a strange feeling," he mused in his diary; "I actually feel like I'm only partly in Vietnam—my mind is still in Sydney."[5]

After all the blondes with blue eyes known for causing car wrecks, he did not even notice the Vietnamese women for several weeks.[6] Remembering the stories of soldiers whose butts were in country but minds still on leave, he did his best to forget about Australia. "Some returnee R&R soldiers daydream too much and step on mines or are killed in firefights," he warned himself as he got his shit wired tight again for the war.[7]

Surprised that nothing had happened during Tet while he was gone (including the usual fireworks, as those had been banned since the 1968 offensive, when the enemy used them to conceal their attack), he landed smack dab into a critical point of the war, that of the SECDEF's second visit to Vietnam, where he decided that

Vietnamization was working. The results of this trip informed and shaped the war effort for the rest of the conflict.

At a press conference on the first day of this trip, before meeting with anyone on the ground, Laird preemptively declared that the advancement towards full Vietnamization of the war had "been adequate." Furthermore, the aim of his trip was not to check on its progress but rather look for ways to improve it and "push it forward to completion." When asked by reporters if Nixon was set on this course of action, Laird responded that at this point Vietnamization could be considered "irreversible."[8] Over this four-day trip, he met with senior military and government officials from whom he desired to learn how the strategy was progressing at the ground level. "The number one national priority is to make Vietnamization work," he adamantly told each of them.[9]

Wearing a black baseball cap and spotless, crisply starched olive drab Army fatigues (with the nametape SECDEF affixed to it where "US Army" would normally go) he visited Trung Lập. Surrounded by a gang of security men, scowling generals, tie-wearing bureaucrats, and the media, SECDEF Laird stepped off a helicopter there to learn about the progress of his brainchild.

In between hand shaking, operational briefings, and troop reviews, Keller, as the leader of Team 99, got a brief moment with the secretary. Unlike the earlier press briefings, Keller was never told why Laird was visiting, but he assumed it was about this thing called Vietnamization that he had heard so much about through unofficial channels. Laird had an old fact sheet that Keller prepared each month that consisted of 145 multiple choice questions that spoke to the progress in the region. "Mr. Secretary," he tried to clarify to Laird about the data he was reviewing, "what you are reading every day about what I'm doing is different from what I'm doing every day." The sheet was a holdover from even before pacification efforts, and the information being collected "had little to do with how things were going or if Vietnamization was working," he explained. It mainly described how much assistance the US was providing but did little to determine if the ARVN would be able to take over once the Americans were gone.[10]

Despite the useless metrics, on his last day In Vietnam, Laird touted his visit to the 25th ARVN at Trung Lập and how they had taken over "another vital area" from American forces fighting the war. "The Vietnamization program is progressing very well … we will be able to continue troop reductions," he confidently stated to the media. "We are ahead or on target with all schedules of Vietnamization."[11]

Via a secret memo, Laird sent Nixon a more candid assessment from his four-day trip to Vietnam, which was not shared with commanders on the ground. "While the progress made in the military aspects of Vietnamization is impressive," he informed the president, "the work remaining is of monumental proportions."[12] He acknowledged the gradual improvements being made militarily, but he had grave concerns about everything else. Namely, the economy, which was almost totally supported by the US, would probably completely collapse if that too was not taken over by the South Vietnamese government soon.[13] Lastly, "the newsmen in South Vietnam," he warned Nixon, "continue to be skeptical, if not cynically pessimistic, about Vietnamization."[14] They needed to watch what they stated publicly on the progress of the effort, he cautioned, less they "elaborate on and, perhaps distort, any temporary setbacks."[15] Privately, Laird thought the "entire thing was a disaster" as he vented to an aide about his actual assessment on Vietnamization.[16]

Squatting in the surrounding rice paddies, my father watched from the perimeter as the stream of helicopters transported Laird's entourage into Trung Lập. As all of this occurred, he and the other advisors had been tasked to surround the base with ARVN troops to protect him during his visit[17]—can't have incoming rockets while the SECDEF was there. Luckily, as Nguyen Charlie's comrade commander told him in that month's cartoon sent home, "That's enough, we have used up our rocket quota for the week."[18]

As grand strategy was discussed, and Laird sought assurances on the success of Vietnamization, my father prevented any indirect fire attacks on the compound. In the process, he lost two men to a booby trap.[19] He tried not to blame the secretary that night as he came back from the field and thumbed through the recently developed pictures of his leave to Australia. With beaches and blondes now ruling his thoughts, he suppressed his anger and tried to sleep. "Only back a little over a week and it seems like two years," he sadly wrote to the family. Oh well, he thought, no big deal—after all, as he reminded them, he was short.[20]

Near Firebase Pershing, Vietnam; February 1970: But how was Vietnamization going at the tactical level? Okay, but not perfect. Team 99 continued to try to get Marvin to take the lead. "You were almost like the Vietnamese Battalion Commander," noted Keller when talking about his time with the ARVN, "because you were training the Vietnamese Infantry Battalion to do things like US Infantry Battalions did." The main difference being that instead of on exercises, you were teaching them how to do it in live combat scenarios. The team also had to realize that the 1/49th was not a US unit and should not be expected to operate like one. Keller understood that his four-man team constantly rotated and had term limits of a year at most. "I knew that I was only going to be able to do a certain amount in the time that was allocated to us," he later stated. "The four of us were not going to be able to change how a culture and a battalion operated in a year's time." The trick was to try to understand their culture and then leverage that to teach them to perform the best they can in the field. After Laird's visit, he was now constantly asked by higher if his battalion had been Vietnamized yet. And if not yet, then when? However, that assessment had no clear definition and was left completely up to him to determine.[21]

Even with my father's pidgin French, language, like culture, was unsurprisingly another barrier. "I tried to sense moods even if I couldn't understand the words,"

Keller remembered. Tone, rapidity of the language, and just a general sense of the atmosphere helped them determine "whether or not we were in danger, whether or not things were going okay" and, most importantly to Keller as the team lead, "whether or not the operation had happened on time."[22]

But back to my father's attempt at Vietnamizing the Vietnamese. To his approval, the shit-bird ARVN commander was finally relieved.[23] It is true that the men that he led and that my father advised were able to fight; however, it takes more than a bayonet-studded rifle to build an effective army. They grappled with logistics—simple things such as water and food for the men on patrol and power in their forward bases were a struggle for them to achieve.[24] Tahir remembers never running out of ammo while on operations, but food and water were a different story. Once they had to survive off green mangoes and water from streams contaminated by the bodies of dead animals and people. Luckily, they had iodine tablets, something the ARVN did not.[25]

Combined arms maneuver and coordination was also still beyond their reach. "I don't know what has to be done to get these people to use their own arty," my father frustratingly jotted down in his diary.[26] He noticed the same things that Laird did, just on a more micro scale. The ARVN could put their boot to a chest with a swift kick, but everything else behind that was tenuous at best.

As February ended, the fighting continued. Helicopter gun and troop ships circled overhead near Firebase Pershing as the pilots directed my father's ARVN unit to squash what looked like ants scurrying about the landscape but that were actually enemy combatants dodging in and out of holes. One was eventually killed before they could disappear back under ground. Unable to resist, a gunship (call sign Stinger 86) landed to play war-tourists. Between posing with the dead body (who turned out to be the local VC postmaster) and taking pictures, the four crewmen traded for souvenirs with the ARVN. For some cartons of cigarettes, they got tore-up enemy clothing, a hat, and a blown-out AK-47 magazine. With the macabre tour over, the air crew left the area to go look for more insects to squash.

To avoid wasting a dead body, just as he did in the 82nd, my father set up an overwatch to see if anyone would come to claim it. Later that night, three VC crept up to their slain postman to do just that. When they were within 15 feet of the body, an ARVN slammed down three times on a claymore clacker, followed by a flurry of hand grenades which ripped the three men off their feet. One was killed instantly while the other two were badly wounded and desperately tried to crawl away. Several ARVN soldiers coolly walked over towards the VC who, now wide-eyed with terror on hearing the footsteps, increased their efforts to drag themselves to safety. Towering over the wounded men, with emotionless faces the soldiers shot the pair in the back with their rifles.[27]

The stats for February: five enemy killed and one captured. One 50-caliber barrel and two pistols were found, along with several caches of ammo. Another VC bamboo viper was also dispatched and civilians scrounging for spent brass and scrap metal were escorted from the restricted areas. They also found two more graves blown from their final resting places. Unfortunately, throughout February eight ARVNs were wounded from booby traps and two were killed.[28] It was a slower month then the previous; however, he had missed the first third of it due to R&R. No worries—just as General Grant once said to Sherman after the failure of the first day at the Battle of Shiloh, as he puffed on his ever-present cigar during our own Civil War, "lick 'em tomorrow though."[29]

Trung Lập, Vietnam; February 1970: While at Advanced Individual Training (AIT) at Fort Sill, Oklahoma on their way to becoming artillerymen, Gary Brown and his best friend James Brewer were presented with an offer they couldn't refuse. Asked if they would like to forgo life as sandbag-filling privates and become shake-and-bake NCOs, how could they say no?[30]

Wearing brand new sergeant stripes, they ended up at Cam Ranh Bay in Vietnam, awaiting transport to their new assignments as artillerymen in Camp Eagle, Phu Bai, near Huế. The city was almost destroyed during the Tet Offensive and was made famous in Stanley Kubrick's *Full Metal Jacket*. Just before they were to depart, Brown and Brewer received the unexpected news that they were being reassigned to MACV as ARVN advisors. In the Army way, which does not allow for asking why or how this happened, they resigned themselves to their fate. That night, over a couple of beers at the NCO club they sought out advice from a group of grizzled veterans who were leaving for home this next morning. They asked them what being an advisor meant and with straight faces the men told them not to worry about it: "You will be titless WACs [Women's Army Corps members], working in air-conditioned offices in Saigon." They probably then laughed themselves to death once the pair of buck-sergeant cherries were out of earshot.[31]

The next day Brown and Brewer caught the same chopper to their new base camps. Brewer hugged his best friend as they promised to link up the next chance they got. He got off outside the village of Tân Mỹ near Trảng Bàng (made famous by the Pulitzer Prize-winning photograph of a burned and naked little girl fleeing a napalm strike on the village), and Brown was flown to Trung Lập.[32] While the enemy was being shot in the back as they tried to crawl away, Team 99 got a new member. An FNG (fucking new guy) cherry to train up—SGT Gary Lee Brown, age 21, from Warren, Ohio. It was a name I heard a couple of times growing up, whispered in hushed tones.

Chapter 25

"We are still killing Cong ..."

PATRICK W. NAUGHTON SR.

The lifeless body lay in the market square of Trung Lâp all week. The ARVN wanted to send a message; what that message was, though, my father was not entirely sure. Either way, a VC village chief who was also the secretary of the Communist Party for the district was killed in an ambush by the ARVN, so there he would lie. Stinking up the square to let everyone know what happens to those who choose to fight the government of South Vietnam.[1]

March was dry, hot, and humid in Vietnam; also known as a month dedicated to the Irish with a day for getting drunk. At least, my father joked to the family, he was always wearing his olive drab green. Besides Vietnamization, more changes were happening in the war—namely, the South Vietnamese military was now starting to strike at the enemy in Cambodia. As had been briefed many times to both Westmoreland and Abrams, "portions of Cambodia are under de factor occupation by the enemy," who used it to supply and insert forces into South Vietnam largely unmolested.[2]

US forces were also now authorized to cross the border if they needed to respond to direct enemy threats—openly announcing for the first time that the war had spread, even though secretly the US had been bombing selected targets in Cambodia for quite some time.[3] After ordering his staff to ask for some aerial photographs to help plan operations there just in case, one general officer remembers how he was denied. "We found out why they didn't want to give them to us," he recalled about the initial rejection. "The photographs of course disclosed these huge craters, that B-52 bombings had been going on for some time—a year or more—and we weren't aware of it."[4] The same was true for my father though; word came down that under no circumstances were American advisors allowed to accompany the ARVN into any neighboring country.[5]

Besides the excitement over Cambodia, no Saint Patrick's Day bar crawls occurred. Instead, the month was filled with ambushes, helicopter assaults, and de bo RIFs looking for a fight—with grenades plopped into every water source to kill all the fish as they went. As always, anyone captured was thrown a beating to try to get a juicy morsel to act on. Lately, the ARVN had landed on a new technique to elicit information—repeated rounds of questioning in-between suffocation with a plastic bag. "The old plastic over the face trick," as my father called it in his diary, had varying degrees of success—just as the beatings did.[6]

Scorching heat during the day followed by soaking-wet night operations hiding in paddies and dykes was getting old. "Boy, I sure wish that date up in the right-hand corner was April instead of March," he wrote home.[7] Especially since his trousers were in such disrepair that they had gaping holes in them—the mosquitoes had direct access to his nuts now. To temper it some, at least the ARVN had worked out some of their resupply issues. For the first time, he got some decent drinking water to put in his canteens that did not need multiple iodine tablets.[8] He also got a hot shower in base camp. No running hot water, no problem—just fill up a garbage pail and let it sit out all day. An instant warm shower when you return. All he needed now was some chow from home. "Her brother can't keep his perfect round shape," he begged the family to remind Momi, "unless she gets on the ball and sends some cookies, mainly chocolate chips."[9]

The occasional thrashings and suffocations did lead the ARVN to some unexpected and ingenious enemy locations. The tunnels found were deep, expansive, and showed up in surprising places. Shockingly, one intricate underground structure was found just 200 meters from the US 25th Infantry Division's Firebase Devon.[10] However, before they could let the 25th know, an Air Force F111 tore in and lined up on them for a bombing run.[11] After another frantic wave off and averted disaster, the US 25th commander made his men comb every inch of ground 1,000 meters around Devon.[12] ARVN operations were paying off it seemed, finding things right in front of the Americans' eyes. They were even getting easier for my father now that SGT Brown was fully trained to advise on his own, including one close call with a white phosphorus booby-trapped grenade which almost seared Brown good.[13]

With Brown pulling some ops now, my father was finally able to catch a break and take a day of rest. He did what many new soldiers do on their first deployment—he bought a car, long distance and tax free. A 1970 American Motors Gremlin. I myself was almost talked into buying a Ford Mustang while in Iraq by a smooth-talking Irishman. With its black interior, matador red exterior with black dual pin stripes, and a tail which looked like someone had kicked in its ass, my father could not wait to be back in the world. The car's unforgettable symbol, he mused, looked "like a fat little Menehune or a wee leprechaun but not a gremlin."[14]

He also used some of his free time to reconnect with his best ARVN friend 1LT Hương Bain, who had just returned to the unit after spending six weeks in hospital recovering from a combat wound. My father was helping him perfect his English and he, his Vietnamese. He was happy to have him back alive to continue the lessons.[15] To help learn, Bain took him to a Vietnamese USO type show, with colorful props and characters. He could not understand the words but was able to generally tell what was happening.[16] Bain also helped him share an article with the other Vietnamese that my grandfather wrote about his time studying rocks brought back from the moon by Apollo 11. Something was lost in translation, though. Their maid claimed my grandfather, with his bald head, mustache, and goatee, was actually Hồ Chí Minh. One swore he was Comrade Lenin and would not believe otherwise. Another ARVN officer politely said that he thought it was nice that his brother was a "moon scientist" before going back to eating.[17]

Finally, my father got to close out the month by covering down for Keller while he was on leave. He was able to spend time in the command-and-control Loach helicopter versus humping it out on the ground, using his aerial viewpoint to direct fire on anybody he saw on the ground in the free-fire zones. "My decision to shoot," he reasoned in his diary, "no qualms, if they run, we shoot."[18] This spurred another movie reminder from my childhood. Who can forget the door gunner in *Full Metal Jacket* as he blasts away at anyone he sees from his helicopter? "Anyone who runs is a VC," he gleefully explains, "anyone who stands still is a well-disciplined VC!"[19]

Final statistics for the month of March: 32 enemy killed and two apprehended. So much for capturing versus killing. Luckily, only 11 ARVN were wounded during operations. Ten AK-47s, one M-16, 9nine rounds of 75-millimeter ammo, one Russian Degtyaryov light machine gun, one M-79, and 20 old Russian bolt-action rifles were the weapons seized. Also seized were tons of documents, 20 broken watches, and some M2A2 gas masks.[20] Finally, in the comic strip that month Nguyen Charlie's boss Comrade Commander was upset because he and his wife had not been invited to the ditch party. The hapless VC had abandoned an attack on the Yang Khi to do a group date night and not invited his boss.[21]

Besides that bit of dry humor, "not much else is happening," my father wrote home to the family. "We are still killing Cong and getting shot at."[22] That was March—monotony interrupted by brief bursts of intense violence, although two events still stuck out to my father.

Ten Kilometers North of Trung Lập near Highway 7A, Vietnam; March 1970: The enemy had messed up. A group of Cobras and Huey gunships were just minding their own business when they received small arms fire from some enemy ground troops. They could not believe their eyes as they saw upwards of 30 enemy soldiers scurrying around. As they circled around to unleash fire from the sky on them, the all-call went out. "Someone, anyone, come get these motherfuckers," broadcasted the message to friendly forces, thus initiating the largest engagement of the month. The closest ground troops? My father and his 24 men jammed into two slicks flying nearby on their way to an unrelated mission.[23] Designed to only hold eight, you could fit just about anything into a chopper bay if you tried. In my day, we once shoved 27 fully loaded soldiers into a Blackhawk helicopter designed to hold 11.

Diverted, he and his men sped towards the contact, knowing that for a little while at least they might be outnumbered. Later, he remembered boasting with the other advisors on the mission about how awesome it was to be first in. Internally he thought differently: "Usually we get in contact so fast that you don't have time to think about it until it is over," he recalled. This time it was different, though. "I knew I was going in after Mr. Charles and frankly I was scared shitless." Landing 500 meters short of the sighting, he got his men online as the gunships fired overhead.[24]

As he advanced, the air cover was so intense that the enemy could barely target the ARVN moving in on them. Luckily, his meager force was augmented by several other helicopters that discharged 96 additional soldiers. The ARVN swarmed the enemy complex, trapping many in the open before they could enter their hidden tunnels. They killed nine before they scurried down their holes—one of which was a woman. In the aftermath, he found identification on two men: Lê Văn Tống and Nguyễn Văn Bách. Tống had a North Vietnamese postage stamp from 1966 which depicts the defense of Con Co island from South Vietnamese airstrikes. This stamp still survives from among my father's war things. Soberingly, he realized for the first time ever that the enemy were real people, with real names.[25]

They remained in the tunnel complex—which ended up being three stories deep at least—all day, trying to ferret out more human moles. However, dangerous booby traps were everywhere. Eventually, the juice was no longer worth the squeeze; just pump them full of smoke and blow the openings, he directed. Interestingly, by this point in his war my father had stopped recording whether the bad guys he faced were VC or NVA. "I usually don't stop to ask until the shooting stops," he finally reasoned, and by that point who cares who they were anyway? He was just happy to be alive.[26] Bad guy note to self—next time let the attack helicopters fly by unmolested when you only have rifles to fire on them.

Gò Nổi, Vietnam; March 1970: Ten days later, the second most memorable event of the month occurred.[27] Curiously, it would be decades before anyone realized the importance of it.

On May 13, 1969, just before the start of the rainy season, Bravo Company, 1st Battalion of the 508th Infantry from the 82nd Airborne, moved in on the Village of Gò Nổi to conduct a search. It was a sister unit to my father's when he was with the 82nd. Machine-gun teams were deployed to cover the flanks as the search was conducted. Nothing found, the company moved on to set in for a night defensive position. It was then that they discovered to their surprise that two soldiers were missing.[28] Unfortunately, the normal platoon leader for the pair was taking his R&R at that time and was shocked to hear what had happened when he returned. "I had made it a habit of making sure all were accounted for before we set out for a new destination," he told me angrily. "How an important machine gun crew could be left behind is beyond belief."[29]

After the US unit had left the area, several villagers rushed excitedly to tell the local VC operatives about an astonishing sight. Two sleeping Americans were resting their heads on an earthen foundation outside of an abandoned house on the outskirts of the village, with an M-60 machine gun in-between them. Not believing the news, Lê Thanh Sơn and Huynh Van Mết stealthily crept up on the unsuspecting duo to investigate closer. As they neared, one of the men stirred, which prompted Mết to swiftly lob three grenades in succession towards the sleeping pair. After the deafening crack of the bombs, Sơn rushed forward through the kicked-up dust and debris and raked the two bodies with AK-47 fire, killing Specialist Robert S. Masuda and Private First Class David L. Munoz where they lay.[30]

The two VC quickly gathered up the usable American weapons, ammo, and gear and fled the area. Before they left, they also took the men's dog tags, identification, and wallets, ultimately hoping they contained money. Later, Sơn and Mết received a Bằng Khen (Certificate of Reward) for their efforts. Before they departed, they did leave behind a message for the Americans. Pleased with their actions, and as is the way with all guerrillas, the two men faded into the background, leaving the villagers to clean up the mess.[31] The local populace is always the loser in an insurgency.

The residents knew they would be screwed when the Americans came back and found the two dead and grenade-mangled bodies. The solution they came up with? Wrap the body parts in plastic sheets and dump them into a nearby well. By the time they started dragging them towards the 5-meter deep well, more local VC had shown up. Their bright idea to help with the situation? Booby-trap the remains. The villagers had no choice but to go along with their plan. The rigged bodies were tossed in and covered with wet soil the best they could.[32]

The next day, aided by helicopters flying overhead broadcasting in Vietnamese a reward for information on the two missing Americans, the 82nd returned.[33] It was then they found the message left by Sơn and Mết before they bolted. A bloody 82nd Airborne patch nailed to a tree with an AK-47 round. They also found a pack of playing cards believed to have belonged to Masuda and a 4-inch piece of scalp covered in black hair.[34]

The Americans also found the well with blood splatter around it. Upset, they attempted to force some of the villagers to enter the hole to investigate, which of course they refused. One of the VC who had killed the pair was hidden in a tree about 100 meters away, from where he watched what happened next. A US soldier cautiously climbed into the well as two others leaned far over the opening to watch. Suddenly, the man in the hole triggered one of the traps; with a roar, the explosion threw all three men out of the well. With three wounded soldiers and deep in enemy territory, the 82nd called it a day. The war took over and the bodies were never recovered, and their exact location was forgotten.[35] Local lore has it that the caved-in well glowed at night for years afterwards due to the phosphorus from the "many bones" that it contained.[36]

"A long time has passed since Robert and David were lost," their old platoon leader sadly told me years later. "I think of them frequently ... such a waste of youth and enthusiasm."[37] Another man from the platoon posted several messages online to their memorial pages. "I went back to look for you," he wrote to Masuda, "damn, why did they pull us out!"[38] Racked with guilt, as he was the last man to leave the village, it haunted him for the rest of his life. "Long nights and hard memories," he further wrote anonymously, "I wish I could have helped."[39] Masuda and Munoz's bodies were never recovered, and they were listed as Missing in Action (MIA) for years. Their names did not appear on the Paris Peace Accords Prisoner of War (POW) lists in 1973.[40] Because of this and the inability to find any remains, in March 1976 both men were categorized as killed in action.[41] This enabled all their past pay, allowances, and gratuities to finally be paid to the families.[42]

What did all of this have to do with my father? In March 1970, his unit received some intel and were sent to dig up the reported remains of two Americans dumped into a well but were pulled away before they could finish. Official records recall the 1969, 1975, 1994, 1999, and 2013 attempts to find their bodies. However, none mention the 1970 attempt by the ARVN my father was with.[43] Masuda and Munoz's cases are still categorized as "Active Pursuit" by the Defense POW/MIA Accounting Agency (DPAA). Even though their files are still open, they do note the extreme challenge behind any attempt to recover them. The area has been cultivated multiple times with fruit, sugar cane, and rubber trees, completely changing the terrain and obscuring any signs of old wells in the area.[44]

The most interesting thing about my father's 1970 search concerns the location. Past reports have generally focused on several grid coordinates as being the location for the well. My father's diary lists a different location; similar, but not an exact match to the past searches.[45] At the time of this publication, with this new information provided by me, the DPAA is writing an excavation proposal to be internally staffed to decide if another physical search should be conducted. I really hope my father's diary helps bring them home.

My generation's wars did not experience the tragedy of soldiers never returning home. Due to technology and the controlled nature of how the conflicts were fought, few found themselves alone and out of touch without some type of coalition support or tracking. This had a direct impact on why no Americans from these wars are still declared as MIA or POWs.

Our most memorable cases, Jessica Lynch and Bowe Bergdahl, both ended up being recovered. This contrasts with Vietnam, where over 1,500 Americans are still unaccounted for.[46] The favorite storyline for a slew of 1980s movies on Vietnam that I grew up on was the US government's conspiracy to avoid admitting that POWs were still being held and the subsequent heroic attempts to recover them while also violently crushing their Vietnamese captors. My friends and I played this same scenario countless times in the jungles surrounding our house in Hawai'i growing up.

Nixon was accused by some of using the POWs' plight to counter the anti-war movement with tales of the North Vietnamese captors' atrocities and of shifting the narrative away from the prolonged war. Nixon disputed this in his 1985 biography, claiming that many in the POW advocacy group the League of Families supported his administration's policies, which rejected the demands of "antiwar politicians that we accept defeat and simply withdraw our forces in exchange for our POWs."[47] Another twisted political game from the Vietnam War.

The only exposure to the MIA phenomenon for my generation has been one probably not even noticed by most. In November 2019, the National POW/MIA Flag Act was signed into law. This act, led by a bipartisan team of senators and representatives, amended Section 902 of Title 36, US Code. It now reads that the flag be displayed every day that the US flag is. Before this law, it was only flown six times a year.[48] Don't believe me? Look around at every federal building and you will see the iconic black and white POW/MIA flag, depicting the head-bowed silhouette of a captive. Show all who will listen, so that we can always remember those who never came home.

Chapter 26

"The most unhappy thing …"

PATRICK W. NAUGHTON SR.

I was with family when the call came on the cold Christmas Eve of 2008. "I need your help, Sir," said the master sergeant (MSG) from my unit on the other end of the line. She had just been designated as a casualty notification officer (CNO): the person tasked by the Army to let the next of kin know that their loved one has lost their life in the line of duty. Usually, a chaplain comes along to offer solace; I don't remember why they couldn't find one, but I was tagged to accompany her as the CNO never went alone. Changed into our dress uniforms, we drove hours through dark, snowy countryside, eventually arriving at an isolated, nondescript house in the middle of nowhere.

The lights from the Christmas tree in the front window illuminated the driveway as our footfalls in the freshly falling snow broke the silence on that quiet night. On ringing the bell, the door was answered by an older man, surprised to see two uniformed soldiers on his doorstep at 11:00pm on Christmas Eve. We inquired as to whether this was the house of the wife of a soldier who, unbeknownst to them at the time, had just died in Iraq. Instead of a yes or no, we got back a slurred, "Well … depends on what you mean by wife," from the man, who identified himself as the father of the house. We immediately realized that the man was falling-down blind drunk.

As we tried to decipher what he was saying, a demure young girl with shoulder-length blond hair appeared at his shoulder. She asked if we were there about a soldier, giving us the name of the man who had been killed. Before we could answer her, the young woman's increasingly belligerent father interrupted, trying to block our access to her. As she now sat, cross-legged, on the floor behind him, staring at the ground in front of her, he continued to answer our inquiries with vague responses and riddles that only made sense to the drunk giving them.

As we stood on the freezing doorstep, answering stupid questions, it started to snow hard. Unsure of what to do now, the MSG and I returned to my truck and called the Casualty Assistance Center (CAC) for further instructions. We explained that unless we could somehow remove the inebriated father, we would not be able to confirm if this was the spouse of the deceased soldier. As we waited for the CAC to call us back with further instructions, the man now stood feet from my driver's side window. Staring at us, he swayed unsteadily back and forth as only seasoned drunks can do.

After what seemed like hours of trying to not make eye contact with the smashed sentinel, the CAC finally called us back. The answer? We were to make the call whether to notify or not. The MSG and I locked eyes, an unspoken understanding passed between us as we both simultaneously exited the vehicle, quickly trudging past the man straight to the young woman in the doorway. We asked her if we could come in just as her staggering and loudly protesting father caught up with us. Finally in the house, the warmth of the room enveloped us as we prepared to make the notification. Before us stood a young girl, probably no more than 19 years old, with big questioning eyes, wondering what was going on.

"The secretary of the army has asked me to express his deep regret," started the MSG before choking up with emotion. She pleadingly looked at me and silently mouthed, "I can't." I took the notification from her and continued to read, "that your husband was killed in action on December 24, 2008 … the secretary extends his deepest sympathy to you and your family in your tragic loss." She just stared at us and said nothing. "Well, they actually are divorced," finally interjected the smashed father with a smug look on his face. What a jerk—he knew all along that this was no longer the soldier's wife. He then told us that he was going to call the soldier's parents to let them know. The Army notifies the immediate next of kin first before moving on. In this case, if they were still married it would have been the wife and then the parents. The soldier had never updated his Department of Defense Form 93, Record of Emergency Data since his divorce—the Army still thought he was married.

We tried to talk him out of it but there was nothing we could do to stop him. Sadly, the parents of the deceased soldier had to find out that their son had died in Iraq on Christmas Eve from his drunken, loudmouthed ex-father-in-law. The family notification of soldiers killed in combat is horrendous.

Cambodian Border with Vietnam; April 1970: My father was short, like a snake-could-crawl-over-him-standing-without-its-belly-ever-leaving-the-ground short (as the saying went from the time). "Until I board the plane, I will be sleeping in flak jacket and steel pot," he half-jokingly told the family. "I'll probably low crawl from Trung Lập to Đức Hòa to Tân Sơn Nhứt to make sure I get there in one piece."[1]

As he counted down the days in single digits, the fighting in Cambodia, where the enemy had often reconstituted unmolested, was heating up. As noted in an official press release by MACV, "The change of government in Cambodia has caused the enemy great concern over the status of his border sanctuaries;" in their words, things had grown quite "tense" at the border.[2] Taking advantage of the government shakeup up and the growing civil war there, two battalions and one cavalry squadron from the regiment chased the enemy back and forth between the two countries for a week. "Charles used to stand on the border and stick his tongue out," my father told the family, but now they were getting their shit pushed in. Forty enemy killed in the first day alone. They also scooped up all kinds of prisoners, captured documents, and even heavy weapons systems such as anti-aircraft guns.[3]

Despite the unique opportunity to strike the enemy in their hideouts, advisors still could not accompany the ARVN into Cambodia. They would participate in the movement towards the border and then be extracted by helicopter 2 kilometers short. In the meantime, they sat at Trung Lập and dodged indirect fire as the ARVN put in work on their own. On the return, the advisors would be reinserted once the ARVN were within 2 kilometers of Vietnamese territory.[4] "I had no feel for US or Vietnamese intelligence or objectives," Keller would later state about their time supporting operations there. "In retrospect," he said, summing up their actions, "I felt this was an incursion into logistical areas to buy time for ARVN to mature Vietnamization and prepare for future fights as the US forces departed Vietnam."[5] Many wondered to themselves why hadn't we gone into Cambodia all along—especially since it was obvious that it was an enemy stronghold based on all the Cambodian cigarette and candy wrappers the ARVN would often find in the tunnels.[6] Abrams too, silently asked himself this very question, clenching his teeth in frustration every time the nation was mentioned.[7]

Regardless of the goals in Cambodia, Vietnamization was accelerating at a rapid clip, driven by political desires to extricate US forces faster than each troop withdrawal timetable originally dictated. Only 429,200 American troops remained in country by mid-April—down 114,282 since my father had arrived a year earlier.[8] Several days later, Nixon, reading from a set of scripted notes, announced via a televised address to the nation that 150,000 additional men would leave Vietnam by next year. His decision, he announced, was "based entirely on the progress of our Vietnamization program."[9]

Despite the lack of clear objectives, the ARVN had done well in Cambodia and had really taken it to the enemy. Keller was excitedly presented with a large, captured solid-red-with-white-hammer-and-sickle international communist flag.[10] Later, Keller would present this flag to an Air Force Cessna O-1 Bird Dog pilot; these were small propeller planes which were used as forward air controllers for ground forces during the war due to their slow speed and ability to easily circle target areas once in contact. In an especially hectic engagement at a tunnel complex near Trung Lập, Keller found himself unable to contact any US artillery or air support. Noticing the Bird Dog far off in the distance, he flashed his handheld survival mirror at him and then popped green smoke. "Guy on the ground, this is guy in the air," soon squelched the radio. Somehow, the pilot had found Keller's frequency and soon poured in all the air support he needed to beat back the enemy who, by this point, had surrounded him. After some research, Keller was able to track down the pilot who saved his unit. Driving to Củ Chi, he presented him with the flag and shared a shot of Scotch with him.[11]

My father received a smaller unit flag with Phạm Văn Cội Unit embroidered on it. It was named after a local VC hero from Củ Chi who was credited with killing many Americans until he was slain in 1967.[12] I possess that small guidon now. As a child, I swore to any friends who would listen that some dirt marks on it were actually enemy blood.

Bình Dương Province, Vietnam; April 1970: There was no time for congratulations on the successes in Cambodia as the day after operations there, SGT Brown steeled himself for his next mission. As the choppers deposited his men in another unnamed patch of dirt in the free-fire zone to look for enemy activity, Brown's eyes and ears adjusted from the noisy helicopters to the quiet countryside as he began his operation with the ARVN company. Half an hour after landing, the whole world unexpectedly opened up on their thus-far peaceful patrol, shattering the stillness. Automatic weapons, recoilless rifles, and B-40 rockets rained in on the surprised company and pinned them down.[13]

My father's war was done. As he sat in the Vietnamese Officer Club drinking a Coke and thinking about the future, someone burst in and said that Brown's group was in deep shit, and that they had negative comms with him.[14] Without any direction and on his own initiative, he quickly organized a rescue mission. He then went a step further and made himself the lead for it. True to his word, he threw on his flak vest, the first time he had ever worn it, jumped into the bird, and flew towards the unknown.[15]

As the helicopter descended towards the hot landing zone, the first thing my father noticed was the crumpled and lifeless naked body of Brown, his pale skin in sharp contrast to the green foliage he lay in.[16] "What the fuck?" he thought—but he had to deal with that later. First step, neutralize the enemy attack. While dodging direct fire, he immediately keyed his most powerful weapon and called in repeated air strikes via jets and gunships until the firing slacked off. He then coordinated the medical evacuation of 13 wounded as the ARVN organized a counterattack, drove the enemy off, and secured the area.[17]

Keller was flying overhead in a command Loach, trying to coordinate between the Vietnamese on the ground and US support channels. The radio chatter was broken by a simple broadcast from my father. Using Brown's call sign, which ended in Kilo, he reported, "Kilo is kilo [for killed]. I'll evacuate him." Keller, as were all the men on the advisory team, was stunned by the news.[18]

As he gingerly loaded Brown's body into the evacuation chopper, he wondered why he was naked. As the noise from the departing bird receded, he looked around at the ARVN, many of whom refused to make eye contact. He quickly realized that they had stripped his body and stolen everything. "Motherfuckers," he thought. They took his entire uniform, boots, web gear, wallet (with $120), watch, and college ring—everything. He informed Keller; however, with his role advising senior ARVN officers he also did his best to persuade them to return the items, but he could not direct them to do anything.

Tahir, in his usual outspoken manner, approached it a little differently. "You sons of bitches, you traitorous assholes," he fumed to the ARVN company commanders, "you give back that shit or I'll never go on another mission with you guys. And if I'm forced to … I'll turn my fucking radio off."[19] Brown's items were slowly returned. First his watch and then his boots, which my father noticed his radiomen wearing as Brown had inked his name on the back of the boot tops.[20] Needless to say, Team 99 was beyond upset.[21]

My father sadly returned to Trung Lập and dropped his gear in his hooch. It was only then that he realized he was dripping with sweat and was on the verge of passing out from the adrenaline drain and the damn flak jacket.[22] "I guess I was afraid of getting killed just before going home," he later reasoned as to why he wore it.[23] He hydrated and prepared himself to go to Saigon to positively identify Brown's body for grave registration.[24] "Much has happened since last I wrote," he dejectedly wrote the family in one of his last letters of the war, "including the most unhappy thing that I've experienced in my year over here."[25] No more Nguyen Charlie cartoons this month to lighten the mood.

My father ended up not having to identify Brown's body as someone beat him to it. Brown's buddy, Jim Brewer, who had gone through basic training and the NCO academy with him before flying in a helicopter to their respective base camps in Vietnam, had just returned from an operation with the ARVN's 3rd Battalion from the 46th Regiment. "My God, Brewer, what are you doing here?" bellowed his shocked team leader upon seeing him. Brewer had been listed as killed in action at headquarters. Turns out that during that chopper ride several weeks earlier, Brown had been dropped off at the 1/49th when he should have been dropped at the 3/46th.[26]

The Army was tracking that Brewer was Brown, and vice versa, and that that he had been killed. Therefore, he was called to Saigon to straighten it all out and identify the body. Trying to find out how his friend died, Brewer and my father spoke years later about what had happened, which helped Brewer get some closure. "In essence," he told me when we connected, "he died in my place."[27] In loving memory of Brown and the friendship he had for him, Brewer named his first son Gary.[28]

In 2012, Keller was video interviewed as part of a Boy Scout Veterans History Project, which was later archived with the Library of Congress. In it, he was asked, "What was the bravest action, friendly or enemy, that you witnessed in your time in Southeast Asia?" This was long before I met him—imagine my surprise as I heard him tell the story of my father organizing the rescue of Brown. Two tours in Vietnam and retiring as a LTG and it was my father and his actions that he remembered the most. "He thought he might be going in there to save him [Brown]," he recalled with a straight face and no embellishment; being only days out from leaving, "he really didn't have to go in there and do that."[29] "I was extremely proud of your Dad," he humbly told me when I asked him about it in person, "on short notice at the end of his tour, doing this courageous thing on behalf of all of us and SGT Brown to recover an American soldier's remains from the battlefield ... it was a tragic time for all of us."[30]

"Your dad's a great guy ... a brave guy," Tahir echoed when I asked him his opinion of my father as a soldier. "He was in the last week of his tour, and we had short timer calendars, and usually in the last week you didn't have to do anything to jeopardize your life," he explained about how my father went above and beyond what was expected of him when he went to get Brown.[31]

For "heroism in connection with military operations against a hostile force" my father was eventually awarded the Bronze Star with V (for Valor) Device.[32] He did not feel like a hero. "Didn't really do much except coordinate gunships and air force strikes," he humbly recorded in his diary; "didn't feel too scared going into area—only after ops was over." Regardless, this was his last time in the field.[33] He never talked about it while I was growing up, and my only knowledge of it was gained by reading the citation as I hid behind the couch as a child. Rereading it as an adult and veteran was a very different experience. For some reason, I remember it being this graphic description of him as a Rambo-type figure jumping into the jungle, carrying out all the wounded singlehandedly while under fire, and then slaughtering all the enemy. The real write-up was, of course, more subdued—it is funny what we remember from our childhood.

He was not presented his award until months later when he was closing out his military time at Fort Benning. Same for his Air Medals, which were eventually sent to the family's address in Hawai'i.[34] Neither would have arrived if Keller had not fought for them. Several months after my father departed Vietnam, Keller went to MACV headquarters for the second time to find out where my father's awards were. Tossing the desks in the admin offices, he found them still sitting there, unprocessed. He took them straight to the senior personnel officer, who then called the CPT in charge and gave him some "pretty specific guidance" to get them completed and mailed out.[35]

Interestingly, as Keller tore the desks apart in the admin office, he found three Purple Hearts and a Bronze Star with V, all in the name of one of the personnel clerks, Darrell Winkler. "The SOB 'won' all of them behind his desk!" wrote Keller to my father. Needless to say, he reported that pogue RAMF right away.[36] I asked my father if this sort of thing was common in Vietnam. "There were a few of these chair-borne awardees around," he told me. When he was XO with the 82nd he always double-checked the award lists to make sure that kind of thing was not happening in his company.[37]

Tahir ran into this same clerk years later at an Army course where Winkler was somehow now a major. Not only was he wearing a slew of unearned combat decorations, but he had also somehow faked an officer's commission.[38] Eventually, the Army caught and confronted him. Rather than be charged, he went AWOL and dropped out of American society. Winkler reappeared years later, representing himself as a mercenary for hire, an ex-US Army major who had done three combat tours in Vietnam. "I resigned from the US Army because I was tired of it," he claimed when asked about his past, conveniently failing to mention that he was kicked out. With his manufactured cover story intact, he maneuvered himself to become the commander of a Rhodesian armored car regiment battling communists in Africa, nicknamed the Black Devils. He was even featured on the cover of *Soldier of Fortune* magazine before disappearing once more, never to be heard from again.[39]

The quest for combat recognition is all-consuming for some. I'll never forget several soldiers I served with in Iraq who were riding in a cargo plane that received AK-47 fire. They immediately demanded that they receive the Army's new Combat Action Badge (CAB). Our commander, rightfully so, told them absolutely not; unless you directly engaged in ground combat you were not getting a CAB. I remember another who was red-faced, muttering curse words under his breath, kicking rocks on the ground like a toddler as he stormed off upon hearing that he was not getting an award he thought he deserved. It seems that these PX Rangers are present in every war, but Winkler by far wins the prize for cheesedick of the century.

Broken little PX Ranger hearts aside, from all of this I only have one hope—that the Brown family had a better notification of his death than the one I participated in. I do know that his eldest sister is in possession of his footlocker, which my father would have inventoried, gone through to remove anything offensive, packed, and then shipped to his family. It is with her still and has never been opened.[40] I tried to contact his other surviving sisters but could not get in touch with them. And I know I have the right contact information for them. "A lot of this stuff is painful," Tahir explained to me on the probable reasons for their lack of replies. "Very painful memories," he said as his voice trailed off.[41]

Gary Brown was 21 when he died—never married and had no kids. He did have a sweetheart who he tried to keep in touch with, but as often happens in those types of relationships, distance and the Army got in the way. They did their best to keep in contact by letters, which slowly drifted off as he did his training and then shipped to Vietnam. Then suddenly, abruptly, she heard that he had been killed. "That broke my heart," she told me about hearing the news. Even after five decades, she still thinks of him, "I've always carried a warm spot in my heart for Gary," she solemnly said, "still do."[42]

Chapter 27

"Vietnam Fini ..."

PATRICK W. NAUGHTON SR.

My return from Iraq was a whirlwind. I was cross leveled into my unit, meaning that I was transferred in from another organization and would not return home with the bulk of the soldiers. The Task Force I was a part of flew together on a charter plane to the then-named Fort Hood, Texas. In the global war on terror, units came and went overseas as one, unlike Vietnam, where individuals deployed by themselves. Along the way, we stopped in Germany, where all the men crowded around several tiny sinks and shared razors to shave so we would look presentable for some reason when we landed in Texas. No one met us on the tarmac, so I am not sure why we all felt that was something important that we needed to do.

Once there, I spent two days out-processing before being dropped off at the Killen airport by myself, with a one-way ticket to Wichita, Kansas. The sunflower state was where I had stored my truck before deployment. I needed to recover it so I could drive across the country to Ohio to meet the movers at my storage unit. Then I had to drive again to report to my new assignment at Fort Douglas, Utah—all in a week's time. Military life can be grand sometimes.

It was a Monday night in Wichita, and I was back from war. Within five days I had gone from the sprawling metropolis of Baghdad, dodging indirect fire, to a small sleepy Kansas town. Obviously, I needed a drink before I drove the next day. After recovering my truck from a storage unit, where I had paid the hillbilly who owned it to start it once a month so it would not die, which he did not do, I had to get it working again. Once that was accomplished, I headed to the nearest bar I could find to hopefully try my luck again by handing out some Saddam money.

Of course, the only open bar within walking distance—this was before the days of Uber—was mostly empty, but that didn't matter. As I nursed my beer alone, I noticed that small groups of men were staring, whispering to each other, and smiling at me, but in a way I was not used to. As I acted like I hadn't noticed, I racked my brain as to what was happening. As I looked around, I slowly noticed rainbow flags arrayed around the room. Oh man, I was in a gay bar—no money to pass out here. It had been so long that my bar identification game was weak. I finished my beer and went to bed. Nothing against the place, just not my scene. I hadn't been in Iraq *that* long.

The next morning, I packed my gear and got ready to leave. My uniform, with its subdued American flag that is only worn when deployed, still lay on the chair where I had left it the night before. I should have driven cross-country in civilian clothes, but for some reason I put it back on. I had devolved into that which I hate the most: a cheesedick starved for attention. To this day I still do not know why I did it. I guess I was not ready to turn it off. I had just spent a year in Iraq and as I drove across America, I guess I just wanted someone to notice me. Someone to ask me how I was doing and where I had been … none of which happened. Life had just gone on as normal for everyone back in the US.

Two weeks later, something monumental did occur, though. On Monday May 2, 2011, Osama bin Laden was killed by US special forces. I was back in Ohio closing out my move when the news broke. I rushed outside my hotel room, thinking that I would walk smack dab into a celebration, like what was being shown on TV. Instead, the streets were dead quiet; nothing was happening. The only bar I could find still open was the one in my hotel lobby. It seemed sitting alone in lonely bars was becoming a habit. As I nursed my drink, trying not to make eye contact with the bartender, who just wanted me to leave so he could close, my thoughts drifted back to all the sacrifices I had seen over the years of conflict. In wars with no triumphs, no parades, and nothing measurable that we could point to as a win, I'm not sure why I expected a victory celebration to spontaneously break out.

Thankfully, I never experienced anti-war demonstrations like my father's generation did. However, I do feel like I experienced anti-war apathy. The all-volunteer force bore the full burden of the war against terror while everyone else went on with their life. I can't blame them I guess; I mean no one forced us to raise our hand. We get lots of discounts and thank-you-for-your-service coffees bought. That is appreciated, but it is hard not to be bitter because you felt pride knowing that we finally got the bastard who attacked us on September 11th only to be met with crazy looks because you wanted to share some high fives. Apathy; better than marches and getting spit on, though.

It's funny, I don't remember any kind of homecoming for me. I was thrown so quickly back into circulation by the Army that I never had a chance to take a pause and reconnect with family. I had just returned from Iraq and was given seven days to report to my new unit. No leave or anything. I am embarrassed to admit that I am not sure why I did not make time for them. It is something I deeply regret.

Honolulu, Hawai'i; April 1970: Just before my father left Vietnam, he wrote his best letter home yet; "See you next week Friday," he simply told the family.[1] Saying goodbye to Team 99, he jumped in a jeep to spend two days clearing at Đức Hòa before flying in his last helicopter to Tân Sơn Nhứt.[2] He then spent another two days at the sprawling air base, taking multiple hot showers and turning in his gear.[3]

Several weeks earlier, he had worked another Hawai'i connection with a local boy who handled transportation. He was able to get my father booked on the shortest flight back home that he could find. The route was the same as when he arrived, only in reverse—Vietnam, Philippines, Guam, then Hawai'i.[4] Only this time, no postcards were sent along the way. Just before he departed, he was given another pamphlet from the Army, called *Tour 365*. It was designed to be handed to the soldiers as they left Vietnam; a feel-good item that recapped the past events of the year and contained a note from the commanding general that acknowledged them for their "help in accomplishing our task in Vietnam and my thanks for a job well done."[5] It was better than anything we got handed on the way home.

As the plane steeply gained altitude to avoid being shot at on the way out, there was no cheering as the aircraft left Vietnamese air space, as some believe. The same stewardess who saw death in the eyes of some departing for Vietnam noticed something else on the way back. "You absolutely saw a different look in their eyes on the way home," she somberly remembered.[6]

Surprisingly, there was another Hawai'i connection on the long flight home on April 24. Sitting next to my father was a Navy officer who the family knew well. He was married to my Uncle John's old high-school sweetheart. In-between reminiscing about people they knew at home, they both caught up on sleep.[7] That is, until my father had his first attack of typhus on the last leg of the flight. Caused by infected fleas, it meant he spent hours huddled under a blanket, racked with chills.[8] Luckily, the attack had passed by the time he landed at 6:00am local time. Due to crossing the international date line, this was one hour earlier than he had left Vietnam.[9]

Unlike most of those on the plane, who still had another flight ahead of them to get to Travis AFB before going home, with the stop in Hawai'i my father was already there. My Tutu, Grandpa, Auntie Momi, Uncle John, and his wife Anne-Marie were all there to greet him with aloha—along with my two toddler cousins Tom and Sean. At Travis, the only thing greeting the soldiers were anti-war protestors outside the airport and the same stewardesses with forced smiles on the tarmac.[10]

A picture exists which captures the moment my father landed. He stands in the same khakis he went to war with, draped in flower leis, arm in arm with my grandfather, both faces gleaming. Tutu is half out of the picture, holding one of the toddlers. She, too, has a smile on her face, all ecstatic that their son had made it home safe. In his right hand, my father holds the captured SKS given to him by the ARVN executive two weeks earlier, which he registered as a war trophy and was able to take home. Long gone are the days when you can just take home a semi-automatic assault rifle from war.[11] He immediately handed the weapon to his brother as a gift.[12] Concerned about having a rifle in their home, my father later took it back. I still remember sneaking away with it as a kid and running around in the woods, chasing imaginary VC with a real weapon that had once belonged to them. Later, my father donated it to his alma mater, the UH ROTC program. A spoil of war, it resides there still.

The family gathered at the Mānoa Valley home and had a large dinner. My father poured out his duffle bag on the living room floor as his two nephews dive bombed into it to play with his uniforms. Both spent hours clomping around the house in his combat boots.[13] I remember my father used to mow the grass in those same boots before they eventually rotted away in the wet Hawai'i climate. In between the celebrations and boot stomping, with a sense of relief, my grandfather finally tucked away his map of Vietnam for good. He used to sit each night glued to the news, using the map to track the fighting in relation to where his son was located—hoping he was okay. Momi remembered that sense of relief he was home, thinking back on all those that they knew who died: "I think we were all so afraid he would not come home, as others we knew didn't."[14]

"I want to emphasize that the most important requirement," stressed SECDEF Laird just after my father left Vietnam, on the key to ending the war favorably, "is to maintain the forward momentum of our Vietnamization program."[15] A statement which rang hollow as my father thought back on Brown and the others he knew who had lost their lives. Regardless, all that was over now. "Vietnam *Fini*," French for finished, made up my father's last diary entry on the day he landed in Hawai'i.[16] If only it were that easy.

Chapter 28

"You don't know what the fuck you're talking about ..."

ALIC TAHIR

My wife and I lived in the Capitol Hill neighborhood of Washington, DC during the height of the coronavirus pandemic. Each night after dinner, we usually went for a walk. We started at Lincoln Park, where we rented, before walking through the charming historic neighborhood via East Capitol Street, trying to peek into the beautiful rowhouses to see how the other half lived before walking down the steep hill on one side of the Capitol Building. We would then head back up the hill on the other side to return home. It was always an inspiring sight—the majestic dome towering over the city.

One thing you get used to when living in DC, especially the Capitol Hill area, is protestors. Just as it was during the Vietnam era, there is always someone marching with signs, screaming to be heard, mainly at the Capitol Building, the Supreme Court, or the White House. The year we lived there was different, though. The normally small crowds of young white professional protesters, men and women who are often paid by special interest groups to demonstrate (how else can you be there every day without some type of income?) were replaced by something else.

Within four days of the brutal murder of George Floyd on May 25, 2020, Washington was flooded with people. By the end of the summer, downtown DC, especially the area around the White House, witnessed almost non-stop demonstrations led by people of all races, ages, and socioeconomic status. Most demanded real change and police reform, while a highly visible minority just longed for an excuse to wreak unchecked mischief. The former demonstrated peacefully, while the latter committed violence, looted, vandalized, and committed arson. For much of it, we were huddled in our rented rowhouse with my loaded shotgun propped next to the bed, hoping it would not spread to our area. Every night we could faintly smell tear gas as it wafted over the neighborhood from the downtown area, and heard yelling in the distance, along with the detonation of flash bang grenades. The National Guard and DC police set up a reaction team in Lincoln Park, right next to our house. All hours of the night, police and military tactical vehicles flew through the streets of the normally quiet neighborhood.

Eventually, this activity subsided as winter set in. We felt safe and began our nightly walks again. It was early one evening on January 5, 2021, during our stroll that we encountered a whole other type of protester. For days, the news had been crying about right-wing factions descending on the city, preparing to contest the election if Trump was declared the loser. We assumed it was more hyperbole by the media—the same ones who used to film 20 paid protesters with signs in front of the Supreme Court and then describe it to the rest of a country as a massive mob overwhelming the Justices and shutting down the city.

As we walked, I noticed that this new breed of activists had traded in their Black Lives Matter t-shirts for various hunting patterned overalls, an assortment of tactical gear, and long beards. I had never seen this type of demonstrator, or even tourist for that matter, in DC before. Most looked like they would be more comfortable in the woods than wandering the streets of a major city. In addition to their attire, they were huddled in small groups, with cheap tourist fold-out maps held out in front of them, pointing out various areas of the Capitol as well as the streets surrounding it. They used handheld radios to communicate within the groups strategically spread out over the grounds about what they were seeing. I turned to my wife and said, "This is different … something may actually happen tomorrow."

The next day, as part of my job working as an Army Liaison in the US Senate, I was watching the Senate floor as Biden's election was set to be certified. Normally a boring time, we usually sat on the floor in case anything of interest to the Army was mentioned. Due to Covid, instead of in person we were doing it from home via the daily live broadcast. As Senator James Lankford of Oklahoma spoke, he was interrupted by a staffer as the chamber abruptly gaveled into recess. Of course, everyone knows what happens next.

The nation watched live as Congress seemed to fall apart, stormed by a mob flying American, Trump, and Confederate flags. Once again, from our living room we heard the roar of flash bang grenades and felt the slight sting of tear gas in our nostrils. Was our country collapsing? Was this a coup? We had no idea what was going on. Eventually order was restored, and Congress reconvened at 8:00pm that night to complete what they had set out to do hours earlier.

Soon, a tall, black metal fence topped with razor wire, patrolled by uniformed national guard soldiers, encircled the entire Capitol grounds. Once, on a lark, I decided to walk the entire perimeter. I did not expect that it would take me over an hour to walk what is normally a 20-minute loop around the capital. For decades, you needed no identification to visit your members' office to have your voice heard. Now, the only way in was if you had an official staff badge. Honestly, I think some members preferred the new standard—they were no longer besieged by needy constituents, crazies, or freelance media bloggers every time they stepped out of their office.

My wife once asked me what Iraq was like. Several weeks later, during Inauguration Day, I finally answered her question. I pointed out the multiple barricades and checkpoints in our neighborhood, the soldiers on every corner, the tactical vehicles traversing the streets and staged at Lincoln Park, the constant helicopters flying overhead; everyone on high alert and jittery. "This is what Iraq looked, felt, and sounded like," I told her as we somberly walked through our own neighborhood.

When people find out that I worked in Congress, they often want to know if I think we are on the verge of another civil war, much like many families did as they witnessed the rise and fall of countercultures and anti-war movements during my father's war. If you had asked the average American in 1969 the same question—if they thought the nation was doomed—many would have probably said yes. Yet we are still here and thriving. The large-scale protests in Vietnam stemmed directly from the earlier Civil Rights public demonstrations, both of which still inform how civil disobedience, either peaceful or violent, is executed today. Despite all the racket and media coverage (who have an interest in sowing division for ratings), I don't think we are anywhere near that type of conflict. Yes, vocal minorities from both sides make it seem that way, but I think the nation is still strong. If anything, the ability to protest is now seen as an embedded American right and has led to positive change in racism and women's rights, to name a few. Vietnam had a part in this.

Looking back at Kennedy's remarks on Vietnam to the 1962 graduating class at West Point, they appear prophetic. "All applaud, and the tide of patriotism runs high," he stated about the pull to serve during a war with a notable enemy in open combat, "but when there is a long, slow struggle, with no immediate visible foe," he continued as he outlined the type of warfare unfolding in Vietnam, "your choice will seem hard indeed."[1] As the war dragged on with no apparent results, public opinion slowly soured against it.

Vietnam will forever be explicably linked to the anti-war protests and the counterculture that accompanied it. Nixon once called them those "bums blowing up the campuses."[2] In his memoirs, General Westmoreland recalled visiting the president in DC in early 1968. "It looked considerably more distressing than Saigon during the Tet offensive," he wrote about the city when flying over it during a violent demonstration.[3] Meanwhile, General Abrams once commented about the cities at home being choked by protestors, "I think President Thiệu is freer to move around his country than President Nixon is in his, you know, the places he can go and so on without having a goddamn riot."[4] Mental images from the war that include massive marches, flag burnings, and peace-loving hippies—they are stereotypes that will forever be coupled with the conflict. A legacy that still haunts many Vietnam veterans.

I was hoping to hear about some stinky, hair-head, hippie spit-in-your-face stories when I asked my father about his experiences with protesters. However, for the most part he and my family witnessed little of it. My Aunt Momi signed some petitions, but that was about the extent of her anti-war efforts. Due to its World War II history, Hawai'i, unlike the mainland, did not witness the mass demonstrations that rocked much of the nation.

Keller, on the other hand, landed at ground zero of the counterculture revolution. After Vietnam he was stationed at the Sixth Army Headquarters at the Presidio of San Francisco, located at the base of the Golden Gate Bridge and only blocks away from the Haight-Ashbury area of the city. "I was stunned by the daily anti-war protests," Keller recalls about his time in the City by the Bay. The daily rallies and marches filled the metropolis and crippled its movements, but due to perimeter security never spilled over into the Presidio where he and his family lived. Unlike Nixon, Keller could exercise simple common sense, like not wearing his uniform in public, to avoid being targeted by any demonstrators.[5]

On his return from Vietnam, Lockaby noted the throng of protestors at the front gate of Travis AFB, but they were secretly spirited out the back. He smartly changed into civilian clothes before continuing his travel home, thereby avoiding any encounters with upset activists.[6] Tahir had a more direct encounter. Landing at Travis on his return from Vietnam, he ignored the advice and went to San Francisco Airport, still wearing his uniform, to travel home. There, an older woman in her 40s sprinted up to him, yelling in his face that he was a baby killer and tried to spit on him. "You're just an old hag," he screamed back at in her in the best response he could come up with on the spot as he dodged the spittle, "and you don't know what the fuck you're talking about!"[7]

Besides being a general nuisance, some also accused the protesters of being communist sympathizers, if not outright agents of the enemy. "Yesterday, you asked me if it is true that we have Vietcong in our battalion, and I did not know what to say," a 25th ARVN soldier once told his American advisor after witnessing mass protests in the US on television. "You may be right," continued the man, "but now I have proof that you have many VC in your country as well."[8] These accusations were flung at higher levels as well. "They have direct contact with leadership of groups in the United States," Abrams angrily stated as he accused anti-war movement groups of directly communicating with the enemy to synchronize messages and activities during a security briefing. "We're involved on a lot of fronts, and so are they," he noted about North Vietnamese efforts.[9]

"From where I sat," noted Kissinger after the war about his time trying to negotiate a peaceful end to the conflict, "the radicalization of the anti-war movement made it more and more an obstacle to negotiation, rather than a help." He recalled how at each meeting with the North Vietnamese representatives, he had to listen for hours about what the latest anti-war movement leaders and even Congressional members against the war had said, claiming "we would be forced by our own domestic opinion sooner or later to accept his demands."[10] A former ambassador to Vietnam expanded on this congressional angle, later explaining in a video interview that "many honorable men," even members of Congress, "got up and made the statement for a great value to the enemy, giving aid and support to the enemy by any interpretation you possibly could."[11]

Supposed direct contact between the enemy, protesters, and Congress aside, after a brief stint teaching at Fort Benning as part of the Recoilless Rifle and Missile Subcommittee, my father honorably separated from the service and went back to school at the University of Alberta in Canada to finish his Geography degree. Unable to find work in Canada as a landed immigrant (equivalent to a US green card holder) he volunteered for the Canadian University Service Overseas (CUSO), which is similar to the US Peace Corps. Originally slated to teach in Sierra Leone in West Africa, after a revolution there he was rerouted to Saint Vincent in the West Indies. A clerical error then saw him redirected again, this time to Jamaica, where he spent the next several years. He taught on the island, where he obtained his PhD and met and married my mother. He then went back to Canada to teach in Newfoundland, where I was born, before finally taking us back to Hawai'i when I was two years old.[12] By the time he came back to the US, the anti-war movement had fizzled out.

My father did relay to me one amusing protest story from his time in Canada. A demonstration was organized at the University of Alberta, where two speakers had been invited. The first was a diplomat from South Africa, who was heckled and attacked over Vietnam. In between shouts, he tried to explain that South Africa was not part of America. Someone saw USA (for the former Union of South Africa) on his resume when they decided to invite him. Imagine their surprise when he accepted—they must have been salivating, assuming that he had once been an American diplomat and so would make for easy fodder to attack over the war.[13]

The second speaker was, surprisingly, a former private from the same time that my father was with the 82nd Airborne. This "bozo," as he called him, riled up the crowd with stories of American atrocities committed against a village in South Vietnam. My father knew what he was saying was total garbage. He was on that same mission, where all the US forces did was emplace an overwatch position and never even entered the village. He smartly kept his mouth shut during the protests, though, amused by the ridiculousness of it. He left the event early as he had to get home to make dinner for a new girlfriend who was coming over.[14] Girls over ill-planned protests—smart man, my father.

Interestingly, when anything on Vietnam is presented in the media or movies, it is almost always accompanied by the anti-war movement and how poorly they treated returning service members. "Of all the American wartime experiences," notes Doctor Christian Appy, renowned Vietnam War historian, "the antiwar movement has perhaps been the most ignored and distorted." Rarely do they appear positively in pop culture, and when they do, they are often "portrayed as frivolous, spoiled, cowardly, self-absorbed draft-dodgers who liked nothing more than spitting upon returning Vietnam veterans."[15]

What is not often shown is the flip side of this, as bashing hippies makes for good character plot: that of the many Americans who supported the fighting men and women in uniform, even if they did not necessarily believe in the war. This was the silent majority that Nixon tried to appeal to in his famous November 1969 speech.[16]

This group did not always quietly sit in the background, a fact which history has overlooked. In my father's last month in Vietnam, the largest pro-war march occurred in DC. There, anywhere from 15,000 to 50,000 (the numbers vary by report) peacefully marched to show their support for the war. One policeman even remarked, "I didn't get called a 'pig' once."[17] More violently, days after the Kent State shooting of protestors by jittery National Guardsmen, a spontaneous mob of hard-helmeted construction workers in New York attacked an anti-war demonstration as they were cheered on from surrounding high-rise office windows. One laborer excitedly commented to the media that "it was about time the Silent Majority made some noise."[18] Twelve days later, a crowd of over 100,000, mostly industrial and office employees, staged their own march in New York in support of the war.[19]

Thankfully, soldier hating has passed. My generation never experienced it—quite the opposite. Once, when I was a brand-new lieutenant stationed briefly in Los Angeles on recruiting duty, I ate lunch in my uniform at a small restaurant on Santa Monica Boulevard. Also eating there was Ed O'Neil, on a break from filming the television show *L.A. Dragnet.* He struck up a conversation with me and thanked me profusely for my service before paying for my meal. It was truly humbling; I mean, Al Bundy was honored to meet me and bought me lunch!

It seems the American people have realized the error of detesting those sent to fight versus the policies that sent them. Recently, I witnessed an Honor Flight landing at Reagan National Airport in DC. Organized by a non-profit of the same name, their mission is to welcome veterans home from past conflicts with a day of honor in the nation's capital. As the flight unloaded its cargo of mostly wheelchair-using heroes, numerous passengers (of all ages, races, and genders) took time from their commute to line the halls and clap for the men and women departing the plane. Most were veterans of the Vietnam War, which their hats and t-shirts advertised. It was truly a heartwarming sight to witness and brought a tear to my eye. Bush senior would be pleased to know that at least one symptom of the Vietnam Syndrome of soldier bashing seems to have been overcome.

Chapter 29

"They threw as much gas on the fire as they could ..."

ALIC TAHIR

For years, Americans have watched grainy videos as rounds from rapid-fire machine guns streak in and tear humans to pieces. Most have crosshairs centered on the screen that focus on dark silhouettes carrying weapons who are involved in some type of nefarious activity against coalition forces. Others track the delivery of smart munitions that zoom in on their target until the screen is filled with static upon impact. Released through official channels and unauthorized leaks, these video clips have recorded America's wars in Iraq and Afghanistan.

I used to watch these safe from home in my living room with glee as I cheered on each shot. In October 2001, my girlfriend at the time and I were visiting my sister and her husband in San Diego, where we watched the US attacks on Afghanistan live. I am embarrassed to say that we got drunk and shouted every time a bomb exploded as though we were watching a sports game. As we celebrated, my girlfriend cried in the other room. Her answer as to why? "People are being killed and I don't want to die." Slightly annoyed by this, I left her and went back to the game of carnage. Later it would come out that while most of these strikes were legitimate, several also struck innocent civilians. Newlyweds, journalists, and civilians just going about their daily lives were killed by thousand-dollar bombs as people like me applauded from home.

I do understand the need for and risk behind airstrikes and precision munitions—only now I just don't root for them as much. Vietnam was the first war broadcasted into homes and seen from the dinner table each evening. The media's obsession with finding unfettered and negative juicy stories of war began here. Those snapshots of blood, gore, and violence (the more the better) morphed into something else altogether for my generation's conflicts. Welcome to war, 21st-century style, where it's disseminated live 24/7 for your viewing and entertainment pleasure—on any platform or venue you desire.

This instant access has consequences. Unlike Vietnam, where My Lai took over a year to come to light, today when an individual makes a mistake at the tactical level it can instantly change the strategic trajectory of an entire conflict. Perfect examples of this are the pixie-faced soldier leading a detainee around like a dog on a leash and posing in front of human pyramids at the Abu Ghraib prison, or Marines urinating on dead bodies. These were events which singularly created more enemies on the ground than anything we did in combat and steadily eroded what little support we had left in the Arab world.

I write all this to note that there is a strong case to make that without the media, there would not have been a massive anti-war movement against Vietnam. "They were watching this war on television every day in their living rooms," later noted Secretary of State Dean Rusk on the American people's view of the conflict. "I don't know what would have happened in World War II if Guadalcanal and the Anzio beachhead and the Battle of the Bulge were on everybody's television every day. It could have made a profound difference to the course of World War II," he concluded.[1]

"The military and the news media had often been at odds in earlier conflicts," wrote William Hammond, author of several seminal works on media and Vietnam, "but both sides had decided during World War II that cooperation held more benefits than confrontation."[2] Hammond believed that the split in Vietnam began with the battle of Ấp Bắc early in the conflict in 1963. There the US government tried to milk a good-news story from a clear debacle, starting the erosion of their credibility with the seasoned journalists present.[3]

By the time my father arrived in Vietnam, a new type of reporter had begun to appear, one which replaced the dogged media professionals and any last vestiges of loyalty to the government party line. According to Hammond, these young hacks, closer to the age of the draftees, "sported the same hairstyles, used the same slang, and, in the case of television correspondents, often played rock and roll as background in their reports." They were also often sympathetic to the antiwar movement, and even participated in antigovernment activities.[4] This changed the nature of reporting on the war for good.

"How does the ongoing exploration for more action, more excitement, more drama serve our national search for internal peace and stability?" a clearly frustrated Vice President Spiro Agnew once publicly asked on the media's seeming obsession with reporting negative stories and its ties to the anti-war movement. "How many marches and demonstrations would we have if the marchers did not know that the ever-faithful TV cameras would be there to record their antics for the next news show?" he asked of the crowd.[5] Nixon himself is reported to have relayed to leaders in Vietnam that, "Our worst enemy seems to be the press."[6]

Politicians were hardly alone in their criticism of the media's wartime coverage. The Joint United States Public Affairs Office held a daily news update on the Voice of America channel during the war. This event soon came to be derisively known as the five o'clock follies by the attending journalists due to the perceived lies about the war's progress that they claimed they were being told by government officials. "One of the problems is that the media had access to anyone and everyone and they had a tendency to find the critics," countered the director of the follies, Barry Zorthian, "I've often said the media would give as much weight to the opinions and judgements of a private first class as they would to General Westmoreland." Of course, these opinions often differed greatly.[7] Later, daily briefings conducted in Iraq by the government would be called the Baghdad follies: a direct throwback to Vietnam.[8]

Westmoreland accused the media of only seeking out negative stories, pointing to the widely photographed burning C-130 during the siege of Khe Sanh. It was the only aircraft destroyed in the attack, which served as the mandatory backdrop for journalists as they claimed the base was on the verge of being destroyed.[9] He further professed "that the more criticism and the more negativism" that a journalist reported on, "the greater the possibly of recognition and reward."[10] Abrams echoed this point: "We're like a half a dozen goldfish, all of us together, swimming around in a goddamn crystal bowl," he fumed to his staff about the media's obsession with always hunting for the negative, "Christ, you can't even take a shower that everybody isn't seeing it."[11] Who can forget the most widely circulated comment on the media which came after a particularly frustrated officer lashed out at them after their reporting may have contributed to a failed operation. "All you press are bastards," he acidly barked, "I blame you for this and you can quote me on it."[12]

Some reporters pushed back on these claims by government officials that they only sought out the negative. "A large part of our problem," argued one editor from the *Washington Post,* "is that we have been bringing you bad news, not for the sheer joy of it, but because the news has been bad." Furthermore, he claimed, many of the stories that journalists conveyed were obtained anonymously from government representatives, politicians, and military officers, who disagreed with what was officially being reported.[13] Another countered that if a reporter "sees himself as an agent of American government, as a promoter of American policies," he then ceases "to be a journalist and becomes instead a propagandist."[14] In his book *Certain Victory: How Hanoi Won the War*, war correspondent Denis Warner noted that Vietnam was probably "the only war ever lost in the columns of the *New York Times*."[15]

When writing about the current lack of government censorship of the media as opposed to previous wars and the tendency towards negative stories, David Lawrence, editor of the *U.S. News & World Report,* scolded his colleagues that this "did not absolve the press from a responsibility to determine for itself at what point an item that may be 'big news' is bound to aid the enemy and possibly lead to a prolongation of the conflict." Lawrence, an old-school diehard in the business since the early 1900s, was one of the few in the media that backed up the military's stance, and he lashed out at fellow reporters. "The press has a duty to keep in mind," he continued with his thrashing, "that wars are fought not merely on the battlefield, but also psychologically in published articles that influence the morale of the peoples in the countries which are engaged in the conflict."[16]

Lawrence also publicly made a bitter connection between free speech and those student protestors on campuses who hid behind it, "adhering to the enemies" of the US and "giving them aid and comfort" through their words and actions.[17] Some military strategists concurred with this connection between the protestor and the enemy, via the media. "It is terribly important for Hanoi to get the war back on the front pages of American newspapers and onto American television," claimed one US official during the start of the US troop drawdown. "Perhaps the main objective—is to win headlines that will stimulate more antiwar pressure on the President."[18]

Retired Army General Douglas Kinnard, in his groundbreaking work on the conflict titled *The War Managers*—a collection of criticisms collected anonymously from American general officers who served in Vietnam—made a startling counter-claim to all this hubbub. "The importance of the press in swaying public opinion was a myth, fostered by the press to increase its importance," Kinnard wrote. It was in the government's interest to support that myth so that they could say "it was not the real situation in Vietnam that the public eventually reacted against, but rather the press portrayal of that situation."[19]

Regardless of which side of the argument one falls on, it is undeniable that the media had a profound impact on the world's perception of the Vietnam War. "The media that was embedded with US forces and observing operations were initially supportive of the military," noted Keller on this phenomenon. However, "as battlefield defeats were observed, and the media was given false, misleading information, the trust in our military and national leaders disappeared."[20] The daily five o'clock follies, compounded by the secretive nature in which the war was expanded by successive administrations, of course resulted in the rise of anti-war sentiments. What else could have been the result? "Yeah, I think they fueled it," Tahir said more simply about the media and protests. "They threw as much gas on the fire as they could."[21]

The media's treatment of the conflict and the anti-war movement some claim it bolstered is still a bitter pill that many Vietnam veterans struggle to swallow. My father's war ended in April 1970, but this resentment is still a long way from over.

Chapter 30

"Still a nightmare that wakes me up ..."

PATRICK W. NAUGHTON SR.

All the skin slowly peeled off my fingertips for years after Iraq. Once, I was at a wedding and it came up in a conversation with someone at my table. She sat with her hands neatly clasped and tucked in her lap as we traded stories about the war. With the astonishment plain on her face when I mentioned my ailment, she stared at me as she slowly opened her hands and showed me her fingers. They looked just like mine. "Iraq," she quietly said. Besides the anti-war legacy and its relationship with the media, which will always stain the national historical psyche, another leftover of wartime service seems to be adverse health effects.

Like many Vietnam veterans, my father was no different, highlighting another vestige of conflict that stuck with him long past the end of his war in April 1970. He suffered from a host of ailments while deployed, including stomach parasites which lasted for years and exposures to bubonic plague and cholera—once he was bit by a rabid dog.[1] He also got typhus, which hospitalized him for two weeks just as he returned home.[2] Lastly, the scourge of Vietnam also impacted him, named after the identifying stripes used on the 55-gallon drums it came in: Agent Orange[3]—the catch-all term for a group of herbicides that the military sprayed to defoliate the tropical jungle.

The theory was that if you removed the dense brush, the enemy would have nowhere to hide. It was not until 2022 that the VA finally recognized that several issues my father was suffering from were due to "herbicide exposure" during the war.[4] He was lucky, though, as his symptoms were not severe. Another of his ROTC classmates died from cancer due to Agent Orange. He and his men used to cut down recently sprayed vegetation to set up their artillery pieces and were drenched with it daily.[5]

Like me, upon their return, numerous global war on terror veterans have had their own weird medical stories to tell. Vietnam had Agent Orange, the Gulf War had its little understood Syndrome, and now my generation has Burn Pits. The smoke and fumes from the burning of trash and toxins in open-air pits that permeated almost every military base in the Middle East are currently being blamed for our complaints.[6]

As for my fingers, I do not attribute it to the pits; rather, I believe it was from the water. Countless liters of drinking water were bottled in plastic containers for allied troops throughout the war. Those containers were then stacked on pallets and placed in open-air storage areas at each base. There were acres and acres of them, glistening in the sun; they could be seen for miles from the air and were left out in the open before being issued to troops. Sometimes they sat exposed like that for years before that happened. With the extreme heat boiling those plastic containers again and again … I just do not see how they could have been safe to drink.

"The Antiwar protesters didn't bother me as much as the way I was treated by the Army and the VA after I was out," Larry Lockeby, my father's old comrade from the 82nd, bitterly relayed to me when talking about this topic. He suffered from PTSD and a host of other issues that no one would address. Fifty years later, he was finally declared 100 percent disabled. "What the fuck?" he noted in dismay. "Do you think they will pay me back pay? I've only been suffering from these maladies for years, right?"[7]

Tahir experienced something similar. After he took medication to control his blood pressure, the VA denied his claims because they stated he had no issues, putting him in a catch-22 type situation. If he stops taking his medication, he will qualify for disability—but then he could die. "A colossal waste of my time," is what he called the VA.[8] This highlights another bitter legacy outside of the protests and the mistrust of the media left over from the Vietnam War.

Another lingering health legacy of war is often one that cannot be seen—one that Lockeby suffered from for years. After World War I it was called shell shock, after World War II and the Korean conflict, battle fatigue; my father's conflict labeled it Post-Vietnam Syndrome. That term morphed into what we call it today: PTSD.[9] "I don't recall your dad talking much about what he went through in Vietnam for a while," my Aunt Momi told me when I asked how he was upon his return, "if at all."[10] I know he suffered some from PTSD but not in the debilitating way that most Vietnam War movies want you to believe.

In a surprising moment of honesty, my normally reserved father bared his soul to me when asked about PTSD and the war. "This is still a nightmare that wakes me up in the middle of the night," he confirmed about his time in the Pineapple coming upon the wet footprint filling up with water.[11] "Sometimes I get flashbacks," he further told me. "I'll get them at night which wakes me (occasionally in a sweat)." He elaborated further on how during the day, these recollections occur as well—triggered by a smell such as rotten flesh from a roadkill or a Huey flying overhead. Thankfully, not many of those helicopters are still in use, so that has lessened some. "This never goes away," he somberly told me.[12]

I remember once as a child, our overactive imaginations had us seeing a giant lizard in the lush jungles we played in daily. We wore our parents down with stories of this supposed animal, so my dad had to come see for himself. As my friends and I led him in from the road, the thick vegetation enveloped us and blocked out the sun, muffling the sound of civilization until all you could hear, see, and smell was the dark forest. Out of nowhere a wild boar charged past us, startled by our intrusion. My father immediately turned around and broke through the brush as he sprinted back to the car and sped down the road. Surprised by his reaction and the fact that he had left us behind, this event faded from my memory, until I asked him about PTSD. I realize now that he must have been terrified; transported alone and unarmed back to Vietnam.

In contrast, I think I am okay. When I tell people that I have been in Iraq, the first question I am often asked is if I am mentally stable. "Oh, don't worry," is my usual smug reply, "I was already fucked up before I left." Those with some type of military exposure break out laughing. Those without look at me horrified, flash an awkward smile, and then try to remove themselves quickly from the conversation. I, selfishly, am glad they feel uncomfortable. I mean, what kind of question is that to ask someone anyway? How about a "Thanks for your service" before you imply that I am one muffler backfire away from losing it?

Can you blame the American populace, though? My father's generation started this stereotype with the 1982 movie *Rambo*—the quiet Vietnam veteran who dropped out of society and lived as a loner because he could not assimilate back into the world. My generation has taken it a step further. Today, we are all just dying to be wronged so that we can use our skills refined in combat to wreak horrendous revenge on whichever crime boss or foul government agents have crossed us—Hollywood's new cliché for the returning veteran.

Once I overheard my father tell a fellow Vietnam veteran how America has forgotten how many of them went on to lead productive lives and become leaders in their communities. PTSD is real, and those who need help should absolutely get it. At the same time, understand that most veterans want nothing more than to fit back into the nation that sent them to war. We are not all one step away from inflicting havoc on the local crime syndicate.

Chapter 31

"I always wear my boots ..."

PRIVATE FIRST CLASS BARRY WINCHELL

One weekend in May 1999, I noticed a private wearing his issued combat boots in civilian clothes as he did his best to fit in with the old hands. In the macho infantry world of the 101st, you had to be careful. If you did not conform, and instead did something to get everyone's attention, your life would be miserable. One sure-fire way to do that was to wear issued clothing off duty.

"I always wear my boots," Private First Class Barry Winchell blurted out to me unsolicited, "my stepdad and I do it at home all the time." I told him I did not care. I was visiting friends in Delta Company's barrack next to mine, so I did not even know who he was. He kept telling me that repeatedly until I finally loudly told him, "dude, enough, I don't care what you wear." With that he slunk off, as the older troopers in Delta Company told me to just ignore the cherry. Two months later, Winchell was dead, beaten to death in his sleep with a baseball bat in a drunken rage by his roommate.[1]

When I look back on it now, I believe he anticipated that I was going to pick on him—just as he had been mercilessly bullied over the last few months by his peers and leaders in the unit. He wanted to get ahead of it before I started because, you see, Winchell was gay. And that was not okay in the "don't ask don't tell" infantry of old. His superiors and soldiers in his unit had found out that he was dating a transitioning man in Nashville and had made their displeasure clearly known. They repeatedly abused him verbally and physically until one early morning his roommate, after getting his ass kicked earlier by Winchell in a fistfight, took a bat to his head while he slept—egged on by another soldier, who cruelly teased him about his loss to Winchell the previous evening. "I won't let a faggot kick my ass," slurred his assailant to his provocateur before stumbling out of his room to attack Winchell.[2]

What does any of this have to do with my father and Vietnam? It speaks to generational expectations about what a nation's military should represent and the human side of service, what some may call "wokeness." Winchell was my first violent exposure to what can happen to someone when they are deemed different. My father's diary and letters were riddled with words and phrases which today would not be considered okay. Dinks and Gooks described the Vietnamese; round-eyes and titless WACs, women; and of course, dandies or nancies for homosexuals. Some claim this is a necessary evil in war; after all, it is much easier "psychologically and morally," claimed one US official, "to kill a 'dink' then it is to shoot a 'Vietnamese.'"[3] General Abrams was frustrated by all of it: "They're all people, they're all human beings," he once fumed about all the derogatory name-calling going on in Vietnam, "just get it out of the damn vocabulary."[4]

Despite official attempts to stop the disdainful defamation and the physical bullying that accompanied it, little changed. Some rode around in "gookmobiles" and neatly painted rows of conical hats on the side of their vehicles for each supposed kill, enemy or not.[5] For fun, Americans were constantly throwing beer cans out of trucks at villagers, running old people off their bicycles, and pulling young girls' pigtails as they passed by, to name just a few of the tamer offences.[6]

As I stumbled across each term and occurrence in my readings, they jumped out at me and hit me with the force of that bat in a Fort Campbell barracks room all those years ago. However, honestly, my generation was little better. We derivatively called Iraqis and Afghanis hajis, hodge, Ali Babas, mujs, or worse, all the while making fun of the women in their hijabs, niqaabs, or burkas. As far as physical abuse goes, we did about the same; running people off roads and even shooting their engine blocks for fun because we claimed they had driven too close to our convoys.

Harsh terms and bullying tactics have changed little from my father's Army to mine, although many other areas have. Back when Winchell was murdered in 1999, there was one female soldier in my entire infantry brigade: one woman surrounded by several thousand males. I will never forget a 101st Division run, where the command sergeant major's (CSM) assistant took it upon herself to call cadence for our infantry company. No one echoed her calls. An awkward silence followed until someone broke it, yelling, "Shut the fuck up, bitch!" She slunk off and we thought nothing of it until later that day when the Division CSM forced all the enlisted soldiers to take turns screaming the same expression, one after the other. It was a line-up of sorts, whose goal was for the reluctant female soldier to pick out her insulter by voice recognition alone. She was not successful, and we all felt demeaned, including her. Something like this abuse and the line-up that followed would never happen in today's Army. And rightfully so.

In Vietnam, there were zero females in combat units. By the time I went to Iraq, a decade after my time in the 101st, women in the military were everywhere and in almost every job. One of my best friends from that time is a 6' African American woman. For many, that would not exactly match the picture of what one thinks of as a war buddy. Some of my most influential mentors have been senior female officers.

Unfortunately, this increased ratio has also brought with it a blight which seems to always be in the news cycle—sexual assaults.

Being in a Medical Task Force, my unit was tasked with trying to tamp down on this surge in Iraq. A stellar NCO and I decided to take it on. Both of us had a martial arts background and decided to put together a self-defense class, open to all female soldiers. First, we examined the history of assaults to determine the types of moves we should teach. Women were being attacked everywhere. In their CHUs, in the latrines, even while they rode in convoys. Several were even assaulted as they lay wounded in the back of field ambulances. How do you sexually attack someone in a convoy moving through hostile territory or who has been injured by enemy fire? Don't women have enough to worry about with IEDs and small-arms fire without adding rape to it? Our first class had three attendees—eight months later, we had upwards of 20 attend each weekly class.

Regrettably, despite heroic efforts on the part of the military, this issue has not gone away, the most famous case now being the recent murder of Vanessa Guillén in a weapons storage room by a fellow soldier who was sexually harassing her. The incident resulted in the eventual passing of the "I am Vanessa Guillén Act" of 2021, which removed the decision to prosecute sexual assault and sexual harassment from the victim's chain of command and into the hands of an independent office. This change seeks to encourage soldiers to come forward when attacked or harassed, and more importantly, feel safe from any retaliation from their leaders. America's daughters (and men) should be able to serve without fear they will be bludgeoned to death in an arms room and then not found for weeks. Shame on us as a military that it took Congress to force us to make a change.[7]

After this act mandated by Congress came another forced transformation which many in my father's generation would have gawked at—that of the complete removal of all things in the military named after the Confederacy. Critics again roared that this was the "woke" mob erasing our history and heritage and undermining the generations of warriors before us. Numerous bases mentioned in this book no longer go by the names those who served in Vietnam knew them as. Fort Benning, where my father and I became soldiers, is now called Fort Moore after Hal and Julie Moore—a deceased LTG and Vietnam veteran who served in the first major battle of the conflict in the Ia Drang valley and his wife who was a tireless advocate for Army families.[8] Hardly a "woke" moniker adjustment.

LGBTQ+ soldiers, women serving in all career fields, sexual assault prevention, name changes, and the general atmosphere of the services trying to clean up their cultures has drastically changed the military since my father's time. The far right has accused certain members of Congress of using the services as their own "woke" petri dish to conduct personal social experiments. This is the same criticism raised during Vietnam. "If the do-gooders will just let the military alone," stated one frustrated Pentagon official in 1969 over the social issues of the day, "the services will be able to handle the situation."[9] These critics seem to forget that the military is fed solely by the society that it fights for. The two are irrevocably connected.

For today's younger generation, what some call "wokeness" is important to them. I don't mean we should kowtow to the extreme left and create a soft military where we all sit around talking about our feelings all the time or undertake unrealistic and counterproductive combat actions such as building separate field accommodations for each letter in the alphabet. Rather, we need to create a military that understands and implements progress that extends basic human dignity to all. One where women are not coddled but rather able to serve while still being kept safe from sexual assault. One where LGBTQ+ soldiers are not called faggots, murdered, or prevented from being themselves. A military that does not erase its history, but rather embraces heroes that its service members can all look to for inspiration and identify with. What the heck have we fought for over generations if not to build a military that lives up to the ideals that the society it serves desires?

The "woke" generation is not unreasonable or weak—many want to wear the uniform. They just have a different outlook on what America should be and, therefore, what its military should reflect. To counter the dismal recruiting problems the services currently face, they need to understand and embrace this. Recruiters during my father's war lamented the new breed of recruit entering the Army. Those who think they are their own "Secretary of State, Secretary of Defense, and Attorney General" and are "superior to any officer alive" as one recruiter from the era raged.[10] It was a nonsensical assessment then, identical to the criticism being leveled against the newest potential recruits now, all fed by simple generational misunderstanding. Today's youth do not desire an easy-going military. Most are not looking for pleasant drill sergeants or gender-neutral latrines. Rather, they just want to know that if they serve, they will not be sexually attacked or murdered while they sleep simply because of their self-identity or beliefs. That their concerns will at least be considered before making personnel decisions. That they will be accepted into the team as they come.

Moreover, unlike my father's and my generation, today's soldiers also want to know why they are doing something. They demand an explanation. When I was a private, if I had asked any leader "why," I probably would have been crushed on the spot. This new desire to understand what is being asked of them is not necessarily a bad thing. Today, leaders must expound on their plans to gain buy-in, which forces them to think through their decisions more thoroughly. But it must be understood that in the heat of a firefight, leaders do not have time to explain themselves, and I think today's youth accept this. However, explaining to soldiers why we are replicating riding on trucks that are supposed to mimic helicopters is not unreasonable and probably even preferred. I wish some of my NCOs and officers had put even a little bit of thought into the things they made me do.

Though all of this might make one warm and fuzzy to read, there is, however, another side that many are afraid to talk about. Many white males now feel that they are no longer welcome in the services—that no matter how hard they work and sacrifice, it no longer matters. The military, when selecting leaders for progressive assignments or command billets, will now always play it safe and cater to the "woke mob." Highly qualified white males will be overlooked for these types of positions in favor of a minority, female, or some other category just so the government can claim that it is diverse—or at least, that is the belief held by many and growing.

Some point to the command climates currently present in most organizations as proof. In contrast to Vietnam's short tours for commanders, today tenures are usually two years and seen as the pinnacle qualifier for an officer's advancement to senior levels of leadership. However, the desire to simply walk away unscathed is even more prevalent than it was in Vietnam. Now, success is measured by being able to simply complete one's tenure without an inspector general or equal opportunity complaint. One wrong word or misconstrued action—or even coming down too hard on a deserving subordinate who has erred—will result in a lodged complaint. If it reaches the level where it enters the court of public opinion or the social media stratosphere (or even if it has the potential to do so), you are done, especially if you are a white male. Even if you were in the right. Most white officers will not admit to this in public; however, behind closed doors, in a safe space, it is all that is talked about.

All this change scares many old soldiers. "A non-gender Army," derisively cried Tahir when I asked him about where the military was headed today. "We're going to teach all this mumbo jumbo shit … you're just wasting your damn time," was his heated answer, "you might as well join the Boy Scouts. Go on a damn jamboree."[11] He went on, as most old soldiers do. About how tough it was in his day and so on. I do the same when talking about the infantry of the 1990s compared to today. His next comments jarred me out of my seat. "These were real soldiers," he said after describing the grizzled NCOs who trained him in basic training, "not this punk-ass bunch. The army of faggots or whatever they want to call themselves." He raged on about how all the "woke" efforts the military is undertaking "has nothing to do with fighting wars. Nothing."[12] His opinion on women in the Army? Sure, they can do jobs in the rear, but not in combat units. "When they're captured, they'll be raped," was his reasoning as to why not.[13]

His comments were shocking for two reasons. One, this is secretly what a large segment of the population thinks. Secondly, he has a point. If an effort has nothing to do with warfighting, why are we expending time, effort, and resources on it? "The money should go to warfighting," raged Tahir about the 82nd Airborne Choir seen on *America's Got Talent*, "not bands and choirs and all this other shit!"[14]

"Wokeness" in the military is nothing new. Each generation goes through it as it adjusts to fit the society it serves. "The Army is always trying to recruit, train and field a combat-ready force that originates off the streets of America," noted Keller when I asked him about this topic, "with all its strengths, weaknesses, and behaviors."[15] Today is no different, a fact which even senior leaders from Vietnam would recognize.

Westmoreland, after several rounds of input from his junior officers on how the Army should operate during the war, dealt with this and had to shut the effort down. "When one enterprising lieutenant set out to unionize all second lieutenants and prepared 'demands' to be presented to senior commanders," he recalled, "the practice had to be discontinued."[16] Others in the Army also tried something similar, forming the American Servicemen's Union, which sought to have officers elected, an end to saluting, and collective bargaining by the rank and file implemented.[17] "Wokeness," 1960s style.

As the chief of staff of the Army, Westmoreland further commented about this in his memoirs, discussing the military shifting to an all-volunteer force. He claimed that it "behooved the Army to be receptive to change" and that the old timers needed to accept it.[18] Speaking out the other side of his mouth, his comments on trying to keep women out of his beloved West Point are rather unpleasant. "Maybe you could find one woman in ten thousand who could lead in combat, but she would be a freak," he stated in 1974, "and we're not running the Military Academy for freaks."[19]

Unfortunately, for all the positive changes that the services are undertaking, many still consider these adjustments as negative and ones that will somehow degrade national security. Regardless, the military is indeed made stronger by diversity and extending basic human dignities to all who want to raise their right hand. One of America's last truly trusted and respected institutions is still a place where young people can go to advance their social standing in life. "As long as it does not degrade combat readiness," should be the mantra when measuring the so-called "woke" changes being proposed and that young people desire. If it cannot pass this basic litmus test, it should not happen.

The warrior caste of today's America is dangerous because it alienates a large portion of society from service; it is time to break that cycle by creating services that attract all types from a true crosscut of US culture. If the military isolates itself from society by making it a welcome home for the few who fit a certain cast type, it ceases to be a servant to that same society. Historical examples have demonstrated that this is not a good thing for democracy.

By most accounts, Winchell was a good soldier; I also heard he was a mean shot with the 50-caliber machine gun. Moreover, women and LGBTQ+ members have proven themselves in combat over the past two decades. If one could go back and tell the men my father knew who died in Vietnam that their lives would be spared by just having one more soldier in the foxhole next to them, I am sure they would not have cared about the name of the base they trained on, or the gender or sexual orientation of that person. Not one bit.

Chapter 32

"We were looking for George Washington …"

AMBASSADOR MAXWELL TAYLOR

As I stared up at it, a yellow flag with three horizontal red strips through the middle snapped in the wind. Only three miles from my home, I must have driven by this flagpole a thousand times before I noticed it peeking above a car dealership; the old flag of South Vietnam. For decades after the fall of the South in April 1975, millions fled the newly formed Socialist Republic of Vietnam any way they could. Some left overland through Thailand, but most left by sea in rickety vessels and are now remembered as the "boat people."[1]

Once in America, like many refugees do, they coalesced around each other, forming communities across the US—just as is occurring today with the Iraqis and Afghans settling in states such as Texas, California, and Michigan. For the Vietnamese, one of the pockets they occupied was the Clarendon neighborhood of Arlington, Virginia just outside of DC, which soon became known as "Little Saigon."[2] Today, much of this once-thriving immigrant community has been taken over by a metro stop and subsequently consumed by the surrounding urban sprawl. What has survived is a shopping plaza called the Eden Center, a thriving mecca for those still alive from the war and their now Americanized children and grandchildren. It was there that I stood gazing up at the yellow-and-red South Vietnamese standard displayed next to the American flag, one of the few places in the world where it still proudly publicly flies.

I was told by many that the surviving ARVN veterans in the US were not interested in talking about the war. I reached out to numerous Vietnamese civic groups and museums, posted social media messages, and even visited places such as the Eden Center, handing out flyers. Once, I connected with a well-known author who wrote about his father's South Vietnamese Army and refugee experience. "No one wants to talk about the war," he told me; furthermore, "No one wants to read about it … Vietnamese or American." Disheartened by what I had hoped would be a positive mentorship experience or tips on how to break into the community, I pressed on.

Due to the passage of time and post-war events, I was never able to find anyone who my father directly advised. Expecting to talk to men bitter about the lost conflict, instead I was surprised by the comments from the few ARVN veterans willing to speak with me. "Thank you for taking the time to learn about a half-century-old war in which 65,000 beloved children of the United States gave their lives to help an ally stop communist aggression," said one veteran who best summed up what most of the men told me. "We hope that your research will help future generations understand."[3] These men forced me to realize that it is impossible to comprehend my father's war without learning the perspective of the ally he advised.

One cannot understand what happened in Vietnam without acknowledging the influence that World War II and the Korean War had on its strategy formulation, which directly informed how the ARVN were structured and trained. "The onslaught of the North Koreans into South Korea in 1950," Secretary of State Rusk explained after the war, "made a major difference to us in our attitude toward events in Asia."[4] With Korea fresh on the mind of military planners, it was thought best to build the ARVN to mirror the US force structure, that of large corps and division-sized combat formations supported by heavy equipment.[5] It was a structure ill-suited to fighting insurgents on the local level. "Let's think about Europe and those good old days of World War II, divisions and corps and tanks and so on," later moaned Ambassador Taylor about the thought process that dominated the formulation of the South Vietnamese military.[6]

"This is a political war, and it calls for discrimination in killing," reportedly said John Paul Vann more candidly about this mismatch. Vann was a former army officer turned civilian with the Agency for International Development, who was well-respected for his views on counterinsurgency. "The best weapon for killing would be a knife," explained Vann. "By giving him [the ARVN] too much gear—airplanes and helicopters—we may be helping them to pick up bad habits instead of teaching them to spend more time in the swamps than the enemy."[7] By 1967, Congress had also noted this discrepancy, entering into the Congressional Record a highly damming article which declared that the ARVN was a Korean-type holdover; an unwieldy, road-bound monstrosity incapable of defeating a growing insurgency in its own country.[8]

In his memoir, General Westmoreland acknowledged this condemnation and offered a fair defense. "What was the alternative?" he demanded. "Small mobile units not unlike guerrilla units ... there is nothing to prevent larger units from being broken into smaller, more mobile forces when the occasion demands." As he further explained, it is much harder to take smaller units and then combine them to create larger ones when faced with conventional forces such as the NVA.[9] Regardless of this criticism, the fact remained: the ARVN were a near replica of US forces. The question now was how to get them to fight like Americans.

The answer to this conundrum was the advisory program. As early as 1950, US officers and NCOs began to advise the South Vietnamese military, first to assist the French and then in support of the American effort. By the time my father joined their ranks, about 13,500 advisors were present in Vietnam.[10] Over the entire conflict, thousands of advisors cycled through these roles, each with their own opinion on how the Vietnamese should fight the war. When writing *The War Managers*, Kinnard received several comments back from the general officers he polled on this topic. Protected by their anonymity, they were brutally honest on the advisory program's shortcomings.

"We never really established rapport," noted one senior officer. He chalked this up to the American obsession with the fact that the American way, "is automatically and unchallengeably the best (really the only) way to do things."[11] Another general noted that a single South Vietnamese commander was exposed to anywhere from eight to 28 different advisors over the years, all with their own unique approach to the same problems.[12]

Civilian participants in the conflict also noticed issues. Richard Holbrooke, an Agency for International Development in Vietnam member before becoming a staff assistant to the US Ambassador, later claimed: "The Vietnamese for their part learned gradually that whether they liked an individual advisor or didn't like him," they had to take at least some of the advice, because it came with perks such as "goods, commodities, money, weapons, [and] ammunition."[13] They could tolerate or placate any advisor they did not get along with; after all, another one would be along in a matter of months to replace them.

The South Vietnamese were not stupid. They clearly understood that material support for the war came with the caveat that they had to tolerate whatever advisor was shoved down their throat. "I don't want you to come in and tell me what to do," chuckled one Vietnamese officer in a TV interview years after the war about how he approached the men advising him. "That condescending attitude, you know, that patronizing attitude," he explained further about the "if you don't do this, we do that" back and forth that constantly ensued.[14] Another ARVN officer elegantly compared the material and advisory relationship to that of a drug addict on opium. "Our people have become dependent upon it," he noted with disgust.[15]

The South Vietnamese military was made from the same stock as their Northern counterparts, only bolstered by US equipment and force structure and advised by the greatest soldiers in the world. The answer as to why they did not act or perform exactly like their American counterparts after whom they were modeled is a complicated one. Westmoreland, in his memoir, may have inadvertently captured it in a sentence, having noticed that numerous captured enemy soldiers had the slogan "Born in the North to die in the South" tattooed on their bodies.[16] Many in the North had adopted a fatalist attitude about life, living by the government slogan: "If you are in love, don't take a fiancé. If you are a fiancé, don't get married.

If you're married, don't have children."[17] Indoctrination and a clear reason to fight was lacking in the South, long overshadowed by the American presence there.

Furthermore, even though the French were gone, many members of the senior officer corps in the South Vietnamese military had worked with them in one form or another. Viewed as traitors, this negative image soon stained all ranks. The South Vietnamese armed forces, especially the ARVN, were seen as the *bộ quân công tác* (an army of collaboration) by the peasants.[18] Prime fodder for a propaganda campaign. "In South Vietnam we did nothing to prepare the countryside for the needed sacrifice," noted one ARVN veteran regretfully about the war and the North's ideological training efforts, which began at birth.[19]

Another described the difference between an 18- to 20-year-old man forcibly drafted from easy city living and forced into the army, versus that of an eight- to ten-year-old taught to fight from an early age and to adopt a religious attitude towards their effort and Hồ Chí Minh.[20] The two produced a drastically different soldier. "I don't think they understood the difference between being commandos and being guerrillas," said renowned journalist David Halberstam years later when interviewed about the lack of appreciation between the two sides of soldiers. "I mean it's one thing to stay out overnight in the boondocks and have all kinds of tricks," he explained, "and it's quite another thing to have a deep political root that the guerrilla has."[21]

Buried in an MACV Combat Experience curricular from 1969 is a shocking picture which further illustrates this difference. It depicts a near-naked NVA infiltrator submerged underwater, floating backwards downstream, breathing through a 20-centimeter garden hose and towing a 300-kilogram explosive charge behind him. This was how bridges in Saigon were sabotaged: operatives trained for two years in underwater operations and explosives in Hanoi before sneaking into the South to blow up bridges.[22] Imagine the dedication and nerve that it takes to execute something like this. We can't even get the common American soldier today to check their mails.

In addition to this lack of indoctrination and motivation, once in the military most men were not treated well. "The average ARVN soldier is not well-supported, makes very little money, and may live in squalor even when he is on leave," bemoaned one veteran after the war when talking about how poorly they were fed, paid, and supported, "and he knows he will be in the army for many years to come."[23] This was in stark contrast to the US soldier, who had an end to look forward to and could leave in a year.

In addition, there was a constant worry of losing their own family members or homes to combat operations. In the North, the heavy bombing campaign could be avoided; however, in the South, the ground conflict was waged among the homes of the very men who served. This, of course, added to the stress of serving in the South Vietnamese military. "We gave up our sons and then had our villages destroyed by our allies," explained one man after the war, "it was a nightmare that never seemed to end."[24]

To their credit, the US did recognize these stressors, especially regarding the rural communities in South Vietnam. Westmoreland attributed the high desertion in the military to a form of what he called "French leave"—men who left the service not because they did not want to fight, but because they had to look after their families.[25] Abrams also realized the impact combat operations in the South were having on desertion rates and morale, briefing his senior leaders that the peasants consider both friendly and enemy forces as equal threats to their safety. As such, commanders must discriminate with their fires as much as possible.[26] "If a mortar shell lands on his house," Abrams explained about this challenge, "it makes no difference to him whether it's an enemy mortar shell or one of ours—it's a disaster."[27]

As Huntington wrote in his *Foreign Affairs* piece on urbanization, besides the destruction wreaked by modern weapons, another threat to the South Vietnamese family in the rural areas was the guerrilla. "The strength of the Viet Cong," he wrote about this lack of security, "is its ability to fill this vacuum of authority."[28] It made it even harder for men in the field to continue fighting this elusive foe when their own families at home were not safe. "Clearly there is very little that can be done economically, socially, psychologically, and politically for the 'hearts and minds' of men," wrote Ambassador Lodge during the war, "if these men have knives sticking into their collective bellies."[29] It was in these rural communities that my father and his teammates mainly operated. They often witnessed the impact of the VCI metaphorical dagger firsthand.

Once, when Tahir was out on an operation, his trusted hooch maid showed up at the compound with a large box of food for him. When the gate guards tried to pilfer some of it, she panicked and ran off in a hurry, dropping the box at her feet. When the guards took a closer look at the package, they found a bomb inside. Upon his return, Tahir mobilized a company of ARVN to go after her in the nearby village. When they entered her hut, they found a large cache of stolen items from the base. Splayed out in the middle of the dwelling was the dead woman, with all her fingers cut off and shoved down her slit throat. She was surrounded by her murdered children—punishment for failing to deliver a bomb to kill an American advisor. Tahir and the company conducted an ambush to see if any VC would return to remove the items she had stolen. Sure enough, later that night they did just that, walking right into the ARVN company waiting for them. Bullets pinged off the pots and pans hanging in the dead woman's kitchen as the VC were mowed down.[30]

"These people would be put under threat," Tahir explained to me about the power and reach of the VCI over the civilian population in the rural areas, "and they were made to do things … you couldn't trust anybody, not even the kids, not even old people." Tahir has long forgiven the maid, knowing that her children were being held by the VC. He believes she ran back to try to save them when she failed to deliver the box, knowing full well that they would probably all be killed. "That's the kind of dirty, dirty war it was," he said with a sigh.[31]

History has not been kind to the South Vietnamese military, especially the ARVN. Given some of the memories being shared in more recent publications such as National Geographic's *Another Vietnam: Pictures of the War from the Other Side*, it is not hard to see why. One image in the collection of mostly propaganda photos from North Vietnam, collated into a coffee-table conversation piece by photographer Dương Thanh Phong, is especially telling. His photo captured hundreds of combat boots left abandoned on a road by fleeing ARVN soldiers who, under fear of capture, discarded their uniforms as quickly as they could once they realized all was lost. "I'll never forget the shoes and the loud 'thump, thump, thump' sound as we drove over them," later recalled the photographer about the surreal scene. It's a popular image still used as propaganda in today's Vietnam.[32]

The codification of the ARVN's shortcomings started very early in the war. The same article, colorfully titled *Their Lions, Our Rabbits*, entered into the Congressional Record in 1967, claimed that most of the young men in South Vietnam were avoiding the army, leaving the fighting to their "big American brothers" to carry the load. "Like the society which created it," declared the piece, whose views many in Congress and the public now subscribed to, the ARVN was "riddled with factionalism, nepotism, corruption, inefficiency, incompetence and cowardice."[33]

The trio of SECDEFs who oversaw the war later confirmed this perspective via books and television interviews. In his memoir, McNamara called the ARVN "tired, passive, and accommodation-prone."[34] Clifford stated that he felt the ARVN never really wanted to fight the war, and that they had hoped that the US would just do it for them.[35] "Well, I don't think we were defeated in Vietnam," Laird noted, adding to the din, "I think the South Vietnamese were defeated." He concluded that the South's military lacked the will and desire to defeat the North.[36]

Even official military histories jumped on the bandwagon. The 2007 book from the Center of Military History on counterinsurgency claimed the ARVN's failure was not due to the way the US executed the war, "but from the army's failure to implement American advice." This, combined with their inability to embrace "calls for vigorous, offensive action, preferring instead the relative safety of their cantonments" ensured defeat was all but certain.[37]

Interestingly, this long-held negative perception is beginning to change, starting with the groundbreaking book *ARVN: Life and Death in the South Vietnamese Army* by Robert Brigham. History is starting to reexamine the ARVN. "In most historical accounts," Brigham writes, the ARVN shoulder much of the blame for losing the war: "Poor political leaders and cowardly, self-interested soldiers were no match for the Communists … and that is why the United States suffered its first defeat." Countering this narrative, Brigham concludes that the real ARVN soldier has simply vanished behind the stereotypes portrayed by the media, books, and in film over the past decades.[38]

"That's actually not accurate," Tahir corrected me in one of our interviews when I repeated some of the harmful comments about the ARVN. "They could fight, and some of the officers were pretty damn experienced and smart." He still marveled at the soldiers' ability to live off the land and survive in some tough terrain, remembering how at each tactical halt the men would pick stuff off trees and bushes to eat as snacks. It was not the enlisted and company grade officers that were found wanting; it was purely the senior leadership.[39] My father wholeheartedly agreed with this assessment.[40]

Keller also backed this up. Having served two tours in Vietnam, he found the common ARVN soldier and company-grade leadership to be quite effective. It was at the division level and higher where the "ARVN seemed disorganized, politicized, without synchronized focus on a battle or war-time strategy." He lamented the dearth of any effective leaders at key echelons that could coordinate and focus the military on any type of winning strategy.[41] Ambassador Taylor said it best years later about the lack of higher echelon talent that never materialized: "We were looking for George Washington under every mango grove in the whole country."[42]

A telling example on the type of senior leaders in the ARVN can be summed up by an experience Tahir had with an American favorite, Dương Văn Minh, also known as Big Minh for his large stature. He was a one-time military advisor to the president of South Vietnam, an ARVN general, and then the actual president when the country fell in 1975. On one hectic operation where Tahir and the ARVN had not eaten for days due to poor resupply, his men killed an NVA general and found a coveted communist pistol and whistle on his body.

Somehow word got back to Big Minh, who soon landed a helicopter in the combat zone, demanding the items for himself. "You tell that big son of a bitch," Tahir angrily replied through an interpreter, "the next time he comes here and gets down on the ground with the rest of us and earns it he can have it." Big Minh, in his clean and starched fatigues, just slyly smiled, promising a Chinook full of food for the ARVN and their families for the items. Stares from the hollow-eyed ARVN now gathered around him bore into Tahir, giving him looks that can only come from hungry bellies that have not eaten for days. Tahir did the only thing he could; he turned over the captured souvenirs to Minh. True to his word, hours later a Chinook landed with the promised food. It only took a pistol and a whistle to get the ARVN what they should have had all along: some basic food to eat.[43]

If history has been unkind to the ARVN, then the end of war and post-war events were downright savage for the average South Vietnamese veteran. By the early 1970s, the ARVN soon realized that the non-stop spigot of American war materiel was slowly being turned off. As such, they needed to ration every shell, bullet, and can of fuel. Tahir witnessed this firsthand just before he left the country for good.

An ARVN 105 howitzer gun crew had a fire mission called off with a round still in the tube. Instead of traversing the barrel to the dump grid to clear the piece, which was standard when the US was present, the men tried to remove the round from the hot tube to save it for later. Unfortunately, it went off, killing all six of the ARVN soldiers. "That's the kind of shit they did," just to stretch out their supplies, Tahir said, as he shook his head.[44]

Are the ARVN solely to blame, as many have suggested, for the swiftness in which South Vietnam was conquered by the North? Or was it due to a deadly combination of events? With Vietnamization, the ARVN became the main effort to wage the war. By then, they were so used to the US taking the lead that they had become dependent on their sustainment, fire support, and air power. Once thrust to the forefront, they were woefully underprepared to assume this role so quickly. Some used what occurred in April 1975 to further counter criticisms of how the US created the ARVN as a mirror image of US forces, stating that it was a "conventional war indeed" which caused their downfall.[45] In other words, their structure was correct from the beginning and it was the ARVN that failed once the North Vietnamese came out of hiding, not the US. Never mind that the ARVN had been subjugated to a minor role for most of the conflict which they were not able to recover from so late in the war.

Despite a body of willing and capable soldiers, due to the loss of US material support and a severe case of pubescent low self-esteem, confidence, and experience at the higher echelons, the ARVN were unable to stand up to the NVA onslaught. As the North Vietnamese conventional forces swarmed south, their rear areas were secured by the VCI and their guerrilla units. Unlike most invading armies, which must slice off pieces to secure these areas and mop up residual enemy elements, the VCI negated this need. This allowed the NVA to retain the entirety of their combat power near the front to easily overwhelm the ARVN. Supported by a secure sustainment pipeline via the unmolested Hồ Chí Minh Trail that was now immune to deep strikes from the Americans, North Vietnam was unstoppable.

The common ARVN soldier was a bad motherfucker, not the duds or cowards that much of history, media, and film have led us to believe. On that, my father and his teammates agree. One former South Vietnamese official described why this might be so. Interviewed years after the war, he included World War II; the Japanese, the French, the Americans; and finally the aftermath of the communist takeover in one succinct statement which encapsulated Vietnam over much of the 20th century: "I was born in the war, grew up in the war, suffered in the war, and lost with the war."[46] This summarized the experiences of an entire generation of Vietnamese, both North and South, who only knew conflict their entire lives.

Chapter 33

"Defend to the death ..."

25TH ARVN DIVISION SLOGAN

But what of the 25th ARVN Division, the unit my father and his team worked so hard to advise? In April 1975, they established a defensive position just outside of Saigon in the hopes of halting the enemy's invasion of the capital. Barbed wire and mined obstacles were erected to both slow the enemy's advance and, reportedly, keep their own soldiers within the perimeter. A slogan was adopted by the division in the final days of South Vietnam: "Defend to the death." After being completely surrounded and cut off from Saigon for several days, at 9am on April 30 they were repeatedly attacked by several NVA divisions with tanks, artillery, and infantry assaults. "The enemy staff fled in confusion," reported one NVA general after his units penetrated the command bunker of the 25th, "the main gate had opened, and the enemy officers and soldiers vaulted past barricades—even barbed wire and minefields—to flee."[1]

At the same time, aided by the VCI, guerrillas from the tunnels of Củ Chi swarmed up from the ground, joined by groups from other local VC elements, all of which caused the 25th to virtually disintegrate within a matter of hours. Some 5,000 men were captured, including the commander. The rest did their best to discard their uniforms and blend back into the population as civilians,[2] adding their boots to the piles in the roads. Witnesses to the events of the 1975 Spring Offensive watched on, bewildered as entire well-armed divisions of Marines and army elements like the 25th were swept aside in the northern onslaught one after the other, "boom, just like that."[3]

My father watched this collapse in safety thousands of miles away. Years later, while working on his PhD, he too struggled to understand what had happened. "The Saigon government fell so swiftly that it stunned everyone," he wrote in a published article on the agricultural systems of the country. "Even the northern victors were not expecting to win so easily and so quickly."[4] Somehow sadly weaving his wartime experiences into an unrelated topic, he wrote that the fall "was more than just a military defeat. It was a collapse of a whole socioeconomic structure."[5]

After the war, thousands of former ARVN soldiers, especially the officers and Hồi Chánh, were either killed or placed in reeducation, forced labor, or political indoctrination camps. Curiously, the anti-war movement was largely silent about the atrocities occurring in South Vietnam to civilians and former military members. The American war was over, and these new rounds of slaughter occurring there, in Cambodia and Laos, were no longer cool to rally against. The West had moved on.

I was unable to find out what happened to any of the officers or men my father advised. However, by examining some of the stories from the Vietnamese diaspora that eventually settled in Northern Virginia near my home, it is possible to piece together what many of them may have experienced as their units crumbled and they tried to shed their identities and blend into the civilian population, trying to save themselves and their families in the post-apocalyptic nightmare that overtook Saigon in April of 1975.

A Fulbright Scholar and graduate of Princeton and Columbia Universities, Nguyễn Ngọc Bích left a job at the Vietnamese Embassy in DC and returned to serve his home nation in 1971 to support President Thiệu as his director general of information. He was a government man through and through; a prime target for capture by the North.[6]

In a last-ditch effort, Thiệu sent Bích and his wife to the US on April 19 to try to obtain American help to thwart the rapid advance of the communists across South Vietnam. A mere two days before, at his public resignation, Thiệu had called the Americans an inhumane ally conducting an inhumane act by abandoning them in their time of need. "The Americans have asked us to do an impossible thing," Thiệu told his fellow countrymen in an incoherent and rambling resignation speech about the failure of Vietnamization. "You have asked us to do something that you failed to do with half a million powerful troops and skilled commanders and with nearly $300 billion in expenditures over 6 long years."[7]

Once in the US, Bích met his old friend Sven Kraemer, then on staff with the National Security Council. "The situation is totally hopeless," Kraemer told Bích as he emotionally embraced him, "there's nothing you can expect ... the hounds are out." Undeterred, Bích transferred his pleas from the White House to Congress and knocked on every door he could in both the House and Senate. Rebuked by the actual members of Congress, the most he received was a sympathetic ear from 20-something interns and low-level staffers.[8]

Realizing that South Vietnam was truly alone, instead of hiding in the US, on April 26 he returned to his country on the last inbound civilian plane. Once on the ground in Saigon, the stewardesses and pilots immediately sprinted down the boarding stairs, leaving the passengers to their fate—no doubt hoping to link up with their families before things got bad. He and his wife, along with several sad

Americans and 40 drunk and celebrating Chinese communists disguised as civilians, joined the fleeing flight crew as they entered the chaotic airport and city.[9]

Returning home, Bích and his wife linked up with 26 other family members and friends, many of whom were soldiers and government officials. Dodging firefights and artillery rounds, they fled south through Saigon towards the coast. From there, the intrepid group commandeered a small boat and ended up on the island of Phú Quốc in the Gulf of Thailand. There they found over 50,000 other refugees all fleeing from the country, joining the mass of prior soldiers, officers, government officials and their families, and civilians, who all feared living under communist rule. Many arrived with only the clothes on their back and nothing else. Huddled on the tiny island that quickly became overwhelmed, Bích's team reboarded their small craft and set out to sea again, praying for some type of rescue.[10]

By then, as part of Operation *Frequent Wind*, the US was leading evacuation efforts of American civilians and at-risk Vietnamese from South Vietnam. The repurposed cargo ship the SS *American Challenger* was transporting refugees from Vũng Tàu, where my father once enjoyed his R&R, to Guam. Luckily, Bích's small craft drifted across the path of the *American Challenger*, where they were plucked from the water. Originally estimated at a transport capacity of 1,000 passengers, Bích's team added to the now 7,000 who were packed into every crevice of the cargo ship.[11]

For the next ten days, as the *American Challenger* chugged towards Guam, the lack of potable water, edible food, or even bathroom facilities made for horrid conditions on the ship. Latrines were rigged from pieces of 2" by 4" wooden beams fastened to hang out over the sides of the ship. As the refugees defecated, schools of sharks rolled and frothed beneath them in a frenzy, gleefully feeding on their waste. Many tried to clean themselves with seawater gathered by bucket, not knowing that when combined with soap, it forms a muddy cake in your hair that cannot be rinsed out. Most stood shoulder to shoulder in a huddled mass on the open deck, hoping for rain so they could get something to drink or those who had unfortunately experimented with soap and seawater could wash the mess from their bodies.[12]

By the time they got to Guam, Bích was black with grime and had lost a lot of weight. With only one pair of shorts and literally nothing else, he disembarked on the island and luckily ran into an American official he knew. Shocked by his appearance, he cut through the red tape and quickly processed Bích and his wife to the refugee camp at Orote Point—the same place where my father had sent a postcard back to the family all those years ago on his way to Vietnam. A week later, Bích and his wife were settled in Northern Virginia with other family members to start their lives anew. Left behind were numerous former ARVN soldiers waiting their turn at a life in the US.[13]

As the daughter of a senior ARVN officer, Anh Thu Lu was used to the good life. Growing up on a private military compound reserved for officers near the Tân Sơn Nhất airbase, she attended school next to the presidential palace which, as it does for all teenagers, made up her world. Consumed by her upcoming final exams, she was vaguely aware of the conversations between her father and other senior officers, none of whom thought the country was on the verge of collapse. Rather, they spent hours huddled around maps in dark smoke-filled rooms planning how they would regroup south of Saigon and conduct a counterattack to drive back the invading force.[14]

Despite this belief, Lu's father still felt it best to evacuate his family to safety, sending his younger children and wife out of the country to France in early April 1975. Lu could not go because she was 16 years old. The South Vietnamese government's rule was that only children under 16 could evacuate. On April 28, Lu went to bed after a stressful day of studying only to be woken by the sounds of explosions in the distance as the communists began to shell Saigon. Her uncle, a government politician, called and told her father that what Americans were left were evacuating. Scratch all delusional counteroffensive fantasies—it was time to go now.[15]

At 6:00am on April 29, Lu, her father, and her uncle loaded into a military jeep with one backpack each and sped out of the military compound she lived on just in time. Moments later, the enemy launched shells directly into the base, destroying most of the structures. Before this attack, the complex was peaceful and orderly, just as it had always seemed to the young girl. The minute they exited the gate they entered a world of complete chaos. Every type of vehicle imaginable, from tiny mopeds to large trucks, was loaded with families and their belongings. All had scared and bewildered looks on their faces; everyone felt they had to run but no one knew where to go. Still in darkness due to overcast conditions, their jeep weaved in and out of bumper-to-bumper traffic as explosions detonated in the distance in every direction.[16]

They too, had no idea where to go; after all, the country was not going to fall so quickly, or so her father and uncle had believed. First, they tried a house in a neighborhood where the US ambassadorial staff used to live. There they found several hundred people milling around the home; apparently all had heard the same rumor about a bus which would supposedly take them to the airport. After about 45 minutes, her father realized no one was coming. Unsure where to go next, her father and uncle knowingly whispered to each other, "Let's go to the river," as they jumped back into their jeep, leaving the confused group behind.[17]

The Soài Rạp river was a major waterway that ran south of Saigon and connected with the South China Sea. Because of this, during the war large barges pulled by tugboats constantly plied its waters to and fro, delivering ammunition and other war commodities during the conflict. "I'd say probably the whole of Saigon was down at the river, trying to get out," Lu recalled years later, "just get out." People lined the riverbanks shoving and pushing each other just to get a chance to be near the riverbank and board a barge. Their three-person party joined the fracas; abandoning their jeep, they fought their way through the crowds on foot. "Listen.

If you don't see me, keep running ahead," Lu's father told her as he grabbed her by the shoulders and yelled in her face. "Don't go back and look for me. Don't ever go back and look for me because I'll take care of myself." Years later, when Lu asked her father what he would have done if he had been left behind, he shrugged his shoulders and said that he had a grenade in his backpack and he would have taken care of himself rather than be captured.[18]

Together, they finally made it to the riverbank as a barge pulled away. An American there with a handheld radio informed them that another one would arrive shortly. As Lu waited, she had a chance to look out over the city as by this time it was midday. It was still overcast, only this time she wasn't sure if it was due to the weather or a result of the countless angry dark black plumes of smoke billowing up from Saigon. As she huddled with the mass of humanity on the riverbank, the crowd emitted shrieks and groans each time a large explosion occurred in the city—which at this point was almost constant.[19]

Finally, another barge maneuvered towards the bank as pandemonium erupted among the throng. People began violently shoving each other as they attempted to be the first to board the craft. Many were knocked down and ground to death between the barge and the bank, the air filling with blood-curdling screams as the boat docked and shifted up and down with the waves. There was one small gate with a gangplank to board the boat. Not willing to wait their turn, Lu's father immediately grabbed her and launched her into the air, hoping to toss her over the side of the barge. "Grab the side," he screamed as she was vaulted toward the top of the 10-foot-high sandbagged barrier which ringed the craft.

Luckily, she grabbed the top of the water-soaked sandbags. With the burlap scratching her skin, she threw herself over the wall and into the barge. She collapsed into a corner and sobbed deeply, hoping that her father would join her soon. He eventually made it onto the boat where he found her in that state. "Let's go home," she begged through tears. "We won't be able to live," he sadly told his daughter, knowing full well what would happen to her as the child and niece of high-ranking military officials. "Who's going to let you live?" he quietly said under his breath to no one in particular.[20]

The sun was setting as their now-packed barge slowly pulled away from the riverbank. As the sky grew dark, Lu noticed that the only lights visible in the sky were the steady stream of American helicopters evacuating personnel from the embassies. The tugboat's engine remained off as both it and the barge drifted downstream with the current. They did not want to get the attention of any communist forces; absolute silence was necessary. As the smoke from the countless fires shrouded them in darkness and they drifted along, the sounds of firefights and artillery shells serenaded them. As they coasted, various soldiers from ARVN units stripped off their gear and uniforms and swam out to the barge to climb aboard. After a terrifying brief moment stuck on a sand bar during low tide, the barge made it out to the open ocean.[21]

Early on April 30, with the tugboat engine at full speed, the barge was pulled into the rough waters of the South China Sea. As they advanced, they passed numerous small fishing boats and other craft all flying or waving white flags, crammed with fleeing people begging to be picked up. Despite the surrender flags, the communists were playing a spirited game of battleship, bracketing their artillery fire onto the tiny boats. Each hit must have been met with cheers by the enemy battery. Luckily, their barge was able to quickly push through the kill zone unscathed.[22]

They soon linked up with the US Navy Cargo Ship *SGT Andrew Miller*, also a part of Operation *Frequent Wind*. As women and children boarded first via the one rope ladder dropped to the barge, Lu watched in horror as a US Huey crashed into the ocean near them. They only later realized that it was probably one of the helicopters that the Americans were abandoning in Vietnam, and that the pilot had jumped before the bird smashed into the sea. She also watched as the elderly and injured struggled to climb the ladder, some even falling to their deaths.[23]

Eventually securing over 6,000 refugees, the *Miller* steamed towards Guam. After processing, Lu, her father, and uncle eventually ended up in Camp Pendleton, California. There, Lu's father was able to find a US Army general who had been his previous advisor, who helped get them sponsored and settled in Northern Virginia. Sadly, the general told them he could not help them financially, just with their entry into the country. "That's fine," Lu's father told him, "we'll take care of ourselves."[24]

Bích's and Lu's stories allude to what may have happened to some of the men and officers of the ARVN's 25th Division. Some may have individually made it to Phú Quốc, Vũng Tàu, or some other coastal area to be picked up by one of the ships supporting Operation *Frequent Wind*; others may have swum the various rivers surrounding Saigon to board the countless numbers of small vessels or barges creeping their way to the Gulf of Thailand or the South China Sea. The story of Liêu Nguyễn, daughter of a rich merchant from Da Nang, offers another intriguing possibility of what may have happened to some of the men from the 25th.

On April 29, the family of 10, two parents and eight kids (including one young son with disabilities), fled to Nhà Bè just south of Saigon to meet a helicopter they had pre-paid for. Unfortunately, they went to the wrong spot and missed the flight. The family then snuck onto a South Vietnamese naval base, thinking that it would be safe there. After spending all night under fire in the bomb shelters, they decided that early on the 30th they needed to find another way out of the country. They fled to a nearby temple, where her father was able to bribe a monk to help them purchase a small fishing boat. Along with about 20 other people they entered the river, where the craft began to leak as those on board became fiercely seasick.

As most on the ship violently emptied their stomachs and bowels, Nguyễn's mother stood on the bow, frantically waving a shirt, hoping for rescue from one of the other ships. As her children bailed out water mixed with vomit and excrement, the mother went to each of the older kids and instructed them to find pieces of wood to hang on to when the ship sank. "Just hang on, and don't worry about dad or mom or anybody else," the scared mother quietly told her eldest children as she instructed them not to worry about any of their brothers and sisters. "Forget about them. Just hang on to that and float for your life." Eventually, Nguyễn realized that her mother had decided that she could not save the youngest children, only the oldest.[25]

Finally, a tugboat stopped to assist the sinking vessel. Luckily, Nguyễn's father had enough money left to pay for the boat to assist them back to the riverbank, where they were able to purchase passage on another run-down ship. After briefly contemplating quitting and returning home to take their chances with the communists, they apprehensively set out on the river again. As they left their lives behind them with no destination in mind, they noticed a large South Vietnamese cargo ship in front of them. With no other options, they decided to head to the large ship as it seemed to have a better chance of surviving the open ocean than their dilapidated craft.[26]

As they neared the large vessel, they were surprised by the crew as their silhouettes slowly materialized in the haze. Instead of the civilian seadogs expected for that type of craft, ARVN soldiers still in their uniforms and field gear peered down at them as they begged to be taken aboard. Rather than dissolving into individuals, an ARVN battalion had decided to stay as a unit. They had fought, bled, and died for one another in the war, and now they would flee together to safety as a team. As the soldiers took them on board, Nguyễn's mother was petrified that the group of men would rape her six daughters, a fear that dissipated as the men embraced the family and treated them as their own.[27]

This new band of expatriates steamed down the river as fast as they could, noticing the communist flags being raised over every population center that they passed. They pushed on downriver as an enemy vessel slowly fell in behind them, gaining ground as they did so. Nguyễn's family huddled together in fear as a floating gunfight ensued. As the ship neared the open ocean, they noticed that the communists had strung a thick steel cable across the mouth of the river to prevent any more boats from fleeing. With bullets peppering their stern, and the banks of the river swarming with enemy troops, the ARVN commander had no choice but to go full steam ahead. As prayers erupted from the Buddhist, Catholic, and any newfound believers on board, the passengers braced for impact. After a brief hesitation and a mournful groan, the cable snapped with a tremendous twang as the ship catapulted past it into the open ocean, leaving their pursuers behind.[28]

Once there, they eventually linked up with two barges, the exact same type as the sandbagged rectangle that Lu had escaped on. The three vessels bobbed in the sea and awaited the slew of US Navy ships that stopped and took aboard who they could. As this occurred, the ARVN soldiers sadly dumped all their gear and uniforms into the ocean. Nguyễn's family gave them what extra clothes they had, which was not a lot. The once brave and proud fighting men in their olive drab issued attire were reduced to wearing one piece of civilian clothing each. Some wore just a shirt and underwear, while others received just a pair of shorts or pants; all to blend in with the surrounding civilians the best they could so they could be rescued. The Nguyễns distributed their clothes amongst the men the best they could.[29]

Like the others, Nguyễn's family was processed through Guam before finally settling in Northern Virginia. It is unknown what happened to that band of warriors who chose to stick together until the end.[30] We will also never know what happened to the men my father advised from the 1/49th Regiment of the ARVN 25th Division. Hearing some of the stories of those who fled, who now live only miles from me, shows what may have occurred. In the end, my father's only hope is that most of them either found a way out or somehow survived the years of camps—living in peace today with the war far behind them.

Chapter 34

"The mission is to destroy the enemy ..."

ALIC TAHIR

I wish I had read Douglas Kinnard's *The War Managers* earlier in my military career instead of some of the other nonsense I was given as part of my professional development. Every single leader deploying to Iraq and Afghanistan should have been forced to digest this book. Many of the strategic bear traps we walked right into were the same in Vietnam and could have been avoided. Shockingly, in *The War Managers* it was claimed that almost 70 percent of the Army generals who led during the war did not understand the objectives they were tasked with achieving. "This mirrors a deep-seated strategic failure," wrote Kinnard, "the inability of policy makers to frame tangible, attainable goals."[1]

How did the US blindly stumble into these quagmires? In hindsight, there were half a dozen clear offramps. But at the time, all was murk, haze, and gloom; compounded by a myriad other issues which made focusing solely on the conflicts nearly impossible. Internal social unrest; rising tensions with North Korea, China, and the then Soviet Union; a Cold War in Europe; an Israeli conflict in the Middle East; criticism over the military-industrial complex; and defense spending, along with severe budget cuts to the DOD framed the backdrop of Vietnam. Ironically, this almost describes the situation today and for the past two decades.

McNamara, whose name is still synonymous with Vietnam, acknowledged the inability of successive administrations to focus solely on crafting responses to the war. "Vietnam was but one of a multitude of problems we confronted," he would later admit.[2] He also forever remained sensitive to accusations on the strategic bankruptcy of the conflict. "Some critics have asserted that the United States lacked a military strategy in Vietnam," he declared. "In fact, we had one—but its assumptions were deeply flawed."[3]

Gathering a cabal of smart people together and siccing them on a national security problem was and still is the most common way to craft strategy. Armed with a host of Ivy League degrees, it is easy to analyze, understand, and formulate responses to a conflict without ever having set foot in the war zone. Holbrooke, from his experience supporting the US ambassador, also noted this phenomenon. "You know, the smartest person in the room wasn't always right," he said years after the war. "Sometimes the best and brightest of the '60s, brilliant as they were, got carried into very serious errors which might have been avoided, had they listened more carefully to slower speaking, less brilliant people who happened to spend part of their lives in the rice paddies or jungles of Southeast Asia."[4] This highlighted a common result when keen minds are gathered together to solve the world's problems: that of bullying or embarrassing—either intentionally or unintentionally—those not as sharp as them into agreeing with their perspective.

This aside, what added to the distraction and further hampered the formulation of a strategy was the fact that war was never officially declared against North Vietnam. "Whom do we declare war against?" Ambassador Taylor reportedly cynically answered when asked. The VC? Hanoi? And what about the impact that would have on the linkage of mutual defense treaties between the Soviets and China, was his usual answer.[5] SECDEF Clifford echoed this concern, recalling how every expert on Southeast Asia queried unanimously declared that an invasion of North Vietnam would unquestionably pull China into the war.[6] McNamara and many others took this concern one step further. Looking past the fear of conventional Soviet and Chinese forces, they were determined that Vietnam would not trigger a nuclear war.[7]

"Influencing many of the decisions was an almost paranoid fear of nuclear confrontation," an infuriated Westmoreland later seethed over this concern and the constant shadow it cast over Vietnam.[8] Secretary of State Rusk acknowledged this, calling everything they did a conscious "limited effort" to avoid the worst. It was also this dread that prevented the total mobilization of American society behind Vietnam. "You didn't see pretty movie stars out selling bonds in factories and things like that, all the things we did during WWII," Rusk later said about the lack of government attempts to whip up a war fever amongst the population, "because we felt that in this nuclear world where thousands of megatons are lying around in the hands of frail human beings it's just too dangerous for entire people to become too angry."[9]

This combined fear of conventional forces and nuclear weapons eventually spawned what became known as the strategy of "graduated response," the implementation of which Westmoreland later labeled as "one of the most lamentable mistakes of the war … bomb a little bit … stop it a while to give the enemy a chance to cry uncle," he described in layman terms in his memoir, "then bomb a little bit more but never enough to really hurt." As he correctly noted, this was no way to win a war.[10]

With a graduated response or not, Westmoreland's leadership ensured that hyper-focused efforts on killing the enemy became the guiding strategic doctrine for much of the war, highlighting the most glaring disconnect between tactics and strategy of any conflict in history. "The fundamental strategic mistake which was made was the idea somehow that the United States could bleed an Asian communist enemy into the point of fading away," later stated Holbrooke. "That was just a basic and profound error."[11] Westmoreland's successor also realized the folly of this. "Shooting them—well that'll stop it," Abrams chastised a group of officers who suggested more killing was the answer to Vietnam. "Christ, these people have been shot at for the last 20 years ... going out there and killing a few of them is not, in my opinion, going to have the effect [of winning the war]."[12]

As Abrams and others recognized, you cannot solely kill your way out of a problem. "We should have just bombed them back into the Stone Age," is something people always tell me when they learn I served in the fight against radical Islam. As anyone who has ever had a murder or successful suicide in their family will tell you, those deaths leave a stain which can fester for generations. For every one enemy killed, 10 more insurgents are created. Twenty, if the person killed was an innocent civilian.

The body count of Vietnam also offers the perfect case study on the obsession of bureaucracies with data, the collection of which, in this case, was supposed to point to when a victory in Vietnam was going to occur. Never mind the usefulness of it—a bubble chart or graph must be filled out each week, no matter what it supposedly depicts. Vietnam was the true birthplace of this fascination with numbers that are meant to somehow make sense of the dark side of human nature. While analyzing data is one tool to measure progress and effectiveness in conflict, it is not the sole one. This passion for metrics as the answer still cripples the military in everything in attempts to do today, in both peacetime and war.

Westmoreland, perhaps unfairly, has borne the brunt of the criticism for the start of today's unquenchable thirst for military data to gauge victory, which then birthed efforts to "cook the books" to tell a positive story. Leslie Gelb, a senior official in the DOD, declared that we all "were well aware of the different calculations from the beginning, and I think also agreed that Westmoreland's figures could not be correct."[13] Holbrooke also noted the credibility gap between the public, military leaders, and Washington politicians that came from this data manipulation, calling it a "product of a system of reporting which emphasized progress at the price of accuracy."[14] Ambassador Taylor bitterly described the volumes of charts and graphs managed throughout the conflict, conceding that "the data upon which they were based were non-existent or thoroughly unreliable."[15] McNamara, the self-avowed numbers guy, also humbly conceded that "many of these measures were misleading or erroneous."[16]

These candid self-reflections from senior officials make for a good read in hindsight, but what of their tangible impacts during Vietnam? "I shudder to think how many of our soldiers were killed on a body-counting mission," anonymously noted one general officer when asked about this as part of the research for *The War Managers*. "What a waste," he cuttingly concluded.[17] My father could very well have been added to this statistic on numerous occasions, most notably in the Pineapple region all those years ago when, separated from his platoon, alone and out hunting for a body, he stumbled upon the footprint rapidly filling up with water.

Interestingly, the topic of data manipulation came up when a retired general spoke to my small group at CGSC. The senior officer claimed that, despite what he had heard, there was no way that anyone in today's Army had ever been ordered or coerced into submitting a false or slanted report. We all nodded our heads in affirmation like good soldiers as he concluded his speech. Once he departed, our instructor asked what we thought. After a moment of awkward silence, one of my classmates blurted out, "That guy is so out of touch." Expressing what we all were thinking, he continued, "There is not a single officer here who has not been ordered to cook the books to make it appear more favorable." In his book, Kinnard gets the final say on this phenomenon, which was kick started in Vietnam: "The immensity of the false reporting is a blot on the honor of the Army."[18]

Perhaps General Keller summed it up best when he and I were reflecting on Vietnam, data-driven conflicts, and my own generation's lack of effective strategic formulation, implementation, and the legacies they left behind. "I do know we entered all these conflicts by the decisions of our political leaders, probably with military cooperation but with unclear objectives," he told me. "As each of them unfolded over time, there was a creeping redefinition of objectives, and the military switched from 'winning America's Wars' to 'establishing stability/restoring governance/training foreign military establishing Democracies'."[19]

Unfortunately, the US could never quite synchronize efforts against whatever they were supposedly trying to collectively achieve.[20] As such, at times it seemed that only the military and heaps of contractors were trying to realize American objectives overseas, pushing trillions in support and goods to fragile, corrupt, and dubious establishments. Furthermore, and more importantly, according to Keller, the constant reshaping of strategies, goals, roles, and missions "led to dishonesty, [and a] loss of trust and divisions in American society that still exist today."[21] "Then," he sadly concluded, "Americans said, 'Let's Get Out' and we left … the aftermath is still unfolding."[22]

Achieving a unity of effort while executing a whole-of-nation approach to conflict are the official strategic buzz phrases that encapsulate everything outlined above. Ultimately, these were lofty goals that were never quite achieved in Vietnam or during my generation's wars.

Westmoreland later commented on these failures in his memoir. He called the Washington, DC-type bureaucracy present in Vietnam a "complex, awkward arrangement."[23] Abrams also commented on this with his staff, noting the great struggle it took to achieve a unified effort from among all the entities present, each "jealous of their own empires."[24]

Comments on the disjointed effort after the war were not confined to military leaders. Holbrooke chastised the uncoordinated efforts between the myriads of federal agencies that had somehow been replicated in Vietnam, calling out the tremendous disputes that occurred as each fought to control programs that overlapped. "Whatever bureaucratic rivalries existed in Washington—and there were plenty of them," Holbrooke explained, "these were mirrored in Saigon."[25] The assistant director of rural affairs in USAID also commented on the massive growth of disjointed programs throughout the conflict: "The bigger it got, the blinder it got," he remembered with regret.[26] Media correspondent Anne Miller supported this view, later recalling what she termed the "little empires" present in Vietnam, operating with no understanding of how their efforts fit into the larger picture. "It just became a sprawl," she ruefully reminisced, "an uncoordinated, undesignated bunch of money, bunch of people, [and] bunch of materials."[27]

Not only were programs in Vietnam poorly coordinated, but they were also inadequately resourced with soldiers. Unlike my wars, where US reserve forces were basically broken with constant deployments—which they are still struggling to recover from today—they were largely not mobilized for Vietnam. This was partly due to the draft and force structure; the reserves were not saturated with the sustainment units needed for combat as they are presently. However, the decision then was primarily influenced by two things. First, the memory of the Berlin crisis of 1961, where the reserves were mobilized for a year, which triggered a growing clamor from the US population to "bring the boys home," forcing swift strategic decisions. Second, calling up the reserves meant that the president would have to declare a national emergency or go to Congress for approval—neither of which was palatable.[28] The result? A broken, tired active Army, with its morale crushed from never-ending deployments, responsibilities across the globe, and unwilling draftees.

Moreover, Vietnam's system of short individual tours did more harm than good. Westmoreland defended this arrangement, believing that the one-year tour gave a soldier a goal, while also sharing the burden equally among volunteers and draftees, thereby improving morale amongst the troops. He also hoped it would prevent pressure from the US population to bring the troops home, as was seen earlier in the Berlin crisis.[29]

Despite Westmoreland's belief, many criticized this practice. One time deputy assistant secretary of defense and later National Security Council member Morton Halperin echoed many in his condemnation of the one-year tour as well as the practice of limiting commissioned officers to just six months of combat. "American casualties were much higher than they had to be," Halperin claimed, "because the critical factor in U.S. casualties was how long the commissioned officer had been in command of the unit."[30] Later studies appeared to back up his claim. One hypothesized that the greater the time spent in Vietnam, the greater one's chances of survival, especially for key leaders. The constant churn of rotating individuals and the steep learning curve that came with each of them worked against this. "Vietnam data," the study concluded, "suggest that the short tour generated additional US casualties."[31]

My generation's wars of one-year rotating units instead of individuals mitigated some of the issues from Vietnam. However, whether it is one person or an entire unit coming and going does not negate the identified learning curve. It is not until at least month six when a unit finally figures out what it is doing, only to depart months later and the process to begin all over again with the incoming organization. Either way, as Westmoreland noted in his defense of the policy, whether unit or individual, one just needs to bide their time. Survive each day and you know you'll be home soon. While this is good for morale, it is horrible for winning a war. As much as I hate to advocate for this stance, units and soldiers must remain in place for the entire (or at least longer than a year) conflict if one ever wants to achieve a true unity of effort within a whole-of-government approach.

Disjointed strategic objectives and policies, poorly coordinated programs, and the constant churn of personnel, each with their own varied knowledge level on the war and how it should be fought, only resulted in one thing—the complete overload of the South Vietnamese government with things not directly related to the conflict. "The total commitment of the North Vietnamese to the war effort led directly to the defeat of the Southern structure," acutely stated my father in a paper while a PhD candidate after the war, "because the latter was divided in its attention to the war and to other societal pursuits."[32]

Secretary of State Rusk echoed my father's assessment. "I think once we counted about forty-four different programs that we were pressing the South Vietnamese to put into effect in South Vietnam in order to strengthen the fiber of the country and mobilize the countryside," Rusk noted years later. "That was simply beyond their governing capacities to handle, and it was indigestible."[33] Official government military histories also acknowledged this problem. A Center of Military History publication credited "a plethora of competing initiatives" with diffusing and overburdening counterinsurgency and South Vietnamese administrative efforts. "There were just too many people charged with stirring the pacification pot, each with his own agenda and chain of command," it concluded.[34]

Finally, even South Vietnamese officials recognized the issue. Vice President Nguyễn Cao Kỳ chastised the priorities of US support to his country, claiming that America placed an emphasis on consumer luxury goods and products over actual industrial enterprises which could support the war effort. "We are at war," he incredulously declared, "and yet we cannot buy equipment for an ammunition factory … at the same time, we have been importing an astounding amount of cars, motorbikes, TV sets, [and] perfumes."[35] President Thiệu supported his colleague's claim, pointing to his war-ravaged nation's requirement to somehow build a sustainable economy while supporting a massive military that went far beyond the ability of a country with only 17 million citizens—while also appeasing incessant American demands.[36]

Even with an executable strategy backed by the full commitment of the nation, would the US have won in Vietnam, and for that matter in Iraq and Afghanistan? Was victory ever even clearly defined? Was it a secure South free from communist meddling, one partially free, or one only moderately free in the loosest sense of the word? Was Vietnam part of a larger communist containment strategy or an action independent of itself? In my generation's wars, were we trying to eradicate radical Islam or just prevent future attacks on the homeland? You could argue that the latter was achieved relatively quickly, so why were we involved there for decades? All of this highlights a persistent problem with vocabulary.

Western military minds, national security experts, the media, and armchair strategists are subliminally obsessed with the quest for Napoleonic decisive battles, and the clearly observable victory that often accompanies them. When the West goes to war, this must be the apparent and immediate outcome. When that does not quickly materialize, doubt and confusion set in. This is further muddied when military and political leaders insist on continuing to use words such as defeat and victory to describe the expected results of the latest action. This cycle of openly communicating to Western populations that we are on the edge of destroying the enemy, which will produce an apparent victory, is a repeated one. Each time it does not transpire, it adds to war fatigue and the perceived incompetence of the government.

When civilians hear these grandiose words to describe actions against an adversary, they instantly think of a flag being flown over Iwo Jima or tanks rolling into Berlin. When the victory parade does not occur and the troops do not come home, they ask themselves, "Wait a minute, I thought we just achieved a victory, why are we still fighting?" This disconnect was evident multiple times throughout the Vietnam War. A perfect example is the 101st Airborne and the bloody battle of Hamburger Hill. After the military touted it as a great victory and then subsequently abandoned Hill 937 a mere two weeks after it had been seized, the American public howled in indignation. "This was a tremendous, gallant victory," angrily fumed the commander of the 101st, Major General Melvin Zais, in response to the inability of the public to understand what had occurred, "and some people are acting like it was a catastrophe."[37]

Ambassador Taylor found himself constantly defending himself against those in Washington who raged over why America could not just win this thing already. "What do you mean by winning?" was his constant response. "Are you talking about an Appomattox or surrender on the deck of the *Missouri* or what are we talking about?" he would annoyingly ask. No one, including him, had an answer.[38] His successor, Ambassador Bunker, would respond to this same question with a more measured answer. "Our objective has never been a military victory in the conventional sense," he stated halfway through my father's year in Vietnam. Rather, the goal was to frustrate as much as possible the North's effort to take over the South. "This may not be a victory in the usual sense of the word," Bunker concluded, "but it is nevertheless success."[39]

In all fairness, by the time my father arrived in Vietnam there were many leaders who had backed off from scheduling ticker-tape parades in Times Square and had recoiled from the language that accompanied them. A month before his arrival, one major newspaper noted the current feeling among many senior leaders in Vietnam, writing that few now spoke of marching into North Vietnam or wiping Hanoi off the map. "That kind of talk faded long ago," it reported.[40] In his memoir, Westmoreland claimed that he consciously avoided using the word victory to describe strategic and operational goals in Vietnam.[41] Despite this claim, his constant whitewashing of the war and use of decisive language painted a picture that the end was always right around the corner.

At the very least Vietnam, Iraq, and Afghanistan must teach us this one lesson: Stop using grandiose terms and grandstanding that convey the wrong message to the American public. Rather, clearly communicate military objectives in realistic and easily understandable terms.

A second lesson has to do with the use of force. "He wanted to achieve his objectives at the cheapest possible cost," Holbrooke scathingly critiqued McNamara after the war. "If the objectives are so important, he shouldn't have been so parsimonious with the resources … if the objectives were only worth limited resources, then the objectives were too limited to be worth going for."[42] In a television interview Westmoreland added to this: "A war winning strategy was not adopted," he said, frustrated about the evolution of the use of force during the conflict; "a strategy of withdrawal was."[43] Interestingly, Kissinger echoed this claim, stating that the only approach that could have changed the outcome of Vietnam would have been to pursue an all-in, gloves-off victory early. "Once we were engaged in a protracted war," Kissinger alleged, "we were playing their ball game."[44]

In one of our many interviews, my father's old friend Tahir once told me, "The mission is to destroy the enemy." Explaining his theory on the misuse of force in Vietnam, the pragmatic old veteran continued, "It's not to open up schools, stores, hospitals, and gas stations, it's just a waste of time."[45] There is some truth to his push-back on the classic "winning the hearts and minds" tenet that defines many counterinsurgency efforts. To their credit, by 1969 military planners understood that the multiple non-combat units in Vietnam were achieving little. It may have been better to embed smaller formations throughout the country in key population enclaves and terrain,[46] although it would have required a million men with an ample conventional reserve force to simultaneously counter NVA regulars, they realistically conceded.[47] In the end though, the limited war effort simply never allowed for this.

While this was a valid assessment, the tooth-to-tail troop ratio deployed in Vietnam remained astronomically slanted towards support elements throughout much of the war. The same can be said for my conflicts. Even while fully acknowledging the need for logistical support, why in the world was I able to swim in a pool, eat pancakes, purchase bootleg DVDs, and participate in a host of other unrelated combat pursuits while in Iraq? Many counter that these activities are needed to maintain and raise the morale of those deployed in an extended conflict. Fair point, but perhaps these conflicts would not have lasted so long if the full weight of the nation's combat forces had been applied initially to achieve clearly defined objectives. Soldiers will accept the lack of niceties if they can clearly see that every single unit and effort is solely devoted to bringing the war to a swift conclusion.

Ultimately, what is most shocking is that if almost everything outlined here about Vietnam was replaced with Afghanistan or Iraq, it would accurately describe what happened there too. Will historians one day point to our ventures during the global war on terror as another waypoint in America's decline? Another activity where good intentions resulted in more turmoil in the world and an even more unstable geopolitical environment? Will correlations be drawn between the abandonment of the South Vietnamese and that of the Kurds and Afghanis? The rise of the Khmer Rouge compared to the Islamic State, the reemergence of the Taliban, and an emboldened Russia and China? Only history will tell.

Epilogue

"Vietnam is still with us ..."

HENRY KISSINGER

I saw nowhere near the amount of combat that my father did. I was not a Navy Seal, a Green Beret, or a Delta Force operative. I was just one of thousands who raised my hand over the last two decades to serve our nation during a time of war—an act I would never have contemplated had my father not been in the Army. My mother backs this belief, claiming that even though my father rarely talked about his time in Vietnam, it was the influence of that conflict that began forging me into the man I am today. In doing so she reminds me of her little boy who played with GI Joe action figures and ran around the woods in mock battles.[1]

With zero help from Saddam's funny money, I met the love of my life at a little-known base near Boston, Massachusetts. The Army and I then dragged her to Texas, Kansas, Washington, DC, back to Texas, where we had our beautiful son, and then to Kansas once again. In between naps and feeding times, he kicked around on his playmat as I wrote this book, the only sound occasionally breaking my concentration being a grunt, giggle, or coo as he tried to raise his head or roll over. This was soon replaced by a baby racing around the room on all fours and eventually by a toddler pulling on my leg saying "Dadda, Dadda, do puzzle or play trains" as I tried to focus. As he did so, I couldn't help but wonder if our wars would one day seduce him to join. Will my son, and the children of others like me, be intrigued by the snippets of military stories and occasional dinner-table flashbacks of faraway and long-ago wars in foreign lands, just as I was?

My mother recoiled when I mentioned this possibility to her. "He is such a delight, I hate to see him walking through mud."[2] When I told her that I had walked through all kinds of mud in the Army, she sheepishly had no reply. Although the night before I was shipped to basic training, I do remember my mother, the smartest and toughest woman I have ever met, one deserving of her own book one day, quietly whispering to my father with red eyes if he thought I would be treated alright. I did not hear his answer; however, I was such a troubled teen that I think both were probably just happy I was finally doing something positive.

The relationship between a father and son can be tricky. Emotions and words are often left unspoken, but the bond is ubiquitous and unbreakable. The slew of Vietnam War movies I grew up watching complicated this further. I somehow believed that unless I joined the military and went to war, he would never see me as an equal. The "bond of brotherhood that can only be formed in combat" nonsense had somehow entrenched itself in my psyche; I have only recently shaken it off. I wonder what ridiculous message will be implanted in my son's head from the future movies, streaming shows, and video games he will eventually be exposed to about my generation's wars.

Just like characters in a film, exploring my father's service introduced me to some Oscar winners: Wilkins, Hindle, and Lockeby, salt-of-the-earth grunts who innocuously faded back into society after their brief brush with history. Then there was Keller, the consummate senior military professional that all officers secretly want to be like. Tahir, the rough and tough, black and white, tells-it-like-it-is combat veteran that America seems good at producing. And then of course my father, considered hilarious by some, a no-nonsense leader by others, and extremely brave by all. The adage rings true here: children never really know their parents. They forget that before their arrival they had their own lives and personalities. Thankfully, through this experience, I am one of the few who really got to know their dad.

What is the final legacy of Vietnam? Speaking of movies, a more recent flick on the conflict that supposedly erased the Vietnam Syndrome gave a subtle nod to this question. "I don't even know what we did here," complained George Clooney's character Major Archie Gates in the 1999 film *Three Kings* about the First Gulf War. "You wanna occupy Iraq and do Vietnam all over again?" annoyingly replied his impatient boss. "Is that your brilliant idea?" His words indirectly implied that the fear of another Vietnam drove all decisions for that conflict, including leaving Saddam Hussein in power. In a different scene, the correlation between the two conflicts is more directly addressed. "You exorcised the ghosts of Vietnam with a clear moral imperative," a reporter declared to a celebrating soldier at the end of the 100-hour ground war; echoing George H. W. Bush's jubilant statement at the end of the conflict. The soldier's surprised response: "Is that what we did?"[3]

Hollywood aside, Westmoreland remembered Vietnam as a "shabby performance by America, a blemish on our history and a possible blight on our future." Due to the abandonment of the South Vietnamese, he ultimately labeled the whole thing a "shameful national blunder."[4] Answering this same question, SECDEF Clifford called it an overall mistake. An honorable and honest one, but a mistake nonetheless.[5] Ambassador Taylor believed the war was like a runaway snowball; irreversibly and forever damaging America's reputation and prestige as it rolled on.[6]

Kissinger was perhaps the most honest in his assessment of the war's legacy. "Vietnam is still with us," he declared in a 1982 television interview. Predicting future American foreign, diplomacy, and domestic policymaking efforts, he explained, "It created doubts about American judgment, about American credibility, and American power ... it has poisoned our domestic debate in which almost every issue now turns more on motives than on substance." He somberly concluded, "This may well be the heaviest price we have paid for the Vietnam War."[7]

But never mind the brilliant theorists, what of the men who waded through the jungles and inundated rice paddies, all while stepping around punji stakes? "Vietnam, Iraq, and Afghanistan," Larry Lockeby, one of the old salts my father served with in the 82nd Airborne, answered when asked about the war's legacy, "dominos, all three that fell anyway." Later marrying a Vietnamese woman and going into the rice business, Lockeby felt that war was for nothing. Vietnam did fall to the communists, but eventually morphed into a close US ally and one of the largest rice distributors in the world, all without firing a shot. It did result in one thing for his family, though. After an Army recruiter persuaded his son into enlisting after high school, Lockeby, remembering his experience in Vietnam, had a private one-on-one talk with the sergeant. His son did not join.[8]

The men with whom my father advised the Vietnamese also struggled with the legacy of the war. Tahir believed that it was the start of the modern disconnect between the use of diplomacy to further the nation's goals versus military action. "You don't break bread and have tea with evil, with dictators, despots and tyrants," Tahir seethed, "you kill them." He labeled politicians today who try to solely use diplomacy and sanctions against American adversaries as gutless wussies.[9] Keller, in his usual way, had a more composed opinion of the war, breaking down the results of Vietnam into strategic, military, financial, and public support bins. His ultimate analysis was negative in all four areas. "America lost trust and faith in its military and civilian leaders," he concluded about the legacy of the conflict. "It caused military service, civil and political divisions that exist today that were exacerbated by Iraq and Afghanistan."[10]

My father echoed these sentiments. "Letting Americans run the war and insisting that the South follow our rules, policies, and strategy was a big mistake," he told me. He further mused that maybe the answer should have been an advisory effort all along, rather than the massive amounts of conventional US troops inserted over the years. "Would the South have won the war if we just advised ... I doubt it," my father eventually concluded. "The domino would have fallen but it would have been less bloody for the Vietnamese and of course Americans."[11] His opinion of the war remained so raw that he once wrote to his family about obtaining Canadian citizenship for his yet unborn children so that they would have a choice in the event of another draft[12]—an action which he actually followed through with for both my sister and me.

One of President Johnson's national security advisors later called the climactic events at the end of the Vietnam War disturbing, and from which the nation has never healed. He referred to the impact the pictures seen on television—of the chaotic withdrawal from Saigon as the US abandoned its allies—had on the American psyche, labeling it a "traumatic event [of] which we haven't yet taken the full measure."[13]

Decades later, one heartbroken father vented his frustration about another outrageous event where the US publicly left its allies to their fate. "Abbey Gate, Abbey Gate," repeatedly screamed Steve Nikoui to President Biden during his March 2024 State of the Union address, interrupting the president's speech in memory of his son Marine Lance Corporal Kareem Nikoui, one of the last 13 US soldiers killed in a terrorist bombing at the entrance to the Hamid Karzai International Airport in Kabul, Afghanistan.[14] I do not care what anyone says: the chaotic withdrawal from Afghanistan looked exactly like Saigon.

The legacy of the war aside, what was the human cost of Vietnam? The full casualties on the Vietnamese side, both North and South, remain unknown. Besides a pair of names gleaned from the captured items off dead enemies, my father never knew who they killed. For Americans, those who died are still missed at the dinner table; however, as their direct loved ones pass on this too will fade with time.

For my family and my father, men such as Thomas Blevins, Gary Funn, Everett Glick, Jan Doxey, Frank Rodriguez, Algernon Ka'akimaka, Herbert Cho, James Rogers, George Gibner, Alton Ellison, Gary Brown—and many of the South Vietnamese grunts that he advised and grew to love whose names he never knew—will never be forgotten. The same can also be said of those I knew in Iraq and Afghanistan.

I have been in the room with some of the most learned national security minds in the nation. They would look at me as though I was crazy if I tried to explain what I call the Brown Principle, named after Gary Brown, the man on my father's advisory team who was killed just before he left Vietnam. The principle is as follows: if you cannot with a straight face explain to hometown ma and pa that a conflict is worth their child's life, then it is not. I think, at its core, that is the main lesson from Vietnam; a much-needed additive litmus test that is often overlooked but should be included with any lofty national security evaluations.

When I was a child, my father took me to the traveling Vietnam Memorial Wall when it came to Hawai'i. I had no idea what the black reflective surface, inscribed with what looked to me like a never-ending list of names, meant. Many of the visitors wore a mismatch of military uniform parts and were either huddled in small groups, embracing one another, or standing off alone in the distance, staring at the glossy panels, fighting back tears. Grown men, rough-looking guys with long hair and leather biker jackets, some with the famed black-and-yellow Koa Puna motorcycle club patch on their backs, had tears streaming down their faces. My father, in his slacks, aloha shirt, and short haircut stood in sharp contrast to these ruffians, yet somehow, he was still one of them. Looking up at my father as I held his hand, clearly noticing the pain on his face, is one of my earliest memories. It confused me greatly.

I watched as families placed small keepsakes such as letters or photographs at the base of the wall under their loved ones' engraved names, somehow hoping that the wall would convey the messages or share the photo with their forever-gone love. During the week when the crowds of tourists disappear, you still see this same thing occur at the memorial in Washington, DC. You can often find a lone, faded photograph of a young soldier staring back at you with a longing look on their face, as if when they took the picture, they somehow knew they would be killed soon after. At the time I had no idea what any of this meant. It is only after my own war and from researching this book that I finally understand. Perhaps one day I, too, will take my own son to see whatever monument ends up honoring my generation's wars. There we will join the throngs of other veterans from all castes of life, united forever by our service. There we will all battle our own demons, trying to understand what happened.

I now own all my father's mementoes from his time in Vietnam. Among my collection of Muslim keffiyehs (headscarves) in both red and white, Iraqi money, crumbling military plaques and flags, and other odds and ends, his items now rest. Plaques given to him by his soldiers in the 82nd Airborne and with Team 99 are falling apart, just like the many I received over the years. They rest safely, cushioned in storage bins by yellowing magazine and newspaper clippings which depict the My Lai massacre, the fall of Saigon, and Nguyen Charlie comic strips, along with old papers from his PhD that mention Vietnam. With them is a tiny cardboard box that contains his dog tags, ribbons, and other bits of medals. One day I will add my own awards to that same box. My son will inherit it all; his very own treasure chest to dig through when he gets older.

Besides a now-shared batch of war memorabilia, where else do our two wars intersect? Strangely, in his memoirs, McNamara unknowingly tied together four more lessons that can be applied to both conflicts. First, "we do not have the God given right to shape every nation in our own image or as we choose," he wrote about the lack of exhaustive efforts to seek resolutions in international forums before going to war.[15] Second, we underestimated the motivation of our adversaries to "fight and die for their beliefs and values."[16] Third, our miscalculations, due to our blissful ignorance of the history, culture, personalities, and politics of the areas we operated in, undermined all our efforts.[17] Finally, we failed to accept that modern high-tech weaponry cannot solve everything, especially in an unconventional conflict against highly motivated insurgents.[18] "Military force, by itself," McNamara accurately summarized about Vietnam and inadvertently about the wars against terrorism, "cannot rebuild a 'failed state'."[19]

"In the scope of history, Vietnam is not going to be a big deal," Westmoreland said irritatingly in a 1993 interview, "it won't float to the top as a major endeavor."[20] This is a statement that has not lasted the test of time. Just as the legacy of Vietnam chased him to his grave, it will be the same for America as a nation. Will history one day remember my generation's wars as just a continuation of Vietnam? A decades-long series of unlearned lessons, shame, wasted opportunities, and deep regret?

My fantasy is that one day, Iraq and Afghanistan, and the other nations roiled by Islamic extremism, will find a peaceful existence. Not a cookie-cutter transplant of American democracy, but some type of peace and prosperity that works for them. I would be honored to say that I had a small part in that.

Although my father was critical of the Vietnam War, he considered his service as one of the defining moments in his life. He matured into a leader and remembers his time in the Army with humble pride.[21] Vietnam remained forever a part of him. As he once wrote to Keller years after the war, he had been bitten by the "Vietnam bug" and would never recover. He voraciously devoured any articles, books, or television programs about the war that he could, trying to understand what happened.[22] This has not happened to me yet. For some reason, I still avoid learning about my generation's conflicts, wary of another living-room breakdown occurring in front of my family.

Despite his insatiable appetite to learn about his war, my father was never one to join veteran organizations, or sport license plates or hats that called attention to his time in the Army. His memorial to his service was instead demonstrated by his desire to be a good man in his community and to his family—something which he did each day. I have always said to anyone who would listen; if I can only be half the man my father was, I will have been extremely successful in life.

In my first several weeks working in Congress, I met my first US senator. We chatted for about two minutes before I mentioned I had served in Iraq. "Oh," they replied, "I'm sorry." Unsure how to respond, I awkwardly smiled as we shook hands and posed for the obligatory selfie. To this day, I don't know what they meant by their comment. I will say that I am not sorry for my service, and neither is my generation. We are not sorry one bit.

Endnotes

Prologue

1 Schwarzkopf, H. Norman, and Peter Petre, *It Doesn't Take a Hero: General H. Norman Schwarzkopf, the autobiography* (New York: Bantam Books, 1992), 381–2.

2 Powell, Colin L., and Joseph E. Persico, *My American Journey* (New York: Random House, 1995), 149.

3 Reagan, Ronald, *An American Life* (Simon & Schuster, Inc., 1990), 451.

4 George H. W. Bush, "Remarks to the American Legislative Exchange Council, March 1, 1991," in Public Papers of the Presidents of the United States: George Bush, 1991, Book I—January 1 to June 30, 1991, 195–7 (Washington, DC: Government Printing Office, 1991).

5 George W. Bush, "Remarks at the Veterans of Foreign Wars National Convention in Kansas City, Missouri August 22, 2007," in Public Papers of the Presidents of the United States: George W. Bush, 2007, Book II—July 1 to December 31, 2007, 1099–1107 (Washington, DC: Government Printing Office, 2007).

6 Joseph Biden, "Sen. Joe Biden Responds to President Bush's Speech on Iraq," Vote Smart, Facts Matter, August 22, 2007, https://justfacts.votesmart.org/public-statement/284316/sen-joe-biden-responds-to-president-bushs-speech-on-iraq.

7 Barack Obama, "Remarks at the United States Military Academy at West Point, New York, December 1, 2009," in Public Papers of the Presidents of the United States: Barack Obama, 2009, Book II—July 1 to December 31, 2009, 1747–54 (Washington, DC: Government Printing Office, 2009).

8 Joseph Biden, "Remarks by President Biden on the Drawdown of U.S. Forces in Afghanistan," The White House, July 8, 2021, https://www.whitehouse.gov/briefing-room/speeches-remarks/2021/07/08/remarks-by-president-biden-on-the-drawdown-of-u-s-forces-in-afghanistan/.

9 Joseph Biden, "Remarks by President Biden on Afghanistan," The White House, August 16, 2021, https://www.whitehouse.gov/briefing-room/speeches-remarks/2021/08/16/remarks-by-president-biden-on-afghanistan/.

10 Charles Creitz, "Trump rips Biden's Afghan actions: 'Our country has never been so humiliated'; 'blows Vietnam away'," Fox News, August 17, 2021, https://www.foxnews.com/media/trump-biden-afghanistan-actions-humiliated.

11 Promulgation of the US Military Assistance Command Vietnam 1969 Command History (Volume I) (San Francisco: USMACV, 1970), ix.

Chapter 1

1 Dwight D. Eisenhower, "Record of News Conference, April 7, 1954," in Public Papers of the Presidents of the United States: Dwight D. Eisenhower, 1954, Book I—January 1 to December 31, 1954, 381–90 (Washington, DC: Government Printing Office, 1954).
2 "Vietnam: A Television History; Interview with Dean Rusk [2], 1981," 04/28/1981, GBH Archives, 2023, http://openvault.wgbh.org/catalog/V_BE368E0B83284807A4F1DFAAFB6B9A8B (accessed September 19, 2024).
3 Schafer, Amy, "Generations of War: The Rise of the Warrior Caste and the All Volunteer Force," Center for a New American Security, May, 2017, https://s3.us-east-1.amazonaws.com/files.cnas.org/documents/CNASReport-WarriorCast-Final.pdf?mtime=20170427115046&focal=none.
4 Jeannie Breeden, interview by author, via Zoom in Falls Church, Virginia, September 20, 2023.
5 Jack Naughton, "II Great Depression Until Moving to Hawaii," January 1980, Honolulu, Hawaii: Transcript from Audio Recording, page 34, Author's Family Private Collection.
6 Momilani Naughton, email message to author, April 9, 2022.
7 Noreen Naughton, email message to author, April 23, 2022.
8 Momilani Naughton, email message to author, April 9, 2022.
9 Patrick W. Naughton Sr., email message to author, February 19, 2022.
10 Lyndon Johnson, "Statement by the President Upon Approving the Reserve Officers' Training Corps Vitalization Act, October 14, 1964," in Public Papers of the Presidents of the United States: Lyndon Johnson 1964, Book II—July 1 to December 31, 1964, 1336–7 (Washington, DC: Government Printing Office, 1965).
11 Patrick W. Naughton Sr., email message to author, August 23, 2023.
12 Patrick W. Naughton Sr., email message to author, December 21, 2021.
13 Ibid.
14 Naughton, Momilani, "Graduation Without Jubilation" (Hawai'i: Roosevelt High School Written Assignment, Unpublished, 1966), 1.
15 Lyndon Johnson, "Why we are in Viet-Nam, July 28, 1965," in Public Papers of the Presidents of the United States: Lyndon Johnson 1965, Book II—June 1 to December 31, 1965, 794, 795 (Washington, DC: Government Printing Office, 1966).
16 Patrick W. Naughton Sr., email message to author, December 20, 2021.
17 Patrick W. Naughton Sr., email message to author, April 7, 2022.

Chapter 2

1 "Why must our men die and kill in Vietnam," Honolulu Star-Bulletin, February 24, 1966, author's private collection.
2 The family generally remembers most people in Hawai'i being supportive of service overall. They credit Pearl Harbor and the 442nd as the main reasons why. Patrick W. Naughton Sr., email message to author, December 20, 2021 and Momilani Naughton, email message to author, December 21, 2021.
3 Momilani Naughton, email message to author, December 21, 2021.
4 Momilani Naughton, email message to author, February 7, 2022.
5 2d Battalion 27th Infantry, *Special Summary of Action—Company A, 2d Battalion, 27th infantry, 5 April 1966 (Operation Circle Pines),* Boyd Bashore. TLIBB-T, APO US Forces, 96225: 1966.
6 Ibid.

7 Bob Jones, "Bloodied 25th Holds the Line," *The Honolulu Advertiser*, April 20, 1966, https://www.newspapers.com/image/260384500/?terms=Bloodied%2025th%20Holds%20the%20Line (accessed February 23, 2023).
8 2d Battalion 27th Infantry, *Special Summary of Action.*
9 Ibid.
10 Jones, "Bloodied 25th Holds the Line."
11 2d Battalion 27th Infantry, *Special Summary of Action.*
12 Ibid.
13 Ibid.
14 "Father Will Accompany Son's Body from Vietnam," *Honolulu Star-Bulletin*, April 7, 1966, https://www.newspapers.com/newspage/270547708/ (accessed February 23, 2023).
15 Joe Arakaki, "Officer saw son die in Vietnam," *Honolulu Star-Bulletin*, April 14, 1966, https://www.newspapers.com/newspage/270568128/ (accessed February 23, 2023).
16 Ibid.
17 "Felt it was his duty, Mrs. Blevins says of son," *The Honolulu Advertiser*, April 7, 1966, https://www.newspapers.com/newspage/260426532/ (accessed February 23, 2023).
18 "Felt it was his duty, Mrs. Blevins says of son," *The Honolulu Advertiser.*
19 Arakaki, "Officer saw son die in Vietnam."
20 Ibid.
21 Stan Dahlin, "Remembrances," Vietnam Veterans Memorial Fund, The Wall of Faces, November 14, 2002, https://www.vvmf.org/Wall-of-Faces/4400/THOMAS-A-BLEVINS/.
22 2d Battalion 27th Infantry, *Special Summary of Action.*
23 "America Second—Humanity First," Rough Rider, Roosevelt High School, April 22, 1966, author's private collection.
24 Momilani Naughton, email message to author, January 17, 2022.
25 "Honolulu Soldier, 18, Killed in War," *Honolulu Star-Bulletin*, August 11, 1966, https://www.newspapers.com/image/270572609 (accessed January 18, 2022).
26 Ibid.
27 Ronald J. Bohanek, "Gary Francis Funn," The Virtual Wall, March 19, 2002, https://www.virtualwall.org/df/FunnGF01a.htm.
28 "Card of Thanks," *Honolulu Advertiser*, August 24, 1966, https://www.newspapers.com/image/260483353/?terms=gary%20funn&match=1 (accessed January 18, 2022).
29 *Ka Palapala* (Hawai'i: Board of Publications for the Associated Students of the University of Hawaii, 1966), 4.
30 Ibid., 118–21.
31 "Island Officer Dies; was Wounded in War," *Honolulu Star-Bulletin*, May 6, 1967, https://www.newspapers.com/image/270370708/?terms=everett%20glick&match=1 (accessed February 27, 2023).
32 Ibid.
33 Ibid.
34 Momilani Naughton, email message to author, January 1, 2023.

Chapter 3

1 Ronald MaGee, "Michael Evarts Obituary," *The Cleveland Plain Dealer*, January 28, 2011 https://obits.cleveland.com/us/obituaries/cleveland/name/michael-evarts-obituary?id=25434466 (accessed March 7, 2023).

2 Cassandra Shofar, "Family, Friends Paint Picture of Fallen Soldier," *The News-Herald*, January 25, 2011, https://www.news-herald.com/2011/01/25/family-friends-paint-picture-of-fallen-soldier/ (accessed March 8, 2023).

3 Cassandra Shofar, "Concord Soldier, Maj. Michael Evarts, Dies in Iraq," *The News-Herald*, January 18, 2011, https://www.news-herald.com/2011/01/18/concord-soldier-maj-michael-evarts-dies-in-iraq/ (accessed March 8, 2023).

4 Bill Debus, "Military Procession set Monday for Maj. Michael Evarts of Concord Township," *The News-Herald*, January 23, 2011, https://www.news-herald.com/2011/01/23/military-procession-set-monday-for-maj-michael-evarts-of-concord-township/ (accessed March 8, 2023).

5 Angela Gartner, "Residents pay their Respects to Fallen Concord Soldier Maj. Michael S. Evarts," *The News-Herald*, January 24, 2011, https://www.news-herald.com/2011/01/24/residents-pay-their-respects-to-fallen-concord-soldier-maj-michael-s-evarts/ (accessed March 8, 2023).

6 Brandon Baker, "Family, Friends, Hundreds More Gather to say Goodbye to Concord Township Soldier (With Videos)," *The News-Herald*, January 30, 2011, https://www.news-herald.com/2011/01/30/family-friends-hundreds-more-gather-to-say-goodbye-to-concord-township-soldier-with-videos/ (accessed March 8, 2023).

7 Shofar, "Family, Friends Paint Picture of Fallen Soldier."

8 Cassandra Shofar, "No Further Results of Investigation of Death of Maj. Michael Evarts Likely to be Released," *The News-Herald*, April 13, 2011, https://www.news-herald.com/2011/04/13/no-further-results-of-investigation-of-death-of-maj-michael-evarts-likely-to-be-released/ (accessed March 8, 2023).

9 Unknown Name, "Michael Evarts Obituary," *The Cleveland Plain Dealer*, March 13, 2013, https://obits.cleveland.com/us/obituaries/cleveland/name/michael-evarts-obituary?id=25434466.

10 Dawn Penn, "Michael Evarts Obituary," *The Cleveland Plain Dealer*, January 27, 2011, https://obits.cleveland.com/us/obituaries/cleveland/name/michael-evarts-obituary?id=25434466.

11 "Department of Defense Annual Report on Suicide in the Military, calendar Year 2021," Department of Defense, Under Secretary of Defense for Personnel and Readiness, https://www.dspo.mil/Portals/113/Documents/2022%20ASR/Annual%20Report%20on%20Suicide%20in%20the%20Military%20CY%202021%20with%20CY21%20DoDSER%20(1).pdf?ver=tat-8FRrUhH2IlndFrCGbsA%3d%3d (accessed March 8, 2023).

12 "2022 National Veteran Suicide Prevention Annual Report," Veterans Affairs Suicide Prevention Office of Mental health and Suicide Prevention, https://www.mentalhealth.va.gov/docs/data-sheets/2022/2022-National-Veteran-Suicide-Prevention-Annual-Report-FINAL-508.pdf (accessed March 9, 2023).

13 Thomas Howard Suitt III, "High Suicide Rates Among United States Service Members and Veterans of the Post 9/11 Wars," Watson Institute International & Public Affairs, Brown University, Costs of War, June 21, 2021, https://watson.brown.edu/costsofwar/papers/2021/Suicides.

14 Defense Suicide Prevention Office, "History and Approach," Defense Suicide Prevention Office, March 9, 2023, https://www.dspo.mil/home/About-DSPO/.

15 "Department of Defense Releases the Annual Report on Suicide in the Military: Calendar Year 2021," US Department of Defense Press Release, October 20, 2022 https://www.defense.gov/News/Releases/Release/Article/3193806/department-of-defense-releases-the-annual-report-on-suicide-in-the-military-cal/ (accessed March 8, 2023).

16 "Veterans Crisis Line Dial 988 Then Press 1," Veterans Crisis Line, https://www.veteranscrisisline.net (accessed March 10, 2023).

17 "Ask. Care. Escort," Army Resilience, https://www.armyresilience.army.mil/ard/pdf/106_CONUS_ACE_Card_FINAL_25JULY2022.pdf (accessed March 10, 2023).

18 Patrick W. Naughton Sr., email message to author, November 14, 2022.

19 Alic Tahir, interview by author, via Zoom in Falls Church, Virginia, August 17, 2023.

Chapter 4

1 Rick McCrabb, "Vietnam Veteran Deserves Ovation," *The Journal-News*, July 26, 2015, https://www.newspapers.com/image/445410717 (accessed January 4, 2022).
2 As explained by Momilani Naughton, email message to author, December 21, 2021, and a fellow classmate: Sandy Erlandson, email message to author, January 3, 2022.
3 Jan Doxey to Momilani Naughton, September 17, 1965. Letter. From author's private collection.
4 Ibid.
5 Joseph Lampara, email message to author, January 13, 2022.
6 Jan Doxey to Momilani Naughton, September 17, 1965.
7 Joseph Lampara, email message to author, January 13 and 18, 2022.
8 "The Situation in Vietnam, February 23, 1968," Central Intelligence Agency, Directorate of Intelligence (Washington, DC: Government Printing Office, 1968), I-3.
9 Ibid., I-2.
10 Rick McCrabb, "Vietnam Veteran Deserves Ovation."
11 Momilani Naughton, email message to author, January 15, 2022.
12 Ibid.
13 Kristl Lee, "Parties Start Summer Fun," *The Honolulu Advertiser*, June 12, 1967, https://www.newspapers.com/image/260402716/?terms="frank%20rodriguez"%20&match=1 (accessed January 31, 2022).
14 George McArthur, "10,000 GIs Take Part in Buildup," *The Sacramento Bee*, December 13, 1967, https://www.newspapers.com/image/619208829/?terms=101st%20&match=1 (accessed March 3, 2023).
15 Ibid.
16 "Westy Calls For the 101st to Live up to Legend," *The Leaf-Chronicle*, December 24, 1967, https://www.newspapers.com/image/353519599/?terms=101st%20westmoreland&match=1 (accessed March 3, 2023).
17 Charlie Gadd, email message to author, March 4, 2023.
18 Ibid.
19 Henry S. H. Young, "Frank Louis Rodriguez," *The Virtual Wall*, April 15, 2018, and June 27, 2018, https://www.vvmf.org/Wall-of-Faces/44105/FRANK-L-RODRIGUEZ/.
20 Bob Boyce, David Compton, and Charlie Gadd, email message to author, March 2, 2023.
21 Charlie Gadd, email message to author, March 4, 2023.
22 "War's Toll of Isle men Rises to 131 Fatalities," *Honolulu Star-Bulletin*, April 2, 1968, https://www.newspapers.com/image/271123631/?terms="frank%20rodriguez"%20&match=1 (accessed January 31, 2022).
23 Darren Pai, "Manoa Protests had big Start in 1968," *The Honolulu Advertiser*, April 29, 1995, https://www.newspapers.com/image/265964517 (accessed April 7, 2022).
24 Jane Evinger, "'Betrayed,' Say Demonstrators," *The Honolulu Advertiser*, May 22, 1968, https://www.newspapers.com/image/261070488/ (accessed April 7, 2022).
25 Momilani Naughton, email message to author, December 21, 2021.
26 Noreen Naughton, email message to author, December 22, 2021.
27 Bruce Dyer, email message to author, January 17, 2022.
28 "Vietnam War Victims were Veteran and Artist," *Honolulu Star-Bulletin*, June 6, 1968, https://www.newspapers.com/image/272040084/ (accessed January 31, 2022).
29 Debby Lada, email message to Bruce Dyer, September 7, 2006, forwarded to author January 17, 2022.
30 Ibid.

31 "Vietnam War Victims were Veteran and Artist," *Honolulu Star-Bulletin.*
32 Gardo, Thomas E., *Vietnam—The Fourth Year, March 68–February 69* (Public Information Office, 173d Airborne Brigade: San Francisco, 1969), 45.
33 Ibid.
34 "Dead Isle Soldier Wanted to Write," The *Honolulu Advertiser*, June 7, 1968, https://www.newspapers.com/image/260396209 (accessed January 31, 2022).
35 Gardo, *Vietnam—The Fourth Year*, 49.
36 Ibid., 81.
37 "Vietnam War Victims were Veteran and Artist," *Honolulu Star-Bulletin.*

Chapter 5

1 U.S. Congress, House Committee on Military Affairs, Army Reorganization: Hearings before the Committee on Military Affairs, 66th Cong., 1st sess., 1919, 755–6.
2 *Platoon*, directed by Oliver Stone (Orion Pictures, 1986), 1:50:12.
3 Patrick W. Naughton Sr., email message to author, December 21, 2021.
4 Halberstam, David, *The Best and the Brightest* (New York: Random House, 1972), 564.
5 Patrick W. Naughton Sr., email message to author, December 20, 2021.
6 Patrick W. Naughton Sr., email message to author, May 28, 2023.
7 Patrick W. Naughton Sr., email message to author, December 20, 2021.
8 "Vietnam War Claims Life of Isle Sergeant," Honolulu Star-Bulletin, September 26, 1968, https://www.newspapers.com/image/271138618/?terms=Herbert%20Cho%20Vietnam&match=1 (accessed February 4, 2022).
9 Ibid.
10 "9th Infantry Division Intelligence Spot Report, September 25, 1968," 9th Infantry Division (1st Battalion 50th Infantry Association Private Collection, 1968).
11 "Vietnam War Claims Life of Isle Sergeant," *Honolulu Star-Bulletin.*

Chapter 6

1 Patrick W. Naughton to Ma, Pop, John, Ami, Sean, Mo, Tommy, & Mele, April 19, 1969. Letter. From author's private collection.
2 Ibid.
3 Patrick W. Naughton to Ma, Pop, John, Ami, Sean, Mo, Tommy, & Mele, April 27, 1969. Letter. From author's private collection.
4 Patrick W. Naughton to Family, April 21, 1969. Postcard. From author's private collection.
5 Patrick W. Naughton to Ma, Pop, John, Ami, Sean, Mo, Tommy, & Mele, April 27, 1969.
6 Ibid.
7 Ibid.
8 Patrick W. Naughton Sr., email message to author, May 14, 2022, and May 15, 2022.
9 Momilani Naughton, email message to author, December 21, 2021.
10 Patrick W. Naughton Sr., email message to author, December 21, 2021, and February 7, 2022.

Chapter 7

1 "What Secretary Laird Learned in Vietnam," *U.S. News & World Report*, March 24, 1969, 27.
2 Patrick W. Naughton to Dr. and Mrs. J. J. Naughton, May 9, 1969. Postcards. From author's private collection.

3 Patrick W. Naughton to Ma, Pop, John, Ami, Sean, Mo, Tommy, & Mele, May 10, 1969. Letter. From author's private collection.
4 Helen Tennant Hegelheimer, in Appy, Christian G., *Patriots: The Vietnam War Remembered from All Sides* (New York, Viking, 2003), 108.
5 Recognizing the 40th anniversary of the withdrawal of United States combat troops from the Vietnam War and expressing renewed support for United States veterans of that conflict, Senate Resolution 280, 113th, 1st Session (2013).
6 Patrick W. Naughton to Ma, Pop, John, Ami, Sean, Mo, Tommy, & Mele, May 10, 1969.
7 Patrick W. Naughton Sr., email message to author, May 25, 2022.
8 Patrick W. Naughton to Ma, Pop, John, Ami, Sean, Mo, Tommy, & Mele, May 10, 1969.
9 Richardson, Walter B., Sentinel to a City: CMAC (San Francisco: US Government Capital Military Assistance Command, 1969), 9–10, 21.
10 Patrick W. Naughton to Ma, Pop, John, Ami, Sean, Mo, Tommy, & Mele, May 10, 1969.
11 Ryan Moore, "Long Binh Post and the Vietnam War," Library of Congress, August 2, 2017. https://blogs.loc.gov/maps/2017/08/long-binh/.
12 Patrick W. Naughton to Ma, Pop, John, Ami, Sean, Mo, Tommy, & Mele, May 10, 1969.

Chapter 8

1 To see an example of GTA 24-01-003 Iraqi Culture Smart Card see: https://irp.fas.org/doddir/usmc/iraqsmart-0506.pdf.
2 Creighton Abrams's comments quoted in Lewis Sorley, ed., *Vietnam Chronicles: The Abrams Tapes 1968–1972* (Lubbock: Texas Tech University Press, 2004), 195.
3 Don Braid, "Khan's Institute to Study Quebec," *The Montreal Star*, April 27, 1977, https://www.newspapers.com/image/742663160/?terms=herman%20kahn%20moat%20saigon (accessed July 29, 2023).
4 Jeffrey Kimball, *Nixon's Vietnam War* (Lawrence: University Press of Kansas, 2004), 163.
5 Morton Halperin, in Appy, *Patriots*, 404.
6 Department of Defense, U.S.-Vietnam Relations, 1945–1967, Vol. 5, Sec. IV.C.6a (Washington, DC: House Committee on Armed Services, 1971), 2.
7 William C. Westmoreland, *A Soldier Reports* (New York: Doubleday and Company, Inc., 1976), 147.
8 Department of Defense, U.S.-Vietnam Relations, 1945–1967, 2.
9 Westmoreland, *A Soldier Reports*, 152.
10 Department of Defense, U.S.-Vietnam Relations, 1945–1967, 5–6.
11 Ibid., 5–6, and "Vietnam: A Television History; Interview with William C. (William Childs) Westmoreland, 1981," 04/27/1981, GBH Archives, http://openvault.wgbh.org/catalog/V_AEA9735AC2664425993A0DE582C3B423 (accessed August 23, 2023).
12 Mao Tse-Tung, *On Guerrilla Warfare* (Frederick A. Praeger: New York, 1961), 93.
13 Robert K. Brigham, *ARVN: Life and Death in the South Vietnamese Army* (University Press of Kansas: Kansas, 2006), 96–7.
14 Mao Tse-Tung, *On Guerrilla Warfare*, 93.
15 "Civilian Casualties a Concern," The Daily Messenger, August 24, 1966, https://www.newspapers.com/image/22404122/.
16 Samuel P. Huntington, "The Bases of Accommodation," *Foreign Affairs* 46, no. 4 (1968): 642–56.
17 Ibid.
18 Ibid.
19 Julian Ewell's comments quoted in Lewis Sorley, ed., *Vietnam Chronicles: The Abrams Tapes 1968–1972* (Lubbock: Texas Tech University Press, 2004), 192.

20 Earle Wheeler's comments quoted in Sorley, ed., *Vietnam Chronicles: The Abrams Tapes 1968–1972*, 277.
21 Townsend Hoopes, *The Limits of Intervention* (David McKay Company, Inc: New York, 1969), 66.
22 Military Assistance Command Civil Operations and Revolutionary/Rural Development Support, Command Information Pamphlet 12–69, Pacification (Washington, DC: US Government, 1969), 2.
23 Ibid.
24 Ibid.
25 Ibid.
26 Ibid., 3.
27 Ibid.
28 Ibid., 8–9.
29 Ibid., 6.
30 Ibid., 3.
31 Walter B. Richardson, *Sentinel to a City: CMAC* (San Francisco: US Government Capital Military Assistance Command, 1969), 1.
32 Ibid., 3.
33 Ibid., 3–4.
34 Written Statement from Vietnam II: 3rd Brigade, 82nd Airborne Division, January 1969 to December 1969 (San Francisco: 82nd Airborne Division, 1969), 1.
35 Richardson, *Sentinel to a City: CMAC*, 5.
36 Don Sockol, "Saigon—Capital of South Vietnam," *The Hurricane: A Publication of II Field Force Vietnam*, January 1970, 18.
37 Brendan Doyle, "Wilfred Burchett: A one-man truth brigade," GreenLeft, January 25, 2008, https://www.greenleft.org.au/content/wilfred-burchett-one-man-truth-brigade (accessed October 11, 2024).
38 Richardson, *Sentinel to a City: CMAC*, 17.
39 Ibid., 16.
40 Robert McNamara, *In Retrospect: The Tragedy and Lessons of Vietnam* (Times Books: New York, 1995), 238.
41 Westmoreland, *A Soldier Reports*, 120–332.
42 Ibid., 273.
43 Wilfred Burchett, *Grasshoppers & Elephants: Why Vietnam Fell* (Urizen Books: New York, 1977), 53–4.
44 Westmoreland, *A Soldier Reports*, 273.
45 Dave Richard Palmer, *Readings in Current Military History* (West Point, Department of Military Art and Engineering, 1969), 94.
46 Creighton Abrams's comments quoted in Sorley, ed., *Vietnam Chronicles: The Abrams Tapes 1968–1972*, 407.
47 Written Statement from: Vietnam II: 3rd Brigade, 82nd Airborne Division, January 1969 to December 1969 (San Francisco: 82nd Airborne Division, 1969), 11.
48 Orientation Issue of the *All American Magazine*, 3rd BDE 82nd ABN DIV (San Francisco: 82nd Airborne Division, 1969), 23.
49 Combat Experiences 4–69: Military Assistance Command Vietnam (Washington, DC: US Government, 1969), 38.
50 Orientation Issue of the *All American Magazine*, 20–1.
51 Written Statement from Vietnam II: 3rd Brigade, 82nd Airborne Division, January 1969 to December 1969 (San Francisco: 82nd Airborne Division, 1969), 1.
52 Ibid., 8.
53 Ibid., 1–2.

54 Ibid., 9.
55 "What Secretary Laird Learned in Vietnam," 27.
56 "Washington Whispers," *U.S. News & World Report*, March 31, 1969, 17.
57 Creighton Abrams's comments quoted in Sorley, ed., *Vietnam Chronicles: The Abrams Tapes 1968–1972*, 192.

Chapter 9

1 Patrick W. Naughton to Ma, Pop, John, Ami, Sean, Mo, Tommy, & Mele, May 11, 1969. Letter. From author's private collection.
2 Patrick W. Naughton to Ma, Pop, John, Ami, Sean, Mo, Tommy, & Mele, May 10, 1969.
3 Patrick W. Naughton Sr., email message to author, May 23, 2022.
4 Earle G. Wheeler. Chairman, Joint Chiefs of Staff Earle G. Wheeler Memorandum For the President, February 12, 1968. From author's private collection.
5 Army Buildup Progress Report, Department of Defense (Washington, DC: US Government, 1968).
6 Patrick W. Naughton Sr., email message to author, May 27, 2022.
7 Patrick W. Naughton to Ma, Pop, John, Ami, Sean, Mo, Tommy, & Mele, May 11, 1969.
8 Patrick W. Naughton Sr., email message to author, May 14, 2023.
9 Department of Defense Pocket Guide-21A, *A Pocket Guide to Vietnam* (Washington, DC: US Government, 1966), 1, 72.
10 Patrick W. Naughton to Ma, Pop, John, Ami, Sean, Mo, Tommy, & Mele, May 10–11, 1969. Letter. From author's private collection.
11 Ibid.
12 Patrick W. Naughton Sr., email message to author, May 25, 2022.
13 Patrick W. Naughton to Ma, Pop, John, Ami, Sean, Mo, Tommy, & Mele, May 15, 1969. Letter. From author's private collection.
14 James H. Willbanks, *Vietnam War Almanac* (New York: Infobase Publishing, 2009), 297.
15 Patrick W. Naughton to Ma, Pop, John, Ami, Sean, Mo, Tommy, & Mele, May 15, 1969.
16 Patrick W. Naughton to Ma, Pop, John, Ami, Sean, Mo, Tommy, & Mele, August 8, 1969. Letter. From author's private collection.
17 Interestingly, the Hawai'i connection occurred here again. The commander of P-Training was a Hawaiian: Charles *Heaukulani.*
18 *Hamburger Hill*, directed by John Irvin (RKO Pictures, 1987), 1:31:15.
19 Patrick W. Naughton to Ma, Pop, John, Ami, Sean, Mo, Tommy, & Mele, August 8, 1969. Letter. From author's private collection.
20 My father does not remember the exact conversation, but from all of BG Dickerson's statements in anything official that was distributed to the unit, the same talking points were driven home. We can imagine this would be the same for new officer introductions; for example, see: George W. Dickerson, Orientation Issue of the *All American Magazine*, 1.
21 Patrick W. Naughton to Ma, Pop, John, Ami, Sean, Mo, Tommy, & Mele, May 17, 1969. Letter. From author's private collection.
22 1/505th Infantry History, an initial draft of the history of the regiment in my father's possession. The final draft, with many of the details of actual combat situations edited out, appears in: Vietnam II: 3rd Brigade, 82nd Airborne Division, January 1969 to December 1969 (San Francisco: 82nd Airborne Division, 1969), 69–77.
23 Patrick W. Naughton Sr., email message to author, May 30, 2022.
24 Patrick W. Naughton to Ma, Pop, John, Ami, Sean, Mo, Tommy, & Mele, May 15, 1969.
25 Patrick W. Naughton Sr., email message to author, December 21, 2021.

Chapter 10

1 Patrick W. Naughton to Ma, Pop, John, Ami, Sean, Mo, Tommy, & Mele, August 8, 1969.
2 Patrick W. Naughton to Ma, Pop, John, Ami, Sean, Mo, Tommy, & Mele, May 27, 1969. Letter. From author's private collection.
3 Patrick W. Naughton to Ma, Pop, John, Ami, Sean, Mo, Tommy, & Mele, May 22, 1969. Letter. From author's private collection.
4 Patrick W. Naughton Sr., email message to author, July 27, 2022.
5 Patrick W. Naughton to Ma, Pop, John, Ami, Sean, Mo, Tommy, & Mele, August 8, 1969.
6 Patrick W. Naughton Sr., email message to author, July 27, 2022.
7 Patrick W. Naughton to Ma, Pop, John, Ami, Sean, Mo, Tommy, & Mele, August 8, 1969.
8 Patrick W. Naughton Sr., email message to author, July 27, 2022.
9 Patrick W. Naughton to Ma, Pop, John, Ami, Sean, Mo, Tommy, & Mele, May 22, 1969.
10 Daniel K. Elder, "Educating Noncommissioned Officers: A Chronological Study on the Development of Educational Programs for U.S. Army Noncommissioned Officers" (US Government: Fort Belvoir, 1999), 22–5.
11 Larry Lockeby, email message to author, September 20, 2023.
12 Patrick W. Naughton Sr., email message to author, July 27, 2022.
13 Ibid.
14 Patrick W. Naughton to Ma, Pop, John, Ami, Sean, Mo, Tommy, & Mele, May 27, 1969.
15 Patrick W. Naughton Sr., email message to author, July 27, 2022.
16 Patrick W. Naughton to Ma, Pop, John, Ami, Sean, Mo, Tommy, & Mele, May 27, 1969.
17 Alic Tahir, interview by author, via Zoom in Falls Church, Virginia, September 20, 2023.
18 Patrick W. Naughton Sr., email message to author, September 29, 2022.
19 Patrick W. Naughton to Ma, Pop, John, Ami, Sean, Mo, Tommy, & Mele, May 27, 1969.
20 Patrick W. Naughton to Ma, Pop, John, Ami, Sean, Mo, Tommy, & Mele, May 30, 1969. Letter. From author's private collection.
21 Patrick W. Naughton to Ma, Pop, John, Ami, Sean, Mo, Tommy, & Mele, May 25, 1969. Letter. From author's private collection.
22 Patrick W. Naughton to Ma, Pop, John, Ami, Sean, Mo, Tommy, & Mele, May 23, 1969. Letter. From author's private collection.
23 Patrick W. Naughton to Ma, Pop, John, Ami, Sean, Mo, Tommy, & Mele, May 10, 1969.
24 Patrick W. Naughton to Ma, Pop, John, Ami, Sean, Mo, Tommy, & Mele, May 23, 1969.
25 Patrick W. Naughton to Ma, Pop, John, Ami, Sean, Mo, Tommy, & Mele, May 25, 1969.
26 Ibid.
27 Patrick W. Naughton to Ma, Pop, John, Ami, Sean, Mo, Tommy, & Mele, June 5, 1969. Letter. From author's private collection.
28 Patrick W. Naughton to Ma, Pop, John, Ami, Sean, Mo, Tommy, & Mele, May 27, 1969.
29 Ibid.
30 Patrick W. Naughton to Ma, Pop, John, Ami, Sean, Mo, Tommy, & Mele, May 30, 1969.
31 Patrick W. Naughton Sr., email message to author, July 27, 2022.
32 Patrick W. Naughton to Ma, Pop, John, Ami, Sean, Mo, Tommy, & Mele, June 2, 1969. Letter. From author's private collection.
33 Westmoreland, *A Soldier Reports*, 273.
34 Patrick W. Naughton to Ma, Pop, John, Ami, Sean, Mo, Tommy, & Mele, June 2, 1969. Letter. From author's private collection.
35 Patrick W. Naughton to Ma, Pop, John, Ami, Sean, Mo, Tommy, & Mele, August 8, 1969.
36 Patrick W. Naughton to Ma, Pop, John, Ami, Sean, Mo, Tommy, & Mele, May 30, 1969.

37 Patrick W. Naughton to Ma, Pop, John, Ami, Sean, Mo, Tommy, & Mele, June 2, 1969. Letter. From author's private collection.
38 Patrick W. Naughton to Ma, Pop, John, Ami, Sean, Mo, Tommy, & Mele, May 25, 1969.

Chapter 11

1 Tom Mangold and John Penycate, *The Tunnels of Củ Chi* (New York: Random House, 1985), 30.
2 Trần Thị Gừng, in Appy, *Patriots*, 17.
3 Westmoreland, *A Soldier Reports*, 56.
4 *Jarhead*, directed by Sam Mendes (Universal Pictures, 2005), 1:31:15.
5 Patrick W. Naughton Sr., email message to author, July 30, 2022.
6 Patrick W. Naughton to Ma, Pop, John, Ami, Sean, Mo, Tommy, & Mele, May 27, 1969.
7 Combat Experiences 4–69: Military Assistance Command, 38–40.
8 Patrick W. Naughton to Ma, Pop, John, Ami, Sean, Mo, Tommy, & Mele, May 27, 1969.
9 Patrick W. Naughton to Ma, Pop, John, Ami, Sean, Mo, Tommy, & Mele, May 23, 1969.
10 Patrick W. Naughton Sr., email message to author, July 30, 2022.
11 Creighton Abrams's comments quoted in Sorley, ed., *Vietnam Chronicles: The Abrams Tapes 1968–1972*, 241.
12 Patrick W. Naughton Sr., email message to author, July 30, 2022.
13 Patrick W. Naughton Sr., conversation with author, January 20, 2023.
14 Patrick W. Naughton to Ma, Pop, John, Ami, Sean, Mo, Tommy, & Mele, May 30, 1969.
15 Handwritten sticky note from Patrick W. Naughton Sr. found in the chapter on the incident as reported in Robert J. Dvorchak, *The Golden Brigade: the Untold Story of the 82nd Airborne in Vietnam and Beyond* (Indianapolis: IBJ Book Publishing, 2020), 405–9.
16 Patrick W. Naughton to Ma, Pop, John, Ami, Sean, Mo, Tommy, & Mele, May 30, 1969.
17 Patrick W. Naughton to Ma, Pop, John, Ami, Sean, Mo, Tommy, & Mele, June 5, 1969. Letter. From author's private collection.
18 Brett Reilly, "The True Origin of the Term 'Viet Cong'," *The Diplomat*, January 31, 2018, https://thediplomat.com/2018/01/the-true-origin-of-the-term-viet-cong/ (accessed June 18, 2023).
19 Patrick W. Naughton to Hi, [unaddressed letter to the family] December 6, 1969. Letter. From author's private collection.
20 "Vietnam: A Television History; America's Enemy (1954–1967); Interview with Duong Long Sang, 1981," 03/10/1981, GBH Archives, http://openvault.wgbh.org/catalog/V_AE9FFF6DEB5B4679B6B6598C9EE6D840 (accessed August 24, 2023).
21 Patrick W. Naughton to Ma, Pop, John, Ami, Sean, Mo, Tommy, & Mele, June 2, 1969. Letter. From author's private collection.
22 Ibid.
23 Burchett, *Grasshoppers & Elephants: Why Vietnam Fell*, 40.
24 "Infantry News," *Infantry*, July–August 1970, 2.
25 Patrick W. Naughton to Ma, Pop, John, Ami, Sean, Mo, Tommy, & Mele, June 5, 1969.

Chapter 12

1 2 Timothy 4:7.
2 Patrick W. Naughton Sr., email message to author, July 27, 2022.
3 Patrick W. Naughton Jr. to Auntie Momi, September 1, 1996. Letter. From author's private collection.

4 "Why Helicopter Losses Are Up," *U.S. News & World Report,* May 19, 1969, 17.
5 Patrick W. Naughton to author, September 18, 2007. Letter. From author's private collection.
6 Burchett, *Grasshoppers & Elephants: Why Vietnam Fell,* 104.
7 Patrick W. Naughton to Ma, Pop, John, Ami, Sean, Mo, Tommy, & Mele, June 8, 1969. Letter. From author's private collection.
8 Patrick W. Naughton to author, September 18, 2007.
9 Patrick W. Naughton to Ma, Pop, John, Ami, Sean, Mo, Tommy, & Mele, June 8, 1969.
10 Patrick W. Naughton to Ma, Pop, John, Ami, Sean, Mo, Tommy, & Mele, May 27, 1969.
11 Larry Lockeby, email message to author, September 20, 2023.
12 Patrick W. Naughton to Ma, Pop, John, Ami, Sean, Mo, Tommy, & Mele, June 8, 1969.
13 Written Statement from: Vietnam II: 3rd Brigade, 82nd Airborne Division, January 1969 to December 1969, 11.
14 Patrick W. Naughton to Ma, Pop, John, Ami, Sean, Mo, Tommy, & Mele, June 10, 1969. Letter. From author's private collection.
15 Patrick W. Naughton to Ma, Pop, John, Ami, Sean, Mo, Tommy, & Mele, June 2 and 5, 1969.
16 Momilani Naughton, email message to author, December 22, 2021.
17 Patrick W. Naughton to Ma, Pop, John, Ami, Sean, Mo, Tommy, & Mele, June 5, 1969.
18 Patrick W. Naughton to Ma, Pop, John, Ami, Sean, Mo, Tommy, & Mele, June 5, 1969.
19 Patrick W. Naughton to Ma, Pop, John, Ami, Sean, Mo, Tommy, & Mele, June 8, 1969.
20 Patrick W. Naughton to Ma, Pop, John, Ami, Sean, Mo, Tommy, & Mele, June 10, 1969.

Chapter 13

1 Momilani Naughton, email message to author, December 21, 2021.
2 Ibid.
3 Patrick W. Naughton Sr., email message to author, February 7, 2022.
4 Patrick W. Naughton to Momilani Naughton, June 12, 1969. Letter. From author's private collection.
5 Patrick W. Naughton, "I am an author writing about my father's experience in Vietnam part of which was with the 82nd (we have the same name, I am a JR). He sent this peace symbol that he bought in Vung Tau back to his sister during the war," Facebook, February 19, 2022, https://www.facebook.com/groups/679983602051459/user/1182769622.
6 Patrick W. Naughton to Momilani Naughton, June 12, 1969.
7 Ibid.
8 Patrick W. Naughton to Family, June 12, 1969. Postcard. From author's private collection.
9 Patrick W. Naughton to Ma, Pop, John, Ami, Sean, Mo, Tommy, & Mele, June 22, 1969. Letter. From author's private collection.
10 Charles Schulz, "Peanuts," Peanuts Wiki, June 13, 1969, https://peanuts.fandom.com/wiki/June_1969_comic_strips.
11 Patrick W. Naughton to Ma, Pop, John, Ami, Sean, Mo, Tommy, & Mele, June 15, 1969. Letter. From author's private collection.
12 Patrick W. Naughton Sr., email message to author, August 26, 2022.
13 Patrick W. Naughton to Ma, Pop, John, Ami, Sean, Mo, Tommy, & Mele, June 26, 1969. Letter. From author's private collection.
14 Patrick W. Naughton to Family, June 12, 1969.
15 Patrick W. Naughton to Ma, Pop, John, Ami, Sean, Mo, Tommy, & Mele, June 15, 1969.
16 Patrick W. Naughton to Ma, Pop, John, Ami, Sean, Mo, Tommy, & Mele, June 15, 1969.
17 Karen Davis Johnson, "Remembrances," Vietnam Veterans Memorial Fund, The Wall of Faces, October 24, 2005, https://www.vvmf.org/Wall-of-Faces/12253/JOHNNY-F-DAVIS/.

18 Patrick W. Naughton to Ma, Pop, John, Ami, Sean, Mo, Tommy, & Mele, June 22, 1969.
19 Patrick W. Naughton to Ma, Pop, John, Ami, Sean, Mo, Tommy, & Mele, June 22, 1969.

Chapter 14

1 Patrick W. Naughton to Ma, Pop, John, Ami, Sean, Mo, Tommy, & Mele, July 16, 1969. Letter. From author's private collection.
2 Doyle Wilkins, email message to author, August 29, 2022.
3 Written Statement from Vietnam II: 3rd Brigade, 82nd Airborne Division, January 1969 to December 1969, 18.
4 Larry Lockeby, email message to author, September 20, 2023.
5 Joe Hindle, "Remembrances," Vietnam Veterans Memorial Fund, The Wall of Faces, June 14, 2004, https://www.vvmf.org/Wall-of-Faces/18411/GEORGE-T-GIBNER/.
6 Doyle Wilkins, email message to author, August 29, 2022.
7 Ibid.
8 Ibid.
9 Ibid.
10 Written Statement from Vietnam II: 3rd Brigade, 82nd Airborne Division, January 1969 to December 1969, 18.
11 Patrick W. Naughton to Ma, Pop, John, Ami, Sean, Mo, Tommy, & Mele, July 2, 1969. Letter. From author's private collection.
12 Patrick W. Naughton to Ma, Pop, John, Ami, Sean, Mo, Tommy, & Mele, July 2, 1969.
13 Patrick W. Naughton Sr., email message to author, July 30, 2022.
14 Ibid.
15 Patrick W. Naughton Sr., email message to author, July 29, 2022.
16 Patrick W. Naughton to Ma, Pop, John, Ami, Sean, Mo, Tommy, & Mele, July 2, 1969.
17 Patrick W. Naughton to Ma, Pop, John, Ami, Sean, Mo, Tommy, & Mele, July 2, 1969.
18 Patrick W. Naughton Sr., email message to author, March 23, 2023.
19 Patrick W. Naughton to Ma, Pop, John, Ami, Sean, Mo, Tommy, & Mele, July 6, 1969. Letter. From author's private collection.
20 Ibid.
21 Patrick W. Naughton Sr., email message to author, September 4, 2022.
22 Ibid.
23 Patrick W. Naughton to Ma, Pop, John, Ami, Sean, Mo, Tommy, & Mele, July 16, 1969.
24 Ibid.
25 Ibid.
26 Patrick W. Naughton Sr., email message to author, July 27, 2022.
27 Patrick W. Naughton to Ma, Pop, John, Ami, Sean, Mo, Tommy, & Mele, July 16, 1969.
28 Ibid.
29 Ibid.
30 Ibid.
31 Ibid.
32 Ibid.
33 Written Statement from Vietnam II: 3rd Brigade, 82nd Airborne Division, January 1969 to December 1969, 76.
34 National Archives, Nixon Presidential Materials, NSC Files, Box 224, Agency Files, DOD, Vol. IV, 1 February 1970–20 April 1970.
35 *Hamburger Hill*, directed by John Irvin (RKO Pictures, 1987), 1:31:15.

Chapter 15

1 Patrick W. Naughton to Ma, Pop, John, Ami, Sean, Mo, Tommy, & Mele, June 22, 1969.
2 Patrick W. Naughton to Ma, Pop, John, Ami, Sean, Mo, Tommy, & Mele, July 6, 1969.
3 Patrick W. Naughton to Ma, Pop, John, Ami, Sean, Mo, Tommy, & Mele, July 27, 1969. Letter. From author's private collection.
4 Ibid.
5 Ibid.
6 Patrick W. Naughton to Ma, Pop, John, Ami, Sean, Mo, Tommy, & Mele, September 1, 1969. Letter. From author's private collection.
7 Patrick W. Naughton to Mo and Tommy, & Mele, July 27 and November 9, 1969. Letters. From author's private collection.
8 Patrick W. Naughton to Ma, Pop, John, Ami, Sean, Mo, Tommy, & Mele, July 27 and August 2, 1969. Letters. From author's private collection.
9 Ibid.
10 Patrick W. Naughton to Ma, Pop, John, Ami, Sean, Mo, Tommy, & Mele, June 22 and 26, 1969. Letters. From author's private collection.
11 Doyle Wilkins, email message to author, March 24, 2021.
12 Patrick W. Naughton to Ma and Pop, August 29, 1969. Letter. From author's private collection.
13 Larry Lockeby, email message to author, September 20, 2023.
14 Patrick W. Naughton Sr., email message to author, September 19, 2022.
15 Doyle Wilkins, email message to author, March 23, 2021.
16 Joe Hindle, email message to author, September 9, 2022.
17 Patrick W. Naughton Sr., email message to author, September 19, 2022.
18 Ibid.
19 Ibid.
20 Patrick W. Naughton to Ma, Pop, John, Ami, Sean, Mo, Tommy, & Mele, August 8, 1969. Letter. From author's private collection.
21 Patrick W. Naughton to Mo and Tommy, & Mele, August 22, 1969. Letter. From author's private collection, and Patrick W. Naughton Sr., email message to author, August 26, 2022.
22 Momilani Naughton, email message to author, August 26, 2022.
23 Patrick W. Naughton Sr., email message to author, August 26, 2022.
24 "The Rev. Delwyn Rayson," Southern New England Conference United Church of Christ. April 2008, https://www.sneucc.org/obituarydetail/94879.
25 Robert Udick, "Church of the Crossroads," *Honolulu Star Bulletin*, August 16, 1969, https://www.newspapers.com/image/273573691/ (accessed September 21, 2022).
26 Eric Cavaliero, "Ministers Voice Mixed Reactions: Ministers Differ on Sanctuary," *The Honolulu Advertiser*, September 13, 1969, https://www.newspapers.com/image/261039436/ (accessed September 21, 2022).
27 Patrick W. Naughton to Mo and Tommy, & Mele, August 22, 1969.
28 "Rogers: 'Hanoi' is Unreasonable," *U.S. News & World Report*, July 28, 1969, 10.
29 "Meanwhile at the Paris Talks …," *U.S. News & World Report*, July 28, 1969, 39.
30 "Nothing but Bodies," *Time Magazine*, August 15, 1969, 24.

Chapter 16

1 Westmoreland, *A Soldier Reports*, 120–360.
2 Douglas Kinnard, *The War Managers: Thirtieth Anniversary Edition* (Naval Institute Press: Maryland, 2007), 111.

3 Ibid., 116.

4 Doyle Wilkins, email message to author, September 20, 2022.

5 Written Statement from Vietnam II: 3rd Brigade, 82nd Airborne Division, January 1969 to December 1969, 14.

6 Ibid., 32.

7 Burchett, *Grasshoppers & Elephants: Why Vietnam Fell*, 108.

8 Ibid., 108.

9 Written Statement from Vietnam II: 3rd Brigade, 82nd Airborne Division, January 1969 to December 1969, 32.

10 1st Battalion 505th Infantry, Daily Staff Journal or Duty Officers Log, 0001 12SEP69 to 2400 12SEP69. From author's private collection.

11 "After Ho: Shift in War?," *U.S. News & World Report*, September 15, 1969, 26.

12 As noted by Abrams's staff in Sorley, ed., *Vietnam Chronicles: The Abrams Tapes 1968–1972*, 254.

13 Written Statement from Vietnam II: 3rd Brigade, 82nd Airborne Division, January 1969 to December 1969, 31–2.

14 1st Battalion 505th Infantry, Daily Staff Journal or Duty Officers Log, 16,17, 26, 30SEP69, 01, 03, 17, 30, 31OCT69. From author's private collection.

15 "Infantry News," *Infantry*, July–August 1970, 3.

16 Patrick W. Naughton to Ma and Pop, October 19, 1969. Letter. From author's private collection.

17 Patrick W. Naughton to Mo and Tommy, & Mele, September 20, 1969. Letter. From author's private collection.

18 Larry Lockeby, email message to author, September 20, 2023.

19 1st Battalion 505th Infantry, Daily Staff Journal or Duty Officers Log, 0001 to 2400 20SEP69. From author's private collection.

20 Patrick W. Naughton Sr., email message to author, September 19, 2022.

21 Joe Hindle, email message to author, September 27, 2022.

22 Ibid.

23 Ibid.

24 Patrick W. Naughton Sr., email message to author, September 29, 2022.

25 Joe Hindle, email message to author, September 27, 2022.

26 Ibid.

27 Ibid; and Written Statement from Vietnam II: 3rd Brigade, 82nd Airborne Division, January 1969 to December 1969, 32.

28 Patrick W. Naughton to Mo and Tommy, & Mele, October 24, 1969. Letter. From author's private collection.

29 Patrick W. Naughton to Mo and Tommy, & Mele, October 9, 1969. Letter. From author's private collection.

30 Patrick W. Naughton Sr., email message to author, September 8, 2022.

31 Ibid.

32 Patrick W. Naughton to Mo and Tommy, & Mele, October 24, 1969.

33 Written Statement from Vietnam II: 3rd Brigade, 82nd Airborne Division, January 1969 to December 1969, 15.

34 Patrick W. Naughton to Ma and Pop, October 19, 1969.

35 Patrick W. Naughton to Mo and Tommy, & Mele, October 24, 1969.

36 Anne-Marie Naughton, email message to author, April 9, 2022.

37 Dvorchak, *The Golden Brigade*, 450.

38 Patrick W. Naughton to Ma, Pop, John, Ami, Sean, Mo, Tommy, & Mele, November 9, 1969. Letter. From author's private collection.

39 Patrick W. Naughton to Ma, Pop, John, Ami, Sean, Mo, Tommy, & Mele, September 1 and October 14, 1969. Letters. From author's private collection.

40 1st Battalion 505th Infantry, Daily Staff Journal or Duty Officers Log, 0001 to 2400 09OCT69. From author's private collection.
41 Larry Lockeby, email message to author, September 20, 2023.

Chapter 17

1 "Texas man brings hope to 'forgotten' disabled Iraqi kids," Good News Network, August 11, 2009, https://www.goodnewsnetwork.org/wheelchairs-for-iraqi-kids/ (accessed October 11, 2024).
2 *Casualties of War*, directed by Brian De Palma (Columbia Pictures, 1989), 1:13:12.
3 Patrick W. Naughton Sr., email message to author, October 1, 2022.
4 Westmoreland, *A Soldier Reports*, 120–427.
5 Earle Wheeler comments quoted in Sorley, ed., *Vietnam Chronicles: The Abrams Tapes 1968–1972*, 271–2.
6 Ibid., 274.
7 Written Statement from Vietnam II: 3rd Brigade, 82nd Airborne Division, January 1969 to December 1969, 50, 54.
8 Patrick W. Naughton to Mo and Tommy, & Mele, September 20, 1969.
9 Patrick W. Naughton to Mo and Tommy, & Mele, October 9, 1969.
10 Patrick W. Naughton to Mo and Tommy, & Mele, October 9, November 30, 1969.
11 Patrick W. Naughton to Folks, November 1, 1969. Letter. From author's private collection.
12 Patrick W. Naughton Sr., email message to author, September 25, 2022.
13 Patrick W. Naughton to Mo and Tommy, & Mele, November 30, 1969. Letter. From author's private collection.
14 Patrick W. Naughton Sr., email message to author, September 25, 2022.
15 Patrick W. Naughton to Mo and Tommy, & Mele, November 30, 1969.
16 Patrick W. Naughton to Ma, Pop et al. November 19, 1969. Letter. From author's private collection.
17 "Vietnam: What's Going on Here?," *Newsweek*, September 22, 1969, 29.
18 "Mr. Nixon in Trouble," *Newsweek*, October 13, 1969, 31.
19 Richard Nixon, "We are not Democrats, or Republicans; we are Americans," *U.S. News & World Report*, November 24, 1969, 69.
20 "Interview with Vice President Agnew," *Newsweek*, October 6, 1969, 37.
21 Patrick W. Naughton to Mo and Tommy, & Mele, November 30, 1969.
22 Patrick W. Naughton to Ma, Pop, and Family, November 14, 1969. Letter. From author's private collection.
23 Patrick W. Naughton to Mo and Tommy, & Mele, June 15, 1969.

Chapter 18

1 Willbanks, *Vietnam War Almanac*, xi–xii.
2 Creighton Abrams's comments on William Rogers quoted in Sorley, ed., *Vietnam Chronicles: The Abrams Tapes 1968–1972*, 192.
3 "Viet War Is 'Wound Up'," *Star-Gazette*, October 16, 1972, https://www.newspapers.com/image/277544815/?terms=bunker%20color%20of%20the%20corpses&match=1 (accessed August 15, 2023).
4 Graham A. Cosmas, *United States Army in Vietnam: MACV The Joint Command in the Years of Withdrawal 1968–1973* (Washington, DC: US Government, 2006), 143–4.
5 Henry Kissinger, *White House Years* (Boston: Little Brown and Company, 1979), 272, and National Security Study Memorandum 36, Vietnamizing the War, April 10, 1969.
6 Westmoreland, *A Soldier Reports*, 120–471.

7 "Based On Paris Progress: No Early Withdrawal-Laird," *Independent*, April 21, 1969, https://newspaperarchive.com/independent-apr-21-1969-p-7/ (accessed January 21, 2023).
8 "Text of Nixon-Thieu Report on Meeting," *Chicago Tribune*, June 9, 1969, https://newspaperarchive.com/chicago-tribune-jun-09-1969-p-1/ (accessed January 16, 2023).
9 "Viet Army Training Stressed Over U.S. Support in the Field," *The Arizona Republic*, October 4, 1969, https://newspaperarchive.com/phoenix-arizona-republic-oct-04-1969-p-8/ (accessed January 21, 2023).
10 Richard Nixon, "Address to the Nation on the War in Vietnam," University of Virginia Miller Center, November 3, 1969, https://millercenter.org/the-presidency/presidential-speeches/november-3-1969-address-nation-war-vietnam (accessed October 11, 2024).
11 Richard Nixon, "President's News Conference," The American Presidency Project, January 30, 1970, https://www.presidency.ucsb.edu/documents/the-presidents-news-conference-142 (accessed October 11, 2024).
12 "Both Sides Ease Up," *Newsweek*, November 3, 1969, 25.
13 Creighton Abrams's comments quoted in Sorley, ed., *Vietnam Chronicles: The Abrams Tapes 1968–1972*, 315.
14 Ibid., 344.
15 Cosmas, *United States Army in Vietnam*,153–4.
16 "Vietnam: A Television History; Interview with Henry Kissinger, 1982," 04/17/1982, GBH Archives, http://openvault.wgbh.org/catalog/V_A4AD7949092D448FBB4E7ECFDC5327F4 (accessed August 25, 2023).
17 Creighton Abrams's comments quoted in Sorley, ed., *Vietnam Chronicles: The Abrams Tapes 1968–1972*, 351.
18 Patrick W. Naughton Sr., email message to author, December 31, 2022.
19 Patrick W. Naughton to Hi, [unaddressed letter to the family] December 6, 1969. Letter. From author's private collection.
20 Patrick W. Naughton Sr., email message to author, December 31, 2022.
21 Patrick W. Naughton to Ma, Pop, Mele and Family, December 3, 1969. Letter. From author's private collection.
22 Patrick W. Naughton Sr., email message to author, December 31, 2022.
23 Patrick W. Naughton to Hi, [unaddressed letter to the family] December 6, 1969.
24 Patrick W. Naughton Sr., email message to author, December 31, 2022.
25 Patrick W. Naughton to Ma, Pop, Mele and Family, December 3, 1969. Letter.
26 Patrick W. Naughton to Mo and Tommy, & Mele, November 30, 1969. Letter. From author's private collection.
27 Patrick W. Naughton Sr., email message to author, December 31, 2022.
28 "Battalion Advisor—Vietnam," *Infantry*, July–August 1970, 49.
29 Ibid., 47–48.
30 Patrick W. Naughton Diary Entry, December 8, 1969. Diary. From author's private collection.
31 Patrick W. Naughton Sr., email message to author, December 31, 2022.
32 Andrew J. Birtle, *U.S. Army Counterinsurgency and Contingency Operations Doctrine 1942–1976* (Washington, DC: US Government, 2007), 322
33 *Full Metal Jacket*, directed by Stanley Kubrick (Stanley Kubrick, 1987), 1:02:10.

Chapter 19

1 Sockol, "Saigon—Capital of South Vietnam," 29.
2 Ibid.

3 Headquarters Military Assistance Command Vietnam, Office of Information Monthly Summary January 1970 (Washington, DC: US Government, 1970), 2.
4 Combat Experiences 4–69, 40.
5 Sockol, "Saigon—Capital of South Vietnam," 30.
6 Ibid., 18.
7 Creighton Abrams's comments quoted in Sorley, ed. *Vietnam Chronicles: The Abrams Tapes 1968–1972*, 199.
8 "Vietnam: A Television History; America's Enemy (1954–1967); Interview with Duong Long Sang, 1981," 03/10/1981, GBH Archives, http://openvault.wgbh.org/catalog/V_AE9FFF6DEB5B4679B6B6598C9EE6D840 (accessed August 24, 2023).
9 Creighton Abrams's comments quoted in Sorley, ed., *Vietnam Chronicles: The Abrams Tapes 1968–1972*, 286.
10 Ibid., 350.
11 Kirk Mitchell, "Boulder Police Make Arrest in 1994 Cold-Case Slaying of Marty Grisham," *The Denver Post*, May 1, 2016, https://www.denverpost.com/2012/01/05/boulder-police-make-arrest-in-1994-cold-case-slaying-of-marty-grisham/ (accessed September 12, 2023).
12 Alic Tahir, interview by author, via Zoom in Falls Church, Virginia, August 17, 2023.
13 Ibid.
14 Ibid.
15 Ibid.
16 Craig R. Whitney, "Truce Holds Little Hope for a Village in Vietnam," *The New York Times*, January 30, 1973, https://www.nytimes.com/1973/01/30/archives/truce-holds-little-hope-for-a-village-in-vietnam-chief-consoles-him.html (accessed January 16, 2023).
17 Patrick W. Naughton Sr., "Territoriality in Counterinsurgent Operations: Geographical Theory in Practice," *Philippine Geographical Journal* 18, no. 3 & 4 (July–December 1974): 53–4.
18 Burchett, *Grasshoppers & Elephants: Why Vietnam Fell*, 105.
19 Naughton Sr., "Territoriality in Counterinsurgent Operations: Geographical Theory in Practice," 54–55.
20 Wolfgang Peter May, *The War Around Us* (Trafford Publishing, 2012), 323–4.
21 Westmoreland, *A Soldier Reports*, 100.
22 May, *The War Around Us*, 325.
23 Alic Tahir, interview by author, via Zoom in Falls Church, Virginia, August 17, 2023.
24 Patrick W. Naughton Sr. and Richard Keller, email messages to author, July 9, 2023.
25 Patrick W. Naughton to Ma, Pop, John, Ami, Sean, Mo, Tommy, & Mele, December 8, 1969. Letter. From author's private collection.
26 Patrick W. Naughton Diary Entry, December 8, 1969.
27 Patrick W. Naughton to Ma, Pop, John, Ami, Sean, Mo, Tommy, & Mele, December 8, 1969.
28 Westmoreland, *A Soldier Reports*, 187.
29 Patrick W. Naughton to Ma, Pop, John, Ami, Sean, Mo, Tommy, & Mele, December 8, 1969.
30 Ibid.
31 Ibid.
32 Patrick W. Naughton Diary Entry, December 8, 1969.
33 Westmoreland, *A Soldier Reports*, 293.
34 Patrick W. Naughton to Ma, Pop, John, Ami, Sean, Mo, Tommy, & Mele, December 8, 1969.
35 Patrick W. Naughton to Ma, Pop, John, Ami, Sean, Mo, Tommy, & Mele, December 20, 1969. Letter. From author's private collection.
36 Patrick W. Naughton Diary Entry, December 8 and 20, 1969. Diary. From author's private collection.
37 Patrick W. Naughton Sr., email message to author, July 9, 2023.

38 Patrick W. Naughton Sr., email message to author, July 9, 2023.

39 Patrick W. Naughton to Ma, Pop, John, Ami, Sean, Mo, Tommy, & Mele, December 8, 1969.

Chapter 20

1 Lyndon B. Johnson, "President's News Conference," The American Presidency Project, April 23, 1964, https://www.presidency.ucsb.edu/documents/the-presidents-news-conference-1046 (accessed October 11, 2024).

2 "As GI's Leave Vietnam—War Roles of the Allies," *U.S. News & World Report,* January 12, 1970, 25.

3 Westmoreland, *A Soldier Reports*, 99–100.

4 "Vietnam: A Television History; Interview with Maxwell D. (Maxwell Davenport) Taylor, 1979 [Part 4 of 4]," 01/30/1979, GBH Archives, 2023, http://openvault.wgbh.org/catalog/V_1AB9782D6F8347D9970744F452D1F0D8 (accessed August 26, 2024).

5 Brigham, *ARVN: Life and Death in the South Vietnamese Army*, 7.

6 Ibid., 12.

7 Westmoreland, *A Soldier Reports*, 69–70 and Kinnard, *The War Managers*, 94–5.

8 Military Assistance Command Civil Operations and Revolutionary/Rural Development Support, Command Information Pamphlet 12–69, *Pacification* (Washington, DC: US Government, 1969), 6–7.

9 Military Assistance Command Vietnam, Lessons Learned Number 75: Cordon and Search Operations (Vietnam: US Government, 1970), 15.

10 Military Assistance Command Civil Operations and Revolutionary/Rural Development Support, Command Information Pamphlet 12–69, *Pacification*, 6–7.

11 Mr. Jacobson and Creighton Abrams's comments quoted in Sorley, ed., *Vietnam Chronicles: The Abrams Tapes 1968–1972*, 292.

12 Military Assistance Command Civil Operations and Revolutionary/Rural Development Support, Command Information Pamphlet 12–69, *Pacification*, 6–7.

13 Military Assistance Command Vietnam, Combat Experiences 5–69 (Vietnam: US Government, 1970), 5.

14 Ibid., i.

15 Military Assistance Command Civil Operations and Revolutionary/Rural Development Support, Command Information Pamphlet 12–69, *Pacification*, 6–7.

16 Military Assistance Command Vietnam, Lessons Learned Number 75: Cordon and Search Operations (Vietnam: US Government, 1970), 14.

17 Ibid.

18 Ibid., 15–16.

19 Richard Keller, email message to author, June 3, 2023.

20 Creighton Abrams's comments quoted in Sorley, ed., *Vietnam Chronicles: The Abrams Tapes 1968–1972*, 351.

21 Military Assistance Command Civil Operations and Revolutionary/Rural Development Support, Command Information Pamphlet 12–69, *Pacification* (Washington, DC: US Government, 1969), 16.

22 Safe Conduct Pass Chieu Hoi Leaflet. Translated by Nhan Phan. From author's private collection.

23 Why Sacrifice Yourself Chieu Hoi Leaflet. Translated by Nhan Phan. From author's private collection.

24 Military Assistance Command Civil Operations and Revolutionary/Rural Development Support, Command Information Pamphlet 12–69, *Pacification* (Washington, DC: US Government, 1969), 16.

25 Military Assistance Command Vietnam, Lessons Learned Number 75: Cordon and Search Operations (Vietnam: US Government, 1970), 16.
26 Military Assistance Command Civil Operations and Revolutionary/Rural Development Support, Command Information Pamphlet 12–69, *Pacification*, 16.
27 *Hamburger Hill*, directed by John Irvin (RKO Pictures, 1987), 1:31:15.
28 J. A. Koch, *The Chieu Hoi Program in South Vietnam, 1963–1971* (1971), Retrieved March 14, 2023, from the RAND Corporation website: https://www.rand.org/pubs/reports/R1172.html.
29 R. F. Keller, J. Boyce, J. Boyce & Boy Scouts of America (1961). Richard F. Keller Collection. Personal narrative. Retrieved from the Library of Congress, https://www.loc.gov/item/afc2001001.84829/ (accessed October 11, 2024).

Chapter 21

1 Patrick W. Naughton Diary Entry, December 16, 1969. Diary. From author's private collection.
2 Ibid.
3 Jeannie Breeden, interview by author, via Zoom in Falls Church, Virginia, September 20, 2023.
4 Patrick W. Naughton Diary Entries, December 9–11, 1969. Diary. From author's private collection.
5 "Dennis Roger Hunsley," The Virtual Wall, https://www.virtualwall.org/dh/HunsleyDR01a.htm.
6 Patrick W. Naughton Diary Entries, December 12–13, 1969. Diary. From author's private collection.
7 Patrick W. Naughton Sr., email message to author, August 26, 2022.
8 Patrick W. Naughton Diary Entries, December 14–15, 1969. Diary. From author's private collection.
9 Patrick W. Naughton Diary Entry, December 16, 1969.
10 Alic Tahir, interview by author, via Zoom in Falls Church, Virginia, August 17, 2023.
11 Patrick W. Naughton to Ma, Pop, John, Ami, Sean, Mo, Tommy, & Mele, December 20, 1969. Letter. From author's private collection.
12 Patrick W. Naughton Diary Entries, December 17–21, 1969. Diary. From author's private collection.
13 Patrick W. Naughton Sr., email message to author, August 16, 2023.
14 Richard Keller, email message to author, May 30, 2023.
15 Richard Keller, email message to author, May 31, 2023.
16 Creighton Abrams's comments quoted in Sorley, ed., *Vietnam Chronicles: The Abrams Tapes 1968–1972*, 325.
17 Patrick W. Naughton to Ma, Pop, John, Ami, Sean, Mo, Tommy, & Mele, December 25, 1969. Letter. From author's private collection.
18 Patrick W. Naughton Diary Entry, December 19, 1969.
19 Patrick W. Naughton Diary Entry, December 14, 1969.
20 William T. Sherman, *Sherman's Civil War: Selected Correspondence of William T. Sherman, 1860–1865*, eds. Jean V. Berlin and Brooks D. Simpson (Chapel Hill, NC: University of North Carolina Press, 1999), 775–7.
21 Patrick W. Naughton Diary Entries, December 20–23, 1969. Diary. From author's private collection.
22 Patrick W. Naughton Diary Entry, December 24, 1969. Diary. From author's private collection.
23 Ibid.
24 Alic Tahir, interview by author, via Zoom in Falls Church, Virginia, August 17, 2023.
25 Patrick W. Naughton Diary Entry, December 24, 1969.
26 Patrick W. Naughton to Ma, Pop, John, Ami, Sean, Mo, Tommy, & Mele, December 25, 1969.

27 Patrick W. Naughton Sr., email message to author, March 21, 2023.
28 Alic Tahir, interview by author, via Zoom in Falls Church, Virginia, August 17, 2023.
29 Richard Keller, email message to author, May 31, 2023.
30 General Order 002/K31CT/TM/TQT/CP, III Corps 25th Infantry Division, January 10, 1970. From author's private collection.
31 Patrick W. Naughton Sr., email message to author, March 21, 2023.
32 Patrick W. Naughton Diary Entry, December 24, 1969.
33 Ibid.
34 Patrick W. Naughton Sr., email message to author, March 21, 2023.
35 Ibid.
36 Patrick W. Naughton to Ma, Pop, John, Ami, Sean, Mo, Tommy, & Mele, December 25, 1969.
37 Captured North Vietnam New Year's Card, Spring 1969. Translated by Nhan Phan. From author's private collection.
38 Ibid.
39 Patrick W. Naughton Sr., email message to author, September 4, 2022.
40 Patrick W. Naughton Diary Entries, December 9, 11, 1969.
41 Alic Tahir, interview by author, via Zoom in Falls Church, Virginia, August 17, 2023.
42 Patrick W. Naughton to Ma, Pop, John, Ami, Sean, Mo, Tommy, & Mele, December 25, 1969.
43 Richard Keller, email message to author, May 30, 2023.

Chapter 22

1 Patrick Hiu, email message to author, March 24, 2023.
2 Ibid.
3 Ibid.
4 Patrick W. Naughton Diary Entry, January 5, 1970. Diary. From author's private collection.
5 Patrick W. Naughton to Ma, Pop, John, Ami, Sean, Mo, Tommy, & Mele, January 1, 1970. Letter. From author's private collection.
6 Patrick W. Naughton Diary Entry, January 1, 1970. Diary. From author's private collection.
7 Patrick W. Naughton Sr., email message to author, March 23, 2023.
8 Patrick W. Naughton Diary Entries, January 9, 10, 23 1970. Diary. From author's private collection.
9 Patrick W. Naughton Diary Entry, December 26, 1969. Diary. From author's private collection.
10 Patrick W. Naughton Sr., email message to author, May 29, 2022.
11 Patrick W. Naughton Diary Entry, January 21, 1970. Diary. Translated by Nhan Phan. From author's private collection.
12 Patrick W. Naughton Sr., email message to author, March 23, 2023.
13 Keller et al. Personal narrative.
14 Patrick W. Naughton Diary Entry, December 28, 1969. Diary. From author's private collection.
15 Patrick W. Naughton Sr., email message to author, August 26, 2022.
16 Ibid.
17 Patrick W. Naughton Diary Entries, December 26, 1969 to January 29, 1970. Diary. From author's private collection.
18 Ibid.
19 Ibid.
20 Tran Van Ban in Appy, *Patriots*, 516.
21 Patrick W. Naughton Diary Entries, December 26, 1969 to January 29, 1970.
22 Stewart Alsop, "They May Make It," *Newsweek,* December 29, 1969, 60.

23 William Rogers, "Changing Role of U.S.: Interview with William P. Rogers, Secretary of State," *U.S. News & World Report*, January 26, 1970, 30.
24 Patrick W. Naughton to Ma, Pop, John, Ami, Sean, Mo, Tommy, & Mele, January 1, 1970. Letter. From author's private collection.
25 Patrick W. Naughton to Ma, Pop, John, Ami, Sean, Mo, Tommy, & Mele, February 15, 1970. Letter. From author's private collection.

Chapter 23

1 Patrick W. Naughton to Ma, Pop, John, Ami, Sean, Mo, Tommy, & Mele, January 1, 1970.
2 DVA (Department of Veterans' Affairs) (2019), "Rest and recreation in Sydney—'R and R'," DVA Anzac Portal, https://anzacportal.dva.gov.au/wars-and-missions/vietnam-war-1962-1975/all-way-lbj/rest-and-recreation-sydney-r-and-r (accessed 7 April, 2023).
3 Military Assistance Command Vietnam, Command Information Pamphlet 37–69, Tet (Washington, DC: US Government, 1969), 2.
4 Ibid.
5 Ibid.
6 Ibid.
7 Westmoreland, *A Soldier Reports*, 333–4.
8 Patrick W. Naughton Sr., email message to author, April 7, 2023.
9 R&R Information: Australia, Volume One, Number Three, Spring–Summer (Sydney: US Government R&R Office, November 1969–April 1970).
10 Ibid., 5, 16.
11 Ibid., 18.
12 Patrick W. Naughton Sr., email message to author, April 7, 2023.
13 Ibid.
14 Patrick W. Naughton Diary Entries, January 30–31, 1970. Diary. From author's private collection.
15 Patrick W. Naughton to Ma and Pop, February 5, 1970. Postcard. From author's private collection; and Patrick W. Naughton to Ma, Pop, and Family, February 9, 1970. Letter. From author's private collection.
16 Patrick W. Naughton to Ma, Pop, and Family, February 9, 1970. Letter. From author's private collection.
17 Patrick W. Naughton Sr., email message to author, April 7, 2023.
18 Patrick W. Naughton Diary Entry, February 7, 1970. Diary. From author's private collection.
19 Patrick W. Naughton Diary Entries, February 1–7, 1970. Diary. From author's private collection.
20 "Note of Caution on Vietnam War," *U.S. News & World Report*, February 9, 1970, 8.
21 Patrick W. Naughton to Ma and Pop, February 5, 1970. Postcard. From author's private collection.

Chapter 24

1 Sarah Stillman, "The Invisible Army: For Foreign Workers on U.S. Bases in Iraq and Afghanistan, War Can be Hell," *The New Yorker*, June 6, 2011, https://www.newyorker.com/magazine/2011/06/06/the-invisible-army (accessed April 14, 2023).
2 *Hamburger Hill*, directed by John Irvin (RKO Pictures, 1987), 1:31:15.
3 Patrick W. Naughton to Ma, Pop, and Family, February 9, 1970. Letter. From author's private collection.
4 Patrick W. Naughton Sr., email message to author, April 7, 2023.

5 Patrick W. Naughton Diary Entry, February 8, 1970. Diary. From author's private collection.
6 Ibid.
7 Patrick W. Naughton Sr., email message to author, April 7, 2023.
8 "Looking for ways to speed up the Vietnamization of the War, Laird Says," *Racine Journal Times*, February 10, 1970, https://www.newspapers.com/image/342578306/?terms=laird&match=1 (accessed April 16, 2023).
9 Melvin Laird's comments quoted in Sorley, ed., *Vietnam Chronicles: The Abrams Tapes 1968–1972*, 371.
10 Keller et al. Personal narrative, and Richard Keller, email message to author, March 19, 2023.
11 Kay Lund, "Vietnamization Progressing Very Well, Laird Asserts," *Honolulu Star-Bulletin*, February 14, 1970, https://www.newspapers.com/image/271122639/?terms=laird&match=1 (accessed April 16, 2023).
12 National Archives, Nixon Presidential Materials, NSC Files, Box 224, Agency Files, DOD, Vol. IV, 1 February 1970–20 April 1970.
13 Ibid.
14 Ibid.
15 Ibid.
16 Paul Warnke in Appy, *Patriots*, 278.
17 Patrick W. Naughton Diary Entries, February 12–13, 1970. Diary. From author's private collection.
18 Patrick W. Naughton Diary Entry, February 15, 1970. Diary. From author's private collection.
19 Patrick W. Naughton Diary Entries, February 12–13, 1970. Diary. From author's private collection.
20 Patrick W. Naughton to Ma, Pop, John, Ami, Sean, Momi, Tommy, and Mele, February 15, 1970.
21 Keller et al. Personal narrative.
22 Ibid.
23 Patrick W. Naughton Diary Entries, February 14, 21, 1970. Diary. From author's private collection.
24 Patrick W. Naughton Diary Entry, February 15, 1970.
25 Alic Tahir, interview by author, via Zoom in Falls Church, Virginia, August 17, 2023.
26 Patrick W. Naughton Diary Entry, February 21, 1970. Diary. From author's private collection.
27 Patrick W. Naughton Diary Entry, February 26, 1970. Diary. From author's private collection.
28 Patrick W. Naughton Diary Entries, February 9–11, 17–28, 1970. Diary. From author's private collection.
29 "Grant and Sherman at Shiloh," *Indiana Democrat*, May 30, 1895, https://newspaperarchive.com/indiana-democrat-may-30-1895-p-1/ (accessed April 19, 2023).
30 James Brewer, email message to author, March 22, 2021.
31 Ibid.
32 Ibid.

Chapter 25

1 Patrick W. Naughton Diary Entry, March 4, 1970. Diary. From author's private collection.
2 Unidentified briefer to Creighton Abrams, quoted in Sorley, ed., *Vietnam Chronicles: The Abrams Tapes 1968–1972*, 376–7.
3 Seymour M. Hersh, "U.S. Confirms Pre-1970 Raids on Cambodia," *The New York Times*, July 17, 1973, https://www.nytimes.com/1973/07/17/archives/us-confirms-pre1970-raids-on-cambodia-bombing-protected-gis-says.html (accessed May 16, 2023).

4 "Vietnam: "A Television History; Cambodia and Laos; Interview with Douglas Kinnard, 1982," 04/01/1982, GBH Archives, http://openvault.wgbh.org/catalog/V_CB4620FF8E474723A6C33BEF61493E13 (accessed August 23, 2023).
5 Patrick W. Naughton to Ma, Pop, John, Ami, Sean, Momi, Tommy, and Mele, March 29, 1970. Letter. From author's private collection
6 Patrick W. Naughton Diary Entry, March 5, 1970. Diary. From author's private collection.
7 Patrick W. Naughton to Ma, Pop, John, Ami, Sean, Momi, Tommy, and Mele, March 24, 1970. Letter. From author's private collection
8 Patrick W. Naughton Diary Entries, March 21, 23, 1970. Diary. From author's private collection.
9 Patrick W. Naughton to Ma, Pop, John, Ami, Sean, Momi, Tommy, and Mele, March 24, 1970.
10 Ibid.
11 Patrick W. Naughton Diary Entry, March 23, 1970. Diary. From author's private collection.
12 Patrick W. Naughton to Ma, Pop, John, Ami, Sean, Momi, Tommy, and Mele, March 24, 1970.
13 Patrick W. Naughton Diary Entry, March 19, 1970. Diary. From author's private collection.
14 Patrick W. Naughton to Ma, Pop, John, Ami, Sean, Momi, Tommy, and Mele, March 29, 1970. Letter. From author's private collection.
15 Patrick W. Naughton to Hi again, [to unaddressed family] March 8, 1970. Letter. From author's private collection.
16 Ibid.
17 Patrick W. Naughton to Ma, Pop, John, Ami, Sean, Momi, Tommy, and Mele, March 13, 1970. Letter. From author's private collection.
18 Patrick W. Naughton Diary Entry, March 28, 1970. Diary. From author's private collection.
19 *Full Metal Jacket*, directed by Stanley Kubrick (Stanley Kubrick, 1987), 45:12.
20 Patrick W. Naughton Diary Entries, March 1–29, 1970. Diary. From author's private collection.
21 Patrick W. Naughton to Ma & Pop et al., March 7, 1970. Letter. From author's private collection.
22 Patrick W. Naughton to Ma & Pop, March 16, 1970. Letter. From author's private collection.
23 Patrick W. Naughton to Ma, Pop, John, Ami, Sean, Momi, Tommy, and Mele, March 13, 1970. Letter. From author's private collection; and Patrick W. Naughton Diary Entry, March 13, 1970. Diary. From author's private collection.
24 Patrick W. Naughton to Ma, Pop, John, Ami, Sean, Momi, Tommy, and Mele, March 13, 1970.
25 Ibid.
26 Ibid., and Patrick W. Naughton Diary Entry, March 13, 1970.
27 Patrick W. Naughton Diary Entry, March 23, 1970. Diary. From author's private collection.
28 *Letters to Wife and Parents*. 1969. Manuscript/Mixed Material. Retrieved from the Library of Congress, www.loc.gov/item/powmia/pwmaster_36320/ (accessed October 11, 2024).
29 Everett Emery, email to author, April 26, 2023.
30 *DRI of Case Conducted During Joint Field Activity 13-3VM*. 2013. Manuscript/Mixed Material. Retrieved from the Library of Congress, www.loc.gov/item/powmia/pwmias141_42/ (accessed October 11, 2024).
31 Ibid.
32 Ibid.
33 Ibid.
34 *Hearsay of Recovery of Remains of an American Serviceman in Song Be Province; Refugee Report & Preliminary Evaluation*. 1987. Manuscript/Mixed Material. Retrieved from the Library of Congress, www.loc.gov/item/powmia/pwmaster_28136/.
35 *DRI of Case Conducted During Joint Field Activity 13-3VM*.

36 *Refugee Report, Remains Discovered in Nez and Buried. Report and Evaluation.* 1979. Manuscript/Mixed Material. Retrieved from the Library of Congress, www.loc.gov/item/powmia/pwmaster_43024/ (accessed October 11, 2024).
37 Everett Emery, email to author, April 26, 2023 and Everett Emery, "Remembrances," Vietnam Veterans Memorial Fund, The Wall of Faces, February 8, 2017. https://www.vvmf.org/Wall-of-Faces/35693/DAVID-L-MUNOZ/ (accessed October 11, 2024).
38 Unknown, "Remembrances," Vietnam Veterans Memorial Fund, The Wall of Faces, September 22, 2009. https://www.vvmf.org/Wall-of-Faces/32915/ROBERT-S-MASUDA/ (accessed October 11, 2024).
39 Unknown, "Remembrances," Vietnam Veterans Memorial Fund, The Wall of Faces, September 22, 2009. https://www.vvmf.org/Wall-of-Faces/35693/DAVID-L-MUNOZ/ (accessed October 11, 2024).
40 *Telegram to Wife and Mother; Serviceman Did Not Appear on List of Captured U.S. Servicemen and Civilians Presented to Paris Negotiations.* 1973. Manuscript/Mixed Material. Retrieved from the Library of Congress, www.loc.gov/item/powmia/pwmaster_36314 (accessed October 11, 2024).
41 *Status Change, MIA to KIA.* 1976. Manuscript/Mixed Material. Retrieved from the Library of Congress, www.loc.gov/item/powmia/pwmaster_36304/ (accessed October 11, 2024).
42 *Letters to Wife and Mother; Termination of Missing Status.* 1976. Manuscript/Mixed Material. Retrieved from the Library of Congress, www.loc.gov/item/powmia/pwmaster_36296/ (accessed October 11, 2024).
43 *DRI of Case Conducted During Joint Field Activity 13-3VM.*
44 Ibid.
45 Patrick W. Naughton Diary Entry, March 23, 1970. Diary. From author's private collection.
46 "Vietnam War Accounting," Defense POW/MIA Accounting Agency, US Government, https://dpaa-mil.sites.crmforce.mil/dpaaFamWebVietnam (accessed April 21, 2023).
47 Richard Nixon, *No More Vietnams* (Arbor House: New York, 1985), 161.
48 "National POW/MIA Flag Act Signed into Law," Senator Elizabeth Warren, US Government, https://www.warren.senate.gov/newsroom/press-releases/national-pow/mia-flag-act-signed-into-law#:~:text=The%20National%20POW%2FMIA%20Flag%20Act%20will%20ensure%20that%20the,already%20designated%20under%20existing%20law (accessed April 21, 2003).

Chapter 26

1 Patrick W. Naughton to Ma, Pop, John, Ami, Sean, Momi, Tommy, and Mele, April 4, 1970. Letter. From author's private collection.
2 Headquarters Military Assistance Command Vietnam, Office of Information Monthly Summary March 1970 (Washington, DC: US Government, 1970), 2.
3 Patrick W. Naughton Diary Entries, March 30 to April 7, 1970. Diary. From author's private collection.
4 Ibid.
5 Richard Keller, email message to author, June 6, 2023.
6 Patrick W. Naughton Sr., email message to author, May 2, 2023.
7 "Southeast Asia: Those Sanctuaries," *Times Magazine,* April 25, 1969, 39.
8 "U.S. Viet Troop Strength Down to 429,200," *Arizona Republic*, April 14, 1970, https://www.newspapers.com/image/9018678/?terms=429%2C200&match=1 (accessed May 16, 2023).
9 Richard Nixon: "Address to the Nation on Progress Toward Peace in Vietnam," April 20, 1970. Online by Gerhard Peters and John T. Woolley, The American Presidency Project. http://www.presidency.ucsb.edu/ws/?pid=2476 (accessed October 11, 2024).

10 Patrick W. Naughton Diary Entry, April 8, 1970. Diary. From author's private collection.
11 Richard Keller, email message to author, June 6, 2023.
12 Patrick W. Naughton Sr., email message to author, May 2, 2023.
13 Headquarters, United States Military Assistance Command, Vietnam, General Orders Number 3004, Award of the Bronze Star Medal with "V" Device, Naughton, Patrick W. From author's private collection.
14 Patrick W. Naughton to Ma, Pop, John, Ami, Mom (2 battered nephews), and Mele, April 12, 1970. Letter. From author's private collection.
15 Patrick W. Naughton Sr., email message to author, September 29, 2022.
16 Patrick W. Naughton to Ma, Pop, John, Ami, Mom (2 battered nephews), and Mele, April 12, 1970.
17 Headquarters, United States Military Assistance Command, Vietnam, General Orders Number 3004, Award of the Bronze Star Medal with "V" Device, Naughton, Patrick W. From author's private collection.
18 Richard Keller, email message to author, June 3, 2023.
19 Alic Tahir, interview by author, via Zoom in Falls Church, Virginia, August 17, 2023.
20 Patrick W. Naughton to Ma, Pop, John, Ami, Mom (2 battered nephews), and Mele, April 12, 1970; and Patrick W. Naughton Sr., email message to author, May 1, 2023.
21 Patrick W. Naughton to Ma, Pop, John, Ami, Mom (2 battered nephews), and Mele, April 12, 1970.
22 Patrick W. Naughton Diary Entry, April 8, 1970. Diary. From author's private collection.
23 Patrick W. Naughton Sr., email message to author, September 29, 2022.
24 Patrick W. Naughton Diary Entries, April 10–20, 1970. Diary. From author's private collection.
25 Patrick W. Naughton to Ma, Pop, John, Ami, Mom (2 battered nephews), and Mele, April 12, 1970.
26 James Brewer, email message to author, March 22, 2021.
27 Ibid.
28 James Brewer, email message to Pam DeWeese, July 9, 2017.
29 Keller et al. Personal narrative.
30 Richard Keller, email message to author, June 3, 2023.
31 Alic Tahir, interview by author, via Zoom in Falls Church, Virginia, August 17, 2023.
32 Headquarters, United States Military Assistance Command, Vietnam, General Orders Number 3004, Award of the Bronze Star Medal with "V" Device, Naughton, Patrick W. From author's private collection.
33 Patrick W. Naughton Diary Entry, April 9, 1970. Diary. From author's private collection.
34 Patrick W. Naughton Sr., email message to author, May 2, 2023.
35 Major Richard Keller to Lieutenant Naughton, June 7, 1970. Letter. From author's private collection.
36 Ibid.
37 Patrick W. Naughton Sr., email message to author, May 2, 2023.
38 Alic Tahir, interview by author, via Zoom in Falls Church, Virginia, September 20, 2023.
39 Robert K. Brown, "Rhodesia's Elite Armored Corps: The Black Devils," *Soldier of Fortune Magazine*, January 1979, 38–43.
40 Pam DeWeese, email message to Jim Brewer, August 5, 2017.
41 Alic Tahir, interview by author, via Zoom in Falls Church, Virginia, August 17, 2023.
42 Karen Wager, email message to author, September 20, 2022.

Chapter 27

1 Patrick W. Naughton to Ma, Pop, John, Ami, Mom (2 battered nephews), and Mele, April 12, 1970.
2 Patrick W. Naughton Diary Entry, April 20, 1970. Diary. From author's private collection.
3 Patrick W. Naughton Diary Entry, April 22, 1970. Diary. From author's private collection.
4 Patrick W. Naughton to Ma & Pop, March 16, 1970. Letter. From author's private collection; and Patrick W. Naughton Sr., email message to author, May 6, 2023.
5 *Tour 365: For Soldiers Going Home*, Summer 1970 Issue (San Francisco: US Army Vietnam, 1970), i.
6 Helen Tennant Hegelheimer, in Appy, *Patriots*, 109.
7 Patrick W. Naughton Diary Entry, April 24, 1970. Diary. From author's private collection; and Patrick W. Naughton Sr., email message to author, May 6, 2023.
8 Patrick W. Naughton Sr., email message to author, May 6, 2023.
9 Patrick W. Naughton Diary Entry, April 24, 1970.
10 Helen Tennant Hegelheimer, in Appy, *Patriots*, 110.
11 War booty: procedures for handling and retaining battlefield objects, U.S. Code 10 (2011), § 2579.
12 Patrick W. Naughton to Ma, Pop, John, Ami, Mom (2 battered nephews), and Mele, April 12, 1970; and Patrick W. Naughton Sr., email message to author, May 6, 2023.
13 Patrick W. Naughton to Ma, Pop, John, Ami, Mom (2 battered nephews), and Mele, April 12, 1970.
14 Momilani Naughton, email message to author, May 11, 2023.
15 Melvin Laird, "Dangers Confronting U.S.: Interview with Defense Secretary Laird," *U.S. News & World Report*, May 11, 1970, 64.
16 Patrick W. Naughton Diary Entry, April 24, 1970.

Chapter 28

1 John F. Kennedy, Remarks at West Point to the Graduating Class of the U.S. Military Academy. Online by Gerhard Peters and John T. Woolley, The American Presidency Project, https://www.presidency.ucsb.edu/node/235775 (accessed October 11, 2024).
2 "GI's Into Cambodia—Americans React," *U.S. News & World Report*, May 11, 1970, 18.
3 Westmoreland, *A Soldier Reports*, 120–440.
4 Creighton Abrams's comments quoted in Sorley, ed., *Vietnam Chronicles: The Abrams Tapes 1968–1972*, 210.
5 Richard Keller, email message to author, May 31, 2023.
6 Larry Lockeby, email message to author, September 20, 2023.
7 Alic Tahir, interview by author, via Zoom in Falls Church, Virginia, August 17, 2023.
8 May, *The War Around Us*, 320.
9 Creighton Abrams's comments quoted in Sorley, ed., *Vietnam Chronicles: The Abrams Tapes 1968–1972*, 189.
10 "Vietnam: A Television History; Interview with Henry Kissinger, 1982."
11 "Vietnam: A Television History; Interview with Maxwell D. (Maxwell Davenport) Taylor, 1979 [Part 4 of 4]."
12 Patrick W. Naughton Sr., email message to author, May 28, 2023.
13 Patrick W. Naughton Sr., email message to author, May 11, 2023.
14 Ibid.

15 Appy, *Patriots*, 264.
16 Richard Nixon, "Address to the Nation on the War in Vietnam." Online by Gerhard Peters and John T. Woolley, The American Presidency Project, https://www.presidency.ucsb.edu/node/240027 (accessed October 11, 2024).
17 "Flags, Pro-War signs Carried by Thousands in Capital Parade," *The Los Angeles Times*, April 5, 1970, https://www.newspapers.com/image/166331694/?terms=prowar&match=1 (accessed May 27, 2023).
18 "Laborers Smash Anti-War Rally," *Newsday* (Suffolk Edition), May 9, 1970, https://www.newspapers.com/image/718888335/?terms=wall%20street&match=1 (accessed May 27, 2023).
19 "Hardhats Jam Park in Support of Nixon," *The Tribune*, May 21, 1970, https://www.newspapers.com/image/322226071/?terms=hardhats&match=1 (accessed May 27, 2023).

Chapter 29

1 "Vietnam: A Television History; Interview with Dean Rusk [2], 1981."
2 William M. Hammond, *Reporting Vietnam* (University Press of Kansas, 1998), ix.
3 Ibid., 9.
4 Ibid., 222.
5 Spiro Agnew, Remarks delivered in Des Moines, Iowa, November 13, 1969. Available online at Otterbein University https://www.otterbein.edu/alumni/wp-content/uploads/sites/4/2021/04/1969-Agnew-Des-Moines-Speech-Handout.pdf (accessed August 16, 2023).
6 Marginal comment, news summary, June 6, 1969, folder News Summaries—June 1969, box 30, President's Office Files (POF), Richard Nixon Presidential Materials, National Archives, College Park, Maryland.
7 Barry Zorthian in Appy, *Patriots*, 290.
8 Richard Engel, *War Journal: My Five Years in Iraq* (New York: Simon & Schuster, 2008), 230.
9 Westmoreland, *A Soldier Reports*, 120–412.
10 Ibid., 79–80.
11 Creighton Abrams's comments quoted in Sorley, ed., *Vietnam Chronicles: The Abrams Tapes 1968–1972*, 194.
12 "Colonel Assails Newsmen," *New York Times*, April 13, 1972, https://www.nytimes.com/1972/04/13/archives/colonel-assails-newsmen.html (accessed October 29, 2023).
13 Philip Geyelin, "The Role of the Press in an Open Society" *Naval War College Review 28*, no. 2 (March–April 1975): 5–6.
14 Richard Harwood, "Vietnam War Reporters Mission," *Washington Post*, March 9, 1971.
15 Denis Warner, *Certain Victory: How Hanoi Won the War* (Sheel Andrews and McMeel, Inc.: Kansas City, Kansas, 1978), 205.
16 David Lawrence, "What's Become of 'Voluntary Censorship'?", *U.S. News & World Report*, September 8, 1969.
17 David Lawrence, "Is Treason Permissible as Merely 'Free Speech'?," *U.S. News & World Report*, March 10, 1969, 108.
18 "Hanoi's Formula: How to Win While Losing," *U.S. News & World Report*, April 6, 1970, 46.
19 Kinnard, *The War Managers*, 135.
20 Richard Keller, email message to author, June 10, 2023.
21 Alic Tahir, interview by author, via Zoom in Falls Church, Virginia, August 17, 2023.

Chapter 30

1 Patrick W. Naughton Diary Entries, February 10, 24 1970. Diary. From author's private collection and Patrick W. Naughton Sr., email message to author, May 11, 2023.
2 Patrick W. Naughton Sr., email message to author, May 2 and 6, 2023.
3 "Agent Orange," U.S. Department of Veterans Affairs, U.S. Government, accessed May 24, 2023, https://www.publichealth.va.gov/exposures/agentorange/ (accessed October 11, 2024).
4 Patrick W. Naughton, Department of Veterans Affairs Rating Decision, May 16, 2022, from author's private collection.
5 Patrick W. Naughton Sr., email message to author, November 14, 2022.
6 "Airborne Hazards and Burn Pit Exposures," U.S. Department of Veterans Affairs, U.S. Government, https://www.publichealth.va.gov/exposures/burnpits/index.asp (accessed May 24, 2023).
7 Larry Lockeby, email message to author, September 20, 2023.
8 Alic Tahir, interview by author, via Zoom in Falls Church, Virginia, September 20, 2023.
9 Sean M. Roche, "The American History of PTSD: Civil War—Vietnam," Master of Military Studies diss., (USMC Command and Staff College, 2011).
10 Momilani Naughton, email message to author, May 11, 2023.
11 Patrick W. Naughton Sr., email message to author, July 30, 2022.
12 Ibid.

Chapter 31

1 Buzz Bissinger, "Don't ask, Don't Kill," *Vanity Fair*, May 2005, https://www.vanityfair.com/news/2000/05/kentucky-murder-200005 (accessed October 11, 2024).
2 United States Appellate v. Justin R, Fisher, Specialist, U.S. Army Appellant, No. 03-0059 Crim. App. No. 20000024 (United States Court of Appeals for the Armed Forces. 2003) https://www.armfor.uscourts.gov/opinions/2003Term/03-0059.htm (accessed October 11, 2024).
3 "GI's in Battle: The 'Dink' Complex," *Newsweek*, December 1, 1969, 37.
4 Creighton Abrams's comments quoted in Sorley, ed., *Vietnam Chronicles: The Abrams Tapes 1968–1972*, 355.
5 "GI's in Battle: The 'Dink' Complex."
6 Creighton Abrams's comments quoted in Sorley, ed., *Vietnam Chronicles: The Abrams Tapes 1968–1972*, 286, 316.
7 I am Vanessa Guillén Act of 2021, S. 1611 (2021), https://www.congress.gov/bill/117th-congress/senate-bill/1611/text (accessed October 11, 2024).
8 Jim Garamone, "DOD Begins Implementing Naming Commission Recommendations," *Department of Defense News*, January 5, 2023, https://www.defense.gov/News/News-Stories/Article/Article/3260434/dod-begins-implementing-naming-commission-recommendations/ (accessed October 11, 2024).
9 "As Race Issue Hits Armed Forces," *U.S. News & World Report*, September 1, 1969, 26.
10 "The Armed Forces—'New Left' Target," *U.S. News & World Report*, May 26, 1969, 60.
11 Alic Tahir, interview by author, via Zoom in Falls Church, Virginia, August 17, 2023.
12 Ibid.
13 Alic Tahir, interview by author, via Zoom in Falls Church, Virginia, September 20, 2023.
14 Ibid.
15 Richard Keller, email message to author, September 3, 2023.
16 Westmoreland, *A Soldier Reports*, 120–362.
17 "Armed Forces: Dissent in Uniform," *Time Magazine*, April 25, 1969, 20.

18 Westmoreland, *A Soldier Reports*, 120–450.
19 Rick Atkinson, *The Long Gray Line* (Boston, New York: Houghton Mifflin Harcourt, 1989), 408.

Chapter 32

1 "Vietnamese Boat People," Vietnamese Boat People, Vietnamese Boat People Non-Profit Organization, https://www.vietnameseboatpeople.org (accessed November 15, 2023).
2 Kim A. O'Connell, "Echoes of Little Saigon," Virginia Foundation for the Humanities, virginia-humanities.org/wp-content/uploads/2016/09/Echoes-of-Little-Saigon.pdf (accessed November 15, 2023).
3 Nguyễn Ngọc Sơn, email message to author, April 3, 2023.
4 "Vietnam: A Television History; First Vietnam War, The (1946–1954); Interview with Dean Rusk [1], 1982."
5 Kinnard, *The War Managers*, 8.
6 "Vietnam: A Television History; Interview with Maxwell D. (Maxwell Davenport) Taylor, 1979 [Part 4 of 4]."
7 David Halberstam, "They Can Win a War if Someone Shows Them How," in *Reporting Vietnam Part I* (The Library of America: New York, 1988), 112.
8 Perry Merton, "Their Lions, Our Rabbits." *Congressional Record* Senate (1967) p. 28248. Text from: https://www.govinfo.gov/content/pkg/GPO-CRECB-1967-pt21/pdf/GPO-CRECB-1967-pt21-4-2.pdf (accessed September 15, 2023).
9 Westmoreland, *A Soldier Reports*, 69–70.
10 J. H. Willbanks, (2009), "The Evolution of the US Advisory Effort in Viet Nam: Lessons Learned," *Journal of Conflict Studies, 29*. Retrieved from https://journals.lib.unb.ca/index.php/JCS/article/view/15238 (accessed October 11, 2024).
11 Kinnard, *The War Managers*, 92.
12 Ibid., 91.
13 "Vietnam: A Television History; Interview with Richard C. Holbrooke [2], 1982," 09/16/1982, GBH Archives, http://openvault.wgbh.org/catalog/V_7C6FB2F0BFE64CC184B4F20495D01537 (accessed August 24, 2023).
14 "Vietnam: A Television History; Interview with Hoang Duc Nha [1], 1981," 05/09/1981, GBH Archives, http://openvault.wgbh.org/catalog/V_9C17ECD0FF9B45D7BDE1A4730F2E0988 (accessed August 23, 2023).
15 William M. Hammond, *Reporting Vietnam* (University Press of Kansas, 1998), 165.
16 Westmoreland, *A Soldier Reports*, 120–306.
17 Phillip Darcourt, "Buildings in Hanoi Crumble … Haiphong is Ruined, Ravaged: interview with a French Authority on Vietnam," *U.S. News & World Report*, December 22, 1969, 39.
18 Brigham, *ARVN: Life and Death in the South Vietnamese Army*, 121.
19 Ibid., 15.
20 Truong Mealy in Santoli, Al, *To Bear any Burden: The Vietnam War and its Aftermath in the Words of Americans and Southeast Asians* (New York: E. P. Dutton, 1985), 61.
21 "Vietnam: A Television History; Interview with David Halberstam, 1979 [part 2 of 5]," 01/16/1979, GBH Archives, http://openvault.wgbh.org/catalog/V_53E871B715174633872DDC-CABF9CC3AA (accessed August 25, 2023).
22 Combat Experiences 3–69: Military Assistance Command Vietnam (Washington, DC: US Government, 1969), 20–3.
23 Brigham, *ARVN: Life and Death in the South Vietnamese Army*, 50.
24 Ibid., 21.

25 Westmoreland, *A Soldier Reports*, 120–1.
26 Donald Marshall comments quoted in Sorley, ed., *Vietnam Chronicles: The Abrams Tapes 1968–1972*, 202.
27 Creighton Abrams's comments quoted in Sorley, ed., *Vietnam Chronicles: The Abrams Tapes 1968–1972*, 347.
28 Huntington, "The Bases of Accommodation."
29 Neil Sheehan, *The Pentagon Papers As Published By the New York Times* (New York, Quadrangle Books, 1971).
30 Alic Tahir, interview by author, via Zoom in Falls Church, Virginia, August 17, 2023.
31 Ibid.
32 Tim Page, *Another Vietnam: Pictures of the War from the Other Side* (Washington, DC: National Geographic Society, Washington, 2002).
33 Merton, "Their Lions, Our Rabbits."
34 McNamara, *In Retrospect: The Tragedy and Lessons of Vietnam*, 267.
35 "Vietnam: A Television History; Tet, 1968; Interview with Clark M. Clifford, 1981," 05/18/1981, GBH Archives, http://openvault.wgbh.org/catalog/V_D949B20587A14B79A0B4293DD23BE385 (accessed August 23, 2023).
36 "Vietnam: A Television History; Peace is at Hand (1968–1973); Interview with Melvin R. Laird, 1981," 06/03/1981, GBH Archives, http://openvault.wgbh.org/catalog/V_D1F9E80249DA419BBFCC019B8B0F3A64 (accessed August 23, 2023).
37 Andrew J. Birtle, *U.S. Army Counterinsurgency and Contingency Operations Doctrine 1942–1976* (Washington, DC: US Government, 2007), 322–3.
38 Brigham, *ARVN: Life and Death in the South Vietnamese Army*, 74.
39 Alic Tahir, interview by author, via Zoom in Falls Church, Virginia, August 17, 2023.
40 Patrick W. Naughton Sr., email message to author, November 13, 2023.
41 Richard Keller, email message to author, July 10, 2023.
42 "Vietnam: A Television History; Interview with Maxwell D. (Maxwell Davenport) Taylor, 1979 [Part 1 of 4]."
43 Alic Tahir, interview by author, via Zoom in Falls Church, Virginia, August 17, 2023.
44 Alic Tahir, interview by author, via Zoom in Falls Church, Virginia, August 17, 2023.
45 Kinnard, *The War Managers*, 8.
46 "Vietnam: A Television History; Interview with Hoang Duc Nha [1], 1981."

Chapter 33

1 Văn Tiến Dũng, *Our Great Spring Victory: An Account of the Liberation of South Vietnam* (Monthly Review Press: New York, 1977), 237–8.
2 Burchett, *Grasshoppers & Elephants: Why Vietnam Fell*, 40.
3 "Vietnam: A Television History; Interview with Hoang Duc Nha [1], 1981."
4 Patrick W. Naughton, "Agricultural System Adjustments in Southern Vietnam: 1975–81" *Agricultural Systems an International Journal* 12, (1983): 114.
5 Ibid., 113.
6 Nguyễn Ngọc Bích, interview by Andrea Dono, November 9, 2014, transcript, Oral History Project "Little Saigon", Arlington Public Library, Arlington, Virginia.
7 Nguyễn Văn Thiệu, "Text of Thieu's Resignation Speech," Central Intelligence Agency, US Government, April 21, 1975, https://www.cia.gov/readingroom/document/loc-hak-244-10-4-5 (accessed October 11, 2024).
8 Nguyễn Ngọc Bích, interview.

9 Ibid.
10 Ibid.
11 Ibid.
12 Ibid.
13 Ibid.
14 Anhthu Lu, interview by Kim O'Connell, March 16, 2016, transcript, Oral History Project "Little Saigon", Arlington Public Library, Arlington, Virginia.
15 Ibid.
16 Ibid.
17 Ibid.
18 Ibid.
19 Ibid.
20 Ibid.
21 Ibid.
22 Ibid.
23 Ibid.
24 Ibid.
25 Liêu Nguyễn, interview by Judd Ullom, March 18, 2015, transcript, Oral History Project "Little Saigon", Arlington Public Library, Arlington, Virginia.
26 Ibid.
27 Ibid.
28 Ibid.
29 Ibid.
30 Ibid.

Chapter 34

1 Kinnard, *The War Managers*, ix.
2 McNamara, *In Retrospect: The Tragedy and Lessons of Vietnam*, 277.
3 Ibid., 210.
4 "Vietnam: A Television History; Interview with Richard C. Holbrooke [2], 1982."
5 "Vietnam: A Television History; Interview with Maxwell D. (Maxwell Davenport) Taylor, 1979 [Part 3 of 4]."
6 "Vietnam: A Television History; Tet, 1968; Interview with Clark M. Clifford, 1981."
7 McNamara, *In Retrospect: The Tragedy and Lessons of Vietnam*, 109.
8 Westmoreland, *A Soldier Reports*, 120–500.
9 "Vietnam: A Television History; Interview with Dean Rusk [2], 1981."
10 Westmoreland, *A Soldier Reports*, 120, 134, 498.
11 "Vietnam: A Television History; Interview with Richard C. Holbrooke [2], 1982."
12 Creighton Abrams's comments quoted in Sorley, ed., *Vietnam Chronicles: The Abrams Tapes 1968–1972*, 213.
13 "Vietnam: A Television History; America Takes Charge (1965–1967); Interview with Leslie H. Gelb, 1982," 08/25/1982, GBH Archives, http://openvault.wgbh.org/catalog/V_80D674B-7F896495F929058E4BC6DDCDD (accessed August 23, 2023).
14 "Vietnam: A Television History; Interview with Richard C. Holbrooke [2], 1982."
15 "Vietnam: A Television History; Interview with Maxwell D. (Maxwell Davenport) Taylor, 1979 [Part 1 of 4]."
16 McNamara, *In Retrospect: The Tragedy and Lessons of Vietnam*, 48.

17 Kinnard, *The War Managers*, 75.
18 Ibid., 75.
19 Richard Keller, email message to author, June 6, 2023.
20 Ibid.
21 Richard Keller, email message to author, June 10, 2023.
22 Richard Keller, email message to author, June 6, 2023.
23 Westmoreland, *A Soldier Reports*, 81, 90, 120, 332, 499.
24 Creighton Abrams's comments quoted in Sorley, ed., *Vietnam Chronicles: The Abrams Tapes 1968–1972*, 287.
25 "Vietnam: A Television History; Interview with Richard C. Holbrooke [2], 1982."
26 Rufus Phillips in Santoli, *To Bear any Burden*, 86.
27 Anne Miller in Santoli, *To Bear any Burden*, 83–4.
28 Kinnard, *The War Managers*, 36, 118–19.
29 Westmoreland, *A Soldier Reports*, 387.
30 Morton Halperin in Appy, *Patriots*, 403.
31 Thomas C. Thayer, *War Without Fronts: The American Experience in Vietnam* (Boulder: Colorado, Westview Press, 1985), 114.
32 Patrick W. Naughton, "Some Comparisons of Higher Education in Vietnam: 1954–1976" Canadian and International Education 8, no. 2 (November 1979): 107.
33 "Vietnam: A Television History; Interview with Dean Rusk [2], 1981."
34 Birtle, *U.S. Army Counterinsurgency and Contingency Operations Doctrine 1942–1976*, 320, 389.
35 Nguyễn Cao Kỳ, "When Will the War End for U.S.: Interview with South Vietnam's Vice President," *U.S. News & World Report*, October 13, 1969, 61.
36 Nguyễn Văn Thiệu, "Can Vietnam go it Alone: Interview with President Thieu," *U.S. News & World Report*, March 16, 1970, 75.
37 "U.S. Commanders Explain: Why the High U.S. Casualties," *U.S. News & World Report*, June 2, 1969, 27.
38 Vietnam: A Television History; Interview with Maxwell D. (Maxwell Davenport) Taylor, 1979 [Part 4 of 4]."
39 Ellsworth Bunker, "A Close Look at Progress Inside Vietnam: Exclusive Interview with U.S. Ambassador to Saigon," *U.S. News & World Report*, November 17, 1969, 46.
40 "Next Turn in Vietnam," *U.S. News & World Report*, March 3, 1969, 29.
41 Westmoreland, *A Soldier Reports*, 277.
42 "Vietnam: A Television History; Interview with Richard C. Holbrooke [2], 1982."
43 "Vietnam: A Television History; Interview with William C. (William Childs) Westmoreland, 1981."
44 "Vietnam: A Television History; Interview with Henry Kissinger, 1982."
45 Alic Tahir, interview by author, via Zoom in Falls Church, Virginia, August 17, 2023.
46 Strategic Objectives Plan as presented during a June 12, 1969 Commanders Conference quoted in Sorley, ed. *Vietnam Chronicles: The Abrams Tapes 1968–1972*, 203.
47 Westmoreland, *A Soldier Reports*, 177–178, 182.

Epilogue

1 Jeannie Breeden, interview by author, via Zoom in Falls Church, Virginia, September 20, 2023.
2 Ibid.
3 *Three Kings*, directed by David Russell (Warner Brothers, 1999), 1:31:15.

4 William Westmoreland, "Vietnam in Perspective," *Military Review* LIX, no. 1 (January 1979): 34–5.
5 "Vietnam: A Television History; Tet, 1968; Interview with Clark M. Clifford, 1981."
6 "Vietnam: A Television History; Interview with Maxwell D. (Maxwell Davenport) Taylor, 1979 [Part 3 of 4]."
7 "Vietnam: A Television History; Interview with Henry Kissinger, 1982."
8 Larry Lockeby, email message to author, September 20, 2023.
9 Alic Tahir, interview by author, via Zoom in Falls Church, Virginia, August 17, 2023.
10 Richard Keller, email message to author, June 10, 2023.
11 Patrick W. Naughton Sr., email message to author, March 4, 2024.
12 Patrick W. Naughton to Ma, Pop, John, Ami, Sean, Mo, Tommy, & Mele, July 6, 1969. Letter. From author's private collection.
13 "Vietnam: A Television History; Tet, 1968; Interview with W. W. (Walt Whitman) Rostow, 1981," 04/20/1981, GBH Archives, http://openvault.wgbh.org/catalog/V_933687866A3B451CAEAE-44C48140DEC2 (accessed August 23, 2023).
14 Luke Barr, "Father of Marine killed in 2021 suicide bomb attack at Afghanistan's Kabul airport arrested at SOTU," ABC News, March 8, 2024, https://abcnews.go.com/Politics/father-marine-killed-2021-suicide-bomb-attack-afghanistans/story?id=107913293 (accessed March 10, 2024).
15 McNamara, *In Retrospect: The Tragedy and Lessons of Vietnam*, 323.
16 Ibid., 322.
17 Ibid.
18 Ibid.
19 Ibid., 330.
20 Jamie C. Ruff, "Vietnam: No One Truth, Colonel Says," *Richmond Times-Dispatch*, September 18, 1993, https://www.newspapers.com/image/832352261/?terms=richmond%20times%20dispatch%20westmoreland (accessed December 22, 2023).
21 Patrick W. Naughton Sr., email message to author, March 4, 2024.
22 Patrick W. Naughton to Colonel Richard Keller, December 21, 1983. Letter. From author's private collection.

Index